# PLEASE DON'T REMAIN CALM

# PLEASE DON'T REMAIN CALM

PROVOCATIONS AND

COMMENTARIES

## MICHAEL KINSLEY

W · W · NORTON & COMPANY

NEW YORK  LONDON

For information about permission to reproduce selections from
this book, write to Permissions, W. W. Norton & Company, Inc.,
500 Fifth Avenue, New York, NY 10110

For information about special discounts for bulk purchases,
please contact W. W. Norton Special Sales at
specialsales@wwnorton.com or 800-233-4830

Manufacturing by The Courier Companies, Inc.
Book design by Margaret M. Wagner
Production manager: Andrew Marasia

Library of Congress Cataloging-in-Publication Data

Kinsley, Michael E.
Please don't remain calm : provocations and commentaries /
Michael Kinsley. — 1st ed.
p. cm.
Includes index.
ISBN 978-0-393-06654-8 (hardcover)
1. United States—Politics and government—1993–2001. 2. United States—
Politics and government—2001– 3. Politicians—United States. 4. Political
corruption—United States. 5. United States—Foreign relations—1989–
6. United States—Social conditions—1980– 7. Kinsley, Michael E. I. Title.
E885.K565 2008
973.929—dc22

2007041570

W. W. Norton & Company, Inc.
500 Fifth Avenue, New York, N.Y. 10110
www.wwnorton.com

W. W. Norton & Company Ltd.
Castle House, 75/76 Wells Street, London W1T 3QT

1 2 3 4 5 6 7 8 9 0

# CONTENTS

## 2001

# INTRODUCTION

At the time of my last collection, in 1995, I was living in Washington, D.C., single, writing for the *New Republic*, the *Washington Post*, and *Time*; appearing five days a week as the liberal "host" on CNN's debate show *Crossfire*; doing a bit of "buckraking" (Jacob Weisberg's term for giving speeches and appearing at conventions for a lot of money); and trying to keep secret the fact that I had Parkinson's disease. In the previous year, I had flubbed the chance to be the editor of *New York Magazine* by accepting the job, then turning it down. (A couple of years later I flubbed an even bigger chance—to be editor of the *New Yorker*—although to this day I'm not sure how. Si Newhouse offered me the job, then enigmatically withdrew the offer the next day.)

Twelve years later, I am living in Seattle, very happily married, and writing full-time for *Time*. I am "out of the closet" with the Parkinson's, had brain surgery last summer to mitigate the symptoms (a great success), and anticipate a more or less normal life span.

In the interim, I got the editorship I hungered for by starting an Internet magazine, *Slate*, for Microsoft Corporation. (My wife, Patty Stonesifer, was on the committee that interviewed me for the job. That is how we met. She now is CEO of the Bill and Melinda Gates Foundation.) Later I left the editorship of *Slate* and then left *Slate* itself to be editorial and opinion editor of the *Los Angeles Times* (a brief but memorable adventure of a year and change, as it turned out). *Slate* was later sold to the Washington Post Company. Under its second editor—the same Weisberg mentioned above—it is profitable and influential.

I even have two terrific stepchildren, Sandy Stonesifer and Matt Stonesifer, and a terrific step-daughter-in-law, Crystal Vancho Stonesifer. My secret for raising terrific children: don't get involved until a week before the youngest finishes high school.

Scott Fitzgerald famously said there are no second acts in American lives, but I'm going on my third or fourth. A lucky man.

On the larger stage, the writings in this book cover the end of the Clinton administration, the stolen election of 2000, and two terms of George W. Bush, including September 11, the war on terror, and the invasion and occupation of Iraq.

The tone of these pieces varies widely. Some are whimsical, some are deadly serious, many are a mixture. Over the years this variety has confused people and put some off. It probably has not helped my career. I thought of putting together a collection of just the outright humor pieces, on the theory that collections of humor pieces are easier to sell. But on reflection, vanity would not allow.

I am grateful to many journalistic colleagues. The list is especially long at *Slate*, but I had better mention Jack Shafer or I'm in trouble. Others I badger for wisdom regularly include Mickey Kaus, Nick Lemann, Tim Noah, Bob Wright, and Jacob Weisberg. I worked with some wonderful people at the *Los Angeles Times* (most of them now gone), starting with the great newspaper editor John Carroll and including Dean Baquet, Andres Martinez, Nick Goldberg, Bob Sipchen, Michael Newman, and Linda Hall. For the three or four minutes I was the American editor of *Guardian.co.uk*, I enjoyed working with Richard Adams and Alan Rusbridger, among others. Conor Clarke helped me to put together this collection.

The people I especially need to thank are not journalists. They are the doctors, physician's assistants, and nurses who truly have made my lucky life possible: the late Dr. Steve Fink at Massachusetts General Hospital; Dr. Tom Chase at the National Institutes of Health; Dr. Jay Nutt and Julie Carter at Oregon Health Sciences University; Dr. John Roberts, Dr. Gary Kaplan, and Dr. Leland Teng at Virginia Mason Clinic; Dr. Ali Rezai and all his colleagues at the amazing Cleveland Clinic, especially Dr. Monique Giroux, Sierra Farris, and Ellen Gooding.

This book is dedicated to Patty. Who else?

PLEASE DON'T REMAIN CALM

# 1995–1999

## Long Sentence

PARSING PAT ROBERTSON.

New Republic, *May 8, 1995*

The controversy continues over whether Pat Robertson's bizarre rantings about the depredations of the Rothschilds and the Warburgs make him an anti-Semite. In a way, this debate has been a useful distraction for Robertson, since it has overshadowed the issue of whether he is a complete nut case. Based on the same evidence, that is a much easier question. Yet, as the leader of the Christian Coalition, he remains the most important person in the most powerful faction within the Republican Party. If this bothers the party's leading lights—let alone its intellectual apologists—they have not said so.

On April 12, the *Wall Street Journal* editorial page published an apologia by Robertson—titled, "a reply to my critics"—which casts light on both the anti-Semitism and lunacy issues. One sentence in particular caught my eye. Wonderfully mad, it is a self-quote from Robertson's 1990 book, *The New Millennium.* In other words, Robertson himself has chosen to highlight this sentence as a sample of his thought, and proof that he is not anti-Semitic. The sentence rewards close textual analysis. Here it is: "Intolerance in any quarter is wrong, but inasmuch as we are able, we must ensure that the trend throughout the 1990s remains in favor of a Jewish homeland in Israel and not for the elimination for the Jews."

Thus sayeth the Rev. Pat Robertson.

It is hard to know where to begin to sample this sentence's delights.

Perhaps it is best, in the Hebrew manner, to start at the end and move backwards. We immediately face a grammatical problem. It should, of course, be "the elimination of the Jews," not "the elimination for the Jews," which is an oddly arch way of putting it. Elimination would not, on balance, be "for" the Jews. To be sure, one might possibly say, "elimination for the Jews," omitting the first "the," in the sense of, "It's curtains for the Jews"—but this would be a rakish construction, surely inappropriate to the subject under discussion.

This brings us to the nub of the matter. Interpretation is always tricky, but Robertson seems to be suggesting here that he opposes the elimination of the Jews. That is nice, and I believe him. He even opposes a "trend" toward the elimination of the Jews, which is especially comforting. But as evidence of an absence of anti-Semitism, it is a bit lacking in oomph. Does Robertson think that anti-Semitism consists of wishing for the "elimination" of the Jews? This is setting the bar awfully high.

Anti-Semitism has, of course, taken that form. But Hitler should not be allowed to spoil anti-Semitism for everyone else. Indeed, the fact that Robertson presents his opposition to the elimination of the Jews as evidence of a lack of anti-Semitism arguably is evidence of the opposite. If someone feels moved to declare, even in a sincere spirit of reassurance, "Look, I really don't want to kill you"—does that demonstrate empathy, or something more sinister?

Then there is Robertson's unusual framework of analysis. There are, apparently, only two options for "the trend throughout the 1990s." One is "a Jewish homeland in Israel." The other is "elimination for the Jews." Between these two options, Robertson declares, he prefers a Jewish homeland over elimination of the Jews. This leaves open the question of how he rates a trend toward elimination for the Jews compared with other possible Jewish trends.

What, after all, does he mean by a trend in favor of a Jewish homeland in Israel? There already is a Jewish homeland in Israel. It is not in need of a trend toward it. The concept is nonsense, unless Robertson means a trend toward Israel becoming *the* Jewish homeland—i.e., a trend toward Jews abandoning other countries and moving to Israel.

There is a strain of fundamentalist Christian thought which holds that the second coming will arrive when all the Jews return to the Holy Land, where they will be destroyed in some sort of cataclysm (thus achieving both of Robertson's options simultaneously). Presumably Robertson is not endorsing that particular theory here. But, at the very least, he seems to be adopting the view of certain Zionist extremists that there can be no safe place for Jews outside of Israel—that the options are Israel or "elimination." Such a view may not be anti-Semitic, even when held by a non-Jew, but it is not exactly the Republican party line. (The Republican party line, of course, is that Jews are perfectly safe outside of Israel, so long as they are carrying a concealed semiautomatic weapon.)

Next, in our backward journey through this remarkable sentence, consider the strange qualifying phrase, "inasmuch as we are able." Inasmuch as we are able, says Pat Robertson, we should strive to avoid the elimination of the Jews. He means, of course, insofar as we are able. "Inasmuch as we are able," read literally, would mean that, since we happen to be able to, we might as well avoid the elimination of the Jews. But Robertson clearly is not saying that. He is suggesting that he is not at all sure we will be able to avoid the elimination of the Jews. Do you detect a note of noble resignation—an almost audible sigh—here? There's a sort of implied advance permission to fail, as if success is a hopeless ideal and the effort is what counts. It reminds me of signs that used to be posted, many years ago, in Harrod's Department Store in London: "Please Try Not to Smoke." Do try not to eliminate the Jews, but, well, flesh is weak, and we are all sinners. A body can only do so much.

Consider, finally, the opening clause: "Intolerance in any quarter is wrong, but inasmuch as we are able" we shouldn't eliminate the Jews, etc., etc. Why "but"? Surely conventional logic would suggest that the proper connector between these two thoughts is "and": intolerance is wrong and we shouldn't eliminate the Jews. (Or possibly even "and therefore" we shouldn't, etc., etc.) What concept is Pat Robertson trying to express when he says that intolerance is wrong but we shouldn't eliminate the Jews?

My only thought here is that perhaps Robertson intended this introductory qualification as a pre-emptive strike against critics who might otherwise accuse him of implicitly condoning other forms of intolerance with his fetishistic insistence that we must strive, as much as we are able, to avoid the elimination of the Jews. As a believer in the true meaning of civil rights—before it was corrupted by civil rights activists—one must be careful not to seem to be endorsing special treatment for any race, creed or color. We must strive toward ensuring that trends run against the elimination of all ethnic groups equally. Of course this equality must be of opportunity, and not of result. Every ethnic group must have an equal opportunity not to be eliminated. Whether they make the most of this opportunity is up to them.

Or something like that.

## CONFESSIONS OF A BUCKRAKER

New Republic, *May 1, 1995*

NOTE: *My buckraking career was quite short. What I don't say in this piece is that I took it up seriously after being diagnosed with Parkinson's, when financial panic made the easy money more alluring. And it didn't last long: when I quit* Crossfire *to start* Slate, *the offers dried up. They only want you if you're on television. I still think that for those who enjoy public speaking, there is nothing wrong with it. I don't much enjoy public speaking, so I don't miss it. Nevertheless, this piece remains the only serious attempt I know of to defend buckraking. I defend it but don't do it. Others do it but don't defend it.*

After years of resisting temptation, I have succumbed to the lecture circuit. What I do mostly is not speeches but staged debates with some conservative journalist or politician. Since the audiences are generally composed of affluent businessmen, my role is like that of the team that gets to lose to the Harlem Globetrotters. But I do it because it pays well, because it's fun to fly around the country and stay in hotels, and because even a politically unsympathetic audience can provide a cheap ego boost.

These are hardly noble reasons. But are they corrupt? Some journalists, and a few gleeful outsiders, think so. Journalistic ethics cops have been very hard on politicians who accept honoraria and campaign contributions from groups with interests before the government. Is it any different when journalists accept handsome fees for addressing conventions, trade associations and so on? The paid lecture circuit is an American tradition, and journalists have always participated—until recently, without controversy. But it has become far more lucrative, and thus more controversial, in recent years.

In a memorable *TNR* article nine years ago, Jacob Weisberg coined the term "buckraking" to describe this new phenomenon. And, to be sure, it is an absurd business in many ways. Anyone whose ego isn't terminally bloated has to be taken aback by the amounts some people are willing to pay for his or her time and thoughts.

Furthermore I, at least, have some doubts about the social utility of the whole conference/convention industry, of which the buckraking circuit is a small part. Buckraking is also a small part of the culture of celebrity, and there is something off-putting about a world of values in which Colin Powell and Kato Kaelin and Gerald Ford and William Safire are all measured—and remunerated—on a single, all-purpose, morally neutral scale of fame. Finally, for a journalist, the buckraking circuit presents a couple of special perils: the distraction of time and energy from the important work of life; and the risk of coming to mistake your prosperous buckraking audiences for a cross-section of America.

All these absurdities and perils are real. But are they severe enough to make buckraking inherently corrupt? In a way, the accusation represents chickens coming home to roost. American journalism has badly overplayed the concept of "conflict of interest"—too easily equating the possibility or opportunity for corruption with corruption itself. An especially lazy ethical shorthand has been the notion of "the appearance of impropriety"—holding, with bootstrap logic, that a situation is wrong if it appears to be wrong. (I'm clean here, having criticized both these journalistic practices often over the years.)

The situation of journalists is different from that of politicians in at least three ways. First, elected officials are public servants. They are employees of the taxpayers, and whatever gives them value as public speakers—whether it is merely their fame, or their inside-Washington insights, or their actual power over the course of the nation—rightly belongs to the public and not to them. Journalists are not public servants. Whether, in taking lecture fees, they are expropriating value that rightly belongs to their employers is a matter for the individual journalist and employer to decide. If a journalist is otherwise performing his or her job, an employer might quite reasonably decide that buckraking is a nice employee perk that costs the employer nothing (or even constitutes free advertising).

Second, politicians run the government. They have real power over people's lives and money. Journalists have no power except the power of words. Now, I wouldn't be in journalism if I thought that the power of words was inconsequential. A Sam Donaldson may well have more influence over the course of events in Washington than some obscure member of Congress. But words only have power to the extent they are persuasive, and abuses of the power of words are, to some extent, self-limiting. Faulty facts or fatuous reasoning can be countered. A politician, by contrast, exercises power directly. Facts and reason may or may not enter into it.

Third, business interests don't even attempt to deny what they're buying when they contribute to a politician's campaign, or pay an "honorarium" for the privilege of eating breakfast with him or her. They are buying, or at least trying to buy, support for their own political agenda. It needn't be as crude as a simple trade of cash for votes. It might be just a trade of cash for an opportunity to persuade. Or, at its most legitimate, it might be a matter of helping to re-elect a politician who already agrees with them on the issues. But the basic purpose of the transaction—buying political support for a private cause—is beyond dispute.

And what are these companies buying when they hire a journalist to speak? Well, maybe I'm naive, or blinded by self-interest, but I honestly believe that a desire to influence what the journalist writes or says on television has nothing to do with it. No group I've spoken to has ever made the slightest effort to ply me with its policy agenda. This really seems to be the furthest thing from anyone's mind (unless these people are a lot more nefarious and subtle than I give them credit for). So what are they buying? They're buying entertainment, insight (they hope), propinquity to someone who's on TV. Are they getting any insight or inside-Washington dope they couldn't get from, say, perusing an issue of *TNR*? Probably not. But then I've often wondered why people would rather listen to a speech than read the same words in print. Yet many do, and always have.

The point is not that journalists are incorruptible. Nor is it that the situation has no corrupting potential. The point is that attempting to close off every avenue of potential corruption is both excessive and futile. Excessive, because journalism—despite the posturing of some practitioners—is just barely a profession, and certainly not a celibate priesthood. Journalists should strive to avoid factual and intellectual dishonesty. But expecting them to avoid all potential occasions of these sins is expecting too much. And it's futile, because no sane set of rules can even begin to foreclose all avenues of potential conflict-of-interest.

Consider James Glassman, a former publisher of *TNR*. Glassman is leading the charge against buckraking. He wrote recently in the *Washington Post* that he is scandalized by journalists taking money for speeches. Glassman spent several years as both editor and publisher of *Roll Call*, a newspaper covering Capitol Hill. He and his wife, Mary, did a brilliant job of reviving this moribund journal. How? Primarily by persuading business interests that *Roll Call* was the perfect medium for sending messages to Congress. At the same time he was selling ads to corporations that were attempting to influence pending legislation, however, Glassman was also supervising *Roll Call*'s coverage of that same legislation. And, based on his success in both roles, *Roll Call* was sold for millions of dollars—of which Glassman got a large chunk.

This dual role surely describes a much more direct temptation to sin—with a much bigger payoff—than that of some TV talking head who accepts a speaking fee from a trade association. Do I have any evidence that *Roll Call*'s coverage was affected by its ads? No. Quite the opposite: to the best of my knowledge, *Roll Call*'s coverage of Capitol Hill was scrupulously honest. Do I think Glassman is corrupt because of the potential corruption of the situation? Not at all. So why won't he extend the same courtesy to lesser buckrakers than himself? Some publications make a big deal about a "church and state" separation of editorial and business staffs. Others bar their reporters from attending political rallies. If rules like these make them feel better, fine. And some rules do make sense, I suppose. For example, you wouldn't want a reporter who covers a specific industry to be getting large checks from that particular industry. But this kind of procedural rule can never catch up with the various ways journalists can be dishonest or blindered or mentally lazy in what they produce. Such rules merely replace the appearance of corruption with the appearance of propriety. Their relation to actual corruption and actual propriety is tenuous at best. What keeps journalists on the straight and narrow most of the time is not a lot of rules about potential conflicts of interest, but the basic reality of our business that a journalist's product is out there for all to see and evaluate. There are no hidden parts.

One rule some moderate buckrakophobes advocate is disclosure. At least, they say, let the readers and viewers know what groups you're speaking to, and let them decide for themselves what conclusions to draw from that. It's hard for a journalist, especially, to argue against the principle that disclosure is good (and my position is, I'll do it if everyone else will). But the widespread resistance to disclosure is perfectly understandable. Why hesitate to disclose your sources of income if you're not ashamed of them? For the same reason you might be embarrassed to display your private parts in public, even if you don't think there's anything wrong with them. And—let's face it—the demand for disclosure derives in large part from a prurient interest in other people's income that is actually quite similar to the prurient interest in other people's private parts. I, for one, would far rather see George Will's income tax returns than his naked body.

What really bothers some Puritans is the very idea of journalists making a lot of money, however they manage to do it. It seems like an inversion of the natural order, and perhaps it is. No one sensible goes into journalism for the money, and no sensible journalist believes he or she is "worth" a fat lecture fee. It's important not to get complacent, and to remember to credit serendipity. But our economy pays many folks—ball-players, business executives, symphony conductors—more than they're worth. Being paid more than you're worth is the American dream. I see a day when we'll all be paid more than we're worth. Meanwhile, though, there's no requirement for journalists, alone among humanity, to deny themselves the occasional fortuitous tastes of this bliss.

## EDITORIAL: A DANGEROUS MEDIUM

Slate, *April 6, 1997*

NOTE: *In the early Internet years, many people thought the World Wide Web was dangerous. This column originally began with a plug for* Slate's *short-lived paper edition.*

We hesitate, frankly, to offer a paper edition of *Slate*. Why? Because paper is a dangerous medium, all too prone to misuse by pedophiles, political extremists, paranoid conspiracy mongers, and purveyors of bad casserole recipes. Hitler's *Mein Kampf* was written on paper. So were many of Stalin's most bestial orders for mass executions. Those of us at *Slate* who are parents must naturally wonder whether paper should be allowed into a house where young children can read or—worse—write on it.

As many newspapers, magazines, and other timber-industry byproducts have pointed out, *Slate*'s preferred medium of the Internet has some darker byways of its own. That's true. But this anti-Internet alarmism is a heavy-handed attempt to distract attention from the really dangerous medium: paper. J'accuse. Quis custodiet ipsos custodes? Et cetera.

The earliest users of paper were ancient Egyptians, with their bizarre worship of the Sun God, Ra. In the modern era, the practice of writing on paper was first taken up, and monopolized for centuries, by Christian monks, all of whom had taken vows of celibacy. Even today, reading paper products is a lonely habit whose practitioners often spend hours or even days at a time silently and obsessively turning pages, immersed in a world of fantasy, isolated from normal society. No wonder some of them lose all grip on reality. Charles Manson was a known book reader. So was Attila the Hun (according to his former political consultant, Dick Morris). Yet society ignored the clues until it was too late.

Mere words cannot describe the vast range of content now available on paper. Much of this, to be sure, is harmless nonsense, such as the installation instructions that come with popular software products. But paper is by far the favorite medium of pornographers.

Ransom notes use paper as well. Several years ago a scientific journal published instructions for building a nuclear bomb. Where? On paper!

In a culture where Internet reality is dismissed as "virtual," the appearance of words on paper lends them instant credibility—credibility that may not be deserved. An irresponsible rumor can be set in type, and then printed and distributed by the millions, with no guarantee whatsoever of its accuracy. And yet people say, "I only know what I read in the papers." At best, paper's materiality creates an unjustified impression of trustworthiness; at worst, paper can be folded into an airplane that can poke someone's eye out.

Paper poses a special peril to children. Unlike a computer, a filthy magazine can easily be snuck into the house in an innocent-looking lunchbox. It can be hidden under a pile of sweat clothes in the bottom dresser drawer. Any page can be folded, placed in a pocket, and secretly transported or shared with other children. Books can even be read by flashlight in bed, long after Dad has requisitioned the family computer and is trying to log on to AOL, naively believing that junior is safe from corruption just because he is tucked in and offline.

It is fine to say that parents are responsible for what their children read. But no parent can realistically patrol a child's access to paper. It's everywhere—even at the library and other taxpayer-supported institutions. Rating systems do not exist. Filtering software is not available.

What is the moral? The first moral is that children are never safer than when staring at a computer screen. At least you know they're not reading a book or anything. Second, government regulation of paper is clearly needed. We look to Congress for a Paper Decency Act, to close the giant loophole left open when last year's Communications Decency Act was limited to electronic media. Third, the recent ruling of the United States Parole Board forbidding paroled federal prisoners to use the Internet must be extended to forbid books, magazines, and newspapers as well. Corrupting influences are everywhere.

## SLATE: A POLICY STATEMENT

Slate, *June 1, 1997*

NOTE: *Microsoft was considered megalomaniacal at this time. The government's antitrust suit against the company turned on the highly Jesuitical question of whether a computer operating system with a browser was one product or two products. The "Justice Department arsonists" in "Bill Clinton's Browser" is a reference to the episode at Waco, when the Justice Department burned down the headquarters of a cult named the Branch Davidians.*

In light of continuing concerns about the power and ambitions of our parent company, the Microsoft Corp., we at *Slate* would like to offer the following declaration of our own policy and goals. This policy statement was prepared without consultation, and applies only to *Slate*.

Our goal at *Slate*, quite simply, is to *own* political and cultural commentary in this country, the industrialized nations, and ultimately in the developing regions as well. The whole world, basically. We will use any means necessary to achieve this end, including competition, both fair and unfair, wholesale buying up of potential rivals, strategic partnerships and alliances, strategic betrayals of partners and allies, theft, bribery, murder, and, if necessary, putting out a high-quality product.

Someday, if you want an opera criticism, an analysis of the latest tax proposal, or a profile of some obscure academic, you'll have no choice but to come to us. Building on our domination of these areas, we will extend our reach into popular culture, gradually monopolizing movie and television reviews and interviews with brainless celebrities. Ultimately, our towering position, as well as economies of scale in the production of opinion and analysis, will make resistance futile. At that point, we will control the industry and be able to extract the rich monopoly profits waiting to be had from poetry, book reviews, essays pleading for entitlement reform, explanations of developments in foreign countries, and similar product lines.

We will, of course, continue to support all platforms: liberal, conservative, libertarian, vegetarian, UNIX. We are committed to producing opinions that are compatible with all standard political labels and work equally well for Democrats and Republicans. We foresee a day when all viewpoints on every subject are equally comfortable for anyone to swallow, and when the frustrating cacophony of today's political and cultural debate is replaced by easy-to-use modules of predigested viewpoints that can be downloaded from the Web with a simple credit-card transaction.

Or at least, that's the plan.


## BILL CLINTON'S BROWSER

Slate, *Jan. 25, 1998*


**W**hom should we run into the other night in T.G.I. Friday's at the mall but Bill Gates and Janet Reno! They were out together celebrating the settlement of their little tiff over that consent decree. Gates' guard dogs snarled as we approached, and so did the crack team of Justice Department arsonists who were standing by, ready to set the whole restaurant on fire at the slightest hint of danger. "Down, Higgins! Down, Ballmer!" said Gates, feeding them small bits of his braised Myhrvold nacho salad and inviting us to pull up a pew. Reno called off her flamethrowers as well, and it was the beginning of a jolly evening. After a few Old Neukom Pale Ales, we couldn't resist asking them what they thought of this latest Clinton brouhaha. Gates observed tartly, "Someone should tell that guy to keep his browser separate from his operating system." Reno guffawed, "Maybe someone should tell him to keep his browser out of other people's operating systems." Gates stared at her briefly, clearly annoyed at having had his metaphor appropriated by the government. But then he relaxed and added with a philosophical chuckle, "Of course in Clinton's case the browser and the operating system seem to be one integrated product."

## In Defense of Matt Drudge

Time, *Feb. 2, 1998*

"Last weekend, there were two extraordinary dramas playing out in Washington." So begins *Newsweek*'s story about President Clinton and the twenty-one-year-old intern. But there was a third extraordinary drama playing out: *Newsweek*'s own agony about whether the story was firm enough to go with. The editors ultimately decided it wasn't and pulled it from last week's issue—only to post it on America Online midweek after Internet scoopmeister Matt Drudge had reported both the story and *Newsweek*'s decision to spike it, and the tale had spread on the Web until it finally surfaced in Wednesday's *Washington Post* and *Los Angeles Times*.

*Newsweek* looks foolish. But was it really so foolish? Even in the pages of a rival, gloating is not called for. *Time* was chasing the same story and never had it to throw away, so hats off to the competition. Furthermore, *Newsweek*'s "mistake" was in being more cautious than Drudge about publishing extremely damaging allegations about the President of the U.S. Even if those allegations are true, was the caution misplaced?

The Internet made this story. And the story made the Internet. Clinterngate, or whatever we are going to call it, is to the Internet what the Kennedy assassination was to TV news: its coming of age as a media force. Or some might say media farce. This story follows several similar episodes of stories pushed into the traditional media after being spread on the Internet—for example, the notion that TWA Flight 800 was shot down by the U.S. Navy—where the stories were nutty and baseless. The Clintern saga certainly is not baseless, although the comic seediness of it, in contrast to the high tragedy of 1963, can be seen as a telling comment on the new medium. After all, the Internet beat TV and print to this story, and ultimately forced it on them, for one simple reason: lower standards.

Let's not give Drudge too much credit. Though he thumbs his nose at traditional news outlets, they supply most of his information. His sources are inside the media, not (usually) inside the institutions they cover. His scoops—including this one—are generally stuff the grownups either have declined to publish or are about to publish. Having pilfered other folks' material, Drudge has the considerable gall to emblazon his own E-mail dispatches with the warning, WORLD EXCLUSIVE. MUST CREDIT THE DRUDGE REPORT.

There is a case to be made, however, for lower standards. In this case, the lower standards were vindicated. Almost no one now denies there is a legitimate story here. Taped conversations and suspected subornation of perjury moved the story safely beyond furtive rumors of sexual dalliance. For Drudge, though, furtive rumors of dalliance are enough.

Even for traditional media journalists, furtive rumors of dalliance are enough—when it comes to trading gossip around the water cooler. There is something slightly elitist about the attitude that we journalists can be trusted to evaluate such rumors appropriately but that our readers and viewers cannot. Actually, though, almost everybody has the same standards—that is, almost none—in passing along juicy rumors to friends and colleagues.

The case for Drudge—who complacently says his reports are 80 percent accurate—is that there ought to be a middle ground between the highest standards and none at all. And the Internet, which can be sort of halfway between a private conversation and formal publication, is a good place for that middle ground. The middle ground, of course, should be acknowledged as such, either explicitly or by convention. People should understand that the information they get this way is middling quality—better than what their neighbor heard at the dry cleaner's but not as good as the *New York Times*. And Internet sites that aspire to the highest standards of traditional media (like *Slate*, where I work) should be held to them. But if Drudge claims only 80 percent accuracy and can make it over that lowered bar, why not?

Well, one reason why not is exactly what seemed to happen last week: journalistic entropy. Everyone sinks to the lowest standard going. It is impossible to maintain a firewall between the *Washington Post* and Matt Drudge. But another way to look at last week is that the firewall held for several days and that the story broke through the firewall only when it became legitimate by any standards. In any event, these are early days still, and the exact relationship of the Internet with older media is still working itself out.

So maybe *Newsweek* was right to get it second and Drudge to get it first. Maybe both staked out their proper places in the media food chain. There will be plenty of times when caution will be rewarded and uncritical insta-printing will look foolish. Or maybe they were both wrong: *Newsweek* to spike a great scoop and Drudge to publish it. The former view is more appealing, and I'm 80 percent sure it's right.

## LIES, DAMNED LIES, AND IMPEACHMENT

FINE. NOW LET'S GO BACK AND IMPEACH REAGAN AND BUSH.

Slate, *Jan. 1, 1999*

NOTE: *This piece applies the standards used to impeach Bill Clinton to his two Republican predecessors. You could also apply those standards forward to impeach George W. Bush, as some want to do. We now know that while the Republican Congress was impeaching Bill Clinton over his affair with Monica Lewinsky, House Speaker Newt Gingrich also was having an affair with a young (though not quite that young) aide. "Flytrap" was* Slate's *name for the Lewinsky scandal. It didn't catch on.*

OK, so it's not about sex. It's about lying under oath, obstruction of justice, and abuse of power. If the standards used to impeach President Clinton for those offenses were applied to his two Republican predecessors, Reagan and Bush, they would have been impeached too. The fact that they weren't owes less to any lack of evidence than to a sense of proportion and respect for the popular will—or call it cowardice, perhaps—in the opposition party (the Democrats), which then controlled Congress.

The only time Ronald Reagan ever talked about Iran-Contra under oath was in a deposition for the criminal trial of his former National Security Adviser John Poindexter. The deposition was in 1990, after Reagan had left office. He claimed that there was not "one iota" of evidence that profits from the sale of arms to Iran had been diverted to the Nicaraguan Contras, that his aides hadn't lied to Congress about the affair, and so on. All this was demonstrably false. The only reason he might not be guilty of perjury is that his mind pretty clearly was going.

But the very fact that Reagan was never forced to testify under oath as president illustrates the double standard that has trapped Bill Clinton. If Iran-Contra Special Prosecutor Lawrence Walsh had operated like Flytrap Special Prosecutor Kenneth Starr, he would have forced Reagan, while president, to repeat or renounce under oath his public lies about Iran-Contra, such as those in his first TV address on the subject, when he declared it "utterly false" that arms had been shipped to Iran in exchange for the release of American hostages. This was as vivid as Clinton's televised finger-wagging "that woman" sound bite, and just as flatly untrue. Reagan had been at several meetings where the arms-for-hostages deal was discussed—and, indeed, where Cabinet members had warned him it was illegal and he'd said he didn't care. If Walsh had been Starr, Reagan would have faced the same excruciating dilemma as Clinton: admit to a spectacular public lie or lie again under oath.

Possibly Reagan was already gaga in 1986, while still president, though this is not an argument the Republicans now pursuing Clinton are likely to want to make (or were heard to make back in 1986). But even before he was officially declared to be losing it, Reagan benefited from a more general double standard about truth telling. Reagan and Clinton both are among the great bullshitters of American history, but somehow Reagan was always regarded as floating above the truth while Clinton is regarded as wallowing beneath it.

Walsh's final report concluded that Reagan "knowingly participated or at least acquiesced in" the Iran-Contra cover-up, which involved, among other things, Oliver North shredding thousands of documents that may well have implicated Reagan more deeply. Any Flytrap cover-up pales in comparison. (The nearest equivalent involves the mysterious appearance—not disappearance—of documents, none of which has turned out to be vital, in a White House closet.) Yet Walsh didn't bring charges against Reagan, or even depose him to squeeze out information or set him up for a perjury rap.

The case against George Bush—by the standards being applied to Bill Clinton—is even stronger. Bush claimed in the 1992 campaign that he'd given sworn testimony hundreds of times conceding that he knew all about the arms-for-hostages deal. In fact, when the story broke in 1986, Bush repeatedly claimed to have been "out of the loop." He knew we were selling arms to Iran—itself flatly illegal and spectacularly in conflict with the administration's public pronouncements—but, he claimed, he had no idea the deal involved paying ransom for hostages.

Specifically, Bush claimed not to have attended a January 1986 meeting at which Secretary of State George Shultz and Secretary of Defense Caspar Weinberger vehemently opposed trading for hostages. When White House logs indicated that Bush was at the meeting, he emended his story to say he hadn't caught the drift of Shultz's and Weinberger's objections. If only he'd known George and Cap were as bothered as he was, Bush said, he would have tried to stop the policy. This was his story until 1992, when Walsh released notes taken by Weinberger at the meeting, recording that "VP approves" of the policy Bush claimed to be both ignorant of and disturbed by.

As president in 1989–93, Bush did his best to thwart Walsh's investigation. He tightened up on the release of classified information. A diary he started keeping in 1986 somehow never materialized until after the 1992 election. And his last-minute pardon of Weinberger, Poindexter, and others, after he'd lost re-election, effectively thwarted Walsh's pursuit of Bush himself, among others. No "obstruction of justice" or "abuse of presidential power" in Flytrap comes close.

So why is Bill Clinton's presidency stamped forever with the shame of impeachment, and why does he face premature removal from office, when impeachment was never seriously considered for Bush and Reagan? Perhaps at this point Clinton's critics would like to revisit their insistence that it's not about sex. The only sensible distinction is that lies about some things matter more than others. Henry Hyde, for example, was quite eloquent back in the Iran-Contra era about how statesmanship and higher principles sometimes require presidents to lie and break the law.

Hyde and others would be tempted to say that lying to free American hostages and breaking the law to protect Latin America from communism are more justified than lies to hide a tawdry affair. I would be tempted to reply that lies and cover-ups intended to thwart the workings of democracy on an important public policy issue seem to me to be a lot worse than lies about an embarrassing personal mess. But perhaps we could agree that David Schippers, the House

Judiciary Committee Counsel, was wrong in his self-righteous pronouncement "Lies are lies are lies."

Schippers himself told a quick series of obvious whoppers during that same impeachment hearing opening statement. "When I appeared in this committee room a little over two months ago," he said (mournful as the Walrus in *Through the Looking Glass*), "it was merely to analyze the [Starr report] referral and to report to you. Today, after our investigation, I come to a point that frankly I prayed I would never reach. It is my sorrowful duty now to accuse President William Jefferson Clinton," etc., etc. Raise your hand if you believe Schippers a) was feeling sorrowful; b) had prayed that his months of effort to nail the president would be in vain; c) was being frank; d) had no settled view on the whole matter even after analyzing the Starr report, until "our investigation" (whatever that consisted of). And while your hand is up, would you care to swear an oath that you believe these unbelievable things?

"Every time a witness lies, that witness chips a stone from the foundation of our entire legal system," Schippers intoned. Or does he make an exception when the witness is himself?

Trent Lott, as Senate majority leader, is overseer of the forthcoming Clinton trial. He was pictured in last Friday's *New York Times* actually wagging his finger, Clinton-"that woman"-style, as he publicly lied to get himself out of a fix. On Wednesday he had said about the Baghdad bombing: "While I have been assured by administration officials that there is no connection with the impeachment process . . . I cannot support this military action in the Persian Gulf at this time. Both the timing and the policy are subject to question." It was immediately clear that Lott should not have said this. So on Thursday, Lott declared that he did support the action, did not suspect any connection with the impeachment process, and had not meant to imply otherwise merely by uttering words whose plain meaning and universal interpretation was the exact opposite. Lott's sushi-master carve-up of the phrase "at this time" was positively Clintonian in its boldness and artistry. Of course he wasn't under oath, so that's OK.

What made the Lott incident especially enjoyable is that Republicans all rallied round the obvious meaning of his original statement even as Lott himself was denying it. Paul Gigot, for example, got trapped midspin-cycle. In his Friday column on the *Wall Street Journal* editorial page, he praised Lott's remark as "an honest, considered judgment." But how could a conservative Republican senator and major flag waver for the original Gulf War honestly oppose punishing Saddam for violating his surrender terms? Easy: "This is the surreal politics Bill Clinton has created. Hawks are now doves and vice versa." But surely, Paul, you don't really believe Clinton bombed Baghdad to affect the impeachment vote? Well, no, but, "The tragedy for American interests is that Mr. Clinton is doubted even when he might be right."

Neato. Clinton is thus responsible not only for his own lies and hypocrisies but also for those of his enemies. No doubt he is somehow to blame for Iran-Contra too.

## The Trouble with Scoops

Time, *March 15, 1999*

We almost had a scoop the other day at *Slate*, the online magazine I edit. We were all terribly excited. The adrenaline was flowing. This is what journalists live for: we were going to grab the world's attention, expose hypocrisy, rectify injustice and draw in new customers. And yet I was only half sorry when the story didn't work out. Scoops are fool's gold in many ways.

The basic premise of a scoop is that you're bringing important facts to public attention. Your philosophical touchstone is Justice Louis Brandeis' bromide that sunlight is the best disinfectant. But you spend much or even most of your energy trying to keep things secret. You're constantly swearing people to silence, making them promise not to tell others so that your scoop doesn't get scooped, and promising for your part to go to jail before revealing your sources.

"We're far more concerned that information like this can be leaked to the press without our authorization," said a spokeswoman for ABC News last week. She was referring to what Monica Lewinsky told Barbara Walters in the exclusive interview for which ABC had fought so hard. She claimed her concern was that the reports were inaccurate. But why should ABC care if other media get the story wrong? The network's real concern was that rivals were getting the story right: scooping ABC's scoop.

Much of the joy of a scoop comes from beating the competition. If *Time* has a story a week earlier than *Newsweek*, there is joy in Rockefeller Center. But what service to humanity are you providing when you reveal some information that is going to come out anyway in a week or a day or (in the case of the Internet) five minutes? The scoops of today's leading scoopmeister, Matt Drudge, consist primarily of beating other media outlets to their own stories: reporting that someone else is about to report something. What's the rush?

ABC's Monica coup illustrates an increasingly common form of dubious scoop, as network newsmagazines proliferate and even real magazines compete for "exclusive" interviews with celebrities and newsmakers. The celebrity interview is exclusive only because the network or magazine has insisted on it or paid for it. Once again, the scoop consists less of producing new information yourself than of keeping others from producing it.

The scoops that come out of celebrity interviews are manufactured. The fact in question comes into existence only to serve as a scoop. There is tremendous pressure on the celebrity to say something interesting. How genuinely interesting can anything said under such pressure actually be?

This dynamic is best seen in the related category of the celebrity book. When, say, a former White House aide hires an agent to peddle a book proposal, the process resembles the legal "proffer" or plea-bargain proposal with which the Lewinsky affair has made us all familiar. The difference is that the client is singing for money instead of immunity. "For X hundreds of thousands of dollars, my client is prepared to say Y." Sometimes Y is an actual fact of historic interest, but often it is some unprovable bit of juicy trivia. ("'Divorce? Divorce is too good for you!' she screamed. Then I heard a crash . . .") And sometimes the scoop consists of nothing more than the former aide's willingness to express a putatively surprising opinion. ("He's a pathological liar, I now realize.")

Book and magazine publishers often follow a hypocritical convention of burying the scoop deep in the text—to signal that they're not really about anything so vulgar and transitory as news. Then they launch a publicity barrage, invariably including a press release written in traditional journalistic "pyramid style"—that is, with the scoop on top, where it belongs. ("ALBRIGHT SAYS CLINTON

NEVER TOUCHED HER. In her just published memoir, *Woman of the World*, former Secretary of State Madeleine Albright denies reports in former White House press secretary Mike McCurry's recent memoir, *The Soul of Discretion*, that President Clinton . . .") In essence the press release is the real reporting medium.

It is a bit hard to understand why this works. Why would anyone pay for a book or a magazine just for scoops you already know about from the publicity? But people do. Partly they've been suckered by the sideshow barker's trick of implying that there's more inside when there ain't. But partly there is pleasure in holding and owning something that's making news, even if it's news you already know. And journalists love producing scoops for something like the same reason. There's a thrill in being the first to report something, even if it's basically trivial, wholly artificial or soon to be universally known anyway.

Which brings up the worst thing about scoops: they come with built-in pressure to exaggerate their own importance. All scoops, even real and important ones, by their nature resist perspective. "In a development that experts say could revolutionize our thinking about toast, XYZ News has learned that . . ." No scoop ever begins, "In a development that may not be any big deal . . ." Thus what starts out as a quest for the truth often ends up just adding to the world's supply of dishonesty.

## EASY ANSWERS

Slate, *March 28, 1999*

NOTE: *In hindsight, the Republican evasions about President Clinton's intervention in Kosovo sound a lot like the Democratic evasions about President Bush's war in Iraq. But Clinton's war was limited and successful. Bush's, to say the least, was not.*

It is often said that there are no easy answers, but in fact there are. In a former life I used to interrogate politicians on television, and in six years there was never a subject on which they were unable to come up with an easy answer. Not necessarily a correct answer—or honest or heartfelt or logically coherent—but easy.

What is an easy answer? An easy answer, for a politician, is one that assures you will never be proved wrong. Or at least that if you seem to have been wrong, another easy answer will be available to explain why you weren't. "There are no easy answers" is itself an easy answer—if you can get away with it. Often, you not only can get away with it, but you can also enhance your reputation for being "thoughtful" (high praise that in the culture of politics means indecisive in a classy way, rather than kindly or considerate of others or anything like that). Sometimes, though, you have to do better, and this is when easy answers become hard work.

War and peace issues are the worst. A famous joke among academics is that scholarly disputes are especially passionate because the stakes are so low. By contrast, when the stakes are as high as they can get, there is a special need for elected officials to avoid having a forthright opinion. Easy answers to the rescue!

The current issue of American military involvement in Kosovo, for example, seems to be a yes-or-no question to which either conventional answer—call them "yes" and "no"—is decidedly uneasy. "Yes" means risking American lives in a faraway land that has no apparent connection to the only thing that really matters, which is the Dow Jones industrial average. "No" means doing nothing, as the world's only superpower, while a thug government commits daily televised atrocities against white people in Europe (not just some unmediated Africans). Unless you're extraordinarily lucky, the outcome of making either choice will leave you morally implicated in some dead bodies.

Fortunately, even for Kosovo there are answers available besides yes and no. They will be familiar from intervention disputes dating back at least to Vietnam, but they are especially useful for the summer-squall-style military actions of today, in which we all agree to be frenzied about the occupation of Kuwait or a drug-smuggling dictator in Panama or warlords in Somalia or genocide in Bosnia on the strict understanding that we will be allowed to forget all about these matters and places in six months, max. Here are half a dozen consumer-tested easy answers on issues like Kosovo:

1. "Well, Cokie, my concern is that if we go into [INSERT LOCATION], we should do so with the resources necessary to get the job

done. Airstrikes alone [or 'only 200,000 troops' or 'a mere half a dozen hydrogen bombs' or whatever is on the menu] just aren't enough. It is immoral to put American soldiers at risk without a guarantee of overwhelming superiority for a certain and speedy victory."

This is perhaps the most prestigious dodge: the Powell Doctrine, named for Gen. Colin Powell. The Powell Doctrine holds that the lesson of Vietnam is do it right or not at all. Go in full force from the beginning rather than escalate yourself into a quagmire. Or don't go in at all. Finish quickly before the public loses patience (or ideally, as in the case of Grenada, before the public has even heard of the place). Or, of course, don't start at all. As to which of these alternatives—all or nothing at all—is the right one in any situation, the Powell Doctrine does not say. So this is a great way to sound tough and sophisticated without actually committing yourself. Since any actual military engagement is not going to involve every last wing nut in the Pentagon's "miscellaneous screws" jar, you are well positioned to say, "I told you so," if things go badly. Yet you never actually opposed the action, so you're OK if things go well. And no one can accuse you of wimping out if the military action doesn't take place: Hey, you wanted to go in with more force!

2. "Where is our exit strategy, Ted? That is what I'd like to know."

"Exit strategy" became a fashionable term during the Gulf War. It really sounds like you know what you're talking about. And what does it mean? As I understand it, an exit strategy is a sort of poor man's Powell Doctrine. It does not demand certain and prompt victory. It merely demands a certain and prompt conclusion to the exercise that is acceptable to the United States. When invoking this concern, it is not necessary to specify—and indeed it is hard to imagine—what conclusion short of victory a guy like you, who flings around terms like "exit strategy," would find minimally satisfactory. And no military action (except for actual movies) can be fully scripted in advance. So you're golden. If things go wrong: "Ted, I pleaded with the president to make sure we had an exit strategy." And if the action goes well or disaster occurs because we didn't intervene: "Ted, I was behind this all the way. I've always said that victory is the best exit strategy."

3. "Tim, I support the president. American credibility is at stake. The commander in chief has made a commitment on behalf of the United States, and the United States must honor that commitment."

This is the sneakiest dodge and probably the most popular—especially among Republicans. You get to be patriotic and hawkish. And if things go well, you were behind the commander in chief all the way. But if things go badly, it is the president's fault for making the commitment. Tragically, you had no choice but to support him once the commitment was made, but of course making it was irresponsible folly. Please note that, like a reheated stew, this dodge works even better after a military action has begun. "Tim, we never should have got into this quagmire, but now we have no choice but to . . ."

4. "I'm not persuaded this is so important, so vital to the nation's interests that we ought to intervene."

That's an almost exact quote from a real senator, Bob Kerrey of Nebraska, and illustrates a nifty linguistic evasion. You don't say you're against it, you say you're "not persuaded" to be for it. Not only do you evade the tough choice, you also evade responsibility for your decision. It's the president's fault, even if he's right, because he didn't persuade you. You can also say (like Sen. Max Baucus of Montana) that there are "unanswered questions." Being undecided and wanting ever more information is another great way to be designated as "thoughtful." And with a bit of skill and a bit of luck, you can keep taking your own temperature until it doesn't matter any more. Meanwhile, you're OK no matter what happens. "Not persuaded" can be spun as a yes or a no. A nice variant is to say, "The American people must be persuaded this is the right thing, and the president hasn't made the case." Not only is whatever happens not your fault (unless it's good), it's not even the public's fault. It's the president's fault, either because we did what he wanted or—if we didn't—because he didn't convince us to do so.

5. "I don't think we should begin bombing unless and until the Serbs really begin a very significant massacre against the people in Kosovo."

That is Don Nickles of Oklahoma in Tuesday's *Wall Street Journal* (where most of these quotes come from). In a way, this is not a dodge. It is a sort of madcap Solomonic approach. Sen. Nickles is saying: "Why must we guess whether Milosevic is going to kill a lot more people? Let's wait and see if he does it! And why must we choose between saving a lot of Kosovars and saving none? Let's split the difference and save half of them." As a bonus, Nickles retains a valuable fudge factor in the question of what qualifies as "a very significant massacre." Depending on what happens, Nickles is in a position to accuse the president of failing to defend American interests and values, or of recklessly endangering American lives on the basis of a massacre that was merely "significant" but not "very significant."

6. "What's happening in [WHEREVER] is a tragedy and an outrage, Wolf. Intervention to stop the bloodshed is absolutely essential. But it's a job for [INSERT NAME OF CLOSER COUNTRY AND/OR REGIONAL GROUP], not for the United States."

This final dodge is slightly different. You're claiming credit for sharing whatever humanitarian or geostrategic concern dictates military action, while opposing the use of the only military power you yourself bear responsibility for. I once interviewed an especially moronic senator, since defeated, who declared that some worthy military action was "a job for the United Nations." I asked him why other countries should risk their soldiers' lives if the United States wouldn't, and he replied, "I didn't say 'other nations,' I said the *United* Nations." When it was pointed out to him that U.N. troops don't come from Mars, he was stymied. That point had never occurred to him.

But exposing the logical flaw here does not depend on any huffing and puffing about America's leadership role. An American pol going on American television to say that the Europeans should tidy up the former Yugoslavia without our help is pointless. When an answer moves beyond difficult to completely impossible, it becomes easy once again.

Watch for these easy answers on the TV talk shows and in the newspaper. Practice on your own. Soon you too can be ducking responsibility like a real-life member of Congress.

## Internet Envy

Slate, *June 11, 1999*

The fact that the Internet will make life better for all humankind has long been noted, even on the East Coast. What seems to have struck the East Coast only recently is that the Internet is making a smaller subset of all humankind—people who start Internet-related companies or join them before they go public—incredibly wealthy. The *New York Times* reported as much on its front page recently, so you know it's probably true.

Out here in cyberland, people have been aware of this fact for several years. Indeed we have talked of little else since about September 1996, which is the last time anyone mentioned a book except in the context of Amazon.com. The basic anecdote—variations on "When I knew him in college he was stoned all the time . . . two years ago he was living in a corrugated box on his ex-wife's compost pile (we all actually pitched in to buy him a new futon!) . . . then last week they had their IPO, and now he's worth $350 million"—declined long ago from fresh conversational gambit through staple to cliché.

So what's new? Money has always been a fraught topic. A New York writer who regularly mines his sex life and longings for material begged off an invitation to write about the Internet IPO phenomenon for *Slate* on the grounds that his feelings about money are too personal and complex. And envy didn't just become a deadly sin when its existence was acknowledged by the *New York Times*. Nevertheless, the arrival of Internet Envy on the Washington–New York buzz axis is new in several ways.

Washington types used to be surprisingly immune to envy of other people simply for being richer. A theory long propounded by Walter Shapiro (*USA Today* political columnist and *Slate* contributor) is that the financial heights of Washington are occupied by high-salaried lawyers and lobbyists, not by real accumulated or inherited wealth as in New York. The lifestyle gap between the middle and upper class does not yawn in front of, say, a *Washington Post* editor every day. Journalists—even print journalists!—and high-level civil servants live in the nicest neighborhoods. More important, of course,

Washington has—or had—a social status ranking independent of money. It's a place where puzzled gazillionaires can find themselves snubbed at dinner parties by deputy assistant Cabinet secretaries and patronized by minor TV talking heads.

Even in New York, where money matters more, there are (unlike in Washington) strong independent subcultures in which a journalist or college professor or unemployed actor can take comfort in an independent value system. They could have been bankers or management consultants but chose not to be. And the people at the top of those heaps, earning plenty to live comfortably, honestly wouldn't trade being, say, curator of dinosaurs at the Museum of Natural History for being just another multimillionaire investment banker. On most days.

So what has changed? One element, obviously, is the size of these Internet fortunes. Hundreds of millions. As syndicated columnist Matt Miller recently pointed out, with numbers like this surging across the *Times* business section, even investment bankers "feel like wage slaves at $10 million a year." (And, poor souls, these investment bankers generally cannot find comfort in an independent value system.) Meanwhile, in Washington, where even New York–style fortunes are rare, it seems that America Online alone (located in D.C.'s Virginia suburbs) has created a vast new social stratum of megamillionaires one has never heard of. Gives one pause.

Second, there's the speed. It's one thing to console yourself that at least you didn't have to spend thirty years doing a job you would hate. That trick is a bit harder when you read that someone (inevitably, someone with the same name as that bozo down the hall sophomore year . . . but it can't be . . . look, here's his picture . . . oh, hell) joined some nothing of a company, sat there through the IPO, and cashed out, all in a couple of years. How awful can a job be?

Answer: maybe not so awful at all. In fact, maybe it's remarkably similar to the job you're doing now. A third startling difference about Internet IPO wealth is that some of it is raining down on journalists! Writing journalists, no less, at places like Amazon and TheStreet and *i*Village (dot-com, dot-com, dot-com). This is something truly new in the history of the known universe. *Slate*'s former "Keeping Tabs" columnist Emily Yoffe observes: "You no longer can say, 'Sure I could have made a lot of money if I'd decided to be a Wall Street money grubber.' And it's not just [a famous TV hack] spending every weekend speaking to the Aluminum Manufacturers for $50,000. We're talking about journalists getting seriously rich just by being journalists."

Thus journalists have joined software engineers and business executives in peddling the other basic Internet Envy anecdote: variations on, "Oh yeah, they offered me the top job at Somedamnedsite. com—begged me to take it, offered me 75 percent of the equity plus options for another 75—but I turned it down." Even during the first few years of Internet frenzy, Internet Envy was not widespread in N.Y.-D.C. buzzworld because the whole thing seemed to be happening on another planet—to people one not only didn't know but could scarcely imagine. Only very recently have lottery winners started popping up in one's own neighborhood.

Internet Envy exists in cyberland itself, too, but it is much more straightforward. Everybody is trying to do the same thing; some succeed, and those who don't are envious. You don't have to pretend that you're not. And there's no queasy feeling that you must have misplaced that notice explaining how the rules were about to change. ("In Paragraph 19, Line 106, replace the words 'Pulitzer Prize for Nonfiction' with the words 'seven hundred fifty million dollars.' ") Also, unlike back East, there's no vertiginous obsession with how young these IPO-heads are, because almost everybody is scandalously young.

The rules have indeed changed. But they're always changing, in a couple of ways. Some changes in personal values are simply part of growing older. Then there are shifts in the values of the general culture.

To oversimplify: In high school the jocks are on top (unless, of course, armed losers storm the cafeteria one day and mow them down). But the smart kids tend to win in adult life. The glow of that happy discovery can last for years, as Nathan Myhrvold explained and simultaneously demonstrated in a recent *Slate* "Book Club." These are folks lucky enough to be able to choose their careers and to have a good shot at success at whatever they choose.

At the crucial moment when they make their choices, many of these people honestly believe that money—beyond the cost of upper-middle-class comfort—is not all that important to them, and most of them may turn out to be right. But some are responding to the fleeting hormonal surges of youthful idealism, or to the special status hierarchy of the academic subculture where they temporarily reside. In the most tragic examples, a charismatic professor will entice them into a lifetime of French medieval history, about which their curiosity is exhausted before they get their Ph.D.s. In less extreme cases, they become writers. Then they discover, in their thirties or forties, that money is important to them after all. This is the moment when reading about some twenty-eight-year-old who's suddenly worth $300 million can have an effect that requires medical attention.

Sometimes this personal process of maturity or decay (take your pick) is reinforced by what's happening in the culture. Money is never unimportant, but there are moments when it is more important than others. This is one of them. Actually, a graph of the changing value of money in the status market would look a lot like a graph of the Dow Jones industrial average: It rose steadily starting about 1982—the year a star *New York Times* reporter shocked his journalist colleagues by quitting the *Times* to become an investment banker—crested and sank briefly in the late 1980s, quickly recovered, and has been hitting new heights ever since. In these days, when even the most softhearted and public-spirited people become venture capitalists, younger readers may find it hard to believe there was ever a time when even an extremely ambitious person, motivated entirely by a desire to do well—rather than to do good, or to do anything in particular—might well decide to be a journalist. But it's true.

Of course it's possible that the stock market and the status market have peaked together again. Price-earnings ratios are perilously high in both. A $400 million fortune gets you about as much status as a mere $50 million got you a decade ago. Speculators in status futures are rumored to be pulling out of money and getting into undervalued properties including kindness, musical talent, and short-term memory. The decline of money is also expected to benefit blue chips such as physical beauty, according to some analysts.

So maybe this is the wrong moment to cash in your reputation as a saint—based on two and a half decades spent bathing patients in a South American leprosy clinic—for a job (with 50 percent equity stake) as CEO of Leper.com (soon to be LPRC on the NASDAQ). In this market as in others, timing is everything.

## GO TO HELL

THE GOSPEL ACCORDING TO GEORGE W.

Slate, *July 24, 1999*

In his current *Slate* "History Lesson" column, David Greenberg compares George W. Bush and John Quincy Adams. John Q.—as he was not known—is the only president's son so far to become president himself. Historian Greenberg finds many parallels but some differences. For example, Q. suffered a "lifelong case of clinical depression," whereas W. has come to "believe that all Jews are bound for hell." While the parallel is unclear, these are certainly two different things. As someone who has long suspected he might be Jewish (based on circumstantial evidence such as his bar mitzvah), I found this latter datum especially interesting. And, of course, it is remarkable to learn that George W. has actual opinions on any subject, let alone strong and controversial ones.

Unless you're a political junkie, or live in Texas, you may have missed this story. The press have reported it, but not with the neurotic intensity you might expect. Why not? Conservative press critics often complain that the media ignore the importance of religion. This may be a case in point, though not one those critics are likely to complain about. Second, there is the inoculation phenomenon: Once a story has "been done," editors and producers don't want to do it again. So, getting it done small is protection against finding it done big. Finally, there may be a feeling among journalists that the whole thing's a bum rap. Which it is and it isn't.

There's no evidence that George W. is an anti-Semite. After college he was even engaged briefly to a half-Jewish woman. Some have suggested that Bush may have dumped her because her father was Jewish, but there's no reason to think he didn't know that all along, if he cared, so the episode weighs in against the anti-Semitism charge, not for it. Bush has had many Jewish business partners and friends. If he believes they're all going to hell, he hasn't held it against them in this life.

So what does he believe? Like the Gospel tales themselves, the story of Bush's views on Jews has several variants. In 1993, discussing his decision around age forty to accept Christ as his personal savior, Bush told a *Houston Post* reporter that—as the reporter paraphrased it—"heaven is open only to those who accept Jesus Christ." So at worst, Bush never condemned Jews to hell specifically, but rather condemned most of humanity (anyone who doesn't accept Christ) to what may be, depending on your point of view, a wider geographical area (anywhere outside heaven). I'm not sure if that's better or worse.

Here's where the gospels differ. According to Fred Barnes of the *Weekly Standard*, Bush says his mother then called Billy Graham to straighten him out. Graham advised him to "never play God" by ruling on who gets into heaven. But according to Sam Howe Verhovek of the *New York Times*, Bush says Graham's intervention occurred earlier, during an informal theological discussion at the Bush Sr. White House. And according to Ken Herman of the *Austin American-Statesman*, Bush actually made his 1993 comment in the course of recounting the Graham episode. In this version, the evangelist's advice was slightly different: "Graham generally agreed with the theory but cautioned against spending much time worrying about it, Bush said."

So, where does this leave us? If Billy Graham actually convinced Bush long beforehand that we don't know who gets into heaven, then the *Houston Post* report of 1993 was flat-out wrong and Bush didn't believe Jews were shut out of heaven even at the time. But Bush has never denied the accuracy of the reporter's paraphrase. Nor, needless to say, has he adopted Version 2 of Graham's advice by declaring that Jews won't get into heaven, but he's too busy to care. Bush now answers all questions on the subject of heaven and its admission requirements with this catechistic formulation: "It is not the governor's role to decide who goes to heaven. I believe that God decides who goes to heaven, not George W. Bush."

This won't do, I'm afraid. It was good enough to get him a kosher certification from the Anti-Defamation League, but it makes no sense. No one is asking Bush to "decide" or "rule on" who gets into heaven. We can stipulate that God decides. (Some people—most Jews, for example—believe in God, but not in heaven. Few, if any, people believe in heaven, but not in God.) The issue is whether God has an admissions policy that excludes Jews and whether George W. has an opinion about what that policy might be.

Surely he does. "My faith tells me that acceptance of Jesus Christ as my savior is my salvation, and I believe that," Bush says. Does he think that this principle only applies to him? Does he think that it's possible for others to achieve salvation without accepting Christ? Even nonrecruiting religions such as Judaism claim to be more than just a personal taste or preference. Born-again Christianity claims to be the right answer to the most fundamental questions. So how can Jews possibly get into heaven without converting? Only two ways that I can see. One is if God allows exemptions. But to avoid offending any religious or nonreligious group, the exception would have to be that anyone who does not accept Christ need not accept Christ, which would destroy the rule. The other way out would be if the entire belief system permits doubt about itself—for example, if it's only 50–50 that accepting Christ is mandatory for salvation for anybody, including George W. himself. Neither of these conditions applies to George W.'s faith, as he describes it.

And so what? Why should anyone care whether he or she will achieve salvation by the terms of someone else's religion? What difference does it make if you can't get into a heaven you don't believe in? As a nonbeliever, I find the conventions of ecumenism baffling. I don't want to tell you people how to run your religions. And obviously we want to avoid an outbreak of religious war, or even lesser forms of intolerance, if possible. But why does tolerance require people to pretend they don't believe what they do? Wouldn't tolerance be easier if it only required agreement to disagree peacefully rather than demanding actual sharing of religious doctrines at some level of abstraction? After all, if Bush really believes that accepting Jesus is the only path to salvation, he is pulling a pretty dirty trick on Jews by telling them otherwise. Putting votes before souls: Talk about political expediency!

George W. is lying either when he professes his faith or when he denies its implications. Or he hasn't really thought it through, which itself would cast doubt on the depth of his faith. But I doubt this particular dishonesty will keep him out of heaven, since it is imposed on every politician—and even every clergyman with ambitions.

To be sure, there is a certain joy in watching a pol caught in pandering gridlock. Bush plays up his born-again faith to the religious right. He uses it even more than bona fide Christian-right pols do, as Fred Barnes points out, in order to allay suspicions that he may be moderate or indifferent on social issues. Then he has to fudge his faith so that people who don't share it won't take it seriously.

And if he gets this balancing act wrong, he must pander even more furiously to make it up. Going for a twofer a couple of years ago, Bush "confided" to Washington political columnist Andrew Glass that "he enjoys hanging out with country music singer [can you guess? well, obviously . . . ] Kinky Friedman, who wrote [uh-oh] 'They Ain't Making Jews Like Jesus Anymore.'"

Does W. agree with this sentiment? Does he have some problem with the quality of Jews being produced in America today?

# 2000

## Six Degrees of America Online

Time, *Jan. 24, 2000*

One thing is clear: This is the make-it-or-break-it millennium for AOL Time Warner. By the year 3000, or maybe even sooner, we will have answers to the questions that plague us this week, such as, Can we talk about something else, please? Is synergy the same thing as convergence or something different but equally wonderful? How many more times in the next thousand years can the same story be told? Tweedy Time Inc. makes a jazzy marriage (a movie studio! a cable-TV network! an Internet dotcom!), a clash of cultures, a triumph of the new media, the death of the old, etc.? And how many times can Old Media, like an actor as the curtain falls, rise from the dead, take a bow and prepare to die again in the next performance?

Above all, Is the agglutination of all telecommunications, media, technology and cinnamon-bun businesses into one sticky, tangled mass a Good Thing or a Bad Thing for everyone besides the three or four white men who have the total power to decide how many times a week *Seinfeld* will be seen on every single television set on the planet?

Actually, I have the answers right now. But first, a few disclosures are necessary. Readers have the right to know that *Time* magazine will be part of AOL Time Warner. The author of this essay, by contrast, has a day job as editor of *Slate*, an online magazine published by Microsoft. Microsoft owns an online service, MSN, that competes with AOL. Microsoft and AOL Time Warner will have competing investments in the cable industry. On yet another hand, Microsoft and Time Warner are co-investors in a high-speed cable-Internet connection business called Roadrunner. On a fourth hand, Microsoft owns a chunk of AT&T, which owns a chunk of Time Warner, which means that after the merger, Microsoft will own a chunk of AOL.

Readers should also take into consideration that Microsoft is a partner with NBC, which is owned by General Electric, in an all-news cable channel, MSNBC, which competes with CNN, which is owned by AOL Time Warner. What's more, the editor in chief of MSNBC. com, the cable channel's affiliated website, is my mother's brother's wife's aunt's husband's nephew, which obviously makes it difficult for me to evaluate objectively the merits of a merger between a company (AOL) that recently bought the company (Netscape) that makes the Internet browser that competes with the browser of the company that employs me, and a company (Time Warner) that owns a studio (Warner Bros.) that made the movie *Wild Wild West*, which I saw on an airplane and which is unforgivable.

This is mitigated, however, by the fact that GE—again, a partner of Microsoft in MSNBC—is also a partner, with Disney and Hearst (which, along with Dow Jones, owns *SmartMoney* magazine; more on that later), in A&E, the Arts & Entertainment cable channel, which is showing a made-for-TV movie starring Jeff Daniels as George Washington, which I haven't seen but which is hard not to hold against these companies anyway. What's worse, GE has direct links, via co-ownership of CNBC, the financial-news cable channel, with Dow Jones, which publishes the *Wall Street Journal*, whose editorial page is a leading cause of heart attacks among sane people.

But wait. It's not that simple, I'm afraid. CNBC competes directly with CNN/fn, the financial-news cable channel that will be owned by AOL Time Warner. I don't need to spell out the implications of that for you, do I? Well, perhaps I do. Look: this very article you are reading is in a magazine published by a company that owns a cable channel that competes with another cable channel that is half owned by a company (Dow Jones) that also half owns a magazine (*SmartMoney*) that competes with another magazine (*Money*) owned by the company that publishes this magazine, and half owned by a company (GE) that also half owns a cable channel (MSNBC) that is half owned by the employer of the author of this article, whose CEO (GE's, that is) nevertheless often appears on the cover of the magazine (*Fortune*) that competes with the magazine (*SmartMoney*) co-owned by the company that also co-owns CNBC with GE.

Here, then, is the guts of the issue. If Jack Welch of GE, whom I've never met, were nonetheless to appear at my door and say, "I hear you're writing about the AOL Time Warner merger. I hope you'll keep in mind that I'm CEO of the company that co-owns a cable channel and a website with the company that writes your paycheck, and the company you're writing about owns a magazine that published a damned fine picture of me recently," would I have the ethical backbone to say, "Obviously that occurred to me, but I have no intention of letting it influence me in any way"? Or would I take the coward's way out and say, "Yes, but your company co-owns Talk City, an Internet-content site, with Hearst and Starbucks"? (And while he was puzzling over the relevance of that, I could make my escape.)

Now you have the information you need to judge my credibility, and we can turn to my analysis of the AOL Time Warner merger. Or we could if there were room.

## McCain's High Horse

Slate, *Feb. 22, 2000*

No man is more entitled to preen about his honor and heroism than John McCain. But honor has its limits, both as a campaign strategy and as a governing philosophy.

To start, there's the danger of overplaying your hand. McCain's constant talk about honor and sly reminders of his own heroism are beginning to resemble that sequence in *Groundhog Day* where Bill Murray tries to seduce Andie MacDowell with sincerity. His first attempt almost succeeds, but repeated efforts get progressively more self-conscious, coarser, and therefore less successful. Yes, Senator, fine, you're Luke Skywalker. Now, can we drop it?

McCain is not above misusing his honor as a blunt instrument. In the South Carolina debate last week, Alan Keyes raised a perfectly legitimate question about McCain's muddled position on abortion. How can McCain believe that fetuses are full human beings and still say that he would allow his daughter to decide for herself whether to kill one? In response, McCain staged an umbrage fit: "I've seen enough killing in my life, a lot more than you have . . . and I will not listen to your lectures about how I should treat this very important issue." Oh, please. McCain cheapens his own heroism when he tries to use five years in a North Vietnamese prison camp as a rhetorical get-out-of-jail-free card.

George W. Bush's widely mocked garble about McCain taking his "high horse" on the "low road" is actually, with a bit of untangling, a pretty good image. It's one thing to drop your negative ads and challenge your opponent to do the same. But it's a bit rich to carry on as if no decent person would ever do what you yourself were doing just a few days before.

The raison d'être of George W. Bush's campaign has been electability, so losing a primary damages him more than it damages McCain. McCain's campaign raison d'être has been honor—he's morally superior to his opponents. So when he and Bush get down and dirty—neither one worse than the other, and in fact neither one especially bad at all by prevailing political standards—it hurts McCain a lot more. It's disingenuous, if not dishonorable, for McCain to insist that he's not going negative when he says, "I won't take the low road to the highest office." For that matter, his very campaign theme of honor implies that the other fella doesn't have it, which is certainly negative.

McCain is hard to nail on hypocrisy because he is so quick with the mea culpa. This too is an honorable habit that becomes cynical with excessive repetition. When McCain says he feels personally dishonored by the corrupt culture of influence peddling in Congress, it's more like an invitation to grant him an exemption ("Oh no, Sen. McCain, not you . . .") than an opportunity to consider the evidence. When he publicly flagellates himself for insufficient stoicism under Communist torture, you are being encouraged to think he must be innocent of any vice or failing he accuses himself of.

The limits of honor as a governing philosophy are best illustrated by McCain's foreign policy. This is the area in which he is considered to be most thoughtful and qualified. But his abstract principles on the question of using American force (as presented in a speech last year) are an unhelpful collection of yin-and-yang bromides. He's proud of the label "internationalist" and rejects calls to "turn inward." But our values and our interests must both be engaged to justify military action. Yet values vs. interests is a "false distinction," since each promotes the other. "Build coalitions to protect our interests and values, don't neglect our interests and values to build coalitions," and so on. McCain's string of "don'ts" may or may not be valid criticisms of the Clinton record, but as a philosophy or guide to decision-making they are worthless. Who is consciously in favor of neglecting our interests and values?

In the South Carolina debate, McCain declared, "We shouldn't have gone into Kosovo" because our interests and values weren't at stake. Last year, he said, "I sincerely believe that Serbia's assault on Kosovo did threaten our national interest"—but only because Presidents Bush and Clinton had put American credibility on the line. He supported Clinton's decision to intervene, but bitterly criticized the bombing as inadequate and the public forswearing of ground troops as cowardly. He has been eloquent about the evils of Milosevic, the suffering of the Kosovars, and the inadequacies of our apparent victory. And yet he apparently thinks a better president would have done nothing about these evils in the first place.

The most coherent gloss you can put on all this is that it is about honor. Honor enters in two ways: First, you need a more honorable president than Bill Clinton, who lacks both the courage to use force and the love for our soldiers not to. And second, the clearest justification for using military force is to preserve national honor. But McCain believes a more honorable president will only put American honor into play where it should be anyway. So the concept of honor tells you nothing in the end about where force should be used.

Then, too, American honor and credibility were the reasons we kept the war in Vietnam going for years after we'd lost interest in any other rationale. No one paid more for that folly than John McCain.

## REPUBLICANS FOR HILLARY

DID WE SAY CHILDREN SHOULDN'T HAVE LEGAL RIGHTS? NEVER MIND.

Slate, *April 24, 2000*

NOTE: *Elián González was a six-year-old Cuban boy whose mother had died trying to bring him to the United States. Elián survived and made it to Miami, but his father wanted him to come home to Cuba. The case became a national obsession, as Republicans self-righteously declared that young Elián had the legal right to make up his own mind.*

"**R**epublicans trust parents and believe that they, not courts and lawyers, know what is best for their children."

So declares the 1992 Republican platform. This ancient document works itself up into quite a froth over what it calls "parental authority." Republicans in those days were specifically alarmed over the notion that children have legal rights independent of their parents—and might even be allowed to bring lawsuits that would break up the nuclear family. "For more than three decades," we learn, "the liberal philosophy has assaulted the family on every side. Today, its more vocal advocates . . . deny parental authority and responsibility, fracturing the family into isolated individuals, each of them dependent upon—and helpless before—government. This is the ultimate agenda of contemporary socialism under all its masks," no less.

Even in a generally hysterical tract, this emphasis on the less-than-pressing issue of lawsuits by children stands out as a bit odd. The explanation is that it was part of an effort to make Hillary Clinton that year's Willie Horton: a symbol of wretched liberal excess. As a law student, Hillary Rodham had published an article arguing that children have legal rights and in some circumstances they should indeed be allowed to sue for separation from their parents. Speaker after speaker at the convention that renominated George H. W. Bush warned that if Hillary's husband was elected president, children would soon be suing their parents for making them do their homework or take out the trash. The Clintons and other Democrats responded that the article was being grotesquely misrepresented (which it was). They weren't about to be trapped defending an idea as un-American as children's independent legal rights.

You see where this is going, of course. But wait: It gets better. The Republicans tried to use a specific case to illustrate the depraved, socialistic road the Hillaryites were leading the country down. It involved a twelve-year-old Florida boy who was suing for the right to remain with a foster family rather than return to his natural parents (or suing to "divorce" his parents, as the headline and talk-show shorthand had it). His mother had repeatedly abandoned him and was living with a man with a criminal record who had recently been arrested for allegedly beating her. His father, the suit alleged, was an alcoholic who had abandoned the family. But the GOP party line was that a twelve-year-old was far too young to decide he'd rather not live with such people and that anyone who wanted lawyers and government to keep these parents apart from their child was a liberal sociopath.

Autres temps, autres moeurs. The harvest of ironic counterpoint from this past Sunday's news and talk shows alone is almost too rich to bear. Republican critics needed a reason why, after five months of fruitless negotiation and brazen defiance of the law by the Miami contingent, Juan Miguel González's obviously loving "parental authority" should not be honored. Most of them grasped onto the circuit court ruling that six-year-old Elián may have an independent legal right to live in the United States, against his father's wish.

There was Rudy Giuliani, of all people, emoting sensitively about the "traumatic damage" that can be caused by forceful police action. (Besides the rule of law and "family values," the whole realm of psychobabble is a subject on which Republicans are sounding distinctly un-Republican these days.) Hillary Clinton's Senate-race opponent declared that Elián's "rights" had been "trampled." He stated flatly that "this boy is entitled to an asylum application in the United States."

Kate O'Beirne, professional Hillary-hater and possibly the most reliable right-wing apparatchik on television: "The child has rights separately distinct from his father."

Perhaps most sublimely, there was Newt Gingrich, reduced to subbing for some Fox News host who wouldn't have been allowed to carry Newt's ego around behind him in a wheelbarrow back in 1992.

After Rep. Ileana Ros-Lehtinen (R-Miami, and therefore not guilty on grounds of constituents' insanity) stated that the courts had given "little Elián" the right to asylum, Gingrich forgot to remind her that "Republicans trust parents and believe that they, not courts and lawyers, know what is best for their children." Instead, he criticized Janet Reno's timing on the adorable grounds that "this is a time for Easter egg hunts. This is a time for the Easter bunny."

George W. Bush also seems to believe in the Easter bunny. He said he was "profoundly saddened and troubled that the administration was not able to negotiate a resolution and instead decided to use force." It would be good to know how much longer than five months President W. would be willing to negotiate and whether he plans to conduct many negotiations by giving up all his leverage in advance. It used to be that Republicans had a better handle on this sort of thing.

All these critics of the operation that reunited father and son seemed more than open to the possibility that the government, or a six-year-old child, or strangers such as themselves, might all be better judges of the child's welfare than the child's one surviving parent. And they may even be right about that. No one ever thought of this particular scenario back in '92. Maybe it's an exception. But then, maybe there are other exceptions, too. In fact, maybe if you've been self-righteously indignant on both sides of an issue, you should conclude that it's not an issue about which self-righteous indignation is called for.

And maybe you should apologize to Hillary.

## THE SECRET SHAME OF THE PROFESSIONAL POLITICIAN

Slate, *June 6, 2000*

Rep. Rick Lazio was carrying on the other day about how he's a genuine New Yorker who rides the subways, whereas Hillary uses a "chauffeured limousine"—a vehicle never previously seen in New

York, apparently—when, according to the *New York Times*, some-one asked him how much a subway card costs. It was slightly a trick question: You can buy them in various amounts. Unfortunately three dollars—Lazio's guess—isn't one of those amounts.

No politician, I presume, ventures into public these days without knowing the price of a gallon of milk. Price, to show that they're regular guys who go grocery shopping and need to worry about what ordinary things cost. Milk, to suggest wholesomeness ("I don't know, but a liter of gin is about fifteen dollars," would not be a good answer, even in New York). A gallon, to signify family man with lots of chil-dren. (Another bad answer: "A half-quart costs about eighty-two cents. If I buy any more it goes sour in the fridge.")

All that knowing the price of milk really proves is that you've got good handlers. Lazio probably was ready for the milk question when he got blindsided by the subway one. Serves him right, of course, for his tiresome harping on what a real New Yorker and regular guy he is. A pro-Lazio TV commercial being run by the Conservative Party mysteriously picks up these very themes, although by law it is supposed to be uncoordinated with the Lazio campaign. It's a photo montage that (according to the voice-over) "could be from any New Yorker's life" or "could be from Rick Lazio's own photo album," but (according to the *Times*) is mostly stock images from ad agency files.

It's true that Lazio was born and raised in New York. Went to col-lege there too (Vassar). He then went to law school in D.C. (Ameri-can University). A stint as a county prosecutor and then, in his early thirties, he was elected to Congress. Now he wants to be a senator and probably dreams of being president. He is, in short, a career poli-tician and has been one his whole adult life. His passions and aspira-tions are in Washington, not New York. If he actually does know the price of milk, he looks forward to forgetting it. He would like to have a job that required you to ride around in a limousine without requir-ing you to admit you like it.

And there's nothing wrong with any of that! Another way to put Lazio's story is that this man decided early on to dedicate his life to public service. That he is directing his brains and ambition toward democracy instead of capitalism. (You get a limo if you win either of these lotteries.) Unfortunately, while our culture currently treats naked business ambition as almost saintlike, it treats naked politi-cal ambition as shameful. In a free-market economy, one person's business success can, and often does, benefit everybody—though it's not clear why we need to be wildly grateful on top of the material rewards. Political success, by contrast, requires at least some direct concern about the general good. Yet political success in America also requires pretending that political success is not your life's goal.

Lazio's party is partly responsible for his tragic inability to come out of the closet and admit his desires. The Republicans have promoted a powerful variant on populism aimed at an elite of politicians, professors, artsy-fartsy types, and suchlike specimens. When this works, as it worked wonderfully from 1980 through 1992, it redirects public resentment from the traditional financial elite and any favors the GOP may be doing for its members at the moment.

Compared with those years, anti-pol populism seems like a spent force. Gosh, remember term limits? What a frenzy that was. We almost had a constitutional amendment! Millions of Americans, most congressional Republicans, not a few Democrats, and George F. Will all became convinced that life was unbearable if anyone could serve in Congress for more than six years. Then Republicans won control of Congress (running on term limits, among other issues), times got good, people got bored, the issue disappeared, life went on. It's now safe for a politician—even one who got elected initially on term limits—to run for a fourth or fifth term. But it's still not safe to openly admit that you're a career politician. Let alone add "and proud of it."

## McCAIN FOR VEEP: IT'S NOT TOO LATE!

WHEN THE PRESS WON'T TAKE NO FOR AN ANSWER.

Slate, *July 25, 2000*

The conventional wisdom among pooh-bahs inside the Beltway is that it is now too late for George W. Bush to select Sen. John McCain as his running mate. This tired consensus is based on the calculation that McCain has repeatedly said—or seemed to say—that he is not interested, capped by the observation that Bush has already chosen someone else.

But that is a naive view. This column has learned that McCain is more willing than previously reported to consider the possibility of becoming the Republican vice-presidential nominee. In an exclusive interview with this column, McCain signaled his continuing interest in the No. 2 slot. McCain is a sophisticated politician whose words must be interpreted with care. But the message he was sending in the following exchange, while subtle, could not be clearer:

THIS COLUMN: Do you rule out any possibility that you might be willing to accept the Republican vice-presidential nomination?

McCAIN: Where have you been? He's already picked someone else.

THIS COLUMN: OK, but suppose he hadn't. Or suppose Bush changes his mind. Or suppose this other guy gets run over by a truck. Yeah, a truck. Would you be willing in that case?

McCAIN: Let me spell it out for you. I would rather spend the next four years back in the Hanoi Hilton than as vice president of the United States.

THIS COLUMN: Does that mean no?

McCAIN: Yes.

THIS COLUMN: Yes? Yes, you would be willing?

McCAIN: No. Yes, that means no.

THIS COLUMN: No?

McCAIN: No!

THIS COLUMN: OK, OK, but suppose this. Suppose this other guy comes down with a horrible fatal disease, and suppose Gov. Bush comes to you on his knees and begs you to run with him for the good of the party and the country? And suppose that a crazed scientist gets hold of a terrible poison, three drops of which are enough to kill millions of people, and suppose he threatens to put it in the water supply of a major city unless you agree to run for vice president. In that case, would you accept the nomination?

McCAIN: Well, in that case I suppose I would have to consider it.

THIS COLUMN: So, in other words, you don't rule out the possibility of running for vice president?

McCAIN: Excuse me, I have another exclusive interview on the other line.

McCain's renewed interest in the No. 2 slot clearly complicates Gov. Bush's decision, which was complicated enough by the fact that he's already made it. Adding further complication is the sudden availability of Gen. Colin Powell. Powell has long indicated—by such statements as "no" and "absolutely not" and "look, can't you get it through your thick skull?"—that he was inclined against running for vice president. But in an exclusive interview with this column, he reopened the door. (The interview was conducted before Bush announced his choice of someone else.)

THIS COLUMN: Will you run for vice president if George W. Bush asks you to?

POWELL: No. Not a chance.

THIS COLUMN: Oh please? Please, please, please?

POWELL: N-O spells no!

THIS COLUMN: Pretty please with sugar on top?

POWELL: Who let you in my house anyway? Get out of here before I call the cops.

It is noteworthy that Powell, a man who chooses his words with care, did not say that he would not run for vice president if George W. Bush did not ask him to. Bush's announcement this week that he has, in fact, asked someone else makes this scenario all the more likely.

Like his decision to call off the Gulf War before reaching Baghdad, Powell's decision to cut off his interview with this column before totally clarifying his availability for the No. 2 slot is a risky strategy that may come back to haunt him during the fall election campaign. Among other difficulties, it creates an opening for Ross Perot, whose expressions of non-interest in the nomination of the Reform Party are widely interpreted as expressions of interest in the nomination of the Reform Party. The widely felt concern (though it has yet to be articulated by anybody, at least on the record) is that without Powell or McCain on the ticket, reform-minded Republicans might desert Bush for Perot.

But is Perot running? Here is what he said in an exclusive interview with this column:

PEROT: No, Larry, I'm not running this year.

THIS COLUMN: My name isn't Larry.

PEROT: Then I'm not talking to you.

The mercurial Perot has often been known to change his mind, however, and there is a widespread belief in the political community that, after taking him seriously in two relatively exciting elections, he owes us a run in this one, when we need him.

In any event, only time will tell whether these new hints of interest by McCain, Powell, and Perot are real or figments of an underactive imagination that won't release its grip on an old story line. But one thing is clear: This column, and the rest of the media, will keep asking until we get the answers we want.

## IT'S AN OUTRAGE (NEVER MIND WHAT)

REPUBLICANS AND WEN HO LEE.

Slate, *Sept. 19, 2000*

NOTE: *Like Elián Gonzaléz, Wen Ho Lee provides a hilarious example of politicians' willingness to exploit the nation's short attention span.*

> SCHIEFFER: You said at one point that this was maybe the biggest security breach of—of our lifetime.
> SEN. LOTT: Yeah, yeah.

That was host Bob Schieffer and Senate Majority Leader Trent Lott on CBS's *Face the Nation* Sunday.

By now Republican criticism of the Clinton administration, and Attorney General Janet Reno in particular, is beyond political calculation and beyond cynicism. They do it by rote, like a ritual incantation of the faith. You would think that even a politician's vestigial sense of irony would give a U.S. senator pause before piling on about the injustice done to Los Alamos nuclear scientist Wen Ho Lee, who was kept in solitary confinement for nine months on lurid charges of spying and then released after pleading guilty to something like pocketing paper clips. There is, after all, plenty of other material available if you wake up one morning and say to yourself, "Y'know, I feel like denouncing the Justice Department today." And if you've run out, someone at Louis Freeh's FBI will be happy to leak you some more. Of all the reasons one might attack the administration, many of them justified, why choose one that puts you at the mercy of any hack columnist with access to Nexis (the news media database)? To do so suggests an unhealthy compulsion, if not severe short-term memory loss.

It was only last June, after all, that Lott was promising to make the Wen Ho Lee case an issue in the election campaign. Way back then—three months ago—the case was said to illustrate the administration's disregard for American national security, not the railroading of a basically innocent man because of his race. "What I want to know is what actions are we going to take to stop this kind of misconduct," Lott huffed, referring to Lee's alleged spying, not the administration's prosecution of him.

Now Lott says the question of Lee's guilt is "not clear," but "there's a real dichotomy" between the way Lee was treated and the wrist-slap for former CIA Director John Deutch, who "apparently did the same thing." No one has ever suggested that Deutch was a superspy for a foreign government, so "the same thing" apparently means that Lott now no longer believes that Lee was a superspy either. "What is the difference?" According to Lott, it's that Deutch is "a buddy of the White House," whereas Lee is Asian-American. (That's actually two differences. But who's counting?) "It's unsettling," Lott piously concluded, though not so unsettling that he had ever bothered to mention it in his many calls for Reno's resignation during the past year.

The day Wen Ho Lee was arrested, Senate Intelligence Committee Chairman Richard Shelby said, "I think they've been too late, or at least very tardy, in doing this." For the next year—while Wen Ho Lee languished in solitary—Chairman Shelby had other concerns. He bounced from talk show to hearing to press conference denouncing administration laxness in cracking down on Chinese spies. "This problem could be more serious, more widespread, and potentially more dangerous than most Americans realize," he foretold.

And now? A modest mea culpa, perhaps? A morsel of apology? Not quite. "All I can say is I thought from the beginning that that was a botched investigation," Shelby said last week, like a man who warned that the *Titanic* was burdened by too many lifeboats.

Sen. Arlen Specter is not a person who brakes for ironies on his way to a microphone. "You have the grandest case of grand larceny in the history of the world on the espionage and the theft of vital American secrets" was his summary of the situation during a

"Media Availability" (actual name of the event) last year. Specter accused the administration of "incredible bungling" that "put millions of Americans at risk." Everyone thought at the time that the "bungling" charge referred to the Clinton administration's failure to arrest Wen Ho Lee, or at least wiretap him, earlier. This might have been a convenient time for Specter to mention his real concern that the only person arrested in this grandest of grand larcenies was an innocent man being railroaded because of his race. If he happened to think so.

But Specter modestly suppressed his civil libertarian concerns until the case against Lee collapsed. Maybe he was waiting for an appropriate occasion. At a recent ceremony for the 213th anniversary of the Constitution, no less, Specter said, "It's hard to understand how a man can be a major threat to national security one day and walk free the next." And lest you think it's the walking free part he objects to now, he added that the Justice Department "threw the book at Dr. Lee to make up for their own failings." Specter promises hearings on this outrage, needless to say.

A year ago Sen. Phil Gramm thought Janet Reno ought to resign because the belated nabbing of the arch-spy Wen Ho Lee added to "the cumulative weight of all her failures." Now Gramm's well-known passion for racial justice makes him even more adamant. "I don't understand an administration that stands up and damns racial profiling and yet engages in it when it suits," he said last week. Reno ought to resign "if she had any honor and any shame," observed this expert on those qualities.

In short, the porridge is too hot. No, wait, it's too cold. Whatever. The important thing is, it's Clinton's fault. Oh yeah, and Reno should resign.

## Frankly, My Dear

POLITICIANS' FAVORITE VERBAL TIC.

Slate, *Sept. 26, 2000*

How can you tell when a politician is lying? Don't say, "When his mouth is open and words are coming out." That is a cheap shot, quite frankly, and unworthy of readers of this column. A better clue is when he or she is using the word "frankly" or—especially—"quite frankly."

A couple of weeks ago, I asserted that this favorite rhetorical device is an example of spin, an attempt to claim courage or originality for a toadying or banal remark. But on reflection, and a bit of research, it appears to be more of an unconscious verbal tic than a conscious strategy. For some pols, it is virtually a throat-clearing device. But isn't it odd, Dr. Freud, that they should choose this particular phrase? And when a pol begins every third sentence with the word "frankly," what are we supposed to assume about the other two?

Appending "frankly" to almost any remark made in public turns that remark into a literal lie in two senses. Regarding the speaker's motive, it implies an artless lack of calculation or an active desire to tell unpleasant truths. And it implies that the remark itself is not merely true but deeply true in some way.

Unless last week is wildly atypical, American politicians use the word "frankly" dozens of times a day. While I wouldn't say the magic word is a clear sign that a lie is attached, there may be a negative correlation between use of "frankly" and actual frankness. On *Meet the Press*, for example, Sen. Dick Durbin, a Democrat, declared—as if these were confessions wrung out of him by Tim Russert's famous tough questioning—that "frankly" the Republicans are adopting positions long held by Democrats, and "frankly" he doesn't care for Bush's policies on various matters. Then, to a question about Al Gore and contributions from trial lawyers, Durbin replied "frankly" that "the Bush campaign looks in the rear-view mirror" whereas "Americans want to talk about where we're headed."

The current king of frankly is Republican vice-presidential candidate Dick Cheney. Last week he said that "frankly" he is astonished that Al Gore would attend a Hollywood fund-raiser. Also, "frankly," he "would expect better of the vice president" than to misrepresent what his dog pays for prescription drugs. "Frankly," the Clinton administration is ducking a fight with Iraq. "Frankly" Clinton's decision to release oil from the Strategic Petroleum Reserve is politically motivated. "Frankly," in fact, it is "not sound policy."

Among other highlights of political frankness last week: Sen. Barbara Boxer alleged that "frankly," voters tell her, "Barbara, we don't want a tax cut." Rep. John Kasich revealed that "frankly, we'll have an election this fall and then, come January, we'll kind of know . . . what we're in for." The political director of the AFL-CIO "frankly" predicted "the greatest union turnout effort ever" this election. However, House Minority Leader Richard Gephardt acknowledged that "frankly" he is more concerned about bipartisan cooperation "to get things done for the American people" than about which party may have a majority in the next Congress.

At a press conference, Sen. Don Nickles scored a spectacular quintuple-frankly, reporting in regard to the administration's oil policy that "frankly" it will lead to price controls, "frankly" it won't work, "frankly" Al Gore and the administration are "part of the problem" because—"frankly"—"politicians like Al Gore" are "not making good economical decisions," and "frankly" this has been a problem with Clinton-Gore for years. In a later at-bat, Nickles added that "frankly" he prefers the marketplace to government price controls (his description of the choice between accepting the OPEC cartel price and trying to break it, for which "frank" is only one word), and "frankly" everything the administration has done about oil has been "counterproductive."

The New York Senate race is producing orgies of frankness. A New York Democratic legislator named Eric Schneiderman, on CNN to defend Hillary Clinton, noted "frankly" that most White House guests were not campaign contributors (the famous most-airplanes-land-safely defense) and even "frankly" acknowledged that her opponent, Rick Lazio, accepts campaign contributions too. Lazio, meanwhile, is a formidable frank-artist in his own right. Last week he confessed that "frankly" Hillary thinks "it only matters what you say when you get caught" and that "frankly" he's too busy running for the Senate to comment about Hillary's exoneration on Whitewater, among other franknesses.

It used to be said that a diplomat's job was to "lie for his country." But now all is frankness. The U.S. ambassador-at-large for war crimes (presumably that should be "against" war crimes) predicted that "frankly" Slobodan Milosevic would have more credibility if he turned himself in. And an international trade official, lobbying Congress for the China pact, testified "frankly" that it was a better deal for us than for them.

These days TV talking heads, not poets (frankly), are the "unacknowledged legislators" of our political system. And increasingly they, too, feel the need to reassure viewers that what they say is actually both sincere and true. TV pundits' own special technique is to preface an assertion—however obviously speculative, tendentious, or flat-out made-up—with the phrase, "The fact of the matter is . . ." But they often resort to the classic "frankly" as well. Last week on CNN's *Capital Gang*, for example, conservative pundit Kate O'Beirne had the guts to admit that "frankly" George W. Bush's "polls started looking good" [*sic*] because "he started talking about . . . what the Bush agenda means for the middle class." Frank talk indeed!

Now financial pundits are horning in. Last week one of them observed that Saddam Hussein "frankly" doesn't care for either American presidential candidate. (He was claiming frankness for himself, of course, not for Saddam Hussein.) And, in what is frankly the frankly of the week, a man named Von Waggoner said on CNN, "Frankly, the optical networking space is a little bit worrisome, just from a valuation standpoint."

How true. How very, very true. And thank goodness someone finally said it. Frankly.

## VOTERS TO DECIDE ELECTION

Slate, *Oct. 3, 2000*

NOTE: *Well the joke turned out to be on me here. In the end, the voters didn't decide the 2000 election. Nevertheless, tautology still played a major role in the election coverage. Both newspaper articles referred to were in the* New York Times.

The key to this election, as some of my colleagues have pointed out, is the undecided voter. Especially the undecided voter in a swing state. A major newspaper made this point over the weekend with exemplary caution, in an article noting that millions of people will be watching the debate Tuesday night. "Yet for all those millions, officials in both campaigns say Mr. Bush and Mr. Gore will focus their messages on the narrow swath of swing voters who are expected to decide the election."

A swing voter is defined by experts as one who could go either way. Such voters, these experts continue, tend to be undecided in the sense that they haven't yet made up their minds. Longtime observers of the political system say that campaign officials tend to concentrate their powers of persuasion on voters whose minds are still open. Experience has shown that these are most often the voters who are undecided and therefore most likely to swing, these observers observe. One rarely acknowledged benefit of our current campaign-finance system, other experts note, is that it enables political campaigns to hire officials smart enough to figure this out.

But what of the alleged expectation, attributed to these campaign officials, that undecided voters will decide next month's election? According to authorities in the field of undecided votership, this expectation may be based on a school of thought discussed at length in the scholarly literature. This literature looks at the non-undecided voter—that is, voters who have already decided how they are going to vote. The central insight, sometimes attributed to Albert Einstein, is that people who are not undecided most likely have already made up their minds. Therefore, the reasoning goes, their decision was made in the past. As such, it is unlikely to change the result in the future. (Unless, Einstein added, a voter is traveling faster than the speed of light. But even in this highly unlikely situation, he noted, the voter probably filed an absentee ballot.)

As another article in a major newspaper reported last month, "The push and pull over these swing voters is particularly intense and of utmost consequence this year because both sides acknowledge that the electoral dynamic has changed considerably." In layperson's terms, it has become a "tight race," defined as one in which either of the two leading candidates has a plausible chance to win. Under such an electoral dynamic, experts say, campaign officials have an even greater incentive to focus their efforts on voters who haven't yet chosen their preferred candidate. "If the result is a foregone conclusion," explains a senior strategist who has served in many presidential campaigns, "you might choose to spend your money on voters who have already made up their minds. But if the election is up for grabs, any campaign official worth his or her salt will zero in where it will have the most impact, and that is on voters who are still undecided." Not to do so would be a mistake "of utmost consequence," this official added.

To be sure, undecided-votership scholars concede, decided voters do sometimes decide the election result. This happens in what experts describe as two very different circumstances. In the first scenario, a majority has already decided in favor of one candidate or the other. In that case, many scholars believe, the strategy of concentrating on the undecided voter may not be effective. But neither will any other strategy, some of these scholars caution.

In the second scenario, voters who normally would fall outside the category of undecided—most often because they have decided—nevertheless change their minds. But experts consider this an exception that proves the rule. "These people may think they've decided, but we would describe them as classic undecided voters," asserts the dean of a leading undecided-voter studies center.

The Electoral College system adds yet another wrinkle to this complex strategic analysis. Many experts believe that a political campaign should concentrate on states where the election result is still undetermined. Those are the states, many believe, that can have the most dramatic effect on the election results—even to the point of causing one candidate to win, rather than the other one.

"The thing to do," one veteran political strategist summarizes, "is to aim all your guns at swing voters in swing states. That is how you get the most bang for the buck. In my early days I used to pour resources into states we were either sure to lose or sure to win. But I've found through bitter experience that if a state can go either way, it tends to be a better investment. And if, within those states, you go after voters who haven't made up their minds, you're going to get the biggest payoff," this strategist added.

To be sure, the importance of the undecided voter can be exaggerated, some analysts point out. In the end, many longtime political observers believe, every election is decided by voters who have already decided. "We don't want you to dither past Election Day," joked one campaign official, adding seriously that voters who don't vote tend to have a smaller effect on the ultimate result than those who do.

But for this official and others of both parties, the ultimate wisdom of going after the undecided voter is, on balance, fairly clear—if only in contrast to the alternative. Concentrating on voters who have already decided how to vote is unlikely to change the total number of people who vote for you, according to political scientists at many universities. And, say these experts, getting more people to vote for you is of utmost consequence to winning elections.

## MY PLAN'S BETTER THAN YOUR PLAN

Time, *Oct. 16, 2000*

NOTE: *The media had accused the presidential candidates of too much symbolism and not enough substance. Big mistake. This was the nightmarish result. The "lockbox" had something to do with Social Security. Or possibly Medicare, I can't remember for sure. But the Democratic presidential candidates felt very strongly about it for a few weeks. Also about testing schoolchildren all the time.*

JIM LEHRER: You recently described your opponent as "a disgusting, wormlike excuse for a human being." What did you mean by that?

THE CANDIDATE: I have never criticized my opponent in personal terms. This election should be about the issues and my plan and his plan. What I was referring to in that remark is the fact that my plan is better than his plan.

Let me tell you about my plan. Under my plan, $17.1 trillion. All current seniors would be put in a lockbox. My opponent has said $63.4 billion, but that's simply wrong. He is misrepresenting my plan. My plan is $17.1 trillion and all seniors in a lockbox. And I will veto anyone—anyone, Jim, I feel very strongly about this—veto anyone who says otherwise. Putting seniors in a lockbox will be my Administration's No. 1 priority.

So you take that $17.1 trillion, saute it lightly for 40 years and divide by 5, by which time 2.3 million schoolchildren will be reaching retirement age without being able to read the labels on their prescription drugs. My opponent's plan would ignore this problem for the first 23 months and then take the first derivative times 6 percent—oh, yes you would! Yes you would! I've read your plan—but under my plan, every citizen of this country would multiply 19 by 7 and get a very large number. And I believe the American people can be trusted to perform this math for themselves, because under my plan they will be tested every 15 minutes, unlike my opponent's plan, which would test them every 20 minutes. Testing every American as often as possible will be my Administration's special No. 1 priority.

Finally, under my plan, I would run my plan past Alan Greenspan and toss the whole thing out if he doesn't like it. My opponent's plan claims to run itself past Alan Greenspan, but if you study the details, it really doesn't. My plan would run my plan past Alan Greenspan at least three and a half times as often as my opponent's plan. Checking with Alan Greenspan will be my Administration's superspecial priority gold No. 1 priority.

Now let me tell you about my opponent's plan. His plan calls for 14 trillion minus 7 in just six years. And no lockbox. Even worse, under my opponent's plan, 81 percent of all seniors. And the square root of 54 whatsoever. In my view, that is totally inadequate. It's not a good plan. We can do better. I wouldn't even call his plan a plan. I'd call it a fuzzy plan. Or no plan at all, because just 6 years from now is 6 years away. The American people are tired.

One of them is in this auditorium. A triple amputee from Benton Harbor, Mich., she used her one remaining hand to drag herself along the interstate all the way to Boston so she could be with us here tonight. And this is her story. She's an heiress of an agribusiness fortune who set up a tax shelter in the Cayman Islands, only to find that she'd missed a filing deadline under the needlessly complex S.A.Y.W.H.A.T. law—and I thank my opponent for supporting this valuable legislation. But I think that's wrong, just plain wrong, and as President I would not interfere.

I know we're 47 minutes over the 2 min. 17.3 sec. allowed under the commission rules for the second rebuttal to the first candidate's

reply to the opponent's indignant explosion of outrage at the first
candidate's outrageous lies and character assassination, but I cannot
let my worthy opponent criticize my plan as he has done. My lovely,
lovely plan. My darling plan. I just love my plan. My plan is better
than his plan, quite frankly.

And let me tell you why. This is a crucial election. My opponent
would use 63.5 percent of the surplus over 23 years. I say that's not
good enough. America's working families are entitled to 64.1 percent
over 26 years. That's a big difference.

And one other thing the American people should know about my
plan: I will never, ever ask working families to entrust their kids' education to an HMO. Under my opponent's plan, HMOs will be free
to continue accepting patients and even to treat their ailments under
some circumstances. That is unacceptable. It is not part of my plan.

It saddens me that my opponent has chosen to engage in negative
personal attacks such as saying my plan isn't better than his plan.
We should be discussing the issues, such as the fact that my plan is a
better plan, not engaging in irresponsible innuendo, such as implying that my plan is not a better plan. Any problems he may have
with my plan are a personal matter and have no place in the public
debate.

## THE EMPEROR'S NEW BRAIN

GEORGE W. AND THE STUPIDITY ISSUE.

Slate, *Oct. 24, 2000*

George W. Bush's handling of the stupidity issue has been nothing
short of brilliant. A Martian watching the last presidential debate
might have concluded that this man would be well-advised not to
put quite so much emphasis on mental testing. But Earth-based commentators mostly shied away from such a conclusion. The rule seems
to be that if a candidate can recite half a dozen policy positions by
rote and name some foreign nations and leaders, one shouldn't point
out that he sure seems a few whereases shy of an executive order.

The problem is probably laziness or complacence rather than actual inability, and journalists' reluctance to call someone who may well be our next commander in chief a moron is understandable. But if George W. Bush isn't a moron, he is a man of impressive intellectual dishonesty and/or confusion. His utterances frequently make no sense on their own terms. His policy recommendations are often internally inconsistent and mutually contradictory. Because it's harder to explain and impossible to prove cold, intellectual dishonesty doesn't get the attention that petty fibbing does, even though intellectual dishonesty indicts both a candidate's character and his policy positions. All politicians, including Al Gore, get away with more of it than they should. But George W. gets away with an extraordinary amount of it.

On Social Security, he continues to say he'll get the trillion dollars needed for his partial privatization "out of the surplus." Does he not understand that the current surplus is committed to future benefits, which will have to be cut to make the numbers work? Or does he understand and not care? When he compares the "paltry 2 percent" return on Social Security with an alleged 6 percent return on private investments, does he know he's leaving out that trillion dollars in one case and including it in the other? Or has this fact failed to penetrate despite repeated exposures?

When he calls the estate tax unfair, especially to farmers and small businesspeople, because it "taxes people twice"—meaning first when they earn the money and again when they die—is he aware that the value of farms and businesses in estates has almost never been taxed as income? Or have his advisers and fellow businessfolks deceived him on this basic point? When he criticizes his opponent for cutting taxes through the use of tax credits, then gives an example of his own tax plan in which most of the cut is through tax credits, is he fooling us? Or is someone fooling him?

When he repeatedly attacks his opponent for "partisanship," does he get the joke? When he blames the absence of a federal patients' rights law on "a lot of bickering in Washington, D.C.," has he noticed that the bickering consists of his own party, which controls Congress, blocking the legislation? When he summarizes, "It's kind of like a political issue as opposed to a people issue," does he mean to suggest anything in particular? Perhaps that politicians, when acting politically, ignore the wishes of the people?

How does he figure? If at all.

When he repeatedly says he has a "clear vision" about the Middle East but never gives a hint what it is, should we assume he has one he's not telling us about? When he complains that there is no general "strategy" for America's role in the world and promises that he'll ask his secretary of defense to come up with one pronto, should we be reassured? When he criticizes the Clinton administration for misusing American soldiers as social workers and promises to get other countries to use their soldiers that way instead, does he notice the logical flaw here?

In the debate, he declared, "I don't want to use food as a diplomatic weapon from this point forward. We shouldn't be using food. It hurts the farmers. It's not the right thing to do." When, just a few days later, he criticized legislation weakening the trade embargo on Cuba—which covers food along with everything else—had he rethought his philosophy on this issue? Or was there nothing to rethink?

When he promises that if he is elected, "we will have gag orders" on doctors and "100 percent" of people will "get the death tax," it's easy enough to figure out that he means we won't have gag orders and nobody will pay the estate tax. But what does he mean when he says that "insurance" is "a Washington term"?

When he promises "to have prescription drugs as an integral part of Medicare," does he comprehend that the exact distinction between his plan and his opponent's is that his is not an integral part of Medicare?

When he says that local control of schools is vital, criticizes his opponent for wanting to "federalize" education, promises as president to impose various requirements on schools, complains that federal money comes with too many "strings," calls for after-school funds to be used for "character education," endorses a federal law forbidding state lawsuits against teachers, and so on, does he have a path through this maze of contradictions? When he promises a federal school voucher program and then deflects criticism by saying "vouchers are up to states," is he being dense or diabolically clever?

In short, does George W. Bush mean what he says, or does he understand it? The answer can't be both. And is both too much to ask for?

## FUN WITH NUMBERS

Slate, *Nov. 8, 2000*

**A** 49–49 tie in a presidential election is irresistibly symbolic. The question is: symbolic of what? Page-one news analyses in this morning's *New York Times* and *Washington Post* are in striking agreement. Times headline: "Voters Remain Divided, to the Very End." Post headline: "Voters' views sharply divided." Both pieces proffer other evidence, but the close vote is the occasion and dramatic centerpiece of the analysis. "[T]he country . . . found it immensely difficult to make up its mind," said the *Times*. "It was as if two nations went to vote yesterday," said the *Post*, and those two nations "agreed only to disagree."

Everyone predicted an election result like this, but no one really believed it would happen. So we're all a bit short of Meaning at the moment, and sympathy is in order for anyone who had to dredge some up on deadline in the wee hours. It might even be true that the nation is divided—or more divided than usual. But the close race is not evidence one way or the other.

Here's an amazing fact worth keeping in mind during the next few days of punditry: Every voter in America, without exception, voted 100 percent for one candidate or another. Not a single voter split his or her vote 49–49 or any other ratio. Nor did any single voter or group of voters cast their votes with the intention of causing a 49–49 tie. Nor did any voter cast his or her vote in a way that communicated ambivalence or difficulty of deciding—because there is no such way.

Here's another amazing fact: A vote cast for Bush by someone who would never vote for Gore in a million years is indistinguishable from a Bush vote by someone who thinks it is a close call. And yet another amazing fact follows from that one: The size of a collection of votes compared with another collection of votes tells you nothing about the intensity of disagreement reflected by either of these piles of votes. A 49–49 split could signify mild disagreement, a deep divide, anything in between, or (most likely) a wide spectrum of views held with no consistent pattern of intensity.

Which leads us to the question of a "mandate." I'm not sure what a mandate is, exactly, but I'm fairly sure that the pundits are wrong in saying that you don't get one in a 49–49 squeaker. Why not? Winning by, say, 54–46 is considered a solid victory, with a mandate included as standard equipment. If turnout is a typical half of the eligible citizenry, this means your hunger for power has been ratified by 27 percent. Winning with 49 percent of a similar turnout (and last night's turnout was higher than normal) gives you the backing of 24.5 percent of the citizenry. The difference: 2.5 percent or 1 voter in 40. Can that possibly be the difference between having authority for bold imposition of your views about how affairs of state should be conducted and being granted permission for no more than amiable accommodation of all sides in a vast centrist love fest of compromise?

Now, getting fewer votes than your opponent does raise some fuzzy mandate issues. But that's a different story.

## Democracy Is Approximate: Live with It

Slate, *Nov. 16, 2000*

NOTE: *So I started out feeling fairly reasonable and statesmanlike about the election result. That didn't last.*

If George W. Bush is sworn in as president even though Al Gore got more votes, Gore voters (including me) will be disappointed. But should we also feel aggrieved? Is it unjust? The truth is, not very.

The Electoral College used to drive me batty. It's so irrational! No one seriously tries to defend it as an exercise in representative government, as if the voters were actually choosing someone else to choose the president for them. The modern case for the Electoral College is that it will lead to an unambiguous result. Even a very close popular vote is likely to produce a solid winner and loser after it's put through this eighteenth-century contraption. But if arbitrary clarity is what you want, why not just flip a coin whenever the vote is close? Stripped of arcane folderol, that's what the Electoral College amounts to. Democracy means majority rule, I thought. Any system that can hand victory to the popular-vote loser is perverse and indefensible.

This time around, the Electoral College delivered on its flaw but not its virtue. It spectacularly failed to banish ambiguity and may well crown the man who got fewer votes. And yet the strange events of the 2000 election make this eccentric arrangement easier to swallow. How? By demonstrating that any perfect measure of the people's will is impossible. Democracy is an approximation, and the Electoral College is probably no more approximate than any other arrangement. Consider some of the flaws in voting itself.

To start, the basic concept of majority rule is arbitrary and unfair. The only perfectly fair voting system is one where all voters get their first choices. In a restaurant, we each vote on what we want for dinner, and there is no need to impose one person's choice on anyone else. But we can't each have our own president. Majority rule is a second-best solution: Less than half the voters are denied their preferences. But "rule by three-quarters" or "rule by everybody" (i.e., requiring unanimity) would thwart the wishes of even fewer people. The only advantage of majority rule over these higher standards of agreement is that a simple majority consensus is easier to achieve. In other words, majority rule is a practical but imperfect mechanism for turning the multiple preferences of millions of people into a clear collective decision. Sort of like the Electoral College.

In practice, furthermore, so-called majority rule rarely gives a majority of voters their first choices. One reason is that what we really have is "plurality rule." In the past three presidential elections, no candidate got a majority of the vote. Most voters' preferences were frustrated. Either Gore or Bush would actually become president with more popular endorsement than Bill Clinton enjoyed. And Election Day is just the last stage of the selection process. As always, millions voted for Gore and Bush only after their real first-choice candidates lost in the primaries. There is a famous scholarly proof that no voting system can sift through multiple preferences with even reasonable efficiency, let alone give most people their first choices.

There was an interesting debate after Nov. 7 about letting contested counties or states vote again. The fairly easy consensus that this would be a bad idea exposes another inherent limit of electoral democracy: An election only reflects voters' opinions at a particular, arbitrary moment. That moment is now gone. The result last week turned on an infinity of factors that cannot be duplicated—the weather, the last TV commercial people happened to see, what they had for lunch. It turned on their not knowing how important their vote would be. None of this can be re-created. And yet there is no inherent reason that voters' preferences on Nov. 7 are more valid than their preferences a couple of weeks later. If anything, the opposite is true: The more recent the sounding, the more likely it is to reflect current opinions. The case against a new election is strong: There are rules, and there has got to be closure. But these necessary practical considerations make an election less accurate, not more so, as an expression of the popular will.

Finally, we've learned striking things in recent days about the limits of elections at even the most mundane level of accurately eliciting voters' current preferences and adding them up. Do you suppose that the elderly citizens of Palm Beach County are the only ones who misunderstood the ballot or marked it incorrectly? Or that Florida is the only state where—with no evidence of fraud—the vote count is off by a few hundred or a few thousand? The sum total of these errors nationwide surely is more than the difference between Bush and Gore in the official count.

Both in theory and in practice, then, elections simply cannot measure the popular will as accurately as last week's results seem to demand. One way or another, it is a flip of the coin. The Electoral College is not a bad way. It's here. It's got a comforting patina of age. And at least it limits the second-guessing to one or two states.

And how unfair is it? No matter how this melodrama ends, the presidential preferences of some forty-seven million people will be thwarted. That's the tragedy of democracy, and this built-in unfairness is true of all elections under any set of rules. The preferences of those who voted for the apparent popular-vote loser are just as valid as the preferences of those who voted for the apparent popular-vote winner. It's simply that there are fewer of the former. So even if the Electoral College ends up satisfying the loser's supporters and thwarting the winner's, how much unfairness does that imply? In an election this close, the answer is "not much." And in any election close enough for the Electoral College to change the result, no other process is likely to be any fairer.

## No Contest

THE MOST OUTRAGEOUS BUSH ARGUMENT YET.

Slate, *Nov. 29, 2000*

The Bush argument for denying Al Gore a fair recount has long since been distilled to a few hard, shiny deceits: We've had plenty of recounts, you don't change the rules in the middle of the game, and so on. Sunday night brought a new one: The Florida results have been certified. Like it or lump it, the game's over. Gore's refusal to give up is bad sportsmanship. In fact, it's downright unpatriotic.

"Now the Gore campaign lawyers want to shift from recounts to contesting the election outcome," sneered James Baker Sunday evening. His client, George W. Bush, said a few minutes later, "Until Florida's votes were certified, the vice president was working to represent the interests of those who supported him." But now? "Now that they're certified, we enter a different phase. If the vice president chooses to go forward, he is filing a contest to the outcome of the election. And that is not the best route for America."

In this hoarse dispute, I've almost given up trying to persuade people of things that seem obvious to me. What difference does it make how many recounts you've already done if they all leave out the same group of ballots? Blah, blah, blah. But this claim that certification should close the issue is so staggeringly dishonest that I'm going to make one more attempt.

Here goes. The right to "contest" an election result after certification was central to every legal argument the Bush side made to get them to their Sunday evening triumph. It was the very reason Secretary of State Katherine Harris said she needed to enforce a strict deadline for certification. It was the reason she gave why Gore would not be unfairly harmed by certification on her schedule. Her briefs criticized Gore for raising issues before certification instead of waiting until afterward, where they belonged. Briefs for George W. Bush endorsed these arguments. Leaving enough time to contest certification was the very reason the Florida Supreme Court gave for setting the Sunday evening deadline!

Harris to the Florida Supreme Court: "The Legislature had good reason to set strict time limits for the certification of election. . . . Importantly, the time for filing an election contest commences upon certification. . . . To delay certification affects the ability to have an election contest heard and possibly appealed and to implement whatever remedy the court might fashion. Each day that certifications are not made and the right to contest is not triggered, the likelihood of a court's ability to effectively deal with a legitimate election failure is adversely affected."

It gets even better. The brief asserts that Gore is "confused" in saying that all the "facts and circumstances" should be known before certification. "This is illogical because such facts and circumstances are usually discovered and raised in a contest action that cannot begin until after the election is certified."

Bush to the Florida Supreme Court: "Florida law provides for contests to be filed after the fact. . . . The contest mechanism provides an adequate and therefore exclusive avenue for relief if Petitioners are correct that the Secretary of State was legally bound to accept late-filed returns."

The Florida Supreme Court ruling: "Accordingly, in order to allow maximum time for contests, . . . amended certifications must be filed with the Election Canvassing Commission by 5 P.M. on Sunday, November 26, 2000 and the Secretary of State . . . shall accept any such amended certifications" up to the same magic moment.

The Harris brief to the U.S. Supreme Court: "The Legislature imposed a deadline for certification because of the short time frame within which to begin and conclude an election contest."

The Bush brief to the U.S. Supreme Court: "That statute [the Florida election law] clearly anticipates that results will be certified in a timely fashion, in order for the results to be contested in court."

The U.S. Supreme Court: yet to be heard from.

So before the certification they argued that Gore had no right to bring up his complaints—or even to establish the "facts and circumstances" of what went on—because all that should wait until after certification. Leaving enough time for him to do this was the very reason certification was so pressing. And the Supreme Court agreed, which is why it laid down the Sunday 5 P.M. deadline that Katherine Harris enforced with such cynical exactitude.

Although certification was delayed, many votes were never counted—or were counted and discarded—to meet the deadline: a deadline allegedly imposed for his benefit. And several reasonable issues have never had their day in court. Yet now Gore is being told he should be ashamed of asserting the right of which Bush and Harris were so solicitous lo, these many days ago.

When a reporter touched on all this in the brief Q and A after James Baker's statement Sunday evening, Baker denied that he meant to suggest that Gore's decision to contest the certification was so much as "inappropriate." Baker said, "I didn't say it was inappropriate, and I didn't say it was not provided for in the statutes of Florida. I did say that it was an extraordinarily unusual approach."

Q: "Could I follow up?"

Baker: "And what I did say was that we've had count after count after recount . . ." Blah, blah, blah.

Of course he and the Bush sound-bite brigade are implying or outright saying that Gore's decision not to give up is a lot worse than "inappropriate." How does he—how do they—do it with a straight face? The answer must be: the same way you get to Carnegie Hall.

## W AND JUSTICE

SO YOU GET TO BE PRESIDENT. JUST STOP YAPPING ABOUT HOW FAIR IT IS.

Slate, *Dec. 8, 2000*

The sharpest analysis of the 2000 presidential election is what Republican Sen. S. I. Hayakawa said in 1977 about the Panama Canal: "We stole it fair and square." The best you can say about what happened since Nov. 7 is that the Republicans managed to bob, weave, and spin their way to victory legally but in defiance of justice and common sense. The worst you can say is . . . a lot worse.

You cannot accurately say what George W. Bush told CBS News on Tuesday: that all the "counts, recounts, legal proceedings . . . will finally verify, once and for all, that the system does work" and that "people will say, 'This has been a fair election.'" No doubt people will say it. No doubt GOP spinners are out saying it at this very moment. But it won't be true. Bush's presumed victory is unfair to

Al Gore and to Gore supporters for two reasons. These are reasons beyond the banal fact that more Americans voted for Gore, which has somehow become something you're not supposed to mention in polite company.

First, Gore deserved to win Florida in a specific sense. It's not just that more Florida voters intended to vote for Gore than for any other candidate. It's that more Florida voters left the voting booth thinking they actually had voted for Gore. (The formulation is from *Slate*'s Jacob Weisberg, who also proves that it's true.) Needless to say—or perhaps not needless—these voters also thought their votes would count. Abstract intention may not matter much in voting, and even sincere attempts to record your intention can't always be honored. You're properly out of luck if you accidentally voted twice or for the wrong guy. And dimpled chads will be puzzling moral philosophers for centuries. But surely, if we're talking fairness, a good measure of fairness in counting ballots is how close the tally comes to reflecting who people honestly thought they'd voted for. By that standard, Florida flunks.

More important, the Bushies worked hard to make sure that Florida would flunk. It might have flunked without their fingerprints, thanks to the muddled voters of Palm Beach County, but the Bushies took no chances. They want the stamp of fairness in hindsight. And many of their efforts had a fairness angle (e.g., it's unfair to count some ballots by hand and not others). But their basic argument, to put it as flatteringly as possible, was one of procedural fairness: deadlines are deadlines, rules are rules. Substantive fairness—counting every ballot; counting them accurately—was quite openly dismissed as an inappropriate consideration.

In my view, the Bush arguments about deadlines and procedures were often wrong. But we won't rehash all that here (you'll be glad to learn). It certainly was one of their most brilliant spinning successes to push for the triumph of procedural rules over substantive fairness, meanwhile nailing the other side for dragging in the lawyers and the courts. If the Bush legal arguments were right, even though they led to a patently unfair substantive result, the least you can say is that the laws Bush took advantage of are flawed. Procedural fairness is supposed to produce substantive fairness, not override it. And the fact that Bush won the legal arguments, correctly or otherwise, certainly doesn't show that the outcome is fair. Quite the opposite.

Furthermore, even if the Bush side is right about every disputed legal issue, the law in its majesty did not compel this result. This is the second reason the Bushies are not entitled to hide behind the law and to claim the result is fair, even procedurally. The law did not say there could not be a statewide manual recount—the obvious fair procedural solution to anyone who had been asked on, say, Nov. 6. The law did not require asininely strict enforcement of deadlines that led ballots not to be counted. The law did not require the state legislature to hold a gun to the heads of the state's judges and justices. The law—if you buy the Bush argument—gives Florida's Republican politicians and political appointees the discretion to do these things. And so they did them.

Of course, in every case they also had the discretion to do the fair thing. You might suppose the realization that as a governing official you have the discretion to decide some matter ought to be the beginning of contemplation, not the end. But, in another brilliant (and ironic) bit of spin, the Bushies convinced the world that the law is a line where contemplation properly stops and unburdened calculation may begin. If the leading politicians of Florida were either Democrats or honest, the result would be the opposite. Even procedural fairness doesn't turn on accidents of party affiliation or moral backbone.

The Bush folk did not rely on the abstract beauty of their legal arguments to carry the day against Gore. They also quite cynically ran out the clock. Not just on time for a fair recount but also on the attention span of the citizenry and the patience of the media. Wednesday's *Washington Post* and *New York Times* op-ed pages ran a total of three virtually identical columns, all saying irritably: He's dead. Why won't he lie down?

How can anyone seriously believe that Al Gore is the one here who wants it too badly and will do anything to get it? George W. Bush clearly wants to become president in the worst way. You finish the joke.

## Equal Protection of Whom? From What?

Slate, *Dec. 15, 2000*

The Equal Protection Clause of the Fourteenth Amendment is the constitutional provision that protects African-Americans and other minorities against official discrimination. In *Bush v. Gore*, the U.S. Supreme Court invoked the Equal Protection Clause to protect . . . whom, exactly? And from what? Don't say, "George W. Bush. From democracy." This is a period of reconciliation and healing the wounds, remember?

And the majority opinion makes clear that the rights at stake are those of voters, not of candidates. So which voters are the victims here? To whom would a recount have been unfair? The court never spells it out, but there are only two possibilities: a) those who are excluded from the recount; and b) those whose votes were already counted correctly before the recount.

The court begins by noting that voting is a fundamental right under the Constitution. It's not easy to get from here to the conclusion that the Constitution therefore requires you to order that thousands of votes must not be counted. The argument is not that there's anything wrong with trying to divine a voter's intent from ambiguous evidence such as dimples and dangling chad. Indeed, the court implicitly assumes the opposite: that the recounts are correct. It argues that any partial recount denies equal protection to those who don't get one. For example, the Florida court's ordered re-examination of undervotes (ballots where the machine detected no choice for president) was unfair to overvotes (ballots the machine disqualified for seeming to contain two choices). But it cannot be an unfair advantage to have your vote credited incorrectly. So the court is assuming that manual recounts are accurate—chad, dimples, and all. Or at least they are more accurate than not doing a recount.

Please note in passing that, in the course of handing Bush the White House on a platter, the court thus rejects some central arguments of his partisans over the past five weeks: Manual recounts are hopelessly inaccurate, ballots the machines couldn't read had nevertheless been "counted," etc., etc. But that is merely infuriating, not illogical. Likewise the court's implied rejection of another pro-Bush sound bite heard ad nauseam—that the Florida court was "changing the rules after the game is over." The U.S. Supreme Court's preferred analysis is (to paraphrase), "You could have done it right, but now it's too late, suckers." And let's not even get into the judicial philosophy President-elect Bush endorsed on the campaign trail: judicial restraint, strict constructionism, states' rights . . .

But what about this newly discovered constitutional right, apparently defined as the right to an equal chance of having your ballot counted correctly? If they're serious, it will keep the justices busy. There are vast differences in voting systems and accuracy among states and within states. Are they now all unconstitutional? In the majority opinion's most fatuous passage, the court breezily suggests that some disparities may be justified by the "expertise" of "local entities."

More important, what sense does it make to address the problem of inaccurate vote counts by requiring any given group's vote count to be just as inaccurate as any other's you can point to? If the court were serious here—which it isn't—the result would be a round robin of lawsuits dragging every vote-counting jurisdiction down to the lowest common denominator.

The majority opinion also suggests, without excessive clarity, that allowing a recount would also be unfair to those whose votes had already been tabulated correctly. How? By "diluting" the value of their votes. This is totally mystifying. Every recorded vote dilutes every other recorded vote equally, whether it is recorded initially or after a recount. Unless there is something independently wrong with counting your vote, how can it be unfair to me just because it dilutes the value of mine?

In a separate opinion, Chief Justice William Rehnquist can't resist quoting the Florida voting instructions about making sure you punch through the card, etc., etc. But even he doesn't suggest that the punishment for failure should be losing your vote. This would be like saying that a sign warning pedestrians to look both ways makes it OK to run them over if they don't. In fact, throw in Equal Protection and—by the court's analysis—it might be unconstitutional not to run them over.

It was George Bush, Katherine Harris, the Republican Florida legislature, and the U.S. Supreme Court itself who prevented the complete and uniform recount that could have met the justices' Equal Protection standards. Meanwhile, through the entire long debate, complaints about lesser recounts—whether complaints about accuracy or complaints about fairness—overlooked the question, "Compared to what?"

The proper comparison is not to some ideal voting system but to what, in the end, we got. Guessing a voter's intent with even 51 percent accuracy—and the guesswork was surely better than that—is fairer and more accurate than assuming in effect that he or she intended not to vote. Even counting votes by a mishmash of different standards would produce a fairer and more accurate result than not counting them at all.

You might think that if voting is a fundamental right, the Constitution would be best served by maximizing the number of citizens whose votes are counted correctly—not by worrying whether each vote has an equal chance of not counting. You might wonder about a use of the Equal Protection Clause that takes away this fundamental right from thousands of voters without extending it to a single one. But if you think like this, you'll never be a Supreme Court justice. At least for the next four years.

## REASONABLE PEOPLE CAN DIFFER?

NOT WITH ME THEY CAN'T.

Slate, *Dec. 22, 2000*

It is often said that reasonable people can differ, but I've never entirely agreed with that. And never before have I felt more strongly that I was surrounded by unreasonable people than during the five weeks after Nov. 7. Or at least never before since I was a teenager.

The Recount may not have been a bigger national obsession than other total-immersion controversies that have become a regular part of our culture in recent years. (We never even came up with a good name for it. "Recount" is exactly what it wasn't.) But for me, at least, it posed the question, "How can reasonable people believe that?" more vividly than any previous contender.

Let's run through the list. Elián González? Question doesn't arise; reasonable people not apparent on other side. Monica? A stew of ambivalence; possibility of reason on the other side all too apparent. O.J.? Nobody reasonable could believe him, and nobody did. Clarence Thomas? Turned on a narrow factual uncertainty; strong beliefs on both sides unreasonable. Bork? Although bitter, a rather high-minded scholarly debate, as these things go. Iran-Contra? What was that all about again?

Even in theory, the notion that reasonable people can differ is a bit lame. On matters you're confident you are right about, it is surely bewildering how others can differ. The temptation is to assume they must be stupid or dishonest, and that is often true. But often it is patently not true. So you wonder: I am not gifted with superhuman vision. Why don't all reasonably intelligent and honest people see things the way I do?

They could of course be blinded by prejudice or predisposition. I think this is often the case, especially about politics. Intelligence and honesty are sometimes no match for comfortable habits of thought. Everyone cannot be expected to rethink his or her entire framework of beliefs every time a new issue comes along. It's possible, I charitably suppose, for even fair-minded people not to realize how wrong they are.

The distressing corollary of this generous thought is that I might be one of these misguided people. I don't think so—but then I wouldn't, would I? And it's also a puzzle what one should do about this possibility. On the one hand, it's important to keep the danger in mind, to take the competition out for a mental road test before you buy an opinion on some issue, and to trade it in at any time if you're persuaded it's a lemon. On the other hand, deriving your specific opinions from a framework of beliefs is a good thing, not a bad one, and excessive self-doubt can be paralyzing and even dishonest in its own way. If you can't decide, maybe you should try harder. And if you're sure you're right . . . well, you're sure you're right, aren't you?

In ordinary times, even the professional opinionizer learns to live with the mystery of how other people can be so wrong. But when so many other people, some of whose honesty you respect (James Baker not included, obviously), seem in all sincerity to believe the unbelievable, that induces epistemological vertigo.

It swept over me one day while watching Bill Bennett being interviewed on CNN. Bennett has, if no more, at least a commercial interest in his reputation for intellectual integrity. And he characteristically began by declaring that he was not in touch with the

Bush campaign. "I don't have talking points." But he had independently come to the conclusions that a) Gore was trying to "change the rules" by asking for a manual recount; and b) manual recounts are a terrible idea "because of the uncertainty in counting by human hands, the subjectivity that's introduced." Asked about the Texas law, signed by Bush, authorizing manual recounts if the machine count is close, Bennett sneered, "I've heard a lot of things from lawyers in the last few weeks," but nothing so ridiculous as the idea that "the law in Texas governs what goes on in Florida."

A clever answer. But an honest answer? One distinctive feature of the Recount episode was the way disagreement on non-ideological issues such as this one split along party lines. (And on some ideological issues—such as states' rights—the parties flipped.) That makes both sides suspect, I suppose. However, either the world is not as I perceive it to be or reasonable people cannot seriously differ that a) manual recounts were uncontroversial standard operating procedure in Florida and elsewhere before Nov. 7; and b) the fact that Bush signed a manual recount law himself is at least relevant evidence that manual recounts can't be the obvious absurdity that Bennett was trying to paint them.

In my world, if you told a couple of reasonable people that there had been an election in Florida, it was very close, and one side wanted to recount certain counties but didn't oppose counting others, while the other side said that all manual recounts were out of the question, these two people could not honestly differ about which side deserved the epithet of trying to "change the rules." And even if you told them that the anti-recount side had a plausible technical legal case—involving various deadlines and the ruthless exercise of "discretion" by officials on their side of the case—these reasonable people would not have differed about which side was more entitled to feel self-righteous. The right to vote and have your vote count seems like an appropriate, or at least explainable, basis for passion. But where do you honestly get passionate intensity about defending the web of technicalities used to defeat that right?

I don't mean to rehash these old arguments. Quite the opposite: My point is that all this seems obvious to me beyond the need for argument. If it doesn't seem that way to you, one of us has a problem with reality. And both of us have a problem with this great national reconciliation everyone is so gung-ho about.

# 2001

## God Bless You And . . .

Slate, *Jan. 26, 2001*

**W**hen did they pass the constitutional amendment requiring every president and would-be president to end every speech with the words, "God bless you, and God bless America"? Even a nonbeliever cannot reasonably object to the sentiment. If I turn out to be mistaken about the central question of the universe, I'll be happy enough that others were doing some celestial lobbying on my country's behalf. And if the words are pouring into an unhearing ether, there's no harm done.

Furthermore, it seems to have worked, so far. But is even God starting to tire of the constant special pleading? This rhetorical sign-off is filtering down from major speeches by national leaders to everyday speeches by members of Congress to casual remarks by local officials. It's starting to be suspicious if a politician doesn't conclude a public statement this way. The missing phrase echoes loud. What's your problem, buddy? You don't want God to bless America?

And how do we even know that the practice is limited to public statements? One imagines the politician at home:

"Pass the salt, honey. God bless you, and God bless America."

"More apple pie, dear? God bless you, and God bless America."

"May I be excused, please, Dad? God bless you."

"Just one moment, young lady. And? And?"

(Sigh.) "And God bless America."

"That's better. You're excused. God bless you, and God bless America."

An unscientific romp through the databases tends to confirm that the great American tradition we had better refer to as GBY/GBA only recently acquired its status as the politicians' answer to "Have a nice day." ("Have a nice day, Senator." "God bless you and God bless America.") The outbreak is worse during election years, of course, and 2000 may have been a milestone. The "Political Transcripts" file of the Federal Document Clearing House shows thirteen uses of GBY/GBA in 1996, eight in 1997, seven in 1998, twelve in 1999 (including, for example, a press conference on impeachment by Rep. Bob Barr), and twenty-seven in 2000. This year has started out with five GBY/GBAs in just the first three weeks: two from President Bush, two from former President Clinton, and one from Sen. Jesse Helms.

The broader Dow Jones Publications Library, tracking hundreds of media outlets around the world, shows 338 uses of the terms "God bless you" and "God bless America" (together) since the beginning of last year. This obviously includes some repetitions, and the database is larger for more recent years, but the historical comparison is nevertheless ominous. A search of the equivalent thirteen-month period in 1990–91 shows only twelve GBY/GBAs. And in the thirteen months from January 1980 through January 1981, as far as the Dow Jones Publications Library is concerned, nobody uttered the magic words at all!

Is it possible, I wondered, that Ronald Reagan didn't end his inaugural addresses this way? Remarkably, Reagan's first inaugural, in 1981, ended with a relatively simple "God bless you, and thank you." His second, in 1985, signed off, "God bless you, and may God bless America"—a subtly less hectorish variant. Nevertheless, I suspect that emulation of the Great Communicator is responsible for this dubious tradition. Imagine if any president from now on tried to get off the swearing-in platform and start trying out all the buttons in the Oval Office without a GBY/GBA. The nation would proclaim in one voice, "Go back. You forgot to say, 'Mother, may I?'"

In another disturbing trend, God is being called on to bless you and then bless various individual states. The Dow Jones database coughs up twenty-one citations for "God bless you, and God bless the state of . . ." plus other direct calls for blessings on "California" and other places self-confident enough to assume that God already knows they are states. There is no record of anybody ever saying, "God bless you, and God bless the District of Columbia."

We seem to be the only country that goes in for this particular formula. A search in English through a U.S.-based media collection has obvious limitations, but nothing turned up for "God bless you, and God bless the United Kingdom" (or Britain or Great Britain or England) or "God bless France" or Russia or Serbia or India or China or Canada. "God bless you, and God bless the European Community"? Zippo.

It's well known that the United States is one of the most religious nations on earth. What GBY/GBA illustrates is that religion is becoming a larger part of our official public life, not a smaller one as many people puzzlingly insist. There's no need to be an ACLU hysteric about this. But it does, for example, make the complaints of some John Ashcroft supporters that he is a victim of the political culture's alleged antipathy to religion hard to take seriously.

And official promotion of religion—even when it's not specific— can reach a point where it infringes on the rights of nonbelievers. President Bush has cut off family planning funds for international organizations that finance abortions on the grounds that money given for one thing frees up money for the other. But he does not apply the same logic to his plans to subsidize church-based education. If a birth-control grant to some agency amounts to taxpayers funding abortions, why isn't a grant to a church school essentially forcing me to pay for candles and incense?

One good thing might come of GBY/GBA, though. If it's going to be our Official Patriotic Sentiment, let's at least make Irving Berlin's tuneful song our national anthem, in place of the unsingable one with the martial lyrics that make no reference to any specific American virtue. Even a nonbeliever will take God's blessing over "bombs bursting in air" any day.

What?

Oh. Almost forgot. God bless you, and God bless America.


## REAGAN'S RECORD

Slate, *Feb. 9, 2001*

Ronald Reagan's ninetieth birthday has set off a national debate about the Reagan presidency. Was it as wonderful as we thought at the time? Or, on the other hand, was it even more wonderful? Happy birthday to Mr. Reagan, a genial, well-meaning, patriotic man, who never (we presume) had oral sex near the Oval Office. A great leader, too, in the general view—and on the question of leadership, the general view is, by definition, hard to dispute. On most other subjects, though, objective fact may be worth consulting as well. On that basis, Reagan's achievements as president appear in hindsight to be just about exactly as wonderful as I thought at the time. Not very.

The nutshell case for Reagan's greatness is: 1) He ended the crisis of stagflation and malaise, restoring our country to prosperity and self-confidence. 2) He cut taxes and reduced the size of government. 3) He rebuilt America's military strength and won the Cold War. 4) He lent dignity to the office, unlike a more recent ex-president one could name.

The case against the case takes a slightly larger nutshell.

Start with the economy. The economic crisis of the late 1970s and early 1980s was double-digit inflation. Double-digit interest rates and a double-dip recession were the medicine we took to cure it. The doctor who administered the medicine was Federal Reserve Chairman Paul Volcker. Volcker was appointed by President Jimmy Carter, who fecklessly allowed inflation to develop and then (nobly? naively?) sacrificed his presidency to stop it. Reagan deserves a couple of points for not complaining too much as Volcker twisted the tourniquet. But Reagan's ultimate thanks was to deny Volcker the third term he wanted.

Reagan hagiographers don't even have a theory, beyond raw assertion, to explain how their man is supposed to have stopped inflation. They are happy enough to blame the pain of the actual cure on his predecessor while claiming credit for the prosperity that followed. That triumph and that prosperity—a record of economic growth over eight years second only to Clinton's!—helped to renew the country's spirit (as did the force of Reagan's sunny personality and our great victory over the island superpower of Grenada). But what caused the prosperity?

Two things that clearly did not cause it are smaller government and lower taxes, because this legendary Reagan revolution barely happened. Federal government spending was a quarter higher in real terms when Reagan left office than when he entered. As a share of GDP, the federal government shrank from 22.2 percent to 21.2

percent—a whopping one percentage point. The federal civilian work force increased from 2.8 million to 3 million. (Yes, it increased even if you exclude Defense Department civilians. And, no, assuming a year or two of lag time for a president's policies to take effect doesn't materially change any of these results.)

Under eight years of Big Government Bill Clinton, to choose another president at random, the federal civilian work force went down from 2.9 million to 2.68 million. Federal spending grew by 11 percent in real terms—less than half as much as under Reagan. As a share of GDP, federal spending shrank from 21.5 percent to 18.3 percent—more than double Reagan's reduction, ending up with a federal government share of the economy about a tenth smaller than Reagan left behind.

And taxes? Federal tax collections rose about a fifth in real terms under Reagan. As a share of GDP, they declined from 19.6 percent to 18.3 percent. After Clinton, they are up to 20 percent. It's hard to think of variations in this narrow range as revolutionary one way or the other. For most working Americans, the share of income going to taxes (including FICA) went up even under Reagan.

Reagan enthusiasts say that what matters is marginal rates, which did decline significantly during his tenure. Of course, rates rose significantly under Clinton, which doesn't seem to have done the economy any harm. Critics say that if Reagan's tax cuts fed the 1980s prosperity, it was as an old-fashioned Keynesian stimulus, caused by the huge deficits the cuts produced. It's easy to throw a party if you're willing to triple the national debt.

But even if Reagan's defenders are right that lower marginal rates were key, they're misstating history a bit to give Reagan credit. The most dramatic rate reductions came in the tax reform of 1986. This bipartisan effort—led by Democratic Sen. Bill Bradley—was a response to public outrage at revelations that Reagan's earlier tax cuts had left many wealthy individuals and profitable corporations paying no taxes at all.

Hey, this is going to take a bigger nutshell than I thought. We'll wrap it up next week. Or maybe we'll wait for the great man's one-hundredth.

## REAGAN'S RECORD II

DID HE WIN THE COLD WAR?

Slate, *Feb. 16, 2001*

"**I**'ve become more and more deeply convinced that the human spirit must be capable of rising above dealing with other nations and human beings by threatening their existence," said President Reagan in his "Star Wars" address of 1983, in which he first proposed to build a defense against nuclear missiles. Its purpose, he said, would be "introducing greater stability" in the relationship between the United States and the Soviet Union. "We seek neither military superiority nor political advantage."

Reagan's hagiographers, currently frolicking in celebration of his ninetieth birthday, now say he was lying about all this. They don't put it that way, of course. But that is the necessary implication of their claim that Reagan's tough rhetoric, his costly defense buildup, and his Strategic Defense Initiative in particular were all part of a successful strategy to defeat communism and win the Cold War.

If Reagan was lying in order to hide an actual intention to destroy the Soviet Union, whom was he trying to fool? Not the enemy, since the whole theory is that Reagan scared the Soviets into giving up. If he was lying, it must have been in order to deceive the American citizenry about the most important issue facing any democracy. Not nice.

But more likely he was telling the truth. In favor of this theory is the fact that in all his denunciations of communism and the Soviet Union, before and during his presidency, the emphasis was on the enemy's enormous and allegedly growing military strength and the need to counter it for our own survival—not the hope, let alone the intention, of toppling it.

The famous exception is his "Evil Empire" speech of 1982, in which he predicted that communism will end up "on the ash heap of history." Reagan's critics wrongly denounced that speech for stating the obvious about who were the good guys and who were the bad guys of the Cold War. But even on this occasion he described the collapse of communism as "a plan and a hope for the long term." He (correctly) gave most credit to communism's own economic and political failures. And the "concrete actions" he advocated to hasten the day (although "we must be cautious about forcing the pace of change") were entirely unmilitary—basically the creation of what became the National Endowment for Democracy.

In the economic sphere (discussed in last week's column), the Reagan hagiographers give him credit for things he intended that never happened, such as smaller government. On the world stage, they credit him for things he never intended that did happen.

Well, so what? Even if Reagan didn't intend his military buildup to achieve victory, that was the happy result—wasn't it? Maybe, maybe not. Certainly the half-century-long bipartisan policy of containment played a role. The effect of variations one way or another is debatable. The notion that Jimmy Carter left us weak and vulnerable is certainly exaggerated. Once you give up the idea that Reagan planned it all, the notion that his buildup (for which we're still paying) made the crucial difference becomes less than obvious.

Some former Soviet apparatchiks have testified that Reagan's policies were devastating. This is oddly persuasive to people who wouldn't have believed a word these guys said when they were following the party line of their previous masters. But it's amazing how credible you can become when you tell me what I want to hear.

Suppose events had played out closer to the way Reagan actually predicted. Suppose that, two decades later, communism's internal collapse was continuing on a long fuse, but meanwhile its military strength had continued to grow. And suppose we had responded with continued Reagan-style increases in defense spending. What would the Reagan hagiographers be saying then? Would they be saying, "Well, he did a lot of great things, but his defense policy doesn't seem to have worked"? No, they would be saying exactly what they're saying now: that history had proved him right.

Winning an argument you refuse to lose is a Pyrrhic victory. If no outcome short of outright defeat or nuclear annihilation would be accepted as evidence that Reagan's policy was a failure, no particular outcome is evidence that it was a success.

One Reagan foreign policy initiative almost no one tries to defend is trading weapons for hostages in Iran-Contra. It was morally contemptible, it violated one of the central principles that got Reagan elected, it trampled the very value of democracy it was ostensibly designed to promote. And it didn't even work.

But the question history must decide is: Was it better or worse than oral sex with an intern? It seems to me that subverting the Constitution on an important policy matter is worse than embarrassing everybody with your private squalor. It seems to others that overzealousness in freedom's cause is easier to forgive than raw self-satisfaction. Whoever is right about that, the mantra of the Lewinsky scandal was that the lying, not the original transgression, is what counts. If so, Reagan's sins are at least equal to Clinton's. He never testified under oath until he was out of office and his claims not to remember things had become sadly believable. But at the height of the scandal Reagan lied to us on television just as spectacularly as Clinton did, with that little shake of the head, rather than a Clintonian bite of the lower lip, as his signature gesture of phony sincerity.

### O'REILLY AMONG THE SNOBS

Slate, *March 1, 2001*

**D**o you believe this story?

Bill O'Reilly, the Fox News talk show host, is in the capital for the Bush inauguration. He is invited to a fancy dinner party. Reluctantly, he accepts, although it is not his kind of thing. According to *Newsweek*, "O'Reilly said he could feel the socialites and bigwigs 'measuring' him. 'They're saying, "What's he doing here?" One couple even got up to leave,' O'Reilly later recalled."

Two people left a Washington dinner party rather than share a table with a prole like Bill O'Reilly? Although I wasn't there, I state baldly: It never happened. That kind of snobbery barely exists in America. (Wednesday's *Wall Street Journal* had a front-page feature on country clubs that exclude Jews, treating the matter—correctly—as an odd cultural cul-de-sac, like a town where everyone plays hopscotch or a Web site devoted to whistling.) Certainly, traditional snobbery cannot hope to compete with today's most powerful social ordering principle: celebrity. O'Reilly, as he himself has been known to admit, has the most popular news show on cable. His book, *The*

*O'Reilly Factor* (named after the show), was a No. 1 best seller. When he appears at an "A-list" (*Newsweek*'s label) social function, nobody wonders, "What's he doing here?"

Yet O'Reilly, like many other people, clings to the fantasy that he is a stiff among the swells. He plays this chord repeatedly in the book, a potpourri of anecdotes and opinions about life in general and his in particular. He had a very strange experience as a graduate student at Harvard's Kennedy School of Government (which let the likes of Bill O'Reilly through its ivy-covered gates, he is careful to note, "in an effort to bring all sorts of people together"). Other Kennedy School students, he says, insisted on being called by three names, none of which could be "Vinny, Stevie, or Serge." Their "clothing was understated but top quality . . . and their rooms hinted of exotic vacations and sprawling family property. Winter Skiing in Grindelwald? No problem." They tried to be nice, but Bill was nevertheless humiliated, in a Thai restaurant, to be "the only one who didn't know how to order my meal in Thai."

I should explain this last one to those who may not have been aware that Thai is the lingua franca of the American WASP upper class. The explanation is simple. American Jewish parents only one or two generations off the boat often spoke in Yiddish when they didn't want their children to understand. Italian-Americans used Italian, and so on. But WASPs only had English. (They tried Latin, but tended to forget the declensions after the second martini.) So they adopted Thai, which they use in front of the servants and the O'Reillys of the world as well. (At least it sounds like Thai after the second martini.) When they turn eighteen, upper-class children attend a secret Thai language school, disguised as a ski resort, in Grindelwald.

The notion that the Kennedy School of Government, populated by swells out of P. G. Wodehouse, reached out to O'Reilly, a poor orphan out of Dickens, as representing the opposite pole of the human experience, would be remarkable enough. But O'Reilly's chapter on "The Class Factor" (Chapter 1, luckily for me) contains some puzzling counterevidence. "I'm working-class Irish American Bill O'Reilly . . . pretty far down the social totem pole," he says. Growing up in the 1960s, he watched his father "exhausting himself commuting from Levittown" to work as an accountant for an oil company. Dad "never made more than $35,000"—which would be $100,000 or more in today's money.

Oh, the shame of it! O'Reilly has been downward social climbing. He is actually—and I wish I could say this in Thai, to avoid humiliating him with the children—m-i-d-d-l-e c-l-a-s-s. He apparently regards that status with just as much horror as do the toffs of his fevered imagination.

Why fake a humble background? Partly for business reasons: Joe Sixpack versus the elitists is a good posture for any talk show host, especially one on Fox. Partly out of vanity: It makes the climb to your current perch more impressive. Partly for political reasons: Under our system, even conservatives need some plausible theory to qualify for victim status, from which all blessings flow. But mainly out of sheer snobbery. And it's the only kind of snobbery with any real power in America today: reverse snobbery. Bill O'Reilly pretends (or maybe sincerely imagines) that he feels the sting of status from above. But he unintentionally reveals that he actually fears it more from below. Like most of us.

This is not a terrible thing. Reverse snobbery, unlike the traditional kind, is a tribute to democracy—it's egalitarianism overshooting the mark. And it is a countervailing social force against growing economic disparity. But when you're faking it, if you're not careful, reverse snobbery can look a lot like the traditional kind. Bill O'Reilly told *Newsweek* he would never patronize a Starbucks, because he prefers a Long Island coffee shop "where cops and firemen hang out." Guess what, Bill?! Cops and firemen like good coffee too! And they can afford it. Starbucks is one of the great democratizing institutions of our time. You'd know that if you went in there occasionally. You snob.

## THE MYSTERY OF THE DEPARTING GUESTS

Slate, *March 22, 2001*

NOTE: *Four years after this episode, O'Reilly publicly fantasized about my decapitation. On his radio show, reacting to some op-ed piece in the* Los Angeles Times *about terrorism, he declared on his radio show, "They'll never get it ["they" meaning liberals and "it" meaning terrorism] until they grab Michael Kinsley out of his little house and they cut his head off. And maybe when the blade sinks in, he'll go, 'Perhaps O'Reilly was right.'" I love that "little house." I assume he is referring to my pied-a-terre in Grindelwald (wherever that is) and not my mansion in Levittown.*

Three weeks ago, writing about reverse snobbery, I took up the case of Fox News talk show host Bill O'Reilly. O'Reilly had told *Newsweek* that two people left a hoity-toity Washington dinner party rather than mix with a working-class guy like him. I asserted, although I was not there, that this could not have happened. I also asserted, based on O'Reilly's own description of his upbringing in his best-selling book—Levittown; father an accountant who commuted to Manhattan; income a pre-inflation $35,000 a year—that he was actually middle class.

O'Reilly had a cow. He denounced me on his show as a liar and as a coward for not daring to come and repeat my aspersions on the air. (And why, other than cowardice, would anyone turn down a chance to be on television? The producer who called with this alluring invitation was told that I was on vacation, but O'Reilly saw through all that.)

So on Tuesday, I went on his show. He called me a liar and a coward again. "You're telling me that I didn't have a modest upbringing?" he raged. "That's the biggest bunk I ever heard in my life." He accused me of childhood affluence. ("That's the truth. I had little, you had a lot. I don't care.") He said that I had no right to call him "middle class" without personally visiting his mother's house in Levittown. But, "You're not invited to dinner because I would never eat with you."

All in all, a fairly dramatic illustration of my thesis that reverse snobbery is a more powerful social force than snobbery of the traditional sort.

But what about the mysterious departing guests? With a flourish, O'Reilly produced what he described as a letter from "the woman who invited me to the dinner party," in which she wrote, "When so-and-so and so-and-so walked out, I was amazed. You were right, you had warned me." I responded that this proved nothing, since the point of the anecdote—his point, as well as mine—was not about whether two people had left this party but about why they had done so. O'Reilly spurned repeated opportunities to engage this argument, although I wouldn't assume that cowardice is the reason. Perhaps he is hard of hearing.

Seeking closure, and curious what O'Reilly might have "warned" her of ("I must warn you, ma'am, that people invariably flee the room when I walk in because I'm from Levittown"), on Wednesday I called the hostess of the party, who said she never wrote such a letter. Apparently, "the woman who invited me" refers not to the hostess but to O'Reilly's own date for the evening, whom O'Reilly understandably does not wish to embarrass by naming. (And what a spectacular act of noblesse oblige on her part to escort the lowly Levittowner around Washington on Inauguration Day!)

My investigators were able to track her down, however. As of this writing, the poor woman has not responded to my phone call and fax. If I were Bill O'Reilly, I would naturally assume that she must be another coward. Join the club! As a weak, woolly liberal, though, I allow the possibility of any number of reasons or no reason at all. Meanwhile, my investigators have obtained more information about this party—including the guest list. Several data points stand out:

- This was not a sit-down dinner, but rather a crowded buffet scene with seating at random. If one were sufficiently paranoid, one might easily misinterpret a decision to go get seconds on that chicken hash as a deliberate insult to the municipality of Levittown.
- Investigators spoke to at least one (i.e., one) of the people assigned to guard the door, who saw no one leaving in anything resembling a huff. At least two (i.e., two) other people involved in staging the party neither saw nor heard of any such incident.
- Close examination of the guest list reveals many other guests with backgrounds more humble than Bill O'Reilly's. Yes, even more humble than an accountant's son from Levittown. We can only hope that they didn't take offense when O'Reilly himself departed.

## CONFESSIONS OF A MCCAIN-FEINGOLD CRIMINAL

Slate, *March 30, 2001*

NOTE: *The crack about pardoning someone's ex-husband refers to Marc Rich, a fugitive pardoned by Bill Clinton in the last moments of his presidency.*

An extremely damaging document has come into my possession. It came in the U.S. mail, actually, calling itself an IRS Miscellaneous Income Form 1099 from the Washington Post Co. According to said document, this private, profit-making corporation paid me several thousand dollars last year to supply a weekly column for the op-ed page of its flagship newspaper. Most of those columns during the tax year 2000, I fear, could be interpreted as efforts to affect the result of the presidential election. Appearances do not deceive: That is, in fact, what they were.

Ever more explicitly as Election Day approached, I urged people to vote against the man who is now president of the United States. (I was operating on the theory that the election results are affected by who gets more votes. This theory has since been discredited, but that's another story.) Meanwhile, this company was not only paying dozens—dozens!—of dollars each time for weekly assaults on a presidential candidate, but it was also spending thousands more to print this electioneering material and to disseminate it to a wide audience. And preliminary research indicates that I am not the only writer whom the Washington Post Co. may have paid to attempt to influence the results of an election. Some of these writers were openly advocating a vote in favor of the ultimate winner. (An unnecessary precaution, as it turned out.) In fact, it appears that, like a K Street lobbying firm, the *Post* routinely spends money on separate attempts to affect election results in favor of both parties' candidates—or even all three—at the same time.

Only two things keep my Form 1099 from being evidence of an "independent expenditure" and a violation of various restrictions and reporting requirements in the McCain-Feingold campaign-finance reform law. One is that McCain-Feingold isn't yet the law. The other is that the campaign-finance laws specifically exempt the media. Current federal regulations declare that the word "expenditure" does not include "any cost incurred in covering or carrying a news story, commentary, or editorial by any broadcasting station (including a cable television operator, programmer, or producer), newspaper, magazine, or other periodical publication" unless it is controlled by a political party or candidate. McCain-Feingold has a similar exemption from its new restrictions on "electioneering communication."

The fiercest critics of campaign-finance reform conclude from all this that the press drumroll on behalf of McCain-Feingold is just a plot to enhance the power of media corporations at the expense of other voices in the political debate. That is silly. The reporters, producers, and editorial writers who are plumping for McCain-Feingold are not pawns of their corporate masters, at least in this regard, and those masters are more interested in profits than in enhancing the political influence of their journalist underlings.

Journalists generally support McCain-Feingold for the same reason other citizens do: They believe—correctly—that the current arrangement stinks. But the media exemption does mean that certain provisions of McCain-Feingold fail the "sauce for the gander" test. These are the same provisions widely acknowledged, even by Sens. McCain and Feingold, as likely to be ruled unconstitutional. But the general media attitude is that this is an unfortunate complication.

For twenty-five years, ever since the Supreme Court first ruled that restrictions on political spending—as opposed to campaign contributions—violate the First Amendment, the *New York Times* editorial page has been ridiculing the idea that "money equals speech." But suppose that Congress decided to restrict the amount of money anyone could spend publishing a newspaper? After all, the *New York Times* is as entrenched an incumbent as any elected politician. It uses its position to raise millions of dollars from other corporations, allowing them in return to flagrantly advance their private agendas in its pages. Limiting what the *Times* can spend might open up room for new voices and liberate the *Times* itself to think more about the public interest and less about how to attract more advertising.

Or suppose Congress merely applied milder impositions resembling those in McCain-Feingold: no editorials endorsing a candidate for office within sixty days of the election; registration and reporting of who writes each editorial, how much that person is paid, what the *Times* charges for those mock-editorial ads on the op-ed page, and so on. All accompanied by detailed rules to enable the government to decide when news analysis crosses over into advocacy. I think the *New York Times* might object.

The Supreme Court's spending/contribution distinction gets attacked from the other side as well. McCain-Feingold's fiercest critics insist that limits on contributions—specifically the closing of the "soft money" loophole—also abridge free speech. But the court got this one right, too. Contributing money may be a way of saying, "I support this candidate," but there's no clear correlation between that message and the size of the contribution. One person's $75 may mean, "I really, really support this candidate," while another person's $1,000 means, "OK, OK, now stop calling me" (and yet another's $500,000 may mean, "Please pardon my ex-husband").

By contrast, when you're spending your own money to promote your own views, every dollar affects your ability to deliver the message. As the *Times,* the *Post,* and all the rest would be explaining today if they weren't exempt.

## It's Not Just the Internet

ALMOST NO ONE PAYS FOR CONTENT IN ANY MEDIUM.

Slate, *May 11, 2001*

The first great cliché of the Internet, carbon-dated back to the mid-1990s, was "information wants to be free." The notion, purged of poetry, was that no one should have to pay for "content"—words and pictures and stuff like that—and, in the friction-free world of cyberspace, no one would have to.

Today, following last year's Great Internet Disillusion, people no longer care what information wants. Information can go inform itself, because information providers want to get paid. Investors are suddenly asking for some plausible theory of how and when a Web site might be expected to make money. And meanwhile, the two most popular answers to those questions—a) advertising; and b) don't bother us about that now, can't you see we're busy?—are met with increasingly impolite skepticism. "You're fired" is how many skeptics now analyze the situation.

The reigning notion today is that the laws of economics are not, after all, suspended in cyberspace like the laws of gravity in outer space. Content needs to be paid for on the Web just as in any other medium. And it probably has to be paid for the same way most other things are paid for: by the people who use it. We tried charging the customers at *Slate*. It didn't work. Future experiments may be more successful, and we at *Slate* encourage others to jump in. We'll watch. But meanwhile, let's look again at this notion that in every medium except the Internet people pay for the content they consume. It's not really true.

Television is the most obvious case. A few weeks ago a producer from *Nightline* contacted *Slate* while researching a possible show on the crisis of content on the Internet. He wanted to know how on earth we could ever be a going business if we gave away our content for free. I asked how many people pay to watch *Nightline*. Answer: none. People pay for their cable or satellite hookup, and they pay for content on HBO, but *Nightline* and other broadcast programs thrive without a penny directly from viewers. There are plenty of differences, of course, and the ability of Web sites to support themselves on advertising is unproved. But *Nightline* itself disproves the notion that giving away content is inherently suicidal.

Now, consider newspapers. Customers do pay, but they're not really paying for the news: They're paying for the paper. Newsprint (which is the paper, not the ink) currently costs around six hundred dollars per metric ton. That's about twenty-seven cents a pound. A weekday edition of the *Washington Post* weighs about a pound and costs twenty-five cents. Not every paper is as weighty as the *Post*. But a recent article in *Presstime*, the house organ of the American Association of Newspapers, reported that a typical newspaper gets about 22 percent of its revenues from readers, while spending 12 percent on paper and ink, 6 percent on running the presses, and 13 percent on delivery and distribution.

That's every penny the newspaper gets from its readers plus another 9 percent of its revenue going to expenses that virtually dis-appear on the Web. Giving up that revenue in exchange for losing those expenses looks like a great way to make money. Once again, no one has managed to make that deal yet (though the *Wall Street Journal* Web edition is reportedly close). But distributing the news for free on the Internet does not seem inherently more absurd than getting twenty-five cents for the same words and pictures on twenty-seven cents' worth of paper.

Finally, look at magazines. And forget about the cost of paper: The money that magazine subscribers pay often doesn't even cover the cost of persuading them to subscribe. A glossy monthly will happily send out twenty dollars of junk mail—sometimes far more—to find one subscriber who will pay twelve or fifteen dollars for a year's subscription. Why? Partly in the hope that she or he will renew again and again until these costs (plus the cost of actually producing and sending the magazine) are covered. But for many magazines—including profitable ones—the average subscriber never pays back the cost of finding, signing, and keeping him or her. The magazines need these subscribers in order to sell advertising.

Most leading print magazines would happily send you their product for free if they had any way of knowing (and proving to advertisers) that you read it. Advertisers figure, reasonably, that folks who pay for a magazine are more likely to read it, and maybe see their ad, than those who don't. So magazines make you pay, even if it costs them more than they get from you.

This madcap logic doesn't apply on the Internet, where advertisers only pay for ads that have definitely appeared in front of someone's "eyeballs." They can even know exactly how many people have clicked on their ads. So far, advertisers have been insufficiently grateful for this advantage. But whether they ultimately come around or not, there will never be a need on the Internet to make you pay just to prove that you're willing.

So maybe the Internet's first great cliché had it exactly backward: Information has been free all along. It's the Internet that wants to enslave it.

## TRIUMPH OF THE RIGHT-WING DORKS

Slate, *May 25, 2001*

**B**ritish Prime Minister Tony Blair is often described as an American-style politician. His opponent in the June 7 election, Conservative Party leader William Hague, seems at first like nothing else on earth, let alone in the United States. Yet Hague is also a recognizable American political type: the dorky right-wing political operative, to be blunt about it. The key difference is that in America these fellows are content to play the role of Rasputin: They don't aspire to be the czar. Precociously possessed by politics; rapturous conspirators and denouncers of conspiracies; middle-aged-looking when young, yet baby-faced as they approach middle age; they leave the actual running for office to less intelligent but glossier specimens with better social skills, like Ronald Reagan and George W. Bush.

Hague is going to lose big—partly because he is such a dork. Nevertheless, it speaks well of British politics—and the British electorate—that an odd duck like Hague should be leading the ticket of a major political party. It shows that the British still have a long way to go if they aspire to the shallowness and professionalization of American politics. It also shows a cultural tolerance for human diversity that is in some ways more valuable than the legally imposed racial consciousness that goes by the term "diversity" in this country.

In fact the British Conservatives have a recent history of leadership by odd ducks. In the 1970s their leader was Ted Heath, a fat bachelor who would be more likely to get arrested than elected if he went around the United States kissing babies. Then, for about four hundred years during the 1980s, there was Margaret Thatcher, who had something closer to hypnosis than a conventional politician's charm. Both of these unusual characters actually led their party to victory—Thatcher seventeen times (or so).

In America, the William Hague types don't run for office, but they do appear on television from time to time. For example, there is the sinister Grover Norquist, who carries half-a-dozen front groups around in his pocket as he pursues his sundry enthusiasms. Turn on Fox News at any hour and you might find Norquist identified as chairman of Citizens against Taxing Rich People. Try again later and he'll be there again, this time as president of the Society for Renaming the Moon after Ronald Reagan.

Then there's John Fund, an editor at the *Wall Street Journal* editorial page with supernatural powers that enable him to plant the exact same thought in the heads of all 147 conservative politicians and commentators appearing on television on any given day. The best-known although least typical example is Bill Kristol, editor in chief of the *Weekly Standard*. Kristol was known as "Dan Quayle's brain" when he served as that vice president's chief of staff. For a while, ABC used Kristol and George Stephanopoulos of the Clinton administration as paired commentators on *This Week*. The glamorous Stephanopoulos is still there; the affable but intellectual (and, worse, intellectual-looking) Kristol was soon dumped.

The emergence of the Right-Wing Dork (RWD) as a recognizable political type, whether running for office in Britain or conspiring behind the scenes in America, is a significant development. (It may even be as significant as the roughly simultaneous emergence of the Leggy Blond Right-Wing Commentatress—a development that has gotten far more attention, for some reason.) Washington has been packed with Left-Wing Dorks since at least the New Deal, but conservatives are supposed to value "real" work in the "real" world and are supposed to hold the capital's leech economy in contempt. Yet the RWD generally discovered politics at a tender age and has never done anything else.

RWDs are drawn unquestioningly to Washington, where they work as aides to real politicians. Or, if they're lucky, they sink into a life of gilded socialism at a conservative think tank. Thanks to the conservative political revival of the past couple of decades, and the growing political activism of big corporations (a development fomented, as it happens, by Irving Kristol, the godfather of neoconservatism and father of Bill), the conservative ideas-and-agitprop industry is now a career track in and of itself. An RWD can go straight from college into a world of seminars, junkets, and political intrigue without ever holding anything most people would recognize as a private-sector job.

There is obvious irony here. But there is poignancy here, too. Are the RWDs hypocrites, or are they selfless martyrs? These are bright, energetic, ambitious people who could probably thrive mightily in the private sector, yet they devote their lives to promoting other people's right to do so. They fight for lower taxes on high incomes that they themselves could earn but choose not to. Selflessly, they promote the cult of the individual. For the good of society, they struggle against dangerous notions like "the good of society." Devoted to reducing the importance of government in our lives, they wallow in public policy so that future generations won't have to. They put up with life in Washington, the better to tear it down.

## TRENT LOTT'S STAGES OF GRIEF

Slate, *June 5, 2001*

Trent Lott is becoming unhinged. At first the former Senate majority leader tried to look on the bright side about his newly reduced status. "There's something liberating about being in the minority," Lott noted philosophically on a call-in radio show. "You're freer to advocate positions and amendments you really think should be adopted."

In suggesting that politicians find it easier to be honest when they're out of power, Lott was not merely saying something we all believe but demonstrating it as well. So it would be unkind to ask what this observation suggests about the "positions" Lott "advocated" before last month, or anything he might say should he become majority leader again.

Acceptance is the last of the famous five stages of grief, as conceived by Elisabeth Kübler-Ross. You're supposed to arrive there after going through Denial, Anger, Bargaining, and Depression. But Lott seems to be doing it backward. Within days, he has slipped from Acceptance back to Anger and even Denial. In a "Call to Action" released by his office (and first reported Sunday in the *New York Times*), the poor man seemed maddened by the loss of power and a sense of betrayal.

"Blow, winds, and crack your cheeks," he declared—No, wait, that was King Lear. Lott merely called for "war" to regain Republican control of the Senate, which had been overturned by a " 'coup of one' that subverted the will of the American voters who elected a Republican majority." Doctors believe this may be a fevered reference to Sen. James Jeffords' switch from Republican to independent, also described by Lott as "the impetuous decision of one man to undermine our democracy."

Republicans must recapture the Senate not just because that would be nice, but because "we have a moral obligation to restore the integrity of our democracy, to restore by the democratic process what was changed in the back rooms in Washington." Democratic "control of the Senate lacks the moral authority of a mandate from the voters."

Lott's notion that Democratic control of the Senate is not merely unfortunate but actually illegitimate is interesting for political reasons as well as the obvious psychiatric ones. The Senate minority leader is not the only one suffering painful symptoms of withdrawal from the drug of political triumphalism. His is not even the most severe case. (Have you been reading the *Wall Street Journal* editorial page?) Republicans and conservatives, somewhat to their credit, are always quick to develop a sense of manifest destiny: a conviction that democracy has anointed them and their agenda forever. They had this feeling, with some justification, throughout the 1980s. They had it again, briefly, in 1994. They had it as recently as two weeks ago, with impressively little factual basis.

Facts are, by definition, a therapy of limited usefulness in cases of advanced delusion. But let us try a few on Sen. Lott's notion that the people have decreed a Republican majority in the Senate and anything that prevents one amounts to a coup d'état. These pills may help others who are less severely afflicted.

One small flaw in Lott's narrative tapestry is that there was not a Republican majority in the Senate even before Jim Jeffords, that impetuous scalawag, betrayed Western civilization. The result was 50–50, remember? It is dubious enough to suppose that when people vote for a particular Senate candidate they are making a conscious decision about which party they wish to see in control. Add in the tie-breaker role of the vice president, especially one elected under the circumstances of this one, and the theory becomes ridiculous.

But suppose that Lott is right and Senate elections are referendums on which party should control the Senate. In that case "the moral authority of a mandate from the voters" belongs to the Democrats, who got 38.38 million votes for senator last November, compared with 37.83 for the Republicans. The fact that states like Montana get just as many senators as New York and California makes it easy for Republicans to have even an actual majority of Senate seats without getting a majority of the vote.

A Republican with a more finely honed sense of irony than Trent Lott's might hesitate before thundering about the moral sanctity of majority rule. Until two weeks ago, the Republicans dominated both elected branches of government without a popular majority in either one. And they were busy with plans to reinforce the effective conservative majority in the third, unelected branch.

American democracy, as we learned last November, is not a system of majority rule. It is majority rule tempered by some purposeful departures enshrined in the Constitution and by some inevitable accidents of history, like the population of North Dakota and the quirky personality of a particular senator from Vermont. They're all part of the system. You cannot reasonably pick and choose among these anomalies, demanding that the other side be good sports about the ones that help you while denouncing the ones that hurt you as betrayals of democracy.

Although they rightly contested an inaccurate vote count in Florida, the Democrats have been very good sports about the basic fact that they lost the presidency while getting a majority of the vote. The Republicans, by contrast, seem to find it inconceivable—and illegitimate—that they should be out of power, even when that result is dictated by both simple majority rule and our system's peculiar departures from it.

And to think these were the people who used to be fixated on the need for term limits.

## PANDORA'S CABLE BOX

Slate, *June 15, 2001*

In the great philosophical dispute of our time—cable or satellite dish?—a big plus for the satellite is that it allows you to live out one of humanity's deepest fantasies: telling the cable company to go away.

It took three visits to get my dish installed, so I had plenty of time for anticipation. Starting cable service had also taken three appointments, with the difference that only the third had resulted in an actual visit. The first two were apparently just tests to see if I would really stay home from work when they asked me to. "Sit!" the cable company had commanded. And, like a dog, I sat.

But now I was through rolling over. No, thank you, I won't reconsider—you see I already have installed the dish . . . Actually, I can get local stations on my dish (no thanks to you bastards lobbying to prevent it, I didn't add) . . . No, I really couldn't ask you to let me have a special "Return of the Prodigal Subscriber" rate . . . Yes, I certainly will keep you in mind if my future needs for cable require me to choose among the only company available. Farewell, then. Be good.

This was so enjoyable that I wasn't even bothered by the news that I would have to return the cable box and remote control to the local cable sales office. (They may have offered another round of guess-if-we're-coming-today as well, but taking the box back myself seemed the more promising method of exorcism.) I didn't even bother to write down the address, figuring I could easily get it on the Web. And with that, the cable company's wicked trap snapped shut. I defy anyone to find this basic piece of information—the address of the local cable sales office in Redmond, Wash., if it exists as alleged—anywhere on the vast Web site of the company that owns the system. I defy you to find it by any other conventional means, such as local directory assistance, or the phone book. No doubt this address is actually hidden in plain sight somewhere, like Poe's Purloined Letter. Perhaps it is scrawled above a urinal in the local bus station. But three hours of earnest effort, building to an Ahablike crescendo of obsession, could not find it.

Despair, O Wanderer Through Hotlink Hell. You are at the mercy of over a century's experience in torturing the customer. Try "Help." Try "Customer service." Try "Search." Try "Contact us." You can even try "Contact your local [cable] office." They laugh at your pitiful mouse clicks. A phone number with a local area code lifts the spirits, only to dash them again when it connects to the same national recording you can already recite by heart.

The cable company is not unique in all this. But it does seem to have mastered all of the state-of-the-art techniques for high-tech aggravation of customers. These include:

- The phone tree. A high-quality phone tree requires a multi-plicity of irrelevant options, offered by an e-x-t-r-e-m-e-l-y s-l-o-w voice; pointless warnings to listen carefully; and espe-cially enraging declarations—each as long as an act of *King Lear*—about how much the company loves you and wants you to be happy. The customer should have to make at least three choices, one of them completely at random, and should have to sit through the first level of options at least twice. Only sissies include a "zero option" to talk to a real human being.

- Hold. This technique is as old as the telephone itself, and most of its conventions are well established, such as recorded mes-sages timed to catch you dozing off so you don't miss a moment of the on-hold experience. Historically, these messages have mostly been unconvincing reassurances that your call is being taken in order. The cable company's brilliant innovation is to nag you to stop bothering them and go to the Web site like a grownup for heaven's sake (or words to that effect). This is the very Web site that drove you to the phone number in despair.

- Information imbalance. Before they'll even consider giving you any information, you must punch in your phone number, a code or password or three, your Social Security number, and the year of your birth divided by three. Then, if you're lucky, a real human being comes on the line asking for your address, account number, and blood pressure. "But all I want is the address of your local office!" She insists that first you must give her all this information. So you do, and of course it's a clas-sic double cross: "Sorry, sucker, I don't have that information. Try the phone number you've already tried eight times. Or be a man and go to the Web site." (Or words to that effect.)

- Scripts and upselling. One voice ran me through a ten-minute sales pitch before admitting that she didn't have a clue about what I wanted to know. They're obviously under orders not to depart from the script. You could be calling to say their build-ing's on fire and they'll linger to tell you about their limited-time offer of HBO plus three channels of yoga for just $8.95.

- Human shields. Phone representatives are instructed to read from scripts because this is cheaper than paying and training them better. But their ignorance and powerlessness are actually a plus for the company. "Sir," they say at any hint of impatience, "I am doing my best to help you." And that's true: There's no point in picking on them. At the cable company, there's an office called "Consumer Complaints," where skilled experts can take any complaint and explain with genuine remorse that they're not authorized to do anything about it.

Anyway, I've got the box if anyone wants it.

## SHINING C

LAND OF OPPORTUNITY, BUSH-STYLE.

Slate, *July 6, 2001*

The most interesting patriotic sentiment of the season was expressed by President Bush last month at Yale's graduation: "And to the C students, I say, you too can be president of the United States." This was intended as a bit of charming self-deprecation: a rhetorical device Bush is quite good at—possibly because he means it. Modesty is one of his better qualities: He seems genuinely comfortable about acknowledging his own limitations. He doesn't evoke a desire to retort, with Golda Meir, "Don't be so humble, you're not that great." Of course, it requires a pretty powerful sense of entitlement to pull this off. There's a real smugness underlying the self-deprecation: Hey, I'm mediocre, and I'm president anyway. (So there, Bill Clinton and Al Gore—study-butts both.)

Sure, a C student can become president. It helps if his father was president first and his grandfather was a senator and he was born into a family that straddles the Northeast WASP aristocracy and the Sun Belt business establishment. And a C student at prep school can get into Yale by adopting a similar action plan of strategic birth control. (That is, controlling whom you're born to.)

By appropriating for himself the magnificent cliché that anyone can become president of the United States, Bush gives it a whole new dimension. Sure, we all know that with gumption and hard work, in this land of opportunity, you can overcome a mountain of life's disadvantages to reach the pinnacle of success. That's one option. But as Bush subtly reminded the Yale graduates, there is another option: With a mountain of life's advantages, you can overcome a disposition against working hard and a cultural distaste for vulgar striving and reach those same pinnacles anyway! Our current president opted for the second strategy, and you cannot begrudge him a splash of smugness in noting that it worked.

What lesson will the Nation's Youth draw from this inspiring tale? It would be tragic if they got the impression that being a lousy student is all it takes. It's a good foundation to build on, but only that. One must also be young and irresponsible until it is time to become old and censorious. "When I was young and irresponsible," Bush has noted, "I was young and irresponsible." And now that he's good, he is very, very good. Bush says he stopped being young and irresponsible on his fortieth birthday. Perfect timing! That happens to be almost exactly when ruining other people's fun starts to be more satisfying—and less exhausting—than having fun of your own. This is another strategy imitators of the Bush Way to Greatness overlook at their peril.

At the Harvard admissions office, they used to have an alleged philosophy they called "the happy bottom quarter." The idea was that Harvard could fill each class, if it wanted to, with nothing but the very top high-school students but that this might be traumatic to those who didn't make it to the top at Harvard. So, the admissions office supposedly reserved about 25 percent of each class for those who could handle the notion of not being a star student.

In practice, this did not mean searching for young folks with a Zenlike acceptance of life's fate, or a profound sense of universal human equality, or enough mathematical wit to appreciate the joke that even at Harvard—unlike Lake Wobegon—everyone cannot be above average. No, "the happy bottom quarter" was a fancy way to make room for alumni sons and athletes and rich kids whose families might give money. These were people who didn't need top grades in order to feel above average. They would be happy with a "Gentleman's C"—meaning both that gentlemen were entitled to no less and that gentlemen strove for no more.

Nicholas Lemann's book *The Big Test* describes how the cozy elite of the Gentleman's C was replaced, in universities and society, by a more rigorous meritocracy of grades and test scores. By the time George W. was in college, that transformation was almost over. "The happy bottom quarter" was just a way to preserve some room for the old America in the new one. Today we like to think we live in an even newer America, where entrepreneurial hustle has replaced test scores and Ivy League degrees as the path to success (and the country's richest person is a Harvard dropout). But George W. Bush's life story of how a C student at Yale became president of the United States illustrates that even the America-before-last hasn't completely lost its grip.

The other day I got a brochure from Harvard, apparently sent to every graduate, inviting me to pay twenty-five dollars to join a computerized mentoring network of Harvard people helping one another to make connections and find jobs. This struck me as a fairly shocking reification of the notion of Harvard as cog in the machinery of a self-perpetuating elite. I'm not sure whether the brazen crudeness indicates self-confidence or a desperate conspiracy of the two older elites against the new one.

President Bush, though, seems to have found a wilier way to protect the older elites from challenge. Let's hope the president's words and example inspire more young Americans to buckle down, get mediocre grades, and party until they're middle-aged.

## EQUALITY AT THE AIRPORT, I

A RELUCTANT CASE FOR RACIAL PROFILING.

Slate, *Sept. 28, 2001*

**W**hen thugs menace someone because he looks Arab, that's racism. When airport security officials single out Arab-looking men for a more intrusive inspection, that's something else. What is the difference? The difference is that the airport security folks have a rational reason for what they do. An Arab-looking man heading toward a plane is statistically more likely to be a terrorist. That likelihood is infinitesimal, but the whole airport rigmarole is based on infinitesimal chances. If trying to catch terrorists this way makes sense at all, then Willie Sutton logic says you should pay more attention to people who look like Arabs than to people who don't. This is true even if you are free of all ethnic prejudices. It's not racism.

But that doesn't make it OK. Much of the discrimination that is outlawed in this country—correctly outlawed, we (almost) all agree—could be justified, often sincerely, by reasons other than racial prejudice. Without the civil rights laws, employers with nothing personal against blacks might well decide that hiring whites is more cost-efficient than judging each jobseeker on his or her individual merits. Universities could base their admissions policies on the valid assumption that whites, on average, are better prepared for college. Even though this white advantage is the result of past and present racism, these decisions themselves might be rational and not racially motivated.

All decisions about whom to hire, whom to admit, whose suitcase to ransack as he's rushing to catch a plane are based on generalizations from observable characteristics to unobservable ones. But even statistically valid generalizations are wrong in particular instances. (Many blacks are better prepared for college than many whites. Virtually every Arab hassled at an airport is not a terrorist.) Because even rational discrimination has victims, and because certain generalizations are especially poisonous, America has decided that these generalizations (about race, gender, religion, and so on) are morally wrong. They are wrong even if they are statistically valid, and even if not acting on them imposes a real cost.

Until recently, the term "racial profiling" referred to the police practice of pulling over black male drivers disproportionately, on the statistically valid but morally offensive assumption that black male drivers are more likely to be involved in crime. Now the term has become virtually a synonym for racial discrimination. But if "racial profiling" means anything specific at all, it means rational discrimination: racial discrimination with a non-racist rationale. The question is: When is that OK?

The tempting answer is *never*: Racial discrimination is wrong no matter what the rationale. Period. But today we're at war with a terror network that just killed six thousand innocents and has anonymous agents in our country planning more slaughter. Are we really supposed to ignore the one identifiable fact we know about them? That may be asking too much.

And there is another complication in the purist view: affirmative action. You can believe (as I do) that affirmative action is often a justifiable form of discrimination, but you cannot sensibly believe that it isn't discrimination at all. Racial profiling and affirmative action are analytically the same thing. When the cops stop black drivers or companies make extra efforts to hire black employees, they are both giving certain individuals special treatment based on racial generalizations. The only difference is that in one case the special treatment is something bad and in the other it's something good. Yet defenders of affirmative action tend to deplore racial profiling and vice versa.

The truth is that racial profiling and affirmative action are both dangerous medicines that are sometimes appropriate. So when is "sometimes"? It seems obvious to me, though not to many others, that discrimination in favor of historically oppressed groups is less offensive than discrimination against them. Other than that, the considerations are practical. How much is at stake in forbidding a particular act of discrimination? How much is at stake in allowing it?

A generalization from stereotypes may be statistically rational, but is it necessary? When you're storming a plane looking for the person who has planted a bomb somewhere, there isn't time to avoid valid generalizations and treat each person as an individual. At less urgent moments, like airport check-in, the need to use ethnic identity as a shortcut is less obvious. And then there are those passengers in Minneapolis last week who insisted that three Arab men (who had cleared security) be removed from the plane. These people were making a cost, benefit, and probability analysis so skewed that it amounts to simple racism. (And Northwest Airlines' acquiescence was shameful.)

So what about singling out Arabs at airport security checkpoints? I am skeptical of the value of these check-in rituals in general, which leads me to suspect that the imposition on a minority is not worth it. But assuming these procedures do work, it's hard to argue that helping to avoid another Sept. 11 is not worth the imposition, which is pretty small: inconvenience and embarrassment, as opposed to losing a job or getting lynched.

A colleague says that people singled out at airport security should be consoled with frequent flier miles. They're already getting an even better consolation: the huge increase in public sensitivity to anti-Muslim and anti-Arab prejudice, which President Bush—to his enormous credit—has made such a focal point of his response to Sept. 11. And many victims of racial profiling at the airport may not need any consolation. After all, they don't want to be hijacked and blown up either.

## WHAT IS TERRORISM?

Slate, *Oct. 5, 2001*

Now may seem like an odd moment to be worrying that one person's terrorist is another person's freedom fighter. If ever there was a man of violence who didn't pose this issue, it is Osama Bin Laden. Bin Laden is triply easy to classify. First, the attack of Sept. 11, assuming he was responsible for it, was on a murderous scale that makes quibbling over definitions seem absurd. Second, his political vision is the opposite of freedom: a repressive clerical state. Third, his method is "terrorism" in the narrowest definitional sense. It is designed to spread terror, almost apart from any larger goal.

Nevertheless, the definition of the word "terrorism" is a problem in what we'd better start calling the war effort. It's a problem for journalists: Reuters has banned the word in reference to Sept. 11, making an admirable concern for the safety of their reporters look like an idiotic moral relativism.

The definition of terrorism is a problem for law enforcement and civil liberties. If we're going to compromise our liberties over it without turning our country into a police state, we want the definition to be as narrow as possible and still do the job. The Justice Department's draft anti-terrorism bill defines terrorism to include "injury to government property" and "computer trespass," which seems way too broad. On the other hand, the *Los Angeles Times* quotes the chairman of the House intelligence committee, Porter Goss, R.-Fla., complaining that the bill could define terrorism to include bombing an abortion clinic—a definition that will not strike many other people as unreasonable.

Above all, the definition of terrorism is a problem because President Bush has chosen to define our mission as a war against "terrorism," not just against the perpetrators of the particular crime of Sept. 11. And he has promised victory. True, he has limited his goal to victory over terrorism of "global reach," but that is presumably a practical limitation, not a moral one.

The advantages of defining the war as one against terrorism, not just Osama Bin Laden, are obvious: It helps in rallying both the American citizenry and other nations to the cause, and if things go well it creates an opportunity to take care of other items on the agenda, such as Saddam Hussein. But the disadvantages are also obvious. First, unlike a war against Osama Bin Laden specifically, a war against "terrorism" is one we cannot win. Terrorism is like a chronic disease that can be controlled and suppressed, but not cured. By promising a total cure, Bush is setting America and himself up to turn victory into the appearance of defeat.

Second, using "terrorism" to win the support of other nations can backfire unless you have a definition you are willing to apply consistently. And there is no such definition. Defining terrorism was a major industry in Washington during the 1980s, when a definition was badly needed to explain why we were supporting a guerrilla movement against the government of Nicaragua and doing the opposite in El Salvador. No definition ever succeeded.

The difficulty is coming up with a definition of terrorism that does not depend on whose ox is gored. Otherwise you are conceding that one person's terrorist is another's freedom fighter. The concept of terrorism is supposed to be a shortcut to the moral high ground. That is what makes it so useful. It says: The end doesn't justify the means. We don't need to argue about whose cause is right and whose is wrong because certain behavior makes you the bad guy however noble your cause.

So what distinguishes terrorism? Is it the scope of the harm? Most terrorist actions are fairly small-scale compared with the death and destruction committed by nation-states acting in their official capacities. Even Sept. 11 killed fewer people than, say, the bomb on Hiroshima—an act that many Americans find easy to defend.

So can "terrorism" mean acts of violence in support of political goals except when committed by a government? This sounds deeply cynical but actually makes a lot of sense. Giving governments a monopoly on violence is how we bring order out of chaos in the world. No matter how successful we are in developing international courts to prosecute official behavior (such as the atrocities of Slobodan Milosevic) as crimes against humanity, governments will be held to a lower standard than free-lance evildoers for the foreseeable future.

The difficulty is that looking for practical ways to get at furtive and elusive terrorists (or looking for sticks to beat other governments with) inevitably leads to the concept of "state-sponsored terrorism." This gives you someone to attack—and is often factually accurate—but is a hopeless conceptual muddle if non-government is the key to defining terrorism. "State-sponsored" also fails to distinguish the anti-Taliban rebel groups we're flooding with help from other groups we're trying to destroy.

So can terrorism be defined as certain gruesome practices that are unacceptable no matter what the cause? As tactics aimed at civilian non-combatants rather than professional soldiers? As strategies literally designed to create terror—fear, panic, despair—as their primary purpose? All these notions are carted out regularly, but none does the trick. All, in fact, are doubly inadequate: They leave out people you wish to include, and they include people you don't think deserve the label "terrorist" (possibly because you are supporting them financially or supplying them with weapons).

The most accurate definition of terrorism may be the famous Potter Stewart standard of obscenity: "I know it when I see it." Unfortunately, that kind of frankness would rob the term of its moral power—and, more important of course, most of its propaganda power as well.

## NEW YORK BECOMES SEATTLE

Slate, *Oct. 12, 2001*

New Yorkers reportedly are being nice to each other these days, and some are finding it strange. On a radio call-in show the other day, a caller described the amazing scene he had witnessed on a crowded subway car. It seems that a woman was sobbing, and not just one but two different people actually approached her to ask if she was OK! Non–New Yorkers might find the amazement more amazing than the incident itself. And of course New York has witnessed many, many acts of genuine heroism and enormous compassion on and since Sept. 11. But New York has never lacked for grand gestures. It is the petty, everyday kindness of strangers that surprises people.

Although New Yorkers seem to be enjoying their niceness epidemic, they may be disconcerted as well. What if this keeps up? Can civilization survive without sharp elbows and tough skins? O! Brave new world, that has nice people in it. What will it be like?

That, I think I can tell you: It will be like Seattle. The shock of adjustment that New Yorkers report undergoing will be familiar to anyone who has moved from the East Coast to the Pacific Northwest. People here really are nicer in the mundane interactions of life. On the highway, they let you cut in if you need to change lanes. At a downtown store, they're happy to make change or let you use the lavatory without buying anything. At the supermarket, the checkout cashier at the end of a long shift is still saying, "Have a nice day," as if she really wants you to. The average person's stockpile of empathy, just sitting there waiting to exude, is enough to win a presidential primary in a midsized East Coast state.

This does not mean that Seattleites are better people in any moral sense. In fact, there are cynics—yes, even in the Pacific Northwest there are cynics—who believe that the shallow surface kindness camouflages a deeper egocentrism and indifference to others. (This directly parallels the belief among some sentimentalists—yes, even in New York there are sentimentalists—that underneath the tough New York hide beats the softest of hearts.) In the early days after Sept. 11—before the patriotism kicked in—some local media and citizens were referring to the catastrophe as "the terrorist attack on the East Coast," which does unintentionally suggest a capacity for psychological distance. But let us assume that people in Seattle and New York share roughly equal amounts of innate goodness per person. Is the Seattlelike veneer of niceness New Yorkers are now enjoying something worth trying to preserve?

Well, there are pros and cons.

On the negative side, it's darned exhausting to be nice all the time, especially if you're not used to it. "How are you" and "Have a nice day" are just the start of what it takes to get into and out of a casual conversation. I'm still working on what to say when someone says, "How are you?" and you say, "Fine. How are you?" and he then says, "Just great! And how are things?" And while I'm not one of those snobs who objects to being invited to have a nice day ("Miss Manners" Judith Martin's classic response: "Thank you but I have other plans"), I really do start to feel oppressed when commanded to have a nice day AND take care of myself AND be good, simultaneously. Who has that kind of time?

New Yorkers also might legitimately worry whether all this niceness will make them soft. Will they still have the moxie they need to deal with other New Yorkers, let alone with Osama Bin Laden? As you get used to people being extraordinarily nice all day, even run-of-the-mill, look-we're-both-busy commercial brusqueness starts to bruise. A full-throated bit of N'Yawk sarcasm is like a knife in the belly.

On the other hand, a culture of niceness is darned pleasant. The pleasure New Yorkers are feeling does not wear off and does not have to be small consolation for a horrible loss in order to be enjoyable. And so what if the niceness is just on the surface? Heck, that is where we spend most of the day anyway.

Another plus: The niceness culture is egalitarian. Cynics (them again) mock practices like waitresses introducing themselves and everybody going by first names, but these things really do break down barriers, in a small way, without being preachy about it. New Yorkers might claim that their (former?) culture of insult is egalitarian too, citing the famous passage in George Bernard Shaw's *Pygmalion* (and in *My Fair Lady*):

LIZA: He treats a flower girl as if she was a duchess.
HIGGINS: And I treat a duchess as if she was a flower girl.

But treating everybody equally badly is not many people's ideal of egalitarian behavior.

Finally, some of all this surface niceness surely must trickle down to deeper places in the communal soul. That's not just a romantic notion. In a famous book published sixteen years ago called *The Evolution of Cooperation*, a game-theory economist named Robert

Axelrod came very close to proving scientifically that niceness can be contagious. It won't work with Osama Bin Laden, but it could well work with the noisy upstairs neighbor.

## An Agenda for Victory

Slate, *Oct. 16, 2001*

NOTE: *Gary Condit was a congressman suspected of murdering a congressional intern.*

At this extraordinary moment, all Americans must put aside partisan differences and special-interest concerns in order to pursue two overwhelming national goals: defeating the evil of terrorism and salvaging our economic prosperity. We must prove to the terrorists that they cannot change our way of life, so this is no time for business as usual. We must be bold and we must be quick: We cannot enjoy the luxury of worrying about matters that occupied our minds just a few short weeks ago. History will not be kind if we allow lesser concerns such as Gary Condit or fiscal responsibility to distract us from the urgent task at hand.

Working together with only minimal partisan bickering, President Bush and the Congress have already produced a bailout for the nation's troubled airlines. They are on the verge of agreement on new anti-terrorism legislation that strikes a necessary balance between the individual's desire for privacy and the government's legitimate need to know everything about you. And President Bush is said to be considering other helpful measures, such as financial subsidies for the hard-hit insurance industry and another round of business tax cuts. Every day's op-ed page, it seems, brings more valuable suggestions from patriotic ideologues, industrialists, and trade organizations.

All this is well and good. But a truly adequate plan for military, economic, and spiritual victory requires us to go much further. For example, bailouts for the business sectors directly affected by the events of Sept. 11 do nothing for sectors that may have been hit just as hard, albeit indirectly. There are many such sectors, but one in particular is especially vital to America's future—and the world's: the Internet. Even before Sept. 11, Internet companies were going under by the dozens every week. Now, hundreds more bankruptcies are threatened as advertising plans are scaled back and investors get even more skeptical than before.

This must not be allowed to continue. It would be a cruel irony indeed if the forces of medievalism were permitted to strangle the infant economy of the future in its bed. What is needed is a carefully targeted tax credit of 50 percent for new or additional investments in Internet startup firms—or for money spent on advertising in online publications. We also need a 100 percent capital-gains-tax exclusion for Internet-related stocks. Nothing would do more to revive what was wrongly dismissed so often as a "speculative bubble" that this misnomer became a self-fulfilling prophecy. (Would that we had such a "speculative bubble" today!) As someone who works in the Internet sector, I can testify that I and all my Internet colleagues are totally dedicated to showing Osama Bin Laden that he cannot drive the American spirit off-line—but we need a little encouragement.

Another essential step in the war against terrorism is for President Bush to order the Justice Department to drop its antitrust suit against Microsoft. As an employee and stockholder, I know the dispiriting effect this litigation is having on people at one of the U.S. economy's most important companies. At a time when the U.S. government is reaching out to Russia (our sworn enemy until recently) and dropping sanctions against Pakistan (which is only building nuclear weapons, f'r Chrissake)—all to strengthen the alliance against terror—our government should not be picking a fight with this American company with so much software to contribute to the war effort.

Third, we need to seriously consider special tax considerations, regulatory relief, and possibly even direct financial subsidies for people named "Mike" or "Michael." In this time of crisis, we cannot allow superficial considerations of fairness to prevent us from doing what is necessary to assure that this essential group of Americans is fully engaged in the war effort.

According to the National Association of Michaels and Allied Names, what is necessary includes, at a minimum, suspension of all automobile speed limits and parking restrictions and a blanket forgiveness for all past tickets, as well as various tax incentives—for Michaels only. In order to have the proper incentive effect, these must be made permanent and not just for the course of the war. We Michaels are not asking for special treatment. At some stage, when fiscal circumstances allow, consideration should be given to extending similar benefits to people with other names.

But government cannot do it all. What can individual citizens—those who are not contributing directly as members of the uniformed services—do to serve the war effort? President Bush has asked us all to do our bit by buying something. A local RV dealer here in Seattle has been invoking this advice in TV commercials urging folks to buy a home on wheels as a patriotic gesture. New York Mayor Rudy Giuliani has said the best thing people can do to help is to visit New York, stay in a hotel, and buy theater tickets.

These are stern challenges, appropriate to the crisis we face. For those who feel they cannot take on this kind of burden, let me suggest an alternative: Send me the money and I will buy an RV in Seattle, drive it to New York, stay in a hotel, see a few shows, eat in some nice restaurants, and buy something there, too. No, don't thank me. As politicians from the president on down have reminded us, sacrifice will be required from every American if this war is going to be won.

## Is Disappearing

Slate, *Nov. 1, 2001*

NOTE: *The tag (ending) of this column refers to a famous parody of* Time *magazine that appeared many years ago in the* New Yorker. *It concluded, "Backward run sentences until reels the mind, and where it will all end, knows God." And where I assert that I did not mean to pick on Lou Dobbs—that's not true.*

To be or not to be? That remaining the question, the answer increasingly clear. The verb "to be" dying out, and the culprit? None other than TV news channels. Taking the place of such cherished words as "is," "are," "am," even "were" and "was": a new verb form that you might call the one-size-fits-all past, present, and future participle. Or you might call it the one-size-fits-all past, present, and future gerund. One of these right and one of them wrong, but which which? Nobody really knowing the difference between a participle and a gerund. Anyone claiming to understand the distinction probably bluffing. So calling it what you wish: Either label doing.

What I talking about? Just listen to Lou Dobbs, the dean of news network anchorpersons, at the top of his show, CNN's *Lou Dobbs Moneyline*, on Tuesday, Oct. 30. Lou saying, "Top government officials today adding their voices to the call for Americans to remain vigilant." (I not kidding: These his opening words on that evening's program.)

Lou continuing, after a couple of clips of politicians talking something close to normal English, "The president planning to do just that [just what not clear in context], scheduled to throw out the first pitch in game three of the World Series . . . ," adding, "And new traces of anthrax, traces found in additional buildings in the nation's Capital today."

Lou Dobbs not alone. (When serving as the lead example in a journalistic trend story, you never alone.) Nor limiting this trend to anchors—who, as gods among us, making their own rules. Ordinary TV reporters doing it, too. First, though, they must paying obeisance to the anchor-god with the magic words, "That's right, Lou" (or whomever—I not meaning to pick on Lou Dobbs). The anchor having just said something like, "And now to Washington, where MSNBC's Amanda Stakeout reporting tonight that President Bush spending the afternoon consulting by telephone with other world leaders. Any hopes for an early agreement, Amanda?"

This known as the "toss." It remaining a point of pride among anchors and those who write their scripts to summarize a reporter's story so succinctly in the toss that he or she having no choice but to begin by saying, "That's right, Lou." The reporter then repeating, murderously, "The president spending this afternoon consulting by telephone with other world leaders. Aides saying tonight hope for an early agreement. Back to you, you [unintelligible] . . . um . . . Lou."

Wonderful about this universal gerundiciple, or whatever we calling it? That it working equally well as a substitute for the traditional past, present, and future tenses. "Madonna entertaining American troops in Peshawar this evening" could refer to something that already happened, something happening now, or something about to happen. The total effect making one dizzy. Past, present, and future melting together as every newsworthy event taking place simultaneously in some dimension beyond the reach of time, where man forever biting dog and yet it remaining news.

What happening here? No easy answers but some uninformed speculation. Long part of vernacular English: referring to the future as the present. ("Honey, I'm meeting with Democratic leaders tonight in a spirit of bipartisan cooperation. Don't wait up.") Add the established convention of newspaper headlines—referring to the past as the present. ("House Passes Tax Cut.") When, as sometimes happens, there remains a need to refer to the present as the present, newspaper headlines leave out the "is" and its variants. ("White House Considering More Tax Cuts.")

So, TV news borrows the conventions of newspaper headlines. These conventions developing out of a need for compression, but after a couple of centuries imparting an automatic sense of drama and urgency. I suspecting the trend of TV news talking in headline-ese traceable to Rupert Murdoch, who buys the *New York Post* many years ago and founding Fox TV News more recently. The *Post* famous for its brilliant headlines. Fox News, though hypocritical about denying its brazen right-wing politics, the most creative of the TV news networks.

But where it all ending? God knowing tonight. Back to you, Lou.

## OSAMA DONE TOLD ME

SO HOW COME MEDIA OBJECTIVITY IS SUDDENLY A BAD THING?

Slate, *Nov. 8, 2001*

Conservative press critics are in another tizzy about objectivity and balance in American journalism. Only this time their complaint isn't the lack of these fine qualities. Their complaint is that there's way too much of the darned stuff. When complaining about it, they don't call it objectivity or balance: They call it neutrality. But it amounts to the same thing. It means an effort to report the facts without developing—or at least without revealing—an opinion about them.

On most days of the week and most subjects, the critics believe that this task is easy to do, highly desirable, and deplorably bungled by the mainstream press. On the subject of Osama Bin Laden (and the current festivities in general), however, the critics are against neutrality and in favor of bias, which on this occasion they call patriotism. They jump on any suggestion that a journalistic outlet or individual journalist might be reluctant to express or act on an opinion: The opinion is that Bin Laden is evil and that at least the broad outlines of the U.S. campaign against him are wise beyond dispute.

Virtually everyone in mainstream journalism does in fact share this opinion, which adds a further irony to the press critics' new gripe. The traditional conservative media critique has no difficulty with the question of motive: Journalists bend the news in a liberal direction because they're liberals. But in the current situation, pro-Osama sentiments are just not a plausible motive. The notion that journalists covertly sympathize with a mass murderer who may well be targeting journalists specifically is too far-fetched even for radio talk shows. So the new gripe doesn't blame ulterior motives. It blames journalistic standards themselves. Journalists are accused of upholding the very standard—neutrality, balance, objectivity, lack of bias, whatever—that they usually are accused of betraying.

It's a bum rap, of course. No one who watches, reads, or listens could have any doubt that the American media are flagrantly biased. They are pro-America and anti-Bin Laden. On a few occasions when media outlets have allowed neutral, objective standards of newsworthiness to trump overt support for the cause—for example, on the issue of broadcasting Bin Laden's propaganda tapes—the journalists have backed down quickly when criticized.

ABC News President David Westin will be licking his wounds and Rush Limbaugh's boots for months after saying that objectivity requires him to have no opinion about whether the Pentagon was a legitimate target. At CNN, meanwhile, they're officially encouraged to remind viewers of how many people died Sept. 11 whenever they report on civilian casualties caused by U.S. bombing in Afghanistan. This is not objectivity or balance. It is pure pro-American bias. No one watching CNN needs to be informed of what happened Sept. 11. And there is no parallel requirement that references to the fatalities on Sept. 11 be balanced with reminders that the United States is killing innocent civilians every day in Afghanistan.

But there's nothing wrong with the media being biased in favor of the United States, against Osama Bin Laden, in favor of freedom, against terrorism, in favor of the Pentagon (as a building, not as a set of policies), and against crashing a plane full of people into it. Whether patriotism alone justifies a degree of media bias is a tricky question: During Vietnam, media skepticism served the country better than unquestioning support would have. But the current situation is an easier case. Though there's lots of room for argument over sub-issues, the basic justice of America's cause is beyond serious dispute. That it's wrong to hijack a plane and crash it into the Pentagon is closer to being a fact than an opinion. The problem with the conservatives' complaints is, first, their insistence against all evidence that the media are being insufficiently biased, and second, their clinging to simple-minded or even fatuous notions about objectivity and media bias that their own current complaints disprove.

The difference between fact and opinion is not a bright line: It is a spectrum. At one end you have "$2 + 2 = 4$," and on the other you have "Social Security should be privatized" (although undoubtedly there are people eager to insist that even the former is just an opinion or that the latter is an incontrovertible fact). In between are most of the issues involved in controversies over media bias. Where you choose to draw your line on that spectrum is not merely a question of judgment on which reasonable people can disagree: It is to some degree a question of taste on which they can all be equally right.

This is not the familiar point that objectivity is impossible because objective reality is an ever-receding mirage or because human beings can never purge themselves of bias. These things may or may not be true, but a newspaper or TV reporter can still try to perceive and convey the facts as neutrally as possible. The point here is that even where objectivity, balance, and all those good things are possible, they're not always wanted—even by those who preach about them the most.

There is nothing inherently contradictory or hypocritical about Rush Limbaugh objecting to media bias in some cases while demanding it in others. Most of us would agree that "terrorism is bad" and "the United States is good" are permissible, indeed admirable biases. It would be nice if the conservative press critics would agree that even justifiable biases don't justify abandoning all skepticism. It would be even nicer if they would agree that their own position is complex and those who think differently may not be morons or traitors.

## THE GENIUS OF ARI FLEISCHER

Slate, *Dec. 6, 2001*

The press briefings of Defense Secretary Donald Rumsfeld are widely acknowledged to be the best show on television, and watching him perform in person is probably even more entertaining. By contrast, it must be hell to be trapped in the White House briefing room with Press Secretary Ari Fleischer. Reading the transcripts of Fleischer's performances on the Web, though, is fascinating. In a review last week of the various war briefers, my colleague David Plotz gave short shrift to Fleischer—dismissing him as an evasive bore. This doesn't give Fleischer nearly enough credit: He is a great evasive bore.

There's a war on, for heaven's sake. The fate of civilization may be at stake, and your job is to tell the world how the war is going. Under these circumstances, how hard is it to be interesting? On the other hand, to be boring and to stay boring—to maintain your rock-solid commitment to the lack of information while fascinating information cascades from the heavens all around you like emergency food parcels—takes discipline. It takes imagination. Let us not flinch: It takes genius.

Rumsfeld's techniques are fairly easy to discern. He gives the impression of enjoying himself. He teases the reporters. He uses vivid language. He seasons the agit-prop with refreshing little truthlets, like the fact that bombs kill people. He says things like "I don't know"—and not just in situations where it's obvious he really does know. He even says that he knows but won't say or that he's still thinking about it, two mental states that journalists have long suspected might exist among Washington officials.

How Fleischer does it is, like all genius, ultimately unfathomable to the rest of us. But we can study the texts, looking for clues. On Wednesday, for example, the question was: Is President Bush "prepared to do some horse trading" to get enhanced trade authority? In reply, Fleischer noted that "the President believes that trade is right on principle," noted it again, then continued:

> Having said that, there are certain elements of trade that are always up for discussion; that there are valid points that members can make that typically do get discussed. And there is a lot of consultation that goes on in the trade process; many members of Congress, in exchange for giving up their right to amend an agreement that is submitted to them, seek an additional role in the negotiations. And so that is not an uncommon request from members of Congress. So the President will continue to act on principle as he works with members of Congress and listens to their ideas.

In other words: yes. Anyone can sound evasive when he's being evasive. It takes talent to sound evasive when you're not being evasive.

Fleischer speaks a sort of Imperial Court English, in which any question, no matter how specific, is parried with general assurances that the emperor is keenly aware and deeply concerned and firmly resolved and infallibly right and the people are fully supportive and further information should be sought elsewhere. Answering a sharp question about whether all the money investors lost in the Enron collapse had any effect on the administration's enthusiasm for privatizing Social Security, Fleischer first (like an unhelpful telephone receptionist) referred the questioner to the Treasury Department, then to the Labor Department, and then delivered a brilliantly bromidic defense of privatization that made no acknowledgment of anything about the question except its general subject matter.

The Middle East? "I think that, as always, the President wants events to develop over time in a way that he hopes will be fruitful . . ." That "as always" is truly bravura banality. Never for one moment has the president wavered in his desire to see events develop in ways he hopes will be fruitful. Logicians may puzzle over how it is even possible to hope that your own hopes be dashed, but in case it is possible, the president is not doing it.

When Fleischer produces a rare vivid image, it appears to be unintentional. But is it? On Wednesday, he was asked about the president's thoughts regarding the American who was caught fighting for the Taliban. Rather than say he didn't know the president's thoughts or that the president had no thoughts—dangerous territory—Fleischer rushed through only a few throat-clearing pieties to declare that "the president hasn't really entered the realm of conjecture." The image lingers, like one of those huge allegorical paintings in art museums: George W. Bush poised at the portals of the Realm of Conjecture. Will he enter? In the background are vignettes of other adventures: in the Land of Deficits, the Precinct of Chad, the National Guard of Texas. A clutch of advisers stands nearby, warning him away. Notice the brilliant blue of Dick Cheney's tie . . .

Don Rumsfeld paints a world reasonably similar to the one we really live in. Ari Fleischer creates an entire alternative universe. That is what makes him the greater artist.

## FORGETTING AFGHANISTAN

AND FORGIVING JOHN WALKER.

Slate, *Dec. 14, 2001*

All red-blooded Americans hate the Taliban. But what did red-blooded Americans think of the Taliban seven months ago? That's about when John Walker, twenty-year-old American citizen, disappeared from sight until he surfaced earlier this month in a prisoner-of-war camp for Taliban fighters who were lucky enough not to have been killed—yet. Now many Americans want Walker tried, punished, executed . . . nothing is too terrible to say about, or contemplate doing to, this traitor who abandoned his country and joined up with that incarnation of evil, that rats' nest of anti-Americanism, that oppressor of women, that harborer of terrorists: the Taliban.

All this about the Taliban was as true seven months ago as it was until last week, when the Taliban's views on women became irrelevant. But most red-blooded Americans had no gripe against the Taliban seven months ago because seven months ago most Americans of all sanguinary hues had never heard of the Taliban. Most probably had heard of Osama Bin Laden and were happy enough to take him for a very bad guy who looked the part, but few could tell you why. Almost no one could identify al-Qaida—let alone spell it. "Harboring" was still widely considered a benign concept, generally thought to involve boats.

Seven months ago "Afghanistanism" still was—as it had been for decades and soon will be again—journalists' slang for pretentiously feigning interest in the goings-on of superfluous faraway nations. The Bush administration's passionate concern about the rights of women in Afghanistan was still being repressed. Even terrorism was not high on its political agenda.

Sept. 11 changed everything. We are all Afghanistanists now. Both sides of this reversal are justified: not just our current obsession, but our previous indifference as well. Although foreign policy fetishists may deplore it (and globalists are right that the world impinges on sovereign nations more and more), the freedom to ignore the rest of the world has always been part of our American Dream. And if you can't ignore Afghanistan, who can you ignore? You could say that this war is about restoring our right to ignore Afghanistan once again.

Meanwhile, the Taliban is well worth hating. What's frightening, though, is how quickly people have forgotten that they didn't always hate the Taliban, and how quickly they will forget about what is now the object of such hatred. (Inevitable Orwell reference, from *1984*: "Oceana is at war with East Asia. Oceana has ALWAYS been at war with East Asia.") Also, how quickly they develop an appetite for heretics.

*Newsweek* reports that Attorney General John Ashcroft wants to "make an example" of Walker. An example to whom? To all the other young Americans who are thinking about joining the Taliban? Was that a serious problem even before last week? Are there thousands or hundreds or dozens or even two U.S. citizens who are now scouring the globe in search of some other fanatical anti-American militia to join? Or is Ashcroft here confirming his reputation as someone who brings more enthusiasm than reflection to the process of trying people and punishing them?

The only voice of perspective has been that of President Bush, who once said of himself, "When I was young and irresponsible, I was young and irresponsible." About John Walker, Bush said that "this poor fellow . . . obviously . . . has been misled."

Walker obviously has been irresponsible in ways the young George W. never contemplated. He is obviously a fool and pretty obviously wished his own country harm. But there is no evidence so far that he actually did the United States any harm. As far as anyone calling for his head knows, he had nothing to do with Sept. 11 or any foreknowledge of it. He told *Newsweek* that he "supported" it in hindsight, which is repellent but not a crime. It is unclear whether he was actually a member of al-Qaida. He played some unknown but small and ineffectual role in defending Afghanistan from an attack by the United States. That attack was justified, but defending a "harborer" is doubly removed from being a terrorist. Walker seems to have played no active role in the prison camp uprising that killed CIA interrogator Mike Spann.

Whatever happens to him now, John Walker will not have avoided his nation's official wrath. Without knowing of his existence, the United States gave this American citizen precisely the same treatment as the thousands of Pakistanis and other nationals who went to defend the Taliban government. That is, for two months we tried hard to kill him. Then, after he and other surviving fighters surrendered, our pals in the Northern Alliance managed to kill a few more by suffocation while transporting them to prison camp in closed container trucks. Nor was Walker given any special treatment when American planes bombed the prison camp to stop the uprising. All fair enough, or at least inevitable, in wartime.

Walker's co-fighters from Pakistan and elsewhere face unpleasant futures, or very short ones, if they are sent back to their home countries. Does John Walker deserve any better because he happens to be a citizen of the United States? Should we show mercy even though the Taliban didn't and Pakistan probably won't? Should we allow him a fancy lawyer and procedural protections undreamed of in the countries he seemed to prefer to his own? Should we even have a bit of understanding about how a troubled teen-ager might be "young and irresponsible" enough to get himself in this fix?

The answer is yes, of course we should. The superior benefits of American citizenship are "why they hate us," as the president points out, and what we're fighting to protect. Now that the Taliban is defeated, even John Walker has the right of every American to forget about Afghanistan.

## In Defense of Denial

Time, *Dec. 17, 2001*

If you're going to get a serious disease—and, unless you'd prefer to die violently and young, you're probably going to—Parkinson's is not your worst choice. It is progressive and, at the moment, incurable. But, like its victims, it tends to move slowly. It is not generally fatal—meaning that there's enough time for something else to get you first. There is also enough time for a cure to come along, which might well happen if politics don't get in the way. And Parkinson's is fashionable these days. It's a hot disease, thanks to celebrity sufferers like the Pope, Billy Graham, Janet Reno, Muhammad Ali and Michael J. Fox. Even, they say, Yasser Arafat.

I might not have chosen to contract this old people's malady at age forty-two, although you must admit it's a pretty good joke on someone who used to like being precocious. If life is a race to the finish line, I'm years ahead now.

There are three ways to deal with news like this: acceptance, confrontation, or denial. Acceptance is an aspiration, not a strategy. Confrontation means putting the disease at the center of your life: learning as much as you can about it, vigorously exploring alternative therapies, campaigning for more research funding and so on. Denial means letting the disease affect your life as little as possible. In fact, it means pretending as best you can that you don't even have it.

To me, confrontation and denial seem like equally valid strategies, and the choice between them is one of personal taste. Most people mix 'n' match. But there is no question as to which approach has society's approval. Our culture celebrates aggressive victimhood. The victim—victim of almost anything—who fights back is one of the master narratives of our time, in plays and movies, on TV talk shows, in books, in politics, in lawsuits. Meanwhile, few things are more socially disapproved than inauthenticity or a refusal to face reality. In choosing confrontation, you embrace the "community" of your fellow victims—another socially approved value. In choosing denial, you are guilty of "self-hatred," like a Jew or an African American putting on Wasp airs or—worse—trying to "pass" as a white Christian.

I don't mean to ridicule these notions. Even eight years along, I can still pass as healthy most of the time, or could until this week; but there has been a slight pang of disloyalty to the cause in doing so. A woman with multiple sclerosis once said to me, unknowingly, about disease activists in general: "We all pray for someone famous to get our disease." Although I am a very minor public figure compared with the Pope—let alone Michael J. Fox!—I haven't been doing my bit.

Nevertheless, when I got the diagnosis eight years ago, I chose denial. If ever you're entitled to be selfish, I thought (and still think), this is it. So I see a good doctor, take my pills most of the time and go about my business. I couldn't tell you some of the most basic things about Parkinson's and how it works. Modern culture may favor confrontation, but we are genetically hard-wired, or at least I am, with a remarkable capacity for denial. It helps, of course, that the symptoms have been mild. Most days for the past eight years I've hardly given a thought to Parkinson's disease.

In the early stages, Parkinson's is mainly a matter of foreboding, which makes denial an especially effective therapy. If you fool yourself skillfully enough, you can banish thoughts of the disease but retain a liberating sense of urgency. It's like having a Get Out of Jail Free card from the prison of delayed gratification. Skip the Democratic Convention to go kayaking in Alaska? Absolutely. Do it now, in case you can't do it later. So what if you had zero desire to kayak in Alaska until faced with the prospect that someday you couldn't? You want to now. And that's good. Although I wouldn't actually recommend Parkinson's for this reason, the diagnosis is a pretty valuable warning shot from the Grim Reaper. The victims of Sept. 11 had minutes to list their regrets. I've got decades to scratch items off the list.

So I recommend denial—and defend it as a legitimate option. To work effectively, though, denial requires secrecy, and secrecy pretty much requires deception. It's simply easier to go through the day not thinking about Parkinson's disease if the people you interact with don't know you have it. This complicates the case for denial. Deceiving yourself may offend the cultural prejudice in favor of relentless self-knowledge, but it does not offend me. What you do with yourself in the privacy of your head is nobody else's business. On the other hand, deceiving those around you is more troublesome. Especially if you're a journalist, whose whole professional value system is wrapped up in the idea of the truth: demanding it of others, telling it yourself.

For eight years I have tried not to tell outright lies, but there have been some Clintonian evasions and prissy parsing. (Q: "You look tired. Are you O.K.?" A: "I feel fine.") And my basic intention has been to deceive. So I'm sorry about that. Some topics—Is it decaf?—require absolute honesty. With others—military secrets, noncontagious diseases—there may be legitimate exceptions.

The least a misfortune can do to make up for itself is to be interesting. Parkinson's disease has fulfilled that obligation, among other ways, by plunging me into a maze of deception and self-deception. I have no idea how well my deception efforts have worked, and I don't intend to believe everyone who claims to have known all along. But in the past couple of years, it seems to me, the symptoms have become more evident. There have been rumors. And the short, somewhat random, list of people who know my secret because I told them has got longer—probably too long for all the pledges of secrecy to hold.

I've come to assume that many or even most of the people I interact with every day actually do know my secret and are pretending not to. It's been like living in that classic childhood fantasy (which was the basis for the Jim Carrey movie *The Truman Show*) that what seems like reality is actually a giant play that everyone else is performing for your benefit. Only this play has a Pirandellian twist: while people are putting on a performance for you, you are putting on a performance for them. Or are they? (And are you?) Even this orgy of mutual pretense was better than facing the truth in every dealing with other people, I thought, and still think.

But eventually, plugging holes in the dike comes to seem more trouble than it's worth. So now I'm out. The next phase will be interesting as well. Call it part two in a controlled experiment testing those fancy French theories about disease as a social construct. I was officially, publicly healthy. Now, with almost no objective medical change, I am officially, publicly sick. How will that change the actual effect of the disease? Without, I hope, distorting the experiment, I predict that this notion of disease as a function of attitudes about disease will turn out to be more valid than I would have suspected eight years ago.

Those around me who knew will be able to stop acting, but my acting burden will probably increase. Everyone I deal with will be scrutinizing me for symptoms—loving friends and relatives most of all—just as I scrutinize friends and relatives who are chronically ill. Up to now my audience has been either nonsuspecting or constrained to pretend it didn't suspect. In the future everyone will all know the script I'm trying not to follow. My performance, to be convincing, will have to be better than normal. If you're normal, or people think you are, you can clear your throat or trip on a rug or complain of a headache without raising alarms or eyebrows. When people know it is partly performance, you can't.

Anyone who develops a chronic disease in mid-career dreads being written off—being thought of prematurely in the past tense. Three years ago, I was offered the editorship of the *New Yorker*. I told the owner I had Parkinson's and invited him to change his mind, but he generously said it didn't matter. A few hours later, though, he withdrew the offer with no explanation. I chose to believe him that the Parkinson's didn't matter. To withdraw the offer for that reason would be, among other things, probably illegal. But I also doubt that he would have made the offer in the first place had he known all along.

Parkinson's is the disease most likely to be cured by stem-cell research, which is enmeshed in controversy. As I wrote in *Time* a few months ago, you can't really criticize people whose reason for opposing research that uses embryos is that they truly believe embryos are fully human beings. But you can criticize politicians who try to escape this yes-or-no dilemma with calls for compromise or delay or prestigious panels to study the situation and report back in a few months. Can't they hear that sound of clocks ticking? Tempus fugit, assholes.

As we've all discovered since Sept. 11, the news is a lot more interesting when your life may depend on it. So that's another little plus of having Parkinson's disease. I don't delude myself that the pluses add up to equal the minuses. Though I may give that a try.

# 2002

## LISTENING TO OUR INNER ASHCROFT

Slate, *Jan. 3, 2002*

As soon as President Bush declared War on Terrorism, culture warriors rushed to their customary battle stations. From satellites hovering in space, a few right-wingers survey the landscape, ready to aim their laser rays and zap any peaceniks who dare to undermine the war effort with their defeatism and moral relativity. Meanwhile, in bunkers deep below the nation's major universities, a few left-wingers huddle around sensitive seismic devices capable of detecting shockwaves from even the slightest formal suppression of dissent.

For both groups, the pickings have been distressingly slim. Early on, TV comedian Bill Maher violated the rhetorical convention that all bad guys are cowards by noting that it's arguably less cowardly to hijack an airliner and fly it to your own certain death than to rain missiles from far away. There was an unholy fuss, Maher's show lost some advertisers and some local stations, but he wasn't fired. All in all, not exactly the Rosenberg case from either camp's perspective. And the selection hasn't gotten much richer since then. Susan Sontag says something dumb and takes it back. A couple of newspaper columnists criticize Bush's leadership and do get fired. A commencement speaker complains about Attorney General John Ashcroft and is heckled off the stage. Ashcroft himself says fatuously that "those who scare peace-loving people with phantoms of lost liberty . . . only aid terrorists" by eroding national unity. But he doesn't propose or even threaten actual restrictions on Americans' freedom to dissent—concentrating instead on novel ways to lock up foreigners.

The grist shortages for both of these mills—the one grinding away at disloyal dissenters and the one grinding away at the smothering of dissent—have the same cause: Almost no one is dissenting. It's hard to dissent from the core proposition that the perpetrators of a crime as monstrous as 9/11 are worthy targets of America's military and diplomatic power. But there has been remarkably little dissent on subsidiary issues, unrelated issues, Bush's leadership in general. Even genial mockery largely dried up for a while, replaced by an unprecedented flood of patriotic gush and mush.

Why? In part because of self-censorship. John Ashcroft can relax because people have been listening to their Inner Ashcroft. I know this for a fact because I'm one of them. As a writer and editor, I have been censoring myself and others quite a bit since Sept. 11. By "censoring," I mean deciding not to write or publish things for reasons other than my own judgment of their merits. What reasons? Sometimes it has been a sincere feeling that an ordinarily appropriate remark is inappropriate at this extraordinary moment. Sometimes it is genuine respect for readers who might feel that way even if I don't. But sometimes it is simple cowardice.

White House Press Secretary Ari Fleischer, with characteristic brilliance, described the situation well when he said early on that in this war Americans "need to watch what they say." He was not referring to national security secrets, and he was not threatening official censorship. He was describing an atmosphere in which clichés are sacrosanct and trying to say something interesting can be more trouble than it is worth. Especially if you go too far or put it badly, as can happen if you're trying to be interesting and not watching what you say.

The right to go too far and the right to put it badly may not seem like terribly crucial rights, but they are. Opening your mouth is not an exact science, and it's harder to do well if you're looking over your shoulder at the same time. Consider an analogy from libel law. The Constitution protects some false statements from libel suits, not for their own sake but to give attempts to tell the truth some necessary room for error. For similar reasons, a healthy political culture has to be able to shrug off some stupid or even offensive remarks. If your main concern is not to say anything offensive or subject to misinterpretation, a lot will go unsaid that is true or even possibly wise. Or at least amusing. Bill Maher has been watching what he says lately, and the nation is poorer for it.

What gets suppressed when you're watching what you say is not formal political dissent or important revelations about government malfeasance. Those things you say with care in any event. It's the lesser criticisms of our government and our leaders, the odd speculative comment that you're not even sure of yourself, the joke that may fall flat. But these are important too. My New Year's resolution for 2002 is to stop listening to my Inner Ashcroft and to be less careful about what I say. How about you?

## THE GOLDBERG VARIATIONS

PLUS: WHAT TO THINK ABOUT LIBERAL BIAS.

Slate, *Jan. 10, 2002*

As a liberal, I had long suspected that we might have a secret coven over at CBS News. It's hard to say why, exactly. Maybe it's that little smirk of Dan Rather's whenever he gets to report something bad happening to America. Or maybe it was the famous episode when Walter Cronkite ended his broadcast by denouncing capitalism as "a system of class oppression that must be destroyed root and branch." But it was only a suspicion.

So I was happy to get confirmation from the current best seller (categorized as nonfiction) *Bias: A CBS Insider Exposes How the Media Distort the News,* by former CBS newsman Bernard Goldberg. The book is rich with anecdotes about the horrors—ideological and otherwise—of working for CBS, culled from Mr. Goldberg's three decades of working for CBS. He must have been chained to his TelePrompTer or something, because a man who "was once rated by *TV Guide* as one of the ten most interesting people on television," as his author ID brags, surely didn't need to spend all those years at a corrupt and dishonest institution.

One story has gotten the most attention. It involves a conversation with CBS News President Andrew Heyward: " 'Look, Bernie,' he said, 'of course there's a liberal bias in the news. All the networks tilt left.' But, 'If you repeat any of this, I'll deny it.'"

Bingo! This was the confirmation that I and every right-wing radio talk show host in America had been waiting for. But then I made the classic journalist's error: I checked it out. First I talked to Goldberg himself. "Look, Mike, of course I made that story up," he said. "It's brilliant, don't you think? If Heyward denies the story, that just confirms it in people's minds. The whole vast right-wing conspiracy has fallen for it. Fox News is so grateful that Roger Ailes is sending me suitcases full of cash. And if you repeat any of this, I'll deny it."

"Of course we haven't fallen for it," Ailes growled. "We just put it out there as prole meat. This Goldberg is what my Communist pals used to call a useful idiot. And what an idiot! They really don't build them like that anymore." Ailes' humor started to improve. Soon tears of happiness were streaming down his cheeks. "I mean, that stuff about CBS execs taking it up the keister from Dan Rather in prison?" He chortled, "I love it, I really do. And who cares if it's all true or not?" He winked. "We report, you decide. By the way, if you repeat any of this, I'll break your legs. And I'll deny it."

Finally, I checked with the chairman of the Vast Conspiracy, *Wall Street Journal* Editor Robert Bartley, who confirmed every detail. "Ailes is a bit of a train wreck himself," Bartley added with a thoughtful wave of his hookah. "Of course if you repeat any of this . . ."

Goldberg's original act of apostasy was in 1996. After managing to hold his tongue for a quarter of a century, he let loose with an op-ed in the *Journal*. To his astonishment, people he thought were his friends turned inexplicably hostile, merely because he had publicly denounced them as betrayers of their profession. Conservative commentary on *Bias* shares Mr. Goldberg's indignation, if not his surprise. Conservatives know the depths of ruthlessness to which the liberal establishment can sink when its supremacy is threatened.

At the *Wall Street Journal* editorial page, presumably, if a colleague announces to the world that he holds the institution and those who work there in contempt, he takes a bit of joshing around the water cooler, then everybody gathers for a group hug and returns to denouncing Tom Daschle. Bernard Goldberg was not so lucky. Trapped in an enraged mob of overpaid, middle-aged white men in suits, he was . . . taken out and tortured? Well, no. Tickled until he begged them to stop? No. Fired? Not at all. Given a cushy job until a bigger pension kicked in at age fifty-five, when he left of his own accord? Yup. Those liberal swine! No wonder Goldberg is regarded (by himself, among others) as a martyr.

OK, OK, Bernard Goldberg may be so dim, or so drunk on self-righteousness, that he can't see the comic futility of trying to insulate a quote from denial by adding a second quote promising to lie about the first one—all in the name of high journalistic standards. (Who is going to doubt the first quote but believe the second?) But he's obviously right about liberal bias, isn't he? Maybe. The point is that this dumb book adds nothing to the argument, and it is the accusers who are offering it as evidence.

Like a stopped clock, Goldberg isn't always wrong. He's probably sincere. But he's remarkably dense. And you have to wonder whether his glorifiers are just as dense, or deeply cynical, or living on a different planet. Do they really think it is devastating evidence of bias that a TV producer would decide to label a full-time ideologue like Phyllis Schlafly as "conservative" but not feel obliged to label avocational activist Rosie O'Donnell as "liberal"?

I don't doubt that Goldberg heard a colleague disparage Gary Bauer as "the little nut from the Christian group." Did he never hear casual disparagement of liberal politicians? "I can't tell you how many times I heard the term 'white trash' thrown around," Goldberg told Howard Kurtz of the *Washington Post*. Was it ever, perchance, applied to Bill Clinton? Goldberg said he "resents" the term "white trash" because of his own lower-middle-class background. His resentment is truly omnivorous. Bernard Goldberg may carry many burdens, but the danger of being considered white trash is not one of them.

Other epithets are available.

## ABOUT LIBERAL BIAS

Warning: What follows is assertion more than argument. Argument seems to be almost pointless on this subject. If you actually believe that CBS News is biased but Fox News tells it straight, our common ground of perceived reality is too small to rumble in. There are all sorts of possible standards for and definitions of bias. There is even a respectable view that Fox News is a terrific innovation in open bias. In fact, that's close to what I believe, though I can also appreciate the view that Fox and CBS are both unacceptably biased, or that CBS is acceptable—B-plus for effort—but Fox is not. What I can't conceive is a serious test of bias that Fox would pass but CBS would flunk. Anyway, for what it's worth, here's what I believe—undefended, but sincere.

1. Are most journalists—on balance, with many exceptions both within and among individuals—inclined to be Democrats? Sure. Just as most corporate executives tend to be Republican. In both cases the reasons are fairly easy to speculate about, mostly involving the psychology of people who are attracted to and do well in these different careers, though in the case of top businesspeople the nexus between political views and self-interest is more obvious.

2. Which has more impact on the shape of society and even the direction of politics: the liberal tendency of journalists or the conservative tendency of business executives? Probably the business folks (through lobbying . . . campaign contributions . . . advertising and PR . . . the general allure of large piles of money), or possibly it's a tie. Unlikely that it is the journalists. Furthermore, even within journalism, the influence of reporters, producers, even anchors is diluted by that of the pundits, the owners, the editorial pages, all of which tend, on average, to be conservative.

3. There is a difference between having an opinion and having a bias. Polls revealing the political preferences of journalists are beside the point. An intelligent and patriotic citizen ought to have informed opinions on the issues of the day, and those opinions—with occasional exceptions—ought to be consistent with one another and with some underlying set of values. Journalists are, by and large, intelligent and patriotic and not exempt from the obligations of citizenship. They also—on average, with exceptions, etc.—tend to be more engaged, both professionally and by disposition, in the issues of the day. So, it is neither practical nor desirable to expect journalists to be ideological eunuchs.

4. The definition of bias depends on the particular institution and the journalist's particular duties. What is bias at a newspaper like the *Washington Post* might not be bias at a magazine like *Time* or *Newsweek*—or a whatever we are at *Slate*. What would be bias at *Slate* might not be at an overtly political journal like the *Nation* or the *National Review*. What is bias for a White House correspondent is proper or even obligatory behavior for an editorial writer. "Liberal bias" obsessives often overlook these distinctions as well as other practical realities of journalism. (The main piece offers some examples.)

5. Most journalists of all political stripes do a pretty good job of preventing their opinions from leading to bias. But no one is perfect and some folks are far from perfect. Since journalists are disproportionately liberal, the bias that creeps in is probably disproportionately liberal as well.

6. Whatcha gonna do about it? If it is wrong for journalists to be disproportionately liberal, what is the proper situation? There are three possible answers, all inadequate. a) Journalists should be ideologically neuter—neither realistic nor desirable, as explained above. b) Journalists should be disproportionately conservative. Many conservative press critics might like this situation, but I cannot imagine a persuasive justification for it. c) The politics of journalists should roughly reflect those of the general population. There is actually an interesting case to be made for this, which I've never seen made. If journalists tend to be disproportionately liberal, achieving ideological balance would require giving hiring preference to conservatives—allowing politics to trump individual merit, if merit is defined as the best possible assessment of a person's potential as a journalist. Actually, I believe that a lot of this goes on already. The constant drumbeat of "liberal bias" has mau-maued many media institutions into actively hiring conservatives. But it's not surprising that conservatives have hesitated to make this argument explicitly, as it inevitably raises the question why they oppose affirmative-action-style favoritism for other underrepresented groups. Somewhat less inevitably, it also raises the question why there shouldn't be favoritism for underrepresented liberals in corporate executive suites.

7. Bottom line: Yes, as a gross generalization, there is some liberal bias in the media. But not nearly enough to explain or justify the obsession with it. Given all the mitigating and complicating and countervailing factors—and assuming that they don't have the stomach for 6 c—liberal-bias obsessives should calm down and learn to live with it. It's really no big deal.

So, that's what I think.

### ARE CONSERVATIVES BRAINIER?

Slate, *Jan. 17, 2002*

Even conservatives generally imagine that liberals are more intellectual. In fact a negative spin on that premise is central to the popular American conservative worldview. To summarize: Liberals are
tweedy, pipe-smoking professors and their '60s-throwback students;
earnest unionized schoolteachers; evil, cunning trial lawyers; head-
in-the-clouds enviro-goofballs; and so on—all of them marinated in
theories out of books and oblivious to the common-sense wisdom of
ordinary folks who may not have a Ph.D. in Advanced Tax-Raising
but have been through the College of Real Life and know a helluva
lot more about how the world works than a bunch of arrogant, elitist
brainiacs.

Liberals also tend to think of themselves as smarter. We are
enlightened; they slog through darkness. This is arrogance, of course,
but it is also naiveté. There is something sweet and innocent about
the notion that people disagree with you because they don't understand the inherent truth of your opinion. Unlike the good old days
when lefties read Karl Marx, it may be conservatives today who are
more likely to see politics as a clash of material interests. This view
can also be a fantasy: It takes real mental energy to persuade yourself
that big corporations, devout Christians, wealthy families, and other
conservative interest groups are the embattled underdogs in a great
power struggle against the tweedy pipe-smokers et al.

And where is the evidence that liberals, for good or ill, are brainier?
("Brainier," of course, confuses very different concepts like innate
intelligence, thoughtfulness, and reading habits. But only some kind
of un-American intellectual pedant would raise that objection.) At
least one good piece of evidence suggests that tarring liberals as the
eggheads around here is a bum rap. As many people, including me,
have suddenly noticed, the nonfiction book best-seller list is dominated by explicitly conservative political tracts. By contrast, there
isn't a single overtly liberal political book on the list.

I noticed this in writing last week about Bernard Goldberg's *Bias*
(about TV news), which is now No. 1. *Final Days* (about the end

of the Clinton administration), by the late Barbara Olson, is No. 7, followed by *The No-Spin Zone* by Fox-TV spin artist Bill O'Reilly. *When Character Was King*, a Peggy Noonan love poem to Ronald Reagan, is No. 10, and Pat Buchanan's latest tract, subtly titled *The Death of the West*, is No. 11. Five out of 15: not bad. And that's not even including the memoir of a TV psychic and a biography of a racehorse, both of which smell pretty conservative to me. (Would a liberal horse be named "Seabiscuit"? C'mon.)

Is it possible that conservatives are actually the intellectuals, reading books and playing with ideas and thinking about issues, while liberals are, at least comparatively, the unreflective know-nothings? I canvassed various liberal friends, who reassured me that it is not possible. Could not be possible. Is unthinkable. Look, let's just not think about it—OK?

They note that most of these conservative best sellers are barely books at all. No sustained argument, but rather sloppy stews of tired anecdote and unsurprising statements about familiar issues. They are bought for comfort and reassurance, not intellectual challenge. That's probably true, but you can't beat a horse with no horse. Even the shoddiest of these books—probably O'Reilly's—is undeniably engaged in ideas, and buying it—let alone reading it—is evidence that the buyer is too. The best-seller list offers no such evidence about liberals.

My friends note that these books tend to be spin-offs of popular conservative TV shows. They point out that liberals don't have a network of lavishly funded propaganda machines passing as foundations that subsidize the production of ideological books. Liberals don't have a pet publisher like Regnery to publish tracts masquerading as tomes. And so on. I do believe that the self-interest of people with money tilts American politics in many ways. But let's face it: You don't have to be rich to buy a book, and these conservative books are meeting the reality test of the market. For that matter, so are the conservative TV shows.

More theories: Liberals read more broadly and deeply, so their intellect infuses the entire catalog, or even all of Western literature, not just a few tawdry best sellers. Or, liberals are buying those conservative books because they have the intellectual integrity to want to test their ideas. Unfortunately, there is no evidence to support these hypotheses, or others of increasing desperation.

If the shoe were on the other foot, conservatives would be scream-ing that book publishers were biased against them. The people in book publishing probably vote Democratic even more heavily than people in the news media. They would measure further left than journalists, on average, by other tests. The fact that conservative books dominate the best-seller list demonstrates how bogus such measures are as evi-dence of bias.

But—pending a better theory of why not—this literary triumph also suggests that conservatives are now the tweedy pipe-smokers, the ivory tower naifs who never lift their eyes from the printed page to let the chill wind of reality smack them in the face, the . . . well, you get the idea.

We liberals have more important things to do than read books.

## DAVOS FOR BEGINNERS

Slate, *Jan. 31, 2002*

The "Newcomers' Guide to the Annual Meeting 2002" kindly sup-plied by the World Economic Forum—aka "Davos"—is written in Globolog, the international language of self-regard, which is simi-lar to English as translated from the original Japanese (perhaps by a European Union functionary in Brussels). "Please note: Sign-up cancellation is not possible. This can only be done at Sign-up Desks." It is impossible, but it can be done—at the appropriate desk. That's the spirit! If we all just put on gray suits and wander the hallways of the Waldorf-Astoria hotel in New York trying to look like the finance minister of Peru . . . why, there's nothing we cannot achieve. We can even "define, discuss and advance key issues on the global agenda."

When an organization parades under a slogan as magnificently banal as "Committed to Improving the State of the World," it is only natural to suspect that something less wholesome is going on. And when important-looking people from around the world gather on a mountaintop in Switzerland—or, this year, in the landscape of police barriers and checkpoints that ordinarily is Midtown Manhattan—

to indulge in "plenary sessions" and other mystic rituals, it is easy enough to believe that this is indeed where the "rich and powerful" come to plot the fate of civilization.

Both the promoters and the critics of Davos are heavily invested in the idea that it is the Central Committee of the Universe. The promoters face the tricky challenge of pooh-poohing this myth without actually undermining it. Fortunately, Globolog is the perfect language for those special moments when you want to be earnest but unconvincing. Elitist? Nonsense: "The World Economic Forum has a long-standing policy of inclusion when it comes to non-government organizations and representatives of civil society, and is working to increase participation within these constituencies."

Yet the Newcomers' Guide is about as frank as Globolog can get about the real purpose of Davos: "Members contribute to the Forum's mission of improving the state of the world while benefiting from unique networking opportunities with other world leaders." One brilliant word transforms this sentence from mundane sales pitch to . . . really great sales pitch. That word, of course, is "other." There are some actual world leaders at Davos, but for most participants it is world leader fantasy camp (like the ones where baseball fanatics pay to attend a mock spring training with actual baseball has-beens). Bring plenty of business cards, the Guide advises, "as people often find that they lack sufficient supply." But do real world leaders hand out business cards? ("John Paul II. Pope. Jp2@vatican.org.")

"There are many possibilities to make yourself available to the media," breathes the Newcomers' Guide, pornographically. And for something a bit kinkier, there's the Garbo option: "Participants may inform the Forum's Media Team that they do not want to have contact with the media. Accordingly, no press conferences, interview requests or personal contact details will be given to journalists."

Journalists are like a drug. Davos invites more of us each year and gets more big-deal treatment as a result. But there's a media equivalent of Heisenberg's uncertainty principle (which holds that the process of observing a scientific experiment can affect the result—or something like that): The more journalists you have hanging around and reporting that Davos is a secret confab of terribly important people, the less true it is. When the media reach a certain critical mass, they start mostly covering themselves.

Allow me to demonstrate.

The Newcomers' Guide is at its most Globologic in the section about the media. The anguish of needing while fearing journalists seeks relief in a comic frenzy of status distinctions. There are "two different types of journalists," the Guide explains. Print and broadcast? Good and evil? No, "Media Fellows and Reporting Press." Except for a Scarlet M, Media Fellows get treated as if they were real people. "They wear white badges on which 'media' is written and have full participant status."

But longtime white badges shouldn't feel too smug. The Guide continues mysteriously, "This year a revised and greatly improved group of Media Fellows and opinion-makers will be present at the Annual Meeting." It is not clear from this whether the individual Media Fellows have greatly improved or whether the selection process has improved to produce a better class of Fellows, but either interpretation is a pretty brutal insult to anyone who has been a Media Fellow before this year. Some of these folks have plenaried their little hearts out year after year to improve the state of the world, and this is the thanks they get?

Still, it could be worse. At least they're not Reporting Press. The Guide is witheringly dismissive. "Familiarly called 'Orange Badges' because of the colour of their badges"—thanks for that explanation, buddy—"are reporters who have limited access to the Meeting." Limited access, the Guide explains, means "they will not have access to . . . the Meeting venue." In other words they can't enter the building, but they're welcome to hang out with their own caste in a "Media Centre" across the street.

As a fellow journalist, I wish to express solidarity with these downtrodden members of my profession. Under our badges, are we not all the same? Has not an Orange Badge eyes? Ears, business cards, sources, a laptop computer? If you cut his piece, does he not whine?

Of course I have a white badge. The canons of journalistic ethics compel me to make this information available to you, the reader. Otherwise I wouldn't mention it since I don't care about such distinctions myself.

## WHAT IS TERRORISM, CONTINUED

THE MORE THINGS YOU CALL TERRORISM, THE FEWER YOU'RE LIKELY TO WIPE OUT.

Slate, *Feb. 7, 2002*

It is not good for North Korea to be developing nuclear weapons, but how exactly is it "terrorism"? The thought of Iran or Iraq as a nuclear power is, if anything, even scarier than the thought of Osama Bin Laden holed up with his dialysis machine in some cave somewhere. But how did the "war on terrorism" change focus so quickly from rooting out and punishing the perpetrators of 9/11—a task that is still incomplete—to doing something—what?—about nuclear proliferation?

As this column and other nit-pickers have noted before, terrorism is a squishy concept. But if the word means anything at all, it embodies the concept that even in war, the end can't justify the means. Terrorism is something-or-other that is bad even when used by the good guys in a good cause. It is a tactic or weapon that is inherently immoral. So shoehorning the problem of nuclear proliferation into the framework of terrorism is especially illogical, since the distinguishing feature of nuclear proliferation as an issue is its asymmetry. It is the United States saying to other countries: We can have nuclear weapons, and so can a few of our old buddies, but you cannot. This imbalance doesn't mean that keeping nukes out of certain hands—even by force if necessary—is a bad idea. It does make terrorism a funny way to think about it.

What is the connection? In his State of the Union speech Jan. 30, President Bush stapled terrorism and proliferation together by declaring that our "goal is to prevent regimes that sponsor terror from threatening America or our friends and allies with weapons of mass destruction." Which is like saying that you want to stop child molesters from robbing banks.

From the beginning, the Bush administration has been admirably clear and consistent that the "war on terrorism" is a long-term project, and not just a matter of nailing Osama Bin Laden. But it has been artfully inconsistent about what that project is. Starting with overwhelming approval for retribution against the perpetrators of

9/11, it has nudged us down the slippery slope from destroying al-Qaida headquarters to destroying the government that "harbored" the headquarters, to invading or bombing other countries where al-Qaida may have operations or that sponsor al-Qaida operations elsewhere, to military action against countries that harbor or sponsor terrorists unconnected to 9/11, to action against countries that do other bad things, like developing nuclear weapons. We haven't actually acted beyond the first two steps, but the administration is building a paper trail that would allow it to claim authority for the whole trip.

Well, so what? Keeping North Korea from going nuclear is a worthy goal, isn't it? Who cares if connecting it to 9/11 is a bit of a stretch? Answer: We should care for three reasons.

The first is advice and consent. Like every modern president, President Bush simply ignored his constitutional obligation to get a formal declaration of war from Congress before—or at least after—invading another country. But he was fully justified in assuming that Congress and the citizenry were behind him in Afghanistan. He would not be justified in assuming similar support for, say, bombing Iran. Imagine if Bush had proposed such a thing on Sept. 10. Yet now he can plausibly claim such support, by association with 9/11. It's been less like a slippery slope than a bait-and-switch. (Conservative pundit William Kristol, writing Jan. 31 in the *Washington Post*, offers another possibility: Bush has been "thinking through the implications" of his original post-9/11 remarks. Anything's possible. Next time, he may even want to try thinking through the implications before announcing the war.)

The second reason Bush's public reasoning matters is that each expansion of the war aims weakens all of them, especially by multiplying the problem of inconsistency. The core commitment to oppose "terror" is problematic in itself: There are terror groups we have ignored or even supported. Our past opposition to nuclear proliferation has been an even wilder festival of double standards—often understandably so as more immediate diplomatic crises have trumped what seemed like a distant concern. The impression that America is motivated by a few immutable principles—not just revenge and not complicated Realpolitik—has been key to both the domestic and the international rallying to the cause. As the cause gets more ambiguous, support will get more ambivalent.

Third, even if you fully support the expansion of the war aims and any action Bush might take in keeping with his latest rhetoric, you ought to be alarmed at the way tacit support for one military action has been converted into implied support for something quite different. That's because the process can keep going. By definition, the first few steps into a quagmire are ones you want to take. If you want to avoid sinking into a quagmire, you have to walk out of it (or at least stop walking into it) *before* taking the step that's regrettable, not afterward. We avoided a quagmire in Afghanistan. Meanwhile, we are taken to have authorized a quagmire of global scale and can only wait and see whether the president—in his wisdom and sole discretion—keeps us out of one.

## Social Hypochondria

Slate, *Feb. 28, 2002*

Something called the National Center on Addiction and Substance Abuse put out a study last week noting with alarm that a quarter of all the alcohol sold in America is consumed by teenagers. The *New York Times* reported on Wednesday that the study was "wrong" because it "had not applied the standard statistical techniques in deriving that number." This makes it sound like the error was arcane and maybe a matter of interpretation, but the *Times* writer, Tamar Lewin, goes on to explain it quite clearly: Forty percent of the survey sample was teenagers, but teenagers are less than 20 percent of the general population. Correcting for this flat-out mistake produces a figure more like 11 percent of alcohol consumption that is by teenagers.

But this raises other questions—or it ought to, but didn't among news organizations that publicized the original number. Shouldn't you want to know what percentage of the population is teenagers before you decide how alarming it is that they consume 25 percent of the alcohol? Yet the Associated Press, CNN, and others passed along the 25 percent figure—and the alarm about it—without even raising this crucial issue.

It is not obviously alarming that teenagers consume 11 percent of the booze if they are 20 percent of the population. But then it would not be obviously alarming that they consumed 25 percent of the booze if they were 40 percent of the population. In other words, the alarm would be dubious even if the original statistic were correct. Now, maybe you believe that teenage drinking is a problem anyway, and maybe you're right. But a news release announcing, "Study Concludes Teenagers Drink Less Than Half as Much as General Population" is not going to rally many new troops to the cause.

In a revised statement on its Web site, the center (which is associated with Columbia University) concedes ungraciously that 11 percent "sets the lower range of estimates." But it goes on to insist that due to a variety of other factors, the teenage share of alcohol consumption may be as high as 30 percent. So where were these other factors when they published the 25 percent figure? It could have been jacked up to 50 percent or 60 percent! Would Joe Califano, the undoubtedly well-meaning Distinguished Former who runs the center, have thought at that point, "Wait a minute, even I don't believe this!"?

This little episode illustrates more than just our national innumeracy—ignorance about math—or the specific credulity of the media about overheated statistics. It is an example of social hypochondria. As a society, we always seem to be obsessing about some problem like teenage drinking or child abuse or immigration or cloning, convinced that it will destroy the country or the world unless it is eliminated. The hypochondria analogy isn't perfect: These diseases tend to be real, not wholly imagined. But a) their perils are exaggerated—at least until they are put aside to make room for other perils; and b) the hope of ever curing them is also exaggerated.

America is not, as it sometimes seems, a society lurching from one acute social crisis to the next. It is a basically healthy society with lots of chronic problems that exist simultaneously, can and should be ameliorated, but will never go away. Nevertheless, a variety of social forces make it hard to see things that way.

One factor is politics. Both major political parties have evolved from collections of people who share a general philosophical framework for looking at the world into coalitions of convenience among people who each feel strongly about one or two particular issues. Direct-mail fund raising, on which both parties rely (and will rely even more if campaign-finance reform succeeds in reducing the role of large donors), works by finding "hot button" issues and exaggerating both their importance and what can be done about them. Special interest groups have actually replaced the parties as the main loyalty of most politically active people. These groups are monomaniacal by definition, and they depend even more on hot-button direct mail.

The media have an obvious vested interest in sowing serial social panic, and that certainly seems to be more true than ever before, though I'm not sure why. What is new is the fad of corporations adopting social issues, then spending millions on them and zillions on bragging about the millions. Also fairly new is the development of social issues—or rather, one good social issue—as a necessary adornment for celebrities from movie stars to first ladies. In fact, issues themselves have become celebrities: each one blindingly famous for fifteen minutes, seen dating Tom Brokaw or Dan Rather, and then brutally dumped and forgotten.

And then there are the lawyers. Suing is our national sport. (Professionals of other sports are among its most enthusiastic practitioners.) If there were an Olympic gold medal for litigation, no other country would have a prayer. Under modern rules like those for class actions, lawsuits are almost an industrial process. Finding or fabricating a social grievance and using it to get the culture of publicity working on your behalf are routine steps. According to a recent study by the respected National Center for Credulity and Alarm, Americans are twice as likely to swallow a phony statistic about a social issue, and almost 2.7 times more likely to find it alarming, as citizens of either the European Union or the former Soviet bloc.

Can you believe that?

## EQUALITY AT THE AIRPORT, II

ARE SHORTER LINES FOR SPECIAL FLIERS FAIR?

Slate, *March 7, 2002*

In the War on Terror, waiting on long lines for security checks at airports is the major war effort imposed on civilians. Though it beats trying to pry martyrdom-crazed al-Qaida fanatics out of caves, trying to get yourself and your luggage from an airport entrance into an actual airplane can be a pretty hellish experience these days. What the demands of security have done since Sept. 11 to make you miserable while heading to the plane nicely complements what the airlines have done in recent years to make you miserable when you're on board.

Unless, of course, you're traveling first-class, or you're a plutonium-level member of the airline's frequent-flier program. In that case your way is eased by, among other perks, special lines—not just at the check-in counter run by the airlines, but at the security checkpoints run by the government. As they inch down endless corridors toward a row of metal detectors shimmering on the distant horizon, juggling possessions and documents according to mystifying rules (laptops must be out of the suitcase . . . cell phones and PalmPilots must be in the suitcase . . . ), the flying masses have both the time and the inclination to wonder: Is this fair?

Special check-in lines are unfair only in the sense that life itself is unfair. The airlines are private companies. They offer better service for a higher price, or for high-volume purchasers, and those who are willing and able to pay more get more. Buying an airplane ticket probably rubs your nose in your financial inferiority—or allows you to wallow in your financial superiority—more forcefully than any other common economic transaction. Probably more than is absolutely necessary. The culture of relentless strategizing, heart-pounding stress, and crushed hopes that has grown up around upgrade certificates is a parody of capitalism's underside. Nevertheless, it's all basically the free market at work.

Special lines to go through airport security are a different matter. It's not just that airport security, as of last month, is run by the federal government. The rules, and thus the inconvenience, have always been mandated by the federal government. And they have always imposed a burden on individuals to benefit the larger society. The new arrangement, and increased burden, just puts the question in sharper perspective. The question is whether money should be able to buy your way out of a social obligation. Or, more grandly, democracy celebrates equality. Capitalism generates inequality. So what do we do, in a democratic-capitalist society, when those forces conflict?

There are two general solutions to this puzzle, neither completely satisfactory. One is: Let capitalism flourish but keep it in its own "sphere" by limiting what money can buy. (*Spheres of Justice* is the title of a book by philosopher Michael Walzer spelling all this out. Another respected book making this case is *The End of Equality*, by *Slate*'s own Mickey Kaus.) If money determines who gets a bigger seat on an airplane, that's OK. But if money determines who fights and dies to protect the country—as it did during the Civil War, when you could buy your way out of the draft by paying someone to take your place—that's not OK. Airline passengers are being drafted, in a small way, in the war on terrorism. Undergoing the hassle is a duty that should be shared as equally as possible, not one you should be able to buy your way out of.

The trouble with this solution is that it bumps up against the powerful moral logic of capitalism: If two people make a deal voluntarily, they both presumably are better off. When you forbid the rich guy to buy something (like a substitute for the draft), you also are forbidding the poor guy to sell something—even though his willingness to sell it proves that he'd rather have the money. So why is that a favor to him? Suppose—to use the classic dorm-room bull-session trump card—he needs the cash to pay for a lifesaving operation on his baby daughter. Yes, of course, he shouldn't have to risk death to get a needed operation for his child. But by closing off one way he can pay for the operation, you're not helping him to get that operation any other way.

The trouble with this second solution is that it "proves too much," in the delightful lawyers' phrase. Should you be allowed to sell an arm or a leg? Sell yourself into slavery? Buy a senator's vote? (I mean buy it directly, rather than through the various indirect methods of our current system.) Should a rich crook or murderer be allowed to hire a substitute for his prison term—or even his execution? Except for nutty Ayn Randists with dollar-sign necklaces, we all have our limits.

In the less melodramatic case of airport security lines, the government's solution involves the splendidly Jesuitical distinction between "lines" and "lanes." The government controls the security lanes themselves, but the airlines control the lines leading up to them. Entry into the lanes is strictly first-come, first-served, in keeping with the principle that the government should treat people equally. How people get to the lanes is up to the airlines, which are free to apply the principle that everything has a price. Of course the net result is that the airlines are free to slice 'n' dice their customers however they wish.

With the tools provided here, you can decide for yourselves whether America's airport terminals have been plunged into moral chaos as well as the physical kind. For myself, I need to think about it for a few more hours. And I think I know where I'll find the time.

## THE JUSTICE'S WIFE'S TALE

Slate, *March 15, 2002*

If you're not careful, you can squander an entire journalistic career swatting flies from the *Wall Street Journal* editorial page. But sometimes resistance to temptation is futile. The question ordinarily posed by these classics is whether the author is staggeringly disingenuous or sincerely addled by ideology. In the case of an op-ed published in the *Journal* last Thursday, though, there is a more benign explanation. This article was an attack on Democrats for opposing President Bush's nomination of Charles W. Pickering for a seat on the Fifth Circuit Court of Appeals. (The Senate Judiciary Committee killed the nomination later that day, on a party-line vote.) The author was Virginia Thomas, wife of Supreme Court Justice Clarence Thomas, whose own famous confirmation ordeal has made him a martyr-saint of American conservatism. Thomas, as you will recall (or if not, his wife will help you), was pummeled so brutally by vicious gangs of Democrats and liberals—who accused him of being a right-wing ideologue with a closed mind about abortion rights, among other vicious lies—that he now lies comatose in the Supreme Court, able only to issue reliably right-wing opinions and vote against abortion rights. Naturally his wife is bitter, and self-righteous bitterness on behalf of an embattled spouse is forgivable, even appealing.

Virginia Thomas is also "director of executive branch relations" at the Heritage Foundation, the well-known right-wing propaganda machine that masquerades as a tax-exempt nonpolitical research institution. ("Director of executive branch relations" is either a joke job or an amusing confirmation of Heritage's true nature.) That a Supreme Court justice's spouse could write this article, and the nation's most influential conservative opinion forum could publish it, illustrates that, for all the talk of the insular, unworldly liberal culture of Washington, there is now a conservative Washington culture large enough and insular enough for its members to live entirely within an echo chamber of their own views.

Or maybe I'm the one who is divorced from reality. But here is reality as I see it. The Constitution gives the Senate the authority to "advise and consent" on the appointment of federal judges. Whatever this means, it must mean more than the obligation to rubber-stamp the president's nominees or merely to pass on their basic competence. Since Ronald Reagan, presidents of both parties have become more careful to nominate judges who reflect their own judicial philosophy—and there is nothing wrong with that. In response, the Senate—especially when controlled by the opposing party—has weighed judicial philosophy more carefully in exercising its advice and consent—and there is nothing wrong with that, either. Each political party opposes nominees from the other one and pompously deplores "politics" when the other party does the same.

Somewhat more tendentiously, it seems to me that Republican presidents have been more disciplined than the one recent Democrat, Bill Clinton, about nominating judges who won't surprise them, which makes the Republican indignation about "ideological" opposition to the president's choices more hypocritical. On the other hand, Democratic politicians and interest groups have been somewhat less principled about distinguishing judicial philosophy—how a judge interprets the law and the Constitution—from the vulgar question of whether they like the outcome. Meanwhile, though, Republicans pretend or imagine that a few magic words like "judicial restraint" and "strict constructionism" add up to a philosophy beyond legitimate dispute—that to believe otherwise is not just misguided but more like cheating—even though it is a philosophy they themselves don't apply with any consistency.

It seems to Virginia Thomas, by contrast, that anyone who opposes judicial nominees of Republican presidents—people like Tom Daschle and other Senate Democrats—represents the "hard left" that cares only "about abortion and homosexuality" and doesn't "think of [opponents] as human." All these accusations are made twice. Oh yes, and these hard leftists "demonize" people they disagree with! (Can you imagine someone doing that?) Whereas "Senate Democrats are actually claiming that some views are so politically incorrect that judges (or others) cannot be allowed to hold them," she and her husband and Judge Pickering are defending "a culture . . . tolerant of philosophical disagreement."

In reality—unless I'm crazy—"hard left" is not an accurate description of the average Democrat on the Senate Judiciary Committee. In reality, both sides of these disputes care disproportionately about abortion. (Homosexuality seems more like a right-wing obsession.) That is why abortion is so contentious. If one side stood for single-issue "litmus tests" and the other stood for "tolerance of philosophical disagreement," we wouldn't be having these set-piece standoffs every few years. The battles happen because both sides have litmus tests, which is another way of saying these are issues they feel strongly about. In Virginia Thomas' opinion, should Republican senators vote to confirm a judicial nominee who believes that *Roe v. Wade* was correctly decided? Or is that view "so politically incorrect that judges (or others) cannot be allowed to hold" it—which is just an overheated way of saying you disagree?

Looking around the real world, it is especially hard to see this martyrdom that Clarence Thomas supposedly has suffered for the sin of holding views that the all-powerful hard left wants to suppress. He had a rough confirmation battle, but now he is a justice of the Supreme Court with a lifetime appointment, even though he clearly lied under oath—or at the very least willfully deceived—in claiming he had never discussed *Roe v. Wade* and had no opinion about it. He probably lied about more notorious matters, too. If he's in pain, it must only hurt when he laughs.


## AN ODE TO MANAGERS

Slate, *April 11, 2002*


All over Washington these days, there are people in suits sitting around conference tables gravely discussing the mess in the Middle East. Some are government officials and politicians. Some are scholars or think-tank pseudo-scholars. Some are journalists. Some of these Mideast discussions are top-secret, while others are actually broadcast live on television. But they all have one thing in common: Nothing will come of it.

The Middle East issue is legendarily intractable. But most such discussions in Washington—even among officials and certainly among scholars and journalists—aren't even intended to solve the problem they are addressing, except in the vaguest of long runs. When, after many years in Washington, I found myself bizarrely employed at a subdivision of a large corporation (Microsoft), the meetings—of which there were plenty—were disorienting. It was not just the dress code: shorts and T-shirts instead of suits and ties. It was not just the subject matter: trivial matters of millions of dollars, instead of billions, or world peace, or something on that order. Finally I figured it out: Not only were these meetings expected to produce decisions, but those decisions were actually expected to produce results.

It was even more shocking to learn how hard it is to get from a decision that something ought to happen to making it happen. In Washington you can make a nice living just calling for things to happen. Or even declaring that it is "unacceptable" for them not to happen. (Arab-Jewish conflict in the Middle East, for example, has been unacceptable according to nearly everybody for the century-plus it has been going on.) Actually making these things happen is usually a hopeless and unnecessary aspiration. Either that or it's just a matter of tidying up after the meeting. But in any case the point is the decision (or often merely the discussion) itself, not anything concrete that might come out of it.

Turning an opinion into a decision and a decision into a result turns out to be a real skill—like writing, except that most writers (including this one) don't have it. As a skill, it is partly an innate gift and partly a set of learnable techniques. It may go too far to call business management a science, and most "how-to" business gurus are surely charlatans, but the premise that management is more than just common sense, and worthy of academic study, no longer seems absurd. Even some of the most easily mockable aspects of business life—meetings to plan for meetings, mission statements, PowerPoint slides, to name but three—are not complete jokes.

Corporate managers don't get enough respect. Their image in the popular culture is still based on the one from the 1950s: A conformist drone doing life-draining work, the man in the grey flannel suit—even if he's a woman and/or gets to dress down on Friday. The anti-corporate 1960s added an element of evil to the image, without any compensating dash of glamour. Starting in the 1980s, general attitudes about business turned positive. But, poignantly—and except for the absurd cult of the CEO—the spotlight of cultural admiration passed right over the corporate manager to focus on the swashbuckling entrepreneur. Even among conservatives today, the midlevel corporate executive is a figure of no cultural interest or value, except as someone with a job the heroic CEO must eliminate to prove his manhood. This is unjust. Even the most brilliant entrepreneur or camera-friendly CEO needs the odd assistant-vice-president or two who probably have skills he or she couldn't duplicate at gunpoint.

One of the nice things about Washington, if you're an egomaniac, is that you can be a big shot without being a boss. The same is true of the literary world and academia and the media. In all these environments, lucky people get all the self-esteem and all the perks of having an important job without needing to take responsibility for the work lives and work product of other people. In fact, the first few employees a rising Washington big shot acquires—a secretary, then another secretary, then maybe a scheduler and a speechwriter—are there to relieve you of responsibility even for yourself. This leaves a false impression of what management is like.

To take the most unpleasant example, have you ever fired someone? In Washington there are people who have fired rockets—and many who have written articles urging others to fire rockets—but have never fired a human being. The natural tendency is to think, "I'm much too nice a person to do that sort of thing"—and to feel superior to anyone without such scruples. Yet in an organization of any size there are going to be people who need or actually deserve to be fired. It is hardly the nicest solution to leave that job to someone nasty enough to enjoy it. The amateur's approach is either to work yourself up into a sadistic fury of your own or to chicken out. Watching a pro get the job done with minimum emotional damage on both sides is impressive. I couldn't do it, and most of you, dear readers, couldn't either.

## LYING IN STYLE

WHAT YOU CAN LEARN ABOUT A PRESIDENT FROM HOW
HE CHOOSES TO DECEIVE YOU.

Slate, *April 18, 2002*

Honest administrations are all alike, but each dishonest administration is dishonest in its own way.

Actually, there are no honest administrations. But each presidency does bring its own unique style to the task of deceiving the citizenry. And at least you can derive some truths about a president from the way he chooses to lie to you. Consider the latest three.

The characteristic lying style of George Bush the Elder derived from his core belief that politics and real life are separate realms. This derived in turn from the cherished preppy-snob distinction between life and games. In life one must be decent and honest and must not seem to be trying too hard. But in games—including politics—one must be ruthless, and one must win. One is not really misbehaving because it's only a game. So the memorable dishonesties of Bush I were highly original artifices on novel or obscure topics, such as Massachusetts prison-furlough policy or teachers who won't pledge allegiance to the flag or how many times Bill Clinton raised taxes as governor of Arkansas. The great ones were often technically true and essentially false at the same time, and the complete performance always included wave upon wave of follow-up obfuscation.

Bush the Elder didn't actually do a lot of the heavy lying himself. He had people for that sort of thing. For Bill Clinton, by contrast, a lie was a seduction—and a personal challenge. Clinton's biggest lie—will it ever be topped?—was a daredevil triple back-flip off the high board. It concerned Topic A on everyone's mind, not some issue invented in the campaign laboratory. It gave him no help in the plausibility department. And yet he offered it boldly, fearlessly, with an actual intention to persuade. And many of us were persuaded.

If the truth was too precious to waste on politics for Bush I and a challenge to overcome for Clinton, for our current George Bush it is simply boring and uncool. Bush II administration lies are often so laughably obvious that you wonder why they bother. Until you realize: They haven't bothered. If telling the truth was less bother, they'd try that too. The characteristic Bush II form of dishonesty is to construct an alternative reality on some topic and to regard anyone who objects to it as a sniveling dweeb obsessed with "nuance," which the president of this class, I mean of the United States, has more important things to do than worry about.

You can just see Bush rolling his eyes at the fuss—small as it is—over his administration's role in the recent military coup in Venezuela. It is unclear what exactly Bush administration officials said to the coup planners in meetings over the past few months. Conflicting anonymous quotes mean that there is some lying of the conventional sort going on. But a simple "Just don't do it: The United States believes in democracy" was obviously not the message or the coup would not have gone ahead.

One problem with reality of the traditional sort is that the pieces have to fit together. In alternative reality there is no such tedious restraint. We brag about our devotion to spreading democracy, especially in Latin America, but we don't care at all for this pesky left-winger these fools in Venezuela seem to have elected. Oh, him? "He resigned," said White House spokesman Ari Fleischer with no basis and no twinkle in his eye. It would be convenient if he had resigned and so: He resigned.

And then two days later the coup fizzled and the elected president was back. I mean, how embarrassing is that? Not very, if you just stick to your story. "The people have sent a clear message . . . that they want both democracy and reform," Fleischer revealed. He went on to lecture the restored president—whose overthrow we at least tacitly supported—about "governing in a fully democratic manner." And National Security Adviser Condoleezza Rice joined in to tell the Venezuelan president not to be so "high-handed." Who could blame the man for thinking, "Only one of us was elected president by majority vote—and it isn't you, George."

Alternative reality can be simple and sleek. That's one thing our Bush du jour likes about it. And simplicity is a genuine virtue in, for example, mobilizing a nation for war. It was quite effective for a while when Bush declared, after Sept. 11, that we were engaged in a Manichaean struggle with a single overarching enemy called terrorism. If anyone had told him it might be more complicated than that, Bush would have smelled nuance and sent the fellow on his way.

But then Reality Classic intrudes. Ariel Sharon says: Hey, I'm fighting an all-out war against terrorism, too. You got a problem with that? And the answer is, yes, we do. But it's hard to say what our problem is without admitting that we're not engaged in a Manichaean struggle with terrorism. American interests and values are more varied and complicated than that.

Another inconvenience of traditional reality is that there can only be one of them at a time. There is no such limit on alternative realities. You can stash them around the house for use as needed, like six-packs in the good old days. So Bush can have one reality where battling terrorism is paramount and another reality where Israel must negotiate and compromise with the sponsors of suicide bombers.

And if he can really juggle all these realities in his head without their bumping up against each other (in a condition known as "irony"), maybe it doesn't even count as dishonest.

## SOME KIND WORDS FOR CARDINAL LAW

Time, *April 29, 2002*

**R**obert Baden-Powell, the British military hero who founded the Boy Scouts, had an intense interest in teenage boys and their bodies. This interest expressed itself with a forthright innocence that to our post-Freudian sensibilities seems to have pretty clear sexual overtones. There is no evidence that Baden-Powell ever acted on this aspect of his enthusiasm for youth, and scouting enthusiasts both deny and resent the implication. But the specter of what was on Baden-Powell's mind might well make modern American parents reluctant to send their sons off for a wholesome weekend in the woods with scoutmaster Bob. And it would probably doom efforts by someone similarly inclined to start an organization like the Boy Scouts today. Would that be a good thing?

Millions of American adults dedicate their lives to serving young people as teachers, coaches or spiritual advisers. Roman Catholic priests, in particular, dedicate themselves to a degree most of us cannot even imagine. Why do they do it? Sheer goodness can explain a lot, but not everything. Even the most saintly among us is moved by a complex stew of motives, some admirable and some less so, some conscious and some unconscious. The sin of pride, for example, helps seduce many into goodness. Fear of real life is part of what tempts some into the cloister. And for a small fraction of those youth-serving millions, sexual longing plays a role.

Even many of those who put themselves among young people for reasons that are partly sexual probably do so with no conscious predatory intention. They may hope to gain some pleasure from mere propinquity, and also from helping young people in wholly admirable ways. Some are fooling themselves, with disastrous consequences. But many undoubtedly succeed in their lifetime project of service and self-denial, doing much good and no harm. They are surely more heroes than predators.

Societies other than the U.S., while not exactly laughing off the sexual abuse of children, manage to acknowledge this reality without the same episodic hysteria. In England, for example, the "randy vicar" is a stock comic character. And even in America we recognize and tolerate the inevitability of certain tendencies that have occasional antisocial consequences. The military services would have a harder time filling their recruiting quotas if they were successful in screening out everyone with an unhealthy enthusiasm for violence. Instead they work to control and channel those impulses, and they largely succeed.

Sure, there is a pretty obvious distinction between thinking illicit thoughts and acting on them. But it is not so easy to purge the actual predators without punishing those heroes of sublimation or losing their valuable contributions to society. Why? Because the line is hard to draw in practice. Is the football coach who spends a bit too long towel snapping in the locker room after the game a predator or a sublimator? Also, because fear of succumbing to temptation must surely plague even those who remain steadfast, and imposing ruination as the cost of succumbing will drive such people away—or condemn them to a lifetime of psychological torture. And because, finally, even this obvious distinction between thinking and acting is being swept away in the nation's current frenzy over predatory priests.

The Roman Catholic Church is far and away America's biggest social-service agency. As such it does a tremendous amount of good:

tending the sick, feeding the hungry, counseling the troubled and running a school system that is the envy of secular educators public and private. So what were Boston's Bernard Cardinal Law and other church officials thinking when they covered up sexual abuse of boys and girls by priests and allowed the offenders to start again in new parishes with fresh, unaware victims?

Maybe they were thinking that God works in mysterious ways and that all this good work may depend in part on people who are doing good for bad reasons. Maybe they were thinking that protecting the church's supply of such necessary people involves a trade-off, a balancing of considerations. There is no question that Law and his colleagues got the balance badly wrong. But at least we should try to understand why they may have thought there was one. Understand, and maybe even sympathize a bit.

## This Throne of Kings

### HOW DID AMERICA GET INTO THE ROYALTY BUSINESS?

Slate, *May 2, 2002*

Is anyone else bothered even a little bit by the idea that the war on terrorism has somehow put the United States in the business of installing a king in Afghanistan? Reinstalling, actually. His name is Zahir Shah, he's eighty-seven years old, and he's been on an extended leave of absence since 1973. But he apparently has used up all his vacation days at last. Or, more to the point, we think he might be useful as a unifying figure during Afghanistan's transition from a hellish cauldron of feuding warlords to a prim parliamentary democracy, which is penciled in for the second half of this year.

The idea, presumably, is not that the king would actually run things but that he and his family could concentrate on the activities we associate with modern royalty—smiling and waving, committing adultery, getting divorced—while the real work of nation-building swirls on around him. We might not want a king ourselves. But Afghanistan, you see, is what one calls a "traditional" culture in which they take innocent pleasure in pretending that some doddering eighty-seven-year-old is better than everybody else because his father was, too. Still, the United States of America was long associated with the idea of rejecting kings. And that "branding strategy," as the business world calls it, worked pretty well. When we find ourselves installing kings instead, the course of human events has taken a strange turn.

When we have tried this sort of thing before, it has sometimes ended in tears. Half a century ago in Iran, a CIA agent shut his eyes, opened the Tehran phone book at random, and chose a family named Pahlavi. (Warning: slight exaggeration.) Before you could say "your majesty," the second so-called shah of Iran had convinced himself that his monarchy dated back thousands of years. He threw himself a huge party full of Hollywood celebrities—today's real royalty—to celebrate that misconception and soon was skewered on his scepter. Iranians decided that, on balance, they would rather be ruled by crazed religious fanatics.

Let's hope that someone has learned from that experience and that this time, in Afghanistan, we have checked the guy out on the Internet to make sure he is the real McCoy. It would be disappointing to learn that he was signed up based merely on his own say-so that he is beloved of his people and the meaningless coincidence that his last name is Shah.

Of course one shouldn't be too snobbish. The ranks of modern royalty are crowded with arrivistes. "King" Fahd, "Crown Prince" Abdullah, "Prince" Bandar, and the thousands of lesser princes who fill the teeming palaces of Saudi Arabia are members of a royal family invented by Western diplomats in the twentieth century. And the "royal" family of Jordan was cobbled together from the leftover scraps.

What's the difference between a desert tribal chieftain who probably couldn't get into the United States on a tourist visa and a royal prince who gets the full state-visit treatment plus quality time pretending to be interested in the landscape around Crawford, Texas? ("Endless flat, parched vistas—how extraordinary, Mr. President! If only we had something like this in Saudi Arabia. . . .") The difference is—well, here's a hint: It's a three-letter word beginning with "o." A royal prince is just a tribal chieftain sitting on a lot of oil.

As Maureen Dowd noted in the *New York Times* the other day, Prince Abdullah's visit with President Bush was the meeting of two dynasts. George W. Bush may even understand the dynastic principle better than he understands the democratic one. "One of the really positive things out of this meeting," Bush said afterward, "was the fact that the crown prince and I established a strong personal bond. We spent a lot of time alone, discussing our respective visions, talking about our families. I was most interested in learning about how he thought about things. I am convinced that the stronger our personal bond is, the more likely it is relations between our countries will be strong."

Bush may have been emphasizing the importance of the personal bond he developed with the prince because he couldn't actually remember any of the specific "things" he allegedly found "most interesting." Or he may really believe that a five-hour friendship between two men who talked about their families and "things" is the most important element in the relationship of two nations with many shared and diverse interests. Probably it's a bit of both.

Judging from small episodes like this and large ones like the recent bungled coup in Venezuela, you begin to suspect that George W. Bush doesn't get it about democracy. He uses the word but doesn't feel it in his bones.

Doesn't our president understand that there are two different kinds of nations in the world? There are nations where the rulers are determined by heredity—where the person in charge is in charge for no better reason than that his or her father was in charge before him. Then there are nations where the rulers are determined by democracy—where the person in charge is in charge because he or she got the most votes in an election among the citizens. And in this great divide, the United States stands proudly on the side of . . . of . . .

Oh, never mind.

## THE HINDSIGHT SAGA

Slate, *May 20, 2002*

NOTE: *Did the Bush administration ignore the signs of a forthcoming terrorist attack? Or are the Democrats who say so being cheap and playing dirty? Yes.*

WASHINGTON—The Bush administration reacted angrily yesterday to renewed accusations that it may have ignored advance warning of the Sept. 11 terrorist attack. The White House reluctantly confirmed that the president received a letter from Osama Bin Laden just days before the attack. The letter, written on stationery labeled "The Caves at Tora Bora: A Luxury Terrorist Headquarters and Spa," is believed by the FBI to be genuine. It said:

> Dear President Bush:
> On September 11, or maybe September 12, I plan to hijack several air-planes and fly them into a building or two in lower Manhattan, and maybe a military facility of some sort in Northern Virginia. Consider yourself warned.
> Yours sincerely,
> Osama

White House spokesman Ari Fleischer rejected any suggestion that this letter should have alerted the administration about Bin Laden's plans for Sept. 11. "Look," he said, "this was a highly ambiguous signal, which was subject to a variety of interpretations. The letter says Sept. 11 or 12. How were we supposed to know that the attack would come on Sept. 11? It might have come on Sept. 12. It would have been the height of irresponsibility to alarm the American people about the possibility of an attack on Sept. 11 when it could just as easily have occurred Sept. 12."

He also noted that there are many buildings in lower Manhattan—"most of which to this very day have never been subject to a terrorist attack of any sort"—and that Northern Virginia contains a variety of military facilities. "It is easy in hindsight to observe that the Pentagon is in Northern Virginia, but there was no way to be certain that Bin Laden knew this. Many foreigners are under the impression the Pentagon is in the District of Columbia.

"Governing is about judgment," Fleischer continued. "It is about filtering the tremendous amount of information that pours in and deciding what is relevant and what is not. Do you know how many letters we get from terrorists every week? No, I'm not saying how many. The point is, you don't know. And you're not going to find out from me. This administration is not afraid to make the tough calls. It doesn't matter whether a call is right or wrong. What matters is that it's tough. Ignoring a clear warning from a known terrorist was one tough call, and this administration is proud to have made it."

National Security Adviser Condoleezza Rice noted in an interview that there are several Osamas listed in the Kabul telephone directory. "If Mr. Bin Laden wished us to take his message seriously, he should have had the common courtesy to sign with his last name. Although the president is a friendly and outgoing person, it would not serve America's interests for him to appear to be on a first-name basis with a terrorist by responding or reacting to Mr. Bin Laden's letter."

The White House later clarified that President Bush had, in fact, responded to Bin Laden's letter, but an official insisted that it was the stock response sent to all letters threatening to hijack airplanes and that there was no special policy applying to letters that also threatened to fly the planes into large buildings. "In fact," the official said, "it's the stock response we use for all letters from wealthy individuals." The response said:

Dear Osama:
Thank you for your generous contribution to the Republican National Committee. With the help of Republicans in Congress, I look forward to signing the legislation you request exactly as you have written it.
Best wishes,
George W. Bush

Vice President Dick Cheney, appearing on eighteen TV talk shows yesterday, called Bin Laden's letter "a cowardly attempt to sow confusion among the forces of civilization and freedom. If the guy had any guts, he would have told us exactly where and when he planned to attack, rather than hiding behind two alternative dates and a variety of possible locations."

Cheney said that by ending his letter with the words, "Consider yourself warned," Bin Laden made it impossible for the administration to take his warning seriously. "For the U.S. government to have indicated in any way that we considered ourselves warned would have been a victory for terrorism. Only by considering ourselves unwarned, and acting as such, could we protect the vital interests of the United States."

Meanwhile on Capitol Hill, hearings continued for the twenty-fifth day on charges that the administration failed to act on warnings from a psychic in Omaha, Neb., last August that "something terrible" was going to happen "sooner or later" on "either the East or the West Coast." Democrats in Congress are charging that this was a clear prediction of the events of Sept. 11.

"I hesitate to criticize or second-guess the president when we are at war with such a sinister foe," said Sen. Joseph Lieberman. "But I am deeply concerned that without a thorough inquiry into this matter, the American people may lose an opportunity for me to be deeply concerned."

## BLAME THE ACCOUNTANT

Slate, *May 30, 2002*

It would have been fun to be a fly on the wall that day in April when Halliburton Co. fired the firm of Arthur Andersen as its auditor. Although the year is not yet half over, this one will be hard to top as Best Capt. Renault Moment of 2002. Like the Claude Rains character in *Casablanca*, the company apparently was "shocked, shocked" to learn what Andersen had been up to.

Of course it's no big deal to fire Arthur Andersen, ever since the firm got cooties last fall in connection with the Enron scandal. By now nearly every company lucky enough to have employed Arthur Andersen has seized the opportunity to establish its own enormous integrity by inviting the beleaguered bookkeepers to drop by for a chat, gently removing their glasses and eyeshades, punching their owlish faces in, and then kneeing them in the double-entry bookkeeping for good measure.

One imagines the scene: an orgy of self-righteousness. "You despicable swine!" these companies shriek at the trembling, cowering number-crunchers. "How dare you sully the sacred title of auditor? We counted on you to stop us from cooking our own books. That's what auditors are paid to do. If you're going to look the other way and then shred documents to cover up our misbehavior, there's no telling the terrible things we might do. Shame on you, Arthur Andersen. Shame! Shame!"

It's not true that some companies attempted to hire auditors from Arthur Andersen just for the thrill of firing them with a sanctimonious flourish. (In fact, no one has even suggested such a thing until this moment.) And it's certainly not necessary to feel sorry for Arthur Andersen. Every company can benefit from a reputation for integrity, but an accounting firm is selling almost nothing except its reputation for integrity. It only takes one pork chop to put a kosher butcher out of business.

Still, Halliburton is a special case, because its CEO during most of those Accounting-a-Go-Go years that climaxed with the Enron scandal was Dick Cheney. Cheney now runs the country, they say, adopting the role of mild-mannered vice president in order to disguise his superpowers. And on Thursday Halliburton revealed that its accounting practices beginning in the Cheney era are under investigation by the Securities and Exchange Commission.

The *New York Times*, which first reported the Halliburton funny business, explained it pretty clearly: The company runs large construction projects, mostly for the government and the oil industry. Apparently, large construction projects work just like small ones, such as remodeling the bathroom. That is, the contractor states a price, runs over budget, then tries to get the customer to fork over the difference. Until 1998 Halliburton had the tact to wait until it got the extra money before putting it on the books. In that year, it began guessing how much of a disputed surcharge would ultimately get paid and crediting itself in advance. Why not? You only live once! This self-administered pick-me-up added $100 million in reported revenues to Halliburton's books.

So where was Arthur Andersen while its client Halliburton was sautéing the spreadsheets? Looking the other way, apparently. Later, when the Enron story broke, Halliburton undoubtedly thought, "Goodness. We'd better get rid of Arthur Andersen and find ourselves an accounting firm with integrity. We certainly don't wish to be associated with an auditor that will allow us to do the kind of thing we're doing." So they fired Arthur Andersen. Too late, too late. Due entirely to Andersen's failure to stop it, Halliburton is now under investigation for doing what it did.

And where was the future vice president while this was going on? The company insists, graciously, that a mere $100 million flyspeck on the company accounts (1999 income: $438 million) was beneath the

notice of a busy CEO like Dick Cheney. This is believable. Cheney's
income in 2000, his last year at Halliburton, was $36 million in sal-
ary, bonuses, benefits, deferred compensation, restricted stock sales,
exercised options, frequent-flier miles, a turkey at Christmas, and
other standard elements of the modern CEO compensation package.
It is a vital responsibility of anyone who is that valuable to remain
completely ignorant of anything improper going on around him. He
owes it to the company to be untainted.

It's true that Cheney was featured in a promotional video for
Arthur Andersen, in which he says, "I get good advice, if you will,
from their people based upon how we're doing business and how
we're operating—over and above just the sort of normal by-the-
books auditing arrangement." The *Wall Street Journal,* which
uncovered this video, had a good time with that patronizing dis-
missal of by-the-books accounting practices. But taken as a whole,
this remark from Cheney is a pretty convincing performance of a
man who doesn't know what the hell he is talking about.

It would be the sheerest demagoguery to suggest that a person
should take the blame for a company's shenanigans just because he
happened to be CEO at the time. Heck, no. That's what accountants
are for.


# KING GEORGE

THE ROLE OF STEPHANOPOULOS IN OUR CONSTITUTIONAL SYSTEM.

Slate, *June 20, 2002*


This is a jittery moment in our country. We await al-Qaida's next
move, while the War on Terrorism has melted into a game of shuffle-
the-boxes on the government organization chart. Every politician in
America has been on television warning Saddam Hussein that he's
got just a few months to use those weapons of mass destruction we're
darned sure he's got. The stock market and the economy are torturing
us with their indecision. And, look, is there global warming or what?

But America is blessed. We have an institution designed to provide a soothing balm of continuity in turbulent times like these. It functions the way the British royal family is supposed to: as a human symbol of the nation. As a sump for adoration that might otherwise be misdirected at political leaders and go dangerously to their heads. As a front of national unity behind which politicians at all levels can bicker and carp.

This institution is, of course, the Television News Anchorhood, of which there are two sorts. Each has its own vital role in our constitutional system. First, there is the Evening News Anchor. This person's burden is to reassure us, by describing all developments in a similar tone for the same block of time every night, that all news is equally important—and therefore not very. Half an hour of Dan Rather's bug-eyed alarm or an hour of Jim Lehrer's wry twinkle: It hardly matters. Consistency is what counts.

Second, there is the Sunday Talk Show Anchor. These Sunday shows have evolved into crucial rituals of democracy in which elected and appointed officials expose themselves publicly to whatever form of humiliation the anchor and a couple of colleagues may devise. (Verbal humiliation only, so far—although CBS is said to be working on an interesting variant.) The Sunday Anchor must embody all the nation's conflicting feelings about those who exercise power over us. Contempt, deference, and bonhomie must all be on display simultaneously. NBC *Meet the Press* anchor Tim Russert's gift for saying, in effect, "With all due respect, Senator, you're a lying bastard. Bowling next Tuesday?"—and not any physical resemblance, which is slight at best—is why so many Americans compare his role in our national life to that of Britain's late queen mother.

But just when we need calm and continuity the most, all is chaos in Anchordom. The last of the classic authority-figure baritones in the tradition of Walter Cronkite, Bernard Shaw of CNN, is already gone. NBC's Tom Brokaw has given us two years to prepare for the shock of his retirement and ascension of Brian Williams, who is regarded as utterly different in ways that may not be apparent to the naked eye. Rather of CBS and Peter Jennings of ABC are also starting to get the "Are you still here?" media treatment.

Most traumatic of all for a nation on edge, the David Brinkley chair at ABC's *This Week* is being entrusted to George Stephanopoulos, the former Clinton administration Wunderkind. All of our fears about the future are currently being sublimated into one nervous question: Can a former partisan political operative rise above politics to perform this crucial monarchial function?

I wouldn't worry about it if I were you. Even the sainted Russert was a Democratic Party apparatchik in his salad days, yet his ideology these days seems to be precisely the vague, sentimental, nonpartisan high-mindedness appropriate to his station. How does this happen?

First, keep in mind that news anchors, like other constitutional monarchs, are primarily figureheads. TV news is an odd business in which one group of people—the on-air "talent"—gets all the appearance and deference and money and perks of being in charge, while another group—the producers—have most of the burden and power of being in charge. America's evening news anchors, unlike the British royals, are capable of intelligent thought, and often prove as much, but their core function of reading a TelePrompTer requires little of it. The Sunday-morning anchors, who ask questions and lead discussions, have more autonomy but less than they appear to have. Especially at first. Stephanopoulos' opportunity to turn *This Week* into Democratic Party propaganda is more limited than it seems.

Second, there is no reason to suppose that Stephanopoulos would sacrifice his commercial interests to his partisan interests. Like everyone else on earth, he wants to be a TV star. And now he has an opportunity to be one. Nothing in his past suggests that he would risk squandering this opportunity in order to advance the agenda of the Democratic Party, even if—unlike everyone else on earth—he knows what that agenda might be.

Third, it would not be so terrible if Stephanopoulos and *This Week* were overtly biased, or the other TV news anchorhoods as well. The TV news anchor I find myself watching most is Brit Hume of Fox News. He brims with bias, and it's a bias I don't share. But his freedom to be biased is also freedom to be intelligent. You get the news as filtered through an interesting mind.

Fox News is a brilliant experiment in overt, honest bias—the broadcast equivalent of its owner Rupert Murdoch's flagship right-wing tabloid newspaper, the *New York Post*. It has stripped a whole layer of artifice from TV news. What almost ruins everything is the network's comically dishonest insistence that it is not what it obviously is. I would love to know what Hume is thinking when he repeats with apparent sincerity the Fox News mantra, "Fair and balanced as always." Fox is usually fair but rarely balanced. In fact it is a good example of how you can be the one without the other.

It's a compliment to Fox, though, that a viewer wonders what its anchor is thinking, rather than whether he is thinking. There is a lesson here for George Stephanopoulos. Or at least for his producers.

## Disabilities and Inabilities

### MUST WE PAY TO HEAR BAD PIANISTS?

Slate, *June 27, 2002*

In the term now ending, the Supreme Court issued three decisions limiting the reach of the Americans with Disabilities Act. My favorite is *Toyota v. Williams*, holding that carpal tunnel syndrome did not qualify as a disability for a woman who worked on an automobile assembly line. The lower court had made the mistake of concluding that the woman was disabled because her condition prevented her from doing her job. That seems sensible, but it's a trap, because if she really can't do her job, the law says it doesn't apply to her.

Trying to interpret a law that expects people to be abled and disabled simultaneously, the court plunges into a festival of Talmudic distinctions. Is "working" a "major life activity"? Do we mean working in a "specific job" or working in a "broad range of jobs"? What about "performing manual tasks"? Is that a "major life activity"? Can it be "specific," or does it need to be a "broad range" like "working"? (The justices' uncertainty about whether working is a major life activity makes you think it must be very pleasant to be a Supreme Court justice.)

Making it illegal to discriminate against people with disabilities is a noble idea, but a peculiar one. After all, forbidding discrimination against people who possess a particular characteristic amounts to forbidding discrimination in favor of people who don't possess that characteristic. If you outlaw discrimination against blacks, you are also outlawing discrimination in favor of whites.

In the case of racial discrimination, that is no problem. But discrimination based on disability is different. The opposite of disability is ability. For millions of years until the ADA was enacted in 1990, discriminating in favor of ability was thought to be a good thing. It still is, most of the time. Employers prefer competent employees to incompetent ones. Sports fans unabashedly show more enthusiasm for more talented athletes. Music enthusiasts shamelessly buy concert tickets for superior performers. Innate ability isn't the only ingredient, but without it even practice, practice, practice won't get you to Carnegie Hall.

Indeed the free-market economic system is a machine for rewarding ability. The more ability, the bigger the reward (at least that is how it is supposed to work). And this is generally regarded as a good thing, not a bad one. It is crucial, in fact, to the prosperity that allows us to indulge in exercises of social justice like laws protecting the disabled.

The ADA was enacted and signed by a Republican president, the elder George Bush, without much controversy compared with the epic struggle over the original Civil Rights Act. But in a couple of ways, it is an even more radical exercise in social engineering. First, it focuses directly on those aspects of the human condition in which we are, in fact, objectively unequal. Second, its implied vision of a society that overcomes differences in ability is far more ambitious than the equivalent visions, implied in earlier civil rights laws, of a society that overcomes differences in race or sex.

The ADA, in fact, neatly exposes the weakness and confusion of "equal opportunity"—the concept invoked in support of all our anti-discrimination laws. The closer we come to eliminating discrimination based on race or sex, etc., the more important innate ability will become in assigning people their stations in life. And if we ever were to eliminate all differences in outcome based on differences in ability, that would not be equal opportunity. That would look more like equality, period. Or, to use the pejorative term, "equality of result."

The ADA itself, of course, does not even aspire to total leveling. Differences in ability only matter to the law if the ability of one person in the comparison falls below a threshold into territory labeled "disability." And the law does exempt disabilities from its protections when they are "job-related." But the line between ability and disability is inherently arbitrary, and the effort to protect disabled people from job discrimination without forcing employers to hire less-qualified candidates is inherently self-contradictory.

Yes, there are cases where an employer won't hire a one-legged man as a typist—where the disability is totally unrelated to the ability required or can be accommodated with almost no burden. That kind of discrimination makes no sense. But discrimination based on ability usually does make sense. That doesn't make it right. Racial discrimination can also make sense sometimes—it might be more efficient for an employer to hire whites only than to consider each candidate individually—and we have no trouble saying too bad: That is unfair, and you cannot do it. But racial prejudice at its heart is irrational, whereas prejudice in favor of ability is not.

A law can do much practical good even if it is logically incoherent, and the ADA certainly falls in that category. And beyond its practical impact, the ADA is noble for its built-in philosophy that rewarding differences in ability is unfair. It's a vision that is unachievable and one that most Americans probably don't even think they share. But the instinctual popularity of the ADA suggests that Americans are more radical believers in equality than they realize.

## It's Good Enough

FREEDOM, JUSTICE, AND MARTHA STEWART.

Slate, *July 3, 2002*

Like every political journalist, I have always wanted to write a cookbook. Mine would be called *The Good Enough Cookbook* (subtitle, "When 'good enough' is good enough") and it would not contain any actual recipes. Instead, it would have detailed instructions for how to skip steps and cut corners and generally simplify the recipes you find elsewhere.

When, for example, can you substitute peanut butter (or those phony liquid eggs in a milk carton, or beer) for ingredients that may require a special trip to the Trendi-Mart? Is there any culinary disaster that cannot be salvaged by liberal dousing with balsamic vinegar? Do you really have to steam the vegetables separately?

The answer to the last question is yes, you do have to, if you want the dish to turn out as the recipe's author intended. But this is dinner, not constitutional interpretation, and the author's original intent doesn't particularly matter. The dish undoubtedly will turn out better if you meld the anchovies, the chocolate, and three teaspoons of vodka, using a mortar and pestle, before gradually stirring in the veal stock, the soy milk, and the rest of that liter of vodka. But if you just dump all the ingredients—minus a few morale-boosting slugs of the vodka—into the blender and then floor it, the result will be OK. More precisely, it will be good enough. Julia Child will not be coming tonight. More important, neither will Martha Stewart.

The guiding philosophy of *The Good Enough Cookbook* is to seek out ways one can, say, put in half the effort and get three-quarters of the desired result. The guiding philosophy of Martha is to seek out ways one can gain a 10 percent better result by doubling the effort put in. It is important to understand that the Martha method is not a complete waste of time. It does make things better. It probably even makes life better. But the Good Enough method is good enough.

So, the media have missed the real significance of the fall of Martha Stewart. As the British writer Geoffrey Wheatcroft once described the joy of American liberals when Nixon resigned, this Martha moment is "a landmark in the history of schadenfreude." But the pleasure Americans feel when they imagine Martha Stewart being led away in (tasteful, homemade, mother-of-pearl) handcuffs is not just about gloating. It is about liberation.

What, after all, do Martha Stewart and the Big Five ( . . . four . . . three . . . ) accounting firms represent in common? No, not greed. Well, not only greed. Anyway, greed is a sentiment as nearly universal as schadenfreude. The correct answer is that they both represent standards. Martha's mission is to impose and enforce impossibly high standards in the details and accoutrements of everyday middle-class life. ("The Queen of Perfection," *Newsweek*'s cover labeled her.) Accountants, especially corporate auditors, are hired almost solely to assure the world that the client's financial disclosures meet not just the highest standards but—more important—the same standards as everyone else, so that comparisons will be valid.

It dawned on the accountants in recent years that being the designated driver during a carnival of financial drunkenness isn't cool, but they could become quite popular by lowering their precious standards just a hair. It remains unclear whether Martha Stewart has done anything actually wrong. But it is apparent that she does not bring to her financial affairs the punctiliousness she displays when wrapping the dog's biscuit in lace or sprinkling oatmeal with gold dust.

So, welcome to the era of lower standards. "It's a good thing" is yesterday. Tomorrow belongs to, "Oh, heck, it's good enough." This doesn't mean it is OK to cook the books. It means that if you do cook the books, it is OK to overcook or undercook them a bit. Either way, it's good enough. Some readers may recall the glorious moment when they realized you don't actually have to use hospital corners when making the bed. From now on, until the culture shifts again, every day will be like that.

What could be more relaxing—or a better gift of freedom, just in time for July Fourth? After all, which is a more oppressive force in the lives of average Americans: some restrictive reading of the First Amendment by the Rehnquist Supreme Court, or the elaborate mythology that has grown around the notion that certain patterns and colors of clothing supposedly "clash" (I believe that is the word) with others?

Breathe free, Americans. In the coming era of Good Enough, nothing clashes. When a man wears a tie, the back part may hang as much as six inches below the front. All gifts will be gratefully received without wrapping paper. Preheating the oven will be exposed for the con that it is.

Thank you, Martha. Thank you.

## WHO WANTS THIS WAR?

Slate, *July 10, 2002*

It was amazing to read the Pentagon's detailed plans for an invasion of Iraq in the *New York Times* last week. The general reaction of Americans to this news was even more amazing: Basically, there was no reaction. We seem to be distant observers of our own nation's preparation for war, watching with horror or approval or indifference a process we have nothing to do with and cannot affect. Which is just about the case.

Who really wants this war? Polls show that a modest and shrinking majority of Americans will choose military action to remove Saddam Hussein when someone holding a clipboard confronts them with a list of options. But does anything like a majority of the citizenry hold this view with the informed intensity that a decision for war deserves? I doubt it. And how many of that pro–"military action" majority imagine that it will be nearly blood-free on our side, based on the experience of the Gulf War, which turned out that way precisely because President Bush's father decided not to try to topple Saddam?

Abroad, nearly all of America's major allies are against it. The Arab states surely dream about being rid of Saddam Hussein. But they won't give public support or permission to use their land and airspace, which is not too much to ask if we're going to save them from a threat as great as Saddam is said to be. Even the Kurdish opposition within Iraq apparently thinks that being liberated by Superpower America, while nice, would be more trouble than it's worth. That's trouble to them, not to us!

Ask around at work, or among your family: Is anyone truly gung-ho? It seems as if true enthusiasm for all-out war against Iraq is limited to the Bush administration and a subset of the Washington policy establishment. The Democratic leadership in Congress feigns enthusiasm, which amounts to the same thing in terms of responsibility for the consequences. You are what you pretend to be. The Democrats feign out of fear of seeming weak-kneed. Bush's enthusiasm seems genuine and is therefore more mysterious. Crude Oedipal theories (triumphing where Dad failed) are tempting, but not as plausible as the simple possibility that he sincerely believes Saddam poses a danger big enough to justify risking massive bloodshed and his own political ruin. And maybe he's right.

Or Bush may be bluffing. At his press conference Tuesday, he blamed the leak of those war plans on "somebody down there at level five flexing some 'know-how' muscle." He may be right about that, too—depending on what on earth he means. Or he may be lying, and the leak may be part of an official strategy of threatening all-out war in the hope of avoiding it, by encouraging a coup or persuading Saddam to take early retirement or in some other way getting him gone without a massive invasion.

Trouble is, it is—or ought to be—very hard for a democracy to make a credible threat that it isn't prepared to carry out. You can't have a vigorous public debate over whether it's worth going to war that reaches the conclusion: Let's pretend we're willing to go to war if necessary and see what happens. But on the issue of war and peace, the United States is no longer a democracy.

The eerie non-debate we're having as vast preparations for battle are made before our eyes is a consequence of a long-running constitutional scandal: the withering away of the requirement of a congressional Declaration of War. Oh, the words are still there, of course, but presidents of both parties flagrantly ignore them—sometimes with fancy arguments that are remarkably unpersuasive, but mainly by now with shrugging indifference. The result is not just a power shift between the branches of government but a general smothering of debate about, or even interest in, the decision to go to war among citizens in general.

It's often said that modern warfare has no place for an eighteenth-century conceit like the declaration of war. (This is said, in fact, by people who usually insist quite strongly that the original intent of the Constitution's framers requires no concessions to modernity.) But despite the modern issues of terrorism and "weapons of mass destruction," there is an old-fashioned quality to our confrontation with Iraq. It is about an imperial power demanding acquiescence from a rogue state. That doesn't make the United States the bad guy. It does mean that events are proceeding in a deliberate, slow-motion way that leaves plenty of time for citizens to debate and decide—if that's the way we want to do it.

## GOVERNMENT BY OSMOSIS

HOW COLIN POWELL SPEAKS WITHOUT MOVING HIS LIPS.

Slate, *Sept. 5, 2002*

It must be hell to disagree with Colin Powell. Powell and Vice President Dick Cheney apparently disagree about Iraq. Cheney thinks that Saddam Hussein must be toppled and any further diddling is pointless. Powell thinks . . . well, something else. Cheney made his opinion known by articulating and defending it in a speech. Powell's view, if you read the papers literally, has spread by a mysterious process akin to osmosis. The secretary of state is "known to believe" or is pigeonholed by unnamed "associates" or (my favorite) has made his opinion known "quietly."

And yet somehow, without an audible peep, Powell has managed to dominate the public debate about whether to make war against Iraq. How does he do it? Maybe, like dogs, State Department reporters can hear frequencies beyond the range available to the normal human ear. Or maybe, just maybe, Powell has made his case using the same basic method as Cheney—that is, by opening his yap and letting words come out—only doing so with small audiences of reliably discreet journalists rather than at a convention of the Veterans of Foreign Wars.

"As the debate over Iraq has intensified in recent weeks," the *New York Times* deadpanned on Tuesday, after days of reporting Powell's opinion, "one voice has been conspicuously absent." The article went on to explore the alleged mystery of Powell's silence, undeterred by the fact that he obviously has not been silent or the strong likelihood that more than one person at the *Times* knows this from personal experience.

A fellow journalist told me the other day that he admires Powell for making his disagreement clear without being publicly disloyal to the president. This is indeed the conventional view among the media. But it is peculiar, if not flatly wrong, on both counts. Clear is exactly what Powell's objection is not. He's against an immediate, irrevocable commitment to off Saddam Hussein. But where he draws the line short of that, and why, are unknown—or at least unreported—and untested. If you don't publicly state your position, you don't have to defend it.

Second, if Powell's view is not that of the president, he is only avoiding "public" disloyalty in terms of the comic distinction—treasured by the media and meaningless to everyone else—between things said publicly and things said "privately" to people who are certain to make them front-page news. If Powell's views were clearly in conflict with those of President Bush, spreading them furtively would be doubly disloyal.

Bush's role in this debate is not to have a clear view of his own.

Until the past few days, his position seemed clear: This Means War. What exactly means war was not entirely clear, but the war part was. Now he has wisely retreated to lack of clarity on both the whether and the why. This allows him to function like a holy rock for which all the squabbling tribal elders can claim to be speaking. The rock is irrevocably committed to "regime change." The rock has never wavered in its call for the return of inspectors. Meanwhile the rock's channeler-in-chief, Ari Fleischer, insists that there is no disagreement even among the rock's advisers. Colin Powell disagrees with him about that.

"Disarray" is the approved label for the peculiar process by which this nation is deciding whether to go to war against Iraq. Enormous power has been vested in the editors of newspaper op-ed pages, who get to decide which former official of the previous Bush administration will get the next opportunity to remind the world that he is still alive. Bush du Jour lets his people squabble in public. All deplorably chaotic to the orderly minds of foreign policy land.

In theory, at least, it's like a high-minded Jeffersonian dream that the national debate about war and peace should be framed by a series of essays penned by former government officials who have withdrawn to their farms, ranches, consulting firms, and suchlike contemplative retreats. In practice, a bunch of turgid, self-regarding pronunciamentos, full of half-hidden agendas, possibly ghostwritten though hardly by Thomas Jefferson's ghost, are not exactly the Federalist Papers.

The general desirability of vigorous debate doesn't solve the puzzle of how a top official who is unhappy about some administration policy should balance the demands of loyalty and honesty. In theory, once again, this one's easy: The official should argue vigorously then rally 'round. In practice, it's trickier. Does arguing vigorously include arguing publicly? Does rallying 'round mean defending a policy you don't believe in? On most issues, there is room for a fudge factor in all of this. But if the issue is war, in which many thousands of people undoubtedly will die, the cause had better be transcendently important.

The Bush administration will decide in the next few weeks that the cause is worth the blood, or that it isn't. In either case, someone in the administration has been leaking that he strongly disagrees. At that point, shouldn't someone resign?

## WHAT TIME IS IT?

Slate, *Sept. 12, 2002*

There just isn't time for all the things it's time for.

"It's time to put sentiment aside," announced *New York Times* columnist Nicholas Kristof one day last month. And who can disagree? Kristof's particular sermon was not about 9/11 or about invading Iraq but about whales, and his view may not be widely shared. (Go ahead and kill a few, he feels.) But on the larger point Kristof speaks for all of us in the business of manufacturing opinions. On all subjects, it is time to put sentiment aside.

You may be thinking that it would have been nice to be alerted back when opinion-makers thought it was OK to wallow in sentiment, so that you could enjoy this opportunity before the time came to put sentiment aside. But there was no such opportunity. Sentiment belongs in a special category, along with partisan differences, of things that exist primarily to be put aside. When sentiment and partisan differences are put aside, there is room for good will and reason and common sense and maybe even a small refrigerator where cooler heads can prevail.

A check of articles in just four major newspapers during the three weeks or so since Kristof's declaration indicates that it is time for literally hundreds of different things, in the view of those who write for or are quoted in the news media. A few of these matters do seem time-sensitive. This may actually be an especially good moment to consider leaving a corporate board of directors or to discuss with a child what he or she is willing to eat for lunch at school. But most of the things it is said to be time for are more like democracy in Pakistan or reviving urban rivers: It is only time for them in the sense that it is never not time for them.

The dean of Stanford Law School, for example, says, "It is time" for America "to hold true to its principles." Was there a time, in her view, when America should not have held true to its principles? By contrast not everyone will agree with the letter-writer to the *Wall Street Journal* who says, "It is time to bring the hierarchy in Rome to its knees to beg forgiveness from the rest of the world for its crimes against humanity." But our view on this subject is unlikely to turn on what time it is.

It may be logically pointless to insist that it's time for something you never think it's not time for, but the "time for" conceit serves various rhetorical purposes. It suggests that you are open-minded and deliberative. You are not saying that your opinion is always and obviously correct. You are saying that you have considered the various options and only now have reached your conclusion, which itself is only tentative and applicable at this point in time.

"It is time to concede that politicians will never understand" the world's major conflicts, writes a *Times* culture critic, who evidently thinks he does understand them. This might seem arrogant, but "it is time" suggests that he decided only lately and reluctantly that his view of geopolitics is superior to that of the politicians. That word "concede" is an especially elegant touch, though one may wonder who forced him to concede the superiority of his own opinion.

"It is time" gives you the credibility of a convert. You are not one of those folks who have always believed unquestioningly that Jews and Christians should "bury old suspicions and fears." Until now, you did not think that Americans should "practice what we preach"—or at least you did not feel strongly about it. But now, "it is time." Your opinion on this subject is fresh and strong.

Third, it creates a sense of urgency. Not merely do you hold a particular opinion, but this is the very moment when your view of things ought to prevail. Yesterday would have been too soon, and tomorrow may be too late. A strong sense of urgency can even help to disguise a certain flabbiness in the opinion itself. According to a *Washington Post* op-ed piece, "now is the time to create a Commission on Privacy, Personal Liberty and Homeland Security." A commission to study the matter is just about the lamest thing you can call for on any subject. But at least "it is time" gives an illusion of vitality.

But where will we find the time for all the things it is time for? Fear not. In recent weeks' newspapers, the list of things it is not or no longer time for is almost as long. German Chancellor Gerhard Schröder says the time for "checkbook diplomacy" is over. Dear Abby says this is no time for feuding—though she also says it is time to face reality, which for most of us will eat up more time than we save by eschewing feuds. A *Los Angeles Times* economic correspondent says it is time for Americans to "drop their infatuation with unfettered markets," while half a dozen others add that it is not the time to raise taxes on business. As if, in their view, it ever could be that time.

With any luck, the time you spend doing the things it is time to start doing and the time you save by not doing things it is time to stop doing ought to be roughly equal. So, please continue to do everything the media tell you to do.

## OURS NOT TO REASON WHY

*Slate, Sept. 26, 2002*

In London Tuesday, Prime Minister Tony Blair declared with fanfare that Saddam Hussein's Iraq has chemical and biological weapons, is ready to use them against other nations, and soon will have nukes as well. In Washington, a reporter asked President Bush why Blair offered no new evidence to explain his newfound conviction on these matters.

THE PRESIDENT: He explained why.

Q: Pardon me, sir?

THE PRESIDENT: Explained why he didn't put new information—to protect sources.

That's a good joke on journalists—"protecting sources" is our religion—and not a bad point on the merits. Much of what our leaders know about Iraq's military capacities and intentions can't be revealed, and how they know it must be secret as well. So, how is a citizen of a democracy supposed to decide the most important question any nation must decide: Should we go to war?

In this case the issues are mainly factual. That is not always so. In Vietnam, though there were factual disputes, the big disagreements were about moral and strategic issues on which the government's policy had no home-team advantage. With Iraq, by contrast there would be almost no opposition to imposing what is being called, with comic delicacy, a "regime change" if Blair and Bush are right that

Western nations are in imminent peril. But this turns on facts and analysis that ordinary citizens must take on trust.

The official U.S. government message on how citizens should decide about going to war is, "Don't worry your pretty little heads about it." Last week the White House issued a sort of Official Souvenir Guide to the Bush administration's national security policy, and it is full of rhetoric about democracy. Yet that policy itself, including at least one likely war, has been imposed on the country entirely without benefit of democracy. George W.'s war on Iraq will be the reductio ad absurdum of America's long, slow abandonment of any pretense that the people have any say in the question of whether their government will send some of them far away to kill and die.

Add it up. You may not agree that the Bush family actually stole the presidency for George W., but you cannot deny that the other guy got more votes. Once installed as president, Bush asserted (as they all do) the right to start any war he wants. Members of Congress can pass a resolution of support if they would like—in fact, he dares them not to—but the lack of one is not going to stop him. You may not agree that this is flagrantly unconstitutional, but you cannot deny that this makes any discussion of the pros and cons outside of the White House largely pointless. Finally, it's already clear that Bush will copy his father's innovation of rigorously controlling what journalists covering the war can see and report. You may not agree that the obvious purpose of this is to protect official propaganda and lies from exposure, but you cannot deny that such will be the convenient effect.

Democracy will be especially missed if "pre-emption"—the hot concept in Bush's national security policy—takes off as his advisers hope. (The Bushies hail pre-emption as a brilliant innovation by The Man, except when they're downplaying it as nothing new to worry about.) If the United States is going to feel free to attack any countries that might attack us, without the inconvenience of waiting to see if they actually do, then putting that decision in one individual's power seems especially reckless. And most of the reasons people give to explain why the Constitution doesn't really mean what it says about Congress having the power to declare war involve things like responding to surprise attacks. These concerns seem especially out of place if America's future wars are going to be chosen off the a la carte menu and then stewed for months or years before they are actually served up.

But let's pretend we actually do have some role in deciding whether our nation goes to war. How should we go about it when our leaders don't come pre-ratified by democracy and when crucial information for an independent decision is unavailable to us? We aren't capable of answering the actual questions at hand: Is Saddam Hussein an imminent threat to our national and personal security, and is a war to remove him from power the only way to end that threat? So, we must do with a surrogate question: Based on information we do have and issues we are capable of judging, should we trust the leaders who are urging war upon us?

The answer to that last one is easy. The Bush administration campaign for war against Iraq has been an extravaganza of disin-genuousness. The arguments come and go. Allegations are taken up, held until discredited, and then replaced. All the entrances and exits are chronicled by leaks to the *Washington Post*. Two overarching concepts—"terrorism" and "weapons of mass destruction" (or "WMD" as the new national security document jauntily acronymizes)—are drained of whatever intellectual validity they may have had and put to work bridging huge gaps in evidence and logic.

The arguments have been so phony and so fleeting that it's hard to know what Bush's real motive is. The lack of any obvious ulte-rior motive, in fact, is the strongest argument for taking Bush at his word.

But it's not strong enough. A quick recap. Knocking off Saddam became a top priority shortly after 9/11. It was part of the "war on terror," though the logical or factual connection between the events of 9/11 and Saddam's depredations was never explained. The admin-istration pounced on suggestions that 9/11 hijacker Mohamed Atta had met with Iraqi agents in Prague—as if discovery of this one meeting retroactively justified the whole hoo-ha—then dropped the allegation (though not the rhetorical connection) when it turned out to be made up. Bush and aides continue to talk ominously about meetings and connections between Iraqis and al-Qaida, continue to supply no details, and continue their relative indifference to greater al-Qaida links with other countries.

According to the 2000 edition of the State Department's annual "Patterns of Global Terrorism" report, issued in April 2001, Iraq has ties to various terrorist groups and does terrible things to dissidents, but "the regime has not attempted an anti-Western terrorist attack since its failed plot to assassinate former President Bush in 1993 in Kuwait." To be sure, for George W., that is a special case. But is it special enough to single out Iraq and ignore other nations that have actually committed successful terrorist acts against the West in the past decade? According to the 2001 State Department terrorism report, issued this past spring, the most enthusiastic state sponsor of terrorism is Iran—an enemy of Iraq that we're now trying to patch things up with.

Iraq's use of poison gas in the Iran-Iraq War of the 1980s is one example always offered to prove Iraq's ability and willingness to use "weapons of mass destruction." The other is the gassing of a Kurdish town called Halabja in 1988. The fact that these episodes happened years ago does not diminish their horror, and there is certainly no reason to think that Saddam has become kinder or gentler over the years. But it does raise the question why now, years later, they are suddenly a casus belli.

"Weapons of mass destruction," like "terrorism," is supposed to convey the idea that certain ways of fighting a war are illegitimate no matter how righteous the cause you are fighting for. It's a problematic notion in any event. The weapons the United States used against Iraqi soldiers in the Gulf War were about as horrific as those Iraq used against Iran. What makes the pretense of moral outrage in 2002 especially dubious, though, is the American attitude while and right after these horrors occurred in 1982–1988.

There is controversy over whether the United States actually supplied ingredients for the gas, or merely supplied helicopters and other useful equipment, or did nothing more than smother the odd unfriendly U.N. resolution. But there is no question that we knew all about it and looked the other way. The administration of the time included some of the same people as the current administration, or their father. Any indignation on this subject that comes without a fairly abject apology is worthless.

But at the time, you see, Iran was our enemy, so we wanted to help Iraq. Now Iraq is the enemy, so we are nuzzling Iran a bit. All very Kissinger and geopolitical and neorealist (or is that a movie genre, not a foreign policy posture?), but hard to reconcile with high dudgeon about terror.

To be sure, the fatuous hypocrisy of the Bush case for war is no reason to let Saddam Hussein drop a nuclear bomb on your head.

Iraq may be an imminent menace to the United States even though George W. Bush says it is. You would think that if honest and persuasive arguments were available, the administration would offer them. But maybe not.

## The Secret Vice of Power Women

Slate, *Nov. 14, 2002*

NOTE: *In the marital relations system, the people are represented by two separate but equally important groups: the wives who watch* Law & Order *obsessively, and the husbands who don't. This is their story. Ka-chunk.*

**R**ecently I got married, fairly late in life for that sort of thing, and have made astonishing discoveries. Most of these revelations turn out to be common knowledge. But one, I believe, has not been widely aired.

People's Exhibit A (my wife), Your Honor, is a formidable, intelligent woman with an important and challenging job and a full private life. (Also undeniable loveliness and charm, which are not strictly relevant to the present case.) She doesn't squander her time. And yet she spends many hours a week watching reruns of *Law & Order*—often back-to-back (the shows, that is).

It would be misleading to call her a fan. *Law & Order,* the long-running crime drama, is not just one of her favorite TV shows, or even her very favorite. Other than reruns of *Law & Order,* she has almost no interest in television at all. Specifically, she has no interest in any of the (to me) barely distinguishable *Law & Order* spin-offs and rip-offs (such as *Law & Order: Special Victims Unit, Law & Order: Criminal Intent, Law & Order: Double-Entry Bookkeeping, CSI, CSI: Miami, Mayberry R.F.D.,* and so on.) She's not even interested in new episodes of *Law & Order* itself. She couldn't tell you what night it's on and has no view about what this country is coming to when a man like Fred Thompson can be plucked from the obscurity of the United States Senate and entrusted with the responsibility of running the prosecutor's office on *Law & Order*.

Nor does she care—or even, possibly, notice—whether it is Michael Moriarty or Sam Waterston who is being unvarnished in any episode she may be watching. Don't ask her whether the female assistant district attorney is the blonde or one of the brunettes. Don't attempt to amuse her by predicting what demographic category the judge will be from. ("They've had four black women in a row, so I'm thinking white man. No, I know, that's ridiculous, so I'll go with white woman—but in a wheelchair. Whaddya think, Honey? Honey?? Ouch, that hurt. OK, never mind.")

Exhibit A and I assumed that this was our little secret. Perhaps it had to do with our weather here in Seattle, which affects some people oddly. Or too much coffee. But then we had a visitor from the East Coast who announced that his wife was about to become the TV critic of a major newspaper. "And the amazing thing," he added, "is that she never watches TV except for reruns of *Law & Order*."

Good grief. I began making discreet inquiries. My closest chum in Washington is a political columnist and TV pundit. I thought I knew her pretty well. Turns out that for years, on all those evenings when I assumed she was at parties to which I wasn't invited, she was at home watching reruns of *Law & Order*. The dean of a major business school poured out a similar confession, as did a senior editor at a newsmagazine. The girlfriend of one of my *Slate* colleagues. Half the women at the University of Texas (according to another *Slate* colleague, who may be exaggerating). Another Washingtonian, this one a prep school dean, though her husband says she is "drifting back to C-SPAN." Always women. Always high-powered. Always *Law & Order*. Always reruns. What on earth is going on?

It is not a cult, because a cult is communal. *Sex and the City* has a cult following: Women, especially, watch it together and/or discuss it the next day at work. New episodes are considered, on balance, a good thing. The obsession with *Law & Order* is something different. Far from discussing it with one another, women seem to watch it alone and may be unaware that anyone else shares the habit.

Exhibit A may be an extreme case. In a rare glimpse into this secret world, Molly Haskell wrote an essay last April for a local section of the *New York Times* in which she frankly and courageously labeled herself a *Law & Order* addict. But she claimed to discuss the show freely with other addicts. She also described her addiction as an essentially New York phenomenon, which suggests that even Haskell does not appreciate the full extent of the situation.

This would all be merely curious except for one ominous recent development. *Law & Order* reruns used to be scattered across the cable schedule like wildflowers. (Or weeds.) To catch them all, you needed to be able to play the remote control like Paderewski. More important, you had to control the remote control. Under these circumstances, only the smarter and more high-powered women were able to indulge this temptation. Now, though, TNT cable has exclusive rights to *Law & Order* reruns and, near as I can tell, runs them more or less all the time. That means *Law & Order* addiction is now available to all women with access to even basic cable.

This presumably is just the kind of chic new social problem the Democrats are being advised to rebuild their party around, now that George W. Bush has solved all the old ones. The new Democratic leader in Congress, Nancy Pelosi, is just the kind of dynamic, smart, take-charge person who can . . .

Uh-oh. Do you suppose . . . ?

## CURSE YOU, ROBERT CARO!

Slate, *Nov. 21, 2002*

My motives were ignoble—mainly vanity and a desire for free books—so, it served me right when the books started rolling in and I realized with horror that I was actually expected to read them: 402 in all. Three FedEx men and our local UPS woman had been retired on full disability by the time all these packages were lugged up our front steps. If you lined up all these books end-to-end, you would just be putting off having to open one and get cracking. Who are you trying to kid?

Agreeing to be a judge of the National Book Awards, nonfiction division, was especially hypocritical because two things I have long claimed to oppose in principle are books and awards. Nonfiction books are especially regrettable. There is too much nonfiction going on in the world already without writers adding to it.

Many years ago, I conducted an experiment of placing a note in copies of several briskly selling books in a local Washington bookstore. The notes had my phone number and offered five dollars to anyone who saw them and called me up. No one called. Though hardly scientific, this tended to confirm my suspicion that people like buying books more than they like reading them. And of course, in the famous formulation (credited to Gloria Steinem, among others), writers don't like writing—they like having written. They like having written under the impression that this means they will be read. The whole book thing is thus based on mutual misunderstanding.

As for awards, they are the purest example of gratuitous or superfluous meritocracy. Life itself is constantly sorting people out, awarding prizes and glory to some and misfortune or ignominy to others. Much of this is inevitable or even necessary: Free-market capitalism, specifically, works well for almost all by rewarding some people more than others. But why look for additional, unnecessary opportunities to say that somebody is better than somebody else? Even if you could say for sure that one nonfiction book published this year is better than all 401 others, what is accomplished by doing so except to make 401 people feel a little worse and one person feel a lot better? Total national feelings remain about the same, but the distribution of good feeling has become less equal. What's the point?

In anointing the best books, as in choosing the best college applicants or the best rhubarb pie at the state fair, the inherent arbitrariness of the process mocks the implicit pretense (often denied but unavoidable) of objectivity about the result. On what sane basis do you judge, say, an indictment of air pollution as better or worse than a biography of Benjamin Franklin or a memoir of life in prewar Central Europe? What is the likelihood that another five people, faced with the same 402 books, would rank them in the same order? How on earth do you do that, anyway?

Well, I can only say how I did it. My fellow panelists were surely more scrupulous. Indeed, leeching on the greater fortitude of colleagues is a key strategy in these circumstances. Bold and fearless procrastination, for example, got the pile winnowed from 402 down to under 50 by others without my having to crack a single spine.

You have to swallow your irritation at the panelist who—like the girl back in high school who always did the extra credit problem in math class—not only has "almost finished" that 1,056-page second (and not final) volume of a Melville biography but has "reread" the first one.

"How do you do it?" the rest of us gasped. "On the StairMaster," she revealed. Like all our meetings until the last one, this was by telephone. When we finally met in person last Wednesday, she looked unbelievably fit.

But the alternative to swallowing your irritation is swallowing those 1,056 pages yourself. Please: No offense intended to the author. His book will probably be read by many people, years after everything I write has been forgotten. Even if people start reading it now, they may be finishing around then. It's just that, you know, I'm still working on *Moby-Dick* . . .

Next, you must put aside any fuddy-duddy notion of not judging a book by its cover, or at least by its title. Does this seem unfair? Well, imagine that you are sitting on the floor, surrounded by clouds of despair and mountains of Styrofoam packing popcorn. You tear open the next shipping envelope and out comes *A Certain Curve of Horn: The Hundred-Year Quest for the Giant Sable Antelope of Angola.* Once again: No offense intended to the author of what may be a brilliant book. But the title seems designed to repel invaders rather than welcome visitors. If, with superhuman energy, you work up enough curiosity about the Giant Sable Antelope of Angola to at least open the book, the phrase "hundred-year quest" will kill it right off. (Rule: Unless it actually is about the Hundred Years' War, never mention any period of time longer than two hours in the title of a book over 150 pages.) And if your interest survives that second wave of defense, it will not, in its weakened state, have a chance against "curve of horn"—a great who-cares phrase made even greater by the modifier "certain," which implies that the differences among curves of horns of animals in Angola that this book is concerned with are not even large or easily noticeable. Expecting us to overcome all these barriers and read the book anyway: That is what's unfair.

Ultimately, though, a book-award judge's fate—like that of the books being judged—depends on luck. Once every seven or eight years, Robert Caro wheels out another gargantuan volume in his legendary biography of Lyndon Johnson, now up to *Vol. 6: The Kin-*

*dergarten Era (Part 1).* When I realized 2002 was one of the fat years, I tried desperately to escape. But it was too late. "Ever heard of a Faustian bargain, fella?" said the man from the National Book Foundation with an evil grin. "Welcome to hell—1,152 pages! Mwahaha . . . hahahahahaha . . ."

So, anyway, we gave the award to Caro. But did I actually read every page? I'll never tell.


## COMPUTERS GO TOO FAR

HEY—THAT'S *MY* JOB YOU'RE AUTOMATING!

Slate, *Nov. 27, 2002*


Google, the popular Internet search engine, now offers a page called Google News, a summary of what's going on in the world produced entirely by computers. Well, I say "entirely," but Google's computers don't actually gather the news. What they do is scan thousands of other Web pages and, using a secret formula, decide what the top stories are.

Then they cleverly lift headlines and other material from different news sources, add links to these and other sites, and come up with what appears to be the Web site of an extremely cosmopolitan newspaper.

It's slightly a bluff. Who knows why the computers chose to feature a New Zealand news site the other day as a way of covering the Miss World imbroglio in Nigeria? But you have to suspect that the explanation lies in the crudeness of the computer's judgment, not its sophistication. Google concedes that its choices of stories and news sources are "occasionally unusual and contradictory" but insists with uncharacteristic pomposity, "It is exactly this variety that makes Google News a valuable source of information on the important issues of the day."

Which is humbug. People still do it better. But not by much. The day is clearly approaching when editors can be replaced by computers. This requires some urgent rethinking.

Throughout the revolution of technology and globalization that has been going on for two decades, responsible mainstream commentators, pundits, analysts, and miscellaneous gasbags (including this one) have taken the view that progress is a good thing. Some people are unfortunately caught in the gears of change, but society as a whole benefits. It's not very complicated if you know a bit of economics. You've got your "invisible hand" (that's free markets), you've got your "comparative advantage" (that's free trade), you've got your "perennial gale of creative destruction" (that's competition and new technology), you've got your "can't make an omelet without breaking eggs" (that's attributed to Stalin, but never mind). The losers in this process deserve sympathy and help, but special pleading must not be allowed to thwart or slow this process.

We must distinguish, however, between special pleading and legitimate alarm about deeply troubling developments. It is one thing to sacrifice textile workers and auto workers on the altar of progress. It is quite another to start throwing journalists into the flames. And the difference is? Well, it's very different. Completely different. Couldn't be more different, quite frankly, my good madam, because . . . because . . . well, it occurs to me that I'm a journalist. This puts the whole situation in a new perspective.

You see, journalists are responsible for reporting and analyzing the "important issues of the day," as the Googlies so eloquently put it. In the prestige ranking of important issues, a key factor is how much an issue actually touches anyone's daily life. The more abstract an issue is from real life, the more prestigious it is. A journalistic career that began covering tornadoes in Iowa and ended writing editorials about the expansion of membership in NATO would be considered a success. One that took the opposite path would not.

We all agree—do we not?—that globalization and technological change remain vitally important issues. In order to assure their continued vitality, therefore, it is essential to guarantee that journalists not be impacted in any way. Abstraction from reality is not just a tradition among journalists: It is an ethical imperative. If an issue actually affects a journalist directly, you see, it becomes a "conflict of interest," which must be avoided. So, you see why we cannot allow technological progress to start displacing journalists. The entire subject would become a conflict of interest.

And what about the computers' conflict of interest? Sure, they're playing it pretty straight now, as the Google folks note. But what happens when all the human editors have been eliminated? We know the answer from the movie *2001*: We will wake up one day to find that all the news is about the parochial concerns of computers ("White House Hard Drives Not Backed Up, Sources Say") while important human developments involving the War on Terrorism and/or Leonardo DiCaprio get ignored.

Until just days ago, it might have been impossible to do anything about this impending crisis due to impediments such as the First and Fifth Amendments. Fortunately, however, we now have the Department of Homeland Security, which must make it an early priority to impose regulations forbidding the use of a computer to perform any functions traditionally performed by human journalists.

Indeed, the regulation should be extended to protect all jobs for which Olympian detachment from reality is an essential requirement. This includes fellows of policy think tanks, heads of nonprofit organizations, and anyone who has been quoted once by the *New York Times* or been a guest on a cable-TV talk show more than twice in the previous quarter.

No doubt there are writers and policy analysts and consultants of all sorts who think today, "They're going after editors, but I can never be replaced by a machine." Ladies and gentlemen, that's what the editors thought.

## WHY INNOCENT PEOPLE CONFESS

Slate, *Dec. 12, 2002*

**D**NA evidence unavailable at the time has now proven conclusively that five teenage boys sent to prison twelve years ago for raping and almost killing a young woman jogger in New York's Central Park were not guilty of that crime (whatever else they may have been up to that evening). What's most shocking is that the boys' convictions were not the result of perjured testimony by racist cops, or manufactured evidence, or jurors addled by some prosecutor's demagogic brilliance. The convictions were based almost entirely on the boys' own confessions. Why would anyone confess to a crime he didn't commit?

DNA testing, which can identify a person indisputably (or indisputably rule that person out) based on a single strand of hair or tiny scrap of skin, has taught us that there are people in prison, including some on death row, who are not just undeserving of their punishment for some legal or political or psychological reason, but plain-and-simple, Perry-Mason not guilty. The Innocence Project at Cardozo Law School, led by Barry Scheck and Peter Neufeld, has achieved a steady stream of murder conviction reversals. As intended, this has given many people pause about an irreversible sanction like the death penalty.

The emphasis on capital crimes is misleading in a couple of ways, though. Crimes like murder and rape are amenable to reversal by DNA testing, but there is no reason to assume that wrongful convictions are more common in DNA-friendly crimes than in others. In fact, there is good reason to assume the opposite. Murder and rape convictions, especially those with a prospect of capital punishment, generally follow a full-dress trial with all its elaborate rights and protections for the defendant. A false confession under these circumstances is highly unusual and highly suggestive that something improper went on at the police station. Even a true confession, for that matter, is a good indication that someone had a lousy lawyer.

But for every one criminal conviction that comes after a trial, nineteen other cases are settled by plea bargain. And when, as part of a plea bargain, innocent people confess to a crime they did not commit, that isn't a breakdown of the system. It is the system working exactly as it is supposed to. If you're the suspect, sometimes this means agreeing with the prosecutor that you will confess to jaywalking when you're really guilty of armed robbery. Sometimes, though, it means confessing to armed robbery when you're not guilty of anything at all.

In 1978 Professor John Langbein, now of Yale Law School, wrote a dazzling and soon-famous article in the *Public Interest* called "Torture and Plea Bargaining." Langbein compared the modern American system of plea bargaining to the system of extracting confessions by torture in medieval Europe. In both cases, the controversial practice arose not because standards of justice were too low, but because they were too high. In medieval Europe, a conviction for murder required either two eyewitnesses or a confession by the perpetrator. This made it almost impossible to punish the crime of murder, which was an intolerable situation. So, torture developed as a way to extract the necessary confessions.

Plea bargaining evolved the same way, Langbein explained. As our official system of justice became larded with more and more protections for the accused, actually going through the process of catching, prosecuting, and convicting a criminal the official way became impossibly burdensome. So, the government offered the accused a deal: You get a lighter sentence if you save us the trouble of a trial. Or, to put it in a more sinister way: You get a heavier sentence if you insist on asserting your constitutional rights to a trial, to confront your accusers, to privacy from searches without probable cause, to avoid incriminating yourself, etc.

Essentially, 95 percent of American criminal defendants are tried under a system entirely different from the one we learn about in school and argue about in politics (liberals celebrating its noble protections, conservatives bemoaning its coddling of criminals). In this real American justice system, your constitutional rights are worth, at most, a few years off your sentence.

Plea bargaining might also be thought of as an insurance policy. Insurance is a way of trading the risk of a large bad outcome (your house burns down and you're out $100,000) for the certainty of a smaller bad outcome (a bill arrives and you're out $850). Plea bargaining is a way of trading the risk of twenty-years-to-life for the certainty of five-seven. But by creating this choice, and ratcheting up the odds to make it nearly irresistible, American justice virtually guarantees that innocent people are being punished.

The five mistaken Central Park jogger convictions weren't officially plea bargains, but unofficial offers of lighter sentences are among the more pleasant theories about how American justice got these teenagers to fabricate confessions. Then in prison, four of the five got stung by the parole system, which is like plea bargaining, Round 2. Their time behind bars was extended because they "declined to accept responsibility" for the rape they didn't commit, as reported in the *New York Times*. Constitutional protections like the right against self-incrimination don't apply to parole hearings, either. You don't have to confess, but extra years of prison are the price if you don't.

## How Reaganomics Became Rubinomics

Slate, *Dec. 19, 2002*

"**Y**ou and I as individuals can, by borrowing, live beyond our means, but for only a limited period of time. Why, then, should we think that collectively, as a nation, we are not bound by that same limitation?"
—*Ronald Reagan's first inaugural address, 1981*

"Glenn Hubbard, chairman of the White House's Council of Economic Advisers . . . derides the 'current fixation' with budget deficits, and labels as 'nonsense' and 'Rubinomics,' the view espoused by former Clinton Treasury Secretary Robert Rubin that higher deficits lead to lower growth."—Wall Street Journal, *Dec. 17*

How in the world did this happen? Once upon a time, federal government deficits were denounced by St. Ronald as a focus of evil barely less threatening than communism itself. Now that concern is mocked by a Republican White House as the nonsensical "fixation" of a previous Democratic administration. In recent weeks the term "Rubinomics" has spread through the press like a rash—promoted by people who apparently believe that the best way to discredit anything is to associate it with Bill Clinton. They are not deterred by the inconvenient fact that the economy did rather well under Clinton and Rubin—better than under either of the Bushes or Reagan himself. Even more astonishing is that the Republican propaganda machine is trying to stamp "Clinton" all over one of the cornerstones of Reaganism.

In fact the coming White House campaign for changes in the tax code is starting to look like a world-class weird combination of extreme frankness and extreme fantasy. For a quarter-century, Democrats have been saying that Republican tax cuts favor the rich, and Republicans have been indignantly denying it. Now, as Tim Noah has been reporting in *Slate*, prominent Republicans are saying: Heck yes, we're out to shift the tax burden from the very affluent to the middle class. White House CEA Chairman Hubbard is one of those who has declared openly that rich folks deserve a break and ordinary folks deserve to pay for it. In an administration where economic advisers are fired merely for wearing a bad tie while loyally mouthing the party line in perfect iambic pentameter, Hubbard is still in good odor. So this bolt of honesty is apparently intentional. It may be brilliant political jujitsu—conceding the opposition's most damning point leaves them with mouths agape and little to say—or it may be nuts. But at least it is honest.

There is an honest element in the new party line about deficits, too. At least the Republicans are no longer pretending that deficits, if they happen to occur, are detritus left behind by the previous administration like all those McDonald's wrappers behind the dresser in the Lincoln Bedroom. Instead, Republicans embrace the coming deficits as their own and pooh-pooh any desire for a balanced budget as some kind of liberal Democratic folly. This is breathtakingly dishonest on three levels.

First is the utter contradiction between the new "deficits don't matter" line and what the Republican Party has claimed to stand for over decades. There is nothing wrong with changing your mind. Indeed that can be one of the nobler forms of intellectual honesty. But if you decide that one of the core values in your political philosophy is misguided, you ought to say so before launching a campaign of ridicule against those who believe what you believed until the day before yesterday. Maybe you even ought to apologize.

Ronald Reagan entered the presidency promising to rid the nation of government borrowing and, of course, ended up tripling the national debt. But Reagan never let his crystalline beliefs be fogged by reality, including the reality of his own behavior.

Even if Republicans hadn't been demonizing deficits for decades, their deficits-don't-matter line would contradict other allegedly core Republican beliefs. That is the second level of dishonesty. The explanation of why deficits allegedly don't matter goes something like this. When the government spends more than it takes in and borrows the difference, this has two potential effects. The borrowing reduces the amount of capital available for private investment, raises interest rates, and makes us poorer. But the extra spending or lower taxes stimulate economic activity and make us richer. The question is: Which effect is bigger?

A battle of empirical studies is going on about whether deficits actually do raise interest rates. And maybe they don't, but only if the law of supply and demand and other basic tenets of free-market capitalism have been repealed, which is an odd position for Republicans to take. Meanwhile the short-term stimulus is a classic "Keynesian" strategy— a word Republicans usually can't even pronounce without a sneer.

Keynes argued that modern economies have a tendency for inadequate demand that can produce a self-feeding spiral into recession or worse and that government deficits can be used as weapons against this danger. Republicans have gone from mocking that idea to parodying it. There hasn't been a moment since 1980 when Republicans thought it was the wrong time for a fiscal stimulus in the form of a tax cut. They were right to eschew Keynesianism—one taste and they became addicts.

But if government borrowing never hurts the economy and if taxes always do, why torture ourselves with taxes at all? Why not borrow the whole cost of government? If you suspect that won't work, you're right—but if the anathematizers of "Rubinomics" have a theory of when deficits can become too big, they haven't shared it. Meanwhile we have the evidence in front of our own eyes that Clinton and Rubin delivered levels of job creation, investment, and economic growth that the current administration would be thrilled to duplicate. And "Rubinomics" did it without the cortisone shots of short-term stimulus that Bush is demanding.

Thus the third level of dishonesty in the newfound Republican fondness for deficits: It conflicts with obvious reality. But I suppose that's a minor consideration.

## LOTT'S ADVENTURES IN GAFFELAND

Time, *Dec. 23, 2002*

NOTE: *Trent Lott seems to run through these pieces like an unexpected leitmotif. I can't explain it—but enjoy!*

If a gaffe is when a politician tells the truth (as someone once said), Senate Republican leader Trent Lott's bizarre endorsement of white racism and segregation does not qualify. An authentic gaffe is more like Lawrence Lindsey's comment that a war against Iraq could cost

$200 billion, which got him fired as President Bush's top economic-policy adviser. Nobody at the White House disputed the figure—they just didn't want it brought up. This is called being off-message, and in Washington that's much worse than being, say, wrong. Lindsey's replacement, investment banker Stephen Friedman, was found to have economic beliefs not always in keeping with the Administration's message (easily summarized in two words: tax cuts). But the important thing is that he will stick to the message from now on, whatever it happens to be.

Lott's comments, by contrast, were certainly not the truth. But they may have revealed a truth. The suspicion is that they bubbled up from his id and escaped through his lips when his guard was down, thereby exposing an important and deeply distressing moral flaw in Lott himself. This process is too serious to label a gaffe. So let's call it a supergaffe. A supergaffe is when a politician says what he really thinks.

Then Washington turns into Gaffeland, and what happens next can be comic. Both kinds of gaffe—regular and supersize—set the stage for festivals of disingenuousness and outright dishonesty. In some ways, the most honest reaction to the brouhaha has been that of Lott himself. His position has been, "Oh, c'mon, I didn't mean it." And surely he didn't mean it, at least consciously. Even if he is a racist, he had no reason to want to say so. Lott must sincerely and understandably feel blindsided. Since when are the fawning remarks of some politician at another politician's birthday party taken seriously? That's cheating! An editorial in the *Washington Post* asks, If he didn't mean what he said, what did he mean? The answer is, he meant nothing at all. Lott, as a Senator whose intellectual integrity may fall only slightly below the median, does not place any great value on his own words. How unfair, he must be thinking, that others do.

And then there are Lott's critics. The politicians and pundits trampling one another in a scramble for the microphones in order to say how deeply offended they were at his comments, how saddened they are by the man's transgression, or how urgently they wish his removal from the Senate leadership—or, if possible, from the solar system—can be divided into two categories. Call them Democrats and Republicans. The Democrats, by and large, are sincerely offended by what Lott said. But they are delighted, not saddened, that he said it. And they are utterly insincere about wanting him to be gone. Like the Republicans during the impeachment of President Clinton, they want to roast their victim in public for as long as possible. Once he goes away, so does the issue.

The Republicans, by contrast, are completely sincere about wanting Lott to be gone, but they are generally insincere about the reason. They want him to be gone for the same reason the Democrats want him to stay: the sooner he's gone, the sooner this nightmarish issue goes away. No one can doubt that Republicans are saddened by the public revelation that Lott shares the views of Strom Thurmond. Yet there are good reasons to doubt that all of them are as offended as they let on, starting with the fact that Thurmond himself has been a Republican Senator in recent centuries.

In fact the timing of the outrage, both long term and short term, raises doubts about everyone's sincerity. Daily and then hourly come new disclosures of old incidents that seem to confirm the beliefs suggested in Lott's remarks. Each new item is a nail in his coffin. But these incidents were publicly known at the time they occurred and have been no secret since. Just as Lott did, the entire Reagan Administration openly supported Bob Jones University in its claim for charitable tax status despite its rule forbidding interracial dating. There is a rarely acknowledged random element in what becomes a big news story and what does not. But moral outrage ought to aspire, at least, to some kind of consistency. The tendency in Washington is the opposite: a new moral norm (don't smoke marijuana; pay your nanny's Social Security tax; don't get misty-eyed about segregation) sweeps into town like a hurricane, knocks a couple of people down, then sweeps out and is forgotten.

The way this story sat around for several days last week before the politicians turned their blood up to boil is also a bit suspicious. Even hair-trigger moralizers like Senators Joe Lieberman and John McCain were slow this time. The President's deliberations were exceptionally deliberate. On Days 5 and 6 after Lott's remarks, the White House shrugged the matter off. On Day 7, Bush declared that Lott's remarks were "offensive." It is hard to understand how anyone can take a week to take offense at a racist remark. A natural suspicion is that the President and the other politicians aren't really as offended as they pretend to be. It is equally possible that they did take offense from the beginning but suppressed it while waiting to see how the story played out. In Gaffeland, there is no penalty for changing your tune as long as you're singing the right one in the end.

# 2003

## Pious Pair

WHAT MAKES SENS. MCCAIN AND LIEBERMAN SO APPEALING
IS ALSO WHAT MAKES THEM SO ANNOYING.

Slate, *Jan. 23, 2003*

**B**ack when I was a co-host on CNN's *Crossfire*, Joe Lieberman and John McCain were known as "7:15 guys"—meaning that the producer could call either of them up at 7:15 P.M., and they'd be on time for a live show at 7:30. (At least, unlike another current senator, they asked what the topic was before dropping important affairs of state and rushing over.) McCain once even came back for a partial rebroadcast at 1 A.M. when, for reasons of verisimilitude, they needed the same senator wearing the same shirt.

To say that two members of the Senate are publicity hounds because they like to be on television is a bit redundant (find a shy senator) and a bit unfair (nobody had a gun to my head either). But even among the self-promoters of Washington, Lieberman and McCain stand out for their enthusiasm and their skill. An important part of that skill, of course, is making enthusiasm look like reluctance. Both are fond of the conceit that they are saddened or alarmed or deeply disturbed by whatever matter impelled them toward the microphones that particular day. The image in your mind, though, if you are an irritated fellow senator or even just a lay cynic, is of Joe or John perusing the newspaper over breakfast coffee as if it were a shopping catalog, looking for something to be saddened by today.

Many a colleague must read a headline like that in the *Times* the other day, "McCain and Lieberman Offer Bill to Require Cuts in [Greenhouse] Gases" and think, "Gasbag, heal thyself."

By any objective standards, Lieberman and McCain are among the very best of our national politicians. They are smarter, more interesting, and probably more honest than most of their colleagues. On the issues they choose to spotlight, they're usually right, often first (or at least ahead of the horde) and occasionally even courageous. It's not surprising that Lieberman is now a front-runner for the 2004 Democratic presidential nomination while Al Gore, who put Lieberman on the map, is gone. Nor is it surprising that dreamers of both parties imagine McCain at the heads of their tickets, rescuing the country from a second George W. Bush turn. Yet there is a mystery to solve about both these virtuous politicians: Why, despite their virtues, are they so annoying?

Obviously it is in part because of their virtues, not despite them. Or rather, it is because of the way they wear their virtues on their sleeves. They are, in a word, pious. If hypocrisy is the tribute vice pays to virtue, piousness is virtue paying tribute to itself.

Lieberman is literally pious—a devout Orthodox Jew—and that is admirable, especially in a politician with the highest ambitions. But he also has the hectoring, bromidic high-rhetorical style reminiscent of an especially pompous clergyman. ("These are not ordinary times for our country. Therefore those of us who seek our highest office or hold it cannot practice ordinary politics." When exactly were these ordinary times when ordinary politics, whatever that means, would have been OK by Joe Lieberman?) His jokes are labored and dutiful. All this melds unattractively with the hair-trigger indignation of a more recent but increasingly familiar social type: the ambulance-chasing state attorney general, always scanning the horizon in search of a reason for a press conference. Greenhouse gases today, violent video games tomorrow, some other alliterative outrage the next.

McCain, by contrast, is the naughty boy who gets too much pleasure out of his reputation for naughtiness. While Lieberman always plays it straight, McCain's performances come with a bit of a wink for those who are looking for one. He makes clear that he gets the joke, which is flattering when you first feel the warmth of his conspiratorial embrace but less so as you come to reflect that the joke may be on you.

Both men are hooked on cheap iconoclasm. How many times can a politician be the rare member of his party who takes the position of the other party on some issue or other before this stops being such a wonderful surprise? McCain and Lieberman have stumbled (perhaps) on a brilliant formula. By being dissidents toward the center, rather than toward the extreme, they get to luxuriate in two of the press's most popular (and, you would have thought, mutually exclusive) categories simultaneously: courageous outsider and moderate voice of reason.

But moderation, far from courageous, can be too easy. Lieberman opposes President Bush's tax plan but "said he was intrigued" (the *Washington Post*) by the idea of tax-free dividends, which is the plan's centerpiece, even though it "doesn't do anything" to help get the economy "out of the rut." Under the nutty conventions of the media, this kind of talk gets you points for statesmanship and sophistication, rather than a penalty for having it every way and a general lack of any meaning whatsoever. McCain, during the Clinton years, used similar techniques to develop a reputation for statesmanship and foreign-policy expertise. His views on the use of American power are easier to admire than to parse.

On the other hand, despite their annoying piousness, either McCain or Lieberman would make a better president than the incumbent or the other obvious alternatives. Now, that's really annoying.

## MORALLY UNSERIOUS

Slate, *Jan. 29, 2003*

The second half of President Bush's State of the Union speech Tuesday night, about Iraq, was a model of moral seriousness, as it should be from a leader taking his nation into war. Bush was brutally eloquent about the cause and—special points for this—about the inevitable cost. It may seem petty to pick apart the text. But logical consistency and intellectual honesty are also tests of moral seriousness. It is not enough for the words to be eloquent or even deeply sincere. If they are just crafted for the moment and haven't been thought through, the pretense of moral seriousness becomes an insult.

In his most vivid passage, Bush listed practices of Saddam Hussein such as destroying whole villages with chemical weapons and torturing children in front of their parents. "If this is not evil, then evil has no meaning," he said, telling "the brave and oppressed people of Iraq" that "the day he and his regime are removed from power will be the day of your liberation."

This is a fine, noble reason to wage war against Iraq. It would have been a fine reason two decades ago, which is when Saddam destroyed those villages and the United States looked the other way because our bone of contention back then was with Iran. It would be a fine reason to topple other governments around the world that torture their own citizens and do other despicable things. Is the Bush administration prepared to enforce the no-torturing-children rule by force everywhere? And what happens if Saddam decides to meet all our demands regarding weapons and inspections? Is he then free to torture children and pour acid on innocent citizens without fear of the United States?

If Saddam's human-rights practices morally require the United States to act, why are we waiting for Hans Blix? Or if the danger that Saddam will develop and use weapons of mass destruction against the United States justifies removing him in our own long-term self-defense, what does torturing children have to do with it? Bush was careful not to say explicitly that Iraq's internal human-rights situation alone justifies going to war—though he was just as careful to imply that it does. But Bush has said clearly and often that Saddam's external threat does justify a war all by itself. So, human-rights abuses are neither necessary nor sufficient as a reason for war, in Bush's view, to the extent it can be parsed. Logically, they don't matter. That makes the talk about the torture of children merely decorative, not serious.

And tell us again why we're about to invade Iraq but we're "working with the countries of the region" to pinion North Korea, which is further along the nuclear trail and can't even be bothered to lie about it. Bush's "axis of evil" coinage last year and recent flagrant North Korean nose-thumbing made it almost impossible for Bush to avoid addressing this logical conundrum. His solution was artful but mysterious: "Our nation and the world must learn the lessons of the Korean Peninsula, and not allow an even greater threat to rise up in Iraq." He seems to be saying here that the United States should have invaded and conquered North Korea years ago. But as Bush sets it out, the "lesson" of Korea seems to be that if you don't go to war soon enough, you might have a problem years later that can be solved through regional discussions. That doesn't sound so terrible, frankly. Regional discussions can be grim, no doubt, but they're more fun than a war. So, what exactly is this lesson the Korean experience is supposed to offer?

There are actually plenty of differences between the situation on the Korean Peninsula and the one in the Middle East, and good reasons why you might decide to bring Iraq to a crisis and steer North Korea away from one. But all these reasons cut against the Manichean notion of an absolute war against an absolute evil called terrorism. Bush is getting terrific credit for the purity and determination of his views on this subject. But either his own views are dangerously simplistic or he is purposely, though eloquently, misleading the citizenry.

Proclaiming the case for war as the second half of a speech that devoted its first thirty minutes to tax cuts and tort reform also makes the call to arms seem morally unserious. Why are we talking about cars that run on hydrogen at all if the survival of civilization is at stake over the next few months? Bush declared that the best thing to do with government money is to give it back to the taxpayers, and then put on his "compassionate conservative" hat and proposed billions in government spending on the environment and on AIDS in Africa and on a program to train mentors for children of prisoners and on and on. The dollars don't exist to either give back or spend, of course, let alone both, so we'll be borrowing them if Bush has his way, a point he didn't dwell upon.

This orgiastic display of democracy's great weakness—a refusal to acknowledge that more of something means less of something else—undermined the moral seriousness of the call to arms and sacrifice that followed. Sneering at the folly of tax cuts spread over several years instead of right away, Bush failed to note that those gradual tax cuts were part of his own previous tax bill. Bragging that he would hold the increase in domestic discretionary spending to 4 percent a year, Bush probably didn't stop to wonder what that figure was under his tax-and-spend Democrat predecessor. Short answer: lower. These are venial sins in everyday politics, but Bush was striving for something higher. He had the right words for it. But words alone aren't enough.

## DESERT SHIELDS

Slate, *Feb. 27, 2003*

**S**addam Hussein, it seems, is not just a dictator and mass murderer. He is a bounder as well. While we amass hundreds of thousands of troops and billions of dollars of military equipment near his borders, with the frank intention of removing him from power and probably from life, he is welcoming a few dozen scraggly Western war protesters to act as "human shields" by planting themselves next to potential bombing targets such as power plants. It's just not cricket, complains Secretary of Defense Donald Rumsfeld. Using civilians as human shields "is not a military strategy." It is "a violation of the laws of armed conflict."

Rumsfeld's indignation is fey. Since the premise and justification for our imminent invasion of Iraq is that Saddam is evil and ruthless, which is certainly true, it would be remarkable if he played the game of war according to Hoyle. Why should he? It's not going to improve his reputation and will do nothing for his life expectancy either. Indeed one of the big surprises of the build-up to Gulf War I was Saddam's sudden decision to release the Western civilians he had initially forced to live near military targets. That certainly made America's job easier. And as a practical matter, it may have cost more civilian lives than it saved, by giving us more freedom to bomb.

Like "terrorism" and like "weapons of mass destruction," the anathema on the use of human shields is an attempt to define certain methods of war as inherently illegitimate, whether the cause for which they are used is legitimate or not. It's a noble effort, but difficult to sustain and may require more intellectual consistency than the current American administration, at least, is capable of. There have been well-documented reports during the past year, for example, that the Israeli army has used Palestinian civilians as human shields. The U.S. reaction has been muted and generalized mumblings of disapproval and calls for all parties to resolve their differences by negotiation in good faith. No high horse to be seen.

Then, too, it is a bit problematic to be invoking international law and insisting on your right to ignore it at the same time, in the same cause, and with the same righteous indignation. International law says, "Thou shalt not use human shields." It also says, "Thou shalt not use military force without the approval of the Security Council—even if thou art the United States of America and some idiot long ago gave veto power to the French." The test of a country's commitment to international law—and the measure of its credibility when it accuses other countries of flouting international law—is whether that country obeys laws even when it has good reasons to prefer not to.

Just like specific instances such as the rule against using human shields, the general regime of international law depends on a willingness to sacrifice short-term goals that may even be admirable for the long-term goal of establishing some civilized norms of global behavior. It sounds naive, and maybe it is. But you're either in the game or you're not. You can't pick and choose which rules to take seriously.

Supporters of the coming war find it maddening that so many people say, "I'm for it if we have U.N. approval, but not if we act unilaterally." This is an awfully convenient resting point for bet-hedging politicians. It also seems to be the most popular position in opinion polls. (And it was the conclusion of a thunderously ambivalent full-page editorial in last Sunday's *New York Times*.) For heaven's sake, this is war we're talking about. And even if we do get international approval, this is overwhelmingly an American show: our initiative, our insistence, our leadership, mostly our money and our blood. Surely, these irritated hawks say, making the right decision is more important than how that decision is made. Putting procedure aside, are you for this war or against it?

But "only if it's multilateral" is not the copout it may seem. Not just because of concern about an anti-American backlash. And not just because obeying international law has an independent value in its own right. In the specific circumstances of this particular war, multilateral procedures can alleviate our substantive doubts.

Like generals, anti-war protesters are always fighting the last war. Or in this case, depending on how you count, the war-before-last. The methods, the style, the arguments, the very language of objecting to war are still stuck in Vietnam. That's why the protests of the past couple of weeks have seemed so lame and retro. The Vietnam debate was primarily a moral one. Although the cost of victory became an important factor as the years went on, it was not the main factor turning people against that war. Americans ultimately decided it was a victory we shouldn't even want. In the case of Iraq, by contrast, few people think the goal of overturning Saddam Hussein is immoral. If we knew for sure it would be as easy and cheap as the administration hopes, few folks would object.

It is often thought that moral questions are inherently fuzzy and uncertain while factual questions are concrete and sharp-edged. But there is always at least the possibility that your strongly held moral view is the right one even when most other folks disagree. Factual predictions about the future, by contrast, will ultimately turn out right or wrong, but meanwhile they are fogged by a more fundamental unknowability. The case for democracy among nations, like the case for democracy within nations, depends in part on this particular human failing. Even if Saddam Hussein were well-meaning, he still wouldn't be all-knowing. The United States actually is well-meaning, but we're not all-knowing either.

## J'ACCUSE, SORT OF

YOU NEVER KNOW WHERE YOU'RE GOING TO FIND ANTI-SEMITIC PROPAGANDA.

Slate, *March 12, 2003*

**R**ep. James P. Moran of Virginia, already a locally famous foot-in-mouther, went national last week by declaring at an anti-war rally that "if it was not for the strong support of the Jewish community," the war against Iraq would not be happening. He said that Jewish "leaders" are "influential enough" to reverse the policy "and I think they should."

The thunderous rush of politicians of all stripes to denounce Moran's remarks as complete nonsense might suggest to the suspicious mind that they are not complete nonsense. Moran himself almost immediately denounced his own words as "insensitive." He said he was using the term "Jewish community" as a shorthand for all "organizations in this country," which would certainly be a first if it were at all plausible.

As others have noted, Moran's words are less alarming for their own direct meaning than for their historic association with some of the classic themes of anti-Semitism: the image of Jews as a monolithic group suffering from "dual loyalty" and wielding nefarious influence behind the scenes. When someone touches even lightly on these themes in public, it's only natural to wonder whether his or her actual views are a lot darker.

Nevertheless, Moran is not the only one publicly exaggerating the power and influence of the Zionist lobby these days. It is my sad duty to report that this form of anti-Semitism seems to have infected one of the most prominent and respected—one might even say influential—organizations in Washington. This organization claims that "America's pro-Israel lobby"—and we all know what "pro-Israel" is a euphemism for—has tentacles at every level of government and society. On its Web site, this organization paints a lurid picture of Zionists spreading their party line and even indoctrinating children. And yes, this organization claims that the influence of the Zionist lobby is essential to explaining the pro-Israel tilt of U.S. policy in the Middle East. It asserts that the top item on the Zionist "agenda" is curbing the power of Saddam Hussein. The Web site also contains a shocking collection of Moran-type remarks from leading American politicians.

Did you know, for example, that former President Clinton once described the Zionist lobby as "stunningly effective" and "better than anyone else lobbying this town"? Former House Speaker Newt Gingrich has gone even further (as is his wont), labeling the Zionists "the most effective general interest group . . . across the entire planet." (Gingrich added ominously that if the Zionist lobby "did not exist, we would have to invent" it.) House Minority Leader Dick Gephardt is quoted saying that if it weren't for the Zionist lobby "fighting on a daily basis," the close relationship between America and Israel "would not be." Sen. John McCain has said that this lobby "has long played an instrumental and absolutely vital role" in protecting the interests of Israel with the U.S. government. There is a string of quotes from leading Israeli politicians making the same point.

According to this Web site, the Zionist lobby is, like most political conspiracies, a set of concentric circles within circles. The two innermost circles are known as the "President's Cabinet" and the "Chairman's Council." Members allegedly "take part in special events with members of Congress in elegant Washington locations," "participate in private conference calls," and attend an annual "national summit." In the past members of these groups have met "in a private setting" with President Clinton, with Vice President Gore, and with the president of Turkey, among others. If this Web site is to be believed, these Zionist-lobby insiders have even enjoyed "a luncheon with renowned author and commentator George Will."

And who is behind this Web site? Who is spreading the anti-Semitic canard that Jews and Zionists influence American policy in the Middle East, including Iraq? It is a group calling itself the America-Israel Public Affairs Committee, or AIPAC, and claiming to be "pro-Israel." They all claim that, of course. But in this case, AIPAC actually is considered to be the institutional expression of the amorphous Zionist lobby. All the foregoing quotes and assertions about the huge Zionist influence with the U.S. government and the lengths to which Zionists go to protect and expand it actually refer to AIPAC itself.

This doesn't make it all true, of course. AIPAC, like any organization, has an institutional interest in exaggerating its own importance. This is especially true of any organization that must raise money to support itself. The "President's Club" and "Chairman's Council" are both fund-raising gimmicks, intended to give donors the feeling that they are in the thick of government policy-making. It's more about being able to say, "As I was saying to Colin Powell" than about trying to say anything in particular to Colin Powell. Another element in AIPAC's braggadocio is rivalry with other Jewish organizations. The American Jewish Committee also has a page of quotes on its Web site about how influential it is. ("We know that yours is the most important and powerful Jewish organization in the United States," says President Jacques Chirac. Maybe it sounds more like a compliment in French.) This evident rivalry undermines any notion of a unified Jewish conspiracy.

Just as African-Americans can use the "n" word when joshing among themselves and it sounds a lot different than when used by a white person, talk about the political influence of organized Jewry sounds different when it comes from Jewish organizations themselves. Nevertheless, you shouldn't brag about how influential you are if you want to get hysterically indignant when someone suggests that government policy is affected by your influence.

## UNAUTHORIZED ENTRY

THE BUSH DOCTRINE: WAR WITHOUT ANYONE'S PERMISSION.

Slate, *March 20, 2003*

Until this week, the president's personal authority to use America's military might was subject to two opposite historical trends. On the one hand, there is the biggest scandal in constitutional law: the gradual disappearance of the congressional Declaration of War. Has there ever been a war more suited to a formal declaration—started more deliberately, more publicly, with less urgency, and at more leisure—than the U.S. war on Iraq? Right or wrong, Gulf War II resembles the imperial forays of earlier centuries more than the nuclear standoffs and furtive terrorist hunts of the twentieth and twenty-first. Yet Bush, like all recent presidents, claims for his person the sovereign right to launch such a war. Like his predecessors, he condescends only to accept blank-check resolutions from legislators cowed by fear of appearing disloyal to troops already dispatched.

On the other hand, since the end of World War II, the United States has at least formally agreed to international constraints on the right of any nation, including itself, to start a war. These constraints were often evaded, but rarely just ignored. And evasion has its limits, enforced by the sanction of embarrassment. This gave these international rules at least some real bite.

But George W. Bush defied embarrassment and slew it with a series of Orwellian flourishes. If the United Nations wants to be "relevant," he said, it must do exactly as I say. In other words, in order to be relevant, it must become irrelevant. When that didn't work, he said: I am ignoring the wishes of the Security Council and violating the U.N. Charter in order to enforce a U.N. Security Council resolution. No, no, don't thank me! My pleasure!!

By Monday night, though, in his forty-eight-hour-warning speech, the references to international law and the United Nations had become vestigial. Bush's defense of his decision to make war on Iraq was basic: "The United States of America has the sovereign authority to use force in assuring its own national security." He did not claim that Iraq is a present threat to America's own national security but suggested that "in one year or five years" it could be such a threat. In the twentieth century, threats from murderous dictators were foolishly ignored until it was too late. In this century, "terrorists and terrorist states" do not play the game of war by the traditional rules. They "do not reveal these threats with fair notice in formal declarations." Therefore, "Responding to such enemies only after they have struck first is not self-defense. It is suicide."

What is wrong with Bush's case? Sovereign nations do have the right to act in their own self-defense, and they will use that right no matter what the U.N. Charter says or how the Security Council votes. Waiting for an enemy to strike first can indeed be suicidal. So?

So first of all, the right Bush is asserting really has no limits because the special circumstances he claims aren't really special. Striking first in order to pre-empt an enemy that has troops massing along your border is one thing. Striking first against a nation that has never even explicitly threatened your sovereign territory, except in response to your own threats, because you believe that this nation may have weapons that could threaten you in five years, is something very different.

Bush's suggestion that the furtive nature of war in this new century somehow changes the equation is also dubious, and it contradicts his assertion that the threat from Iraq is "clear." Even in traditional warfare, striking first has often been considered an advantage. And even before this century, nations rarely counted on receiving an enemy's official notice of intention to attack five years in advance. Bush may be right that the threat from Iraq is real, but he is obviously wrong that it is "clear," or other nations as interested in self-preservation as we are (and almost as self-interested in the preservation of the United States as we are) would see it as we do, which most do not.

Putting all this together, Bush is asserting the right of the United States to attack any country that may be a threat to it in five years. And the right of the United States to evaluate that risk and respond in its sole discretion. And the right of the president to make that decision on behalf of the United States in his sole discretion. In short, the president can start a war against anyone at any time, and no one has the right to stop him. And presumably other nations and future presidents have that same right. All formal constraints on war-making are officially defunct.

Well, so what? Isn't this the way the world works anyway? Isn't it naive and ultimately dangerous to deny that might makes right? Actually, no. Might is important, probably most important, but there are good, practical reasons for even might and right together to defer sometimes to procedure, law, and the judgment of others. Uncertainty is one. If we knew which babies would turn out to be murderous dictators, we could smother them in their cribs. If we knew which babies would turn out to be wise and judicious leaders, we could crown them dictator. In terms of the power he now claims, without significant challenge, George W. Bush is now the closest thing in a long time to dictator of the world. He claims to see the future as clearly as the past. Let's hope he's right.

## UNSETTLED

Slate, *April 10, 2003*

NOTE: *Hard to believe now, but there really was a moment when the Iraq war appeared to be "won." This piece mistakenly allowed Bush to define "victory" in Iraq as victory over Saddam. But it got the basic point—that dislodging Saddam was just the beginning of our troubles—right.*

So, we've won, or just about. There is no quagmire. Saddam is dead, or as good as, along with his sons. It was all fairly painless—at least for most Americans sitting at home watching it on television. Those who opposed the war look like fools. They are thoroughly discredited and, if they happen to be Democratic presidential candidates (and who isn't these days?), they might as well withdraw and nurse their shame somewhere off the public stage. The debate over Gulf War II is as over as the war itself soon will be, and the anti's were defeated as thoroughly as Saddam Hussein.

Right? No, not at all.

To start with an obvious point that may get buried in the confetti of the victory parade, the debate was not about whether America could topple the government of Iraq if we chose to make the attempt. No sane person doubted that the mighty United States military machine could conquer and occupy a country with a tiny fraction of our population and an even tinier fraction of our wealth—a country suffering from over a decade of economic strangulation by the rest of the world.

Oh, sure, there was a tepid public discussion of how long victory might take to achieve, in which pro's and anti's were represented across the spectrum of opinion. And the first law of journalistic dynamics—The Story Has to Change—inevitably produced a couple of comic days last week when the media and their rent-a-generals were peddling the Q-word. No doubt there are some unreflective peaceniks still mentally trapped in Vietnam, or grasping at any available argument, who are still talking quagmire. But the serious case against this war was never that we might actually lose it militarily.

The serious case involved questions that are still unresolved. Factual questions: Is there a connection between Iraq and the perpetrators of 9/11? Is that connection really bigger than that of all the countries we're not invading? Does Iraq really have or almost have weapons of mass destruction that threaten the United States? Predictive questions: What will toppling Saddam ultimately cost in dollars and in lives (American, Iraqi, others)? Will the result be a stable Iraq and a blossoming of democracy in the Middle East or something less attractive? How many young Muslims and others will be turned against the United States, and what will they do about it?

Political questions: Should we be doing this despite the opposition of most of our traditional allies? Without the approval of the United Nations? Moral questions: Is it justified to make "pre-emptive" war on nations that may threaten us in the future? When do internal human rights, or the lack of them, justify a war? Is there a policy about pre-emption and human rights that we are prepared to apply consistently? Does consistency matter? Even etiquette questions: Before Bush begins trying to create a civil society in Iraq, wouldn't it be nice if he apologized to Bill Clinton and Al Gore for all the nasty, dismissive things he said about "nation-building" in the 2000 campaign?

Some of these questions will be answered shortly, and some will be debated forever. This doesn't mean history will never render a judgment. History's judgment doesn't require unanimity or total certainty. But that judgment is not in yet. Supporters of this war who are in the mood for an ideological pogrom should chill out for a while, and opponents need not fold into permanent cringe position.

Of course opponents have been on the defensive since the day the fighting started, forced to repeat the mantra that we "oppose the war but support the troops." Critics mock this formula as psychologically implausible if not outright dishonest, but it's not even difficult or complicated. Most of the common reasons for opposing this war get more severe as the war grows longer. Above all is the cost in human lives, especially the lives of American soldiers. (And most American war opponents share with American war supporters—with most human beings, for that matter—an instinctively greater concern for the lives of fellow nationals, however illogical or deplorable that might be.) Unlike Vietnam, where opposition barely existed until the war had been going on for several years, this is a war in which calling for a pullout short of victory would be silly. So, once the war has started, no disingenuousness is required for opponents to hope for victory, the quicker the better.

What is an honest opponent of a war supposed to do? Since even the end of this war won't settle most of the important arguments about it, dropping all opposition at the beginning of the war would surely be more intellectually suspicious than maintaining your doubts while sincerely hoping for victory. Inevitably, more than one supporter of this war has taunted its opponents with Orwell's famous observation in 1942 that pacifists—the few who opposed a military response to Hitler—were "objectively pro-fascist." The suggestion is that opposing this war makes you objectively pro-Saddam. In an oddly less famous passage two years later, Orwell recanted that "objectively" formula and called it "dishonest." Which it is.

The psychological challenge of opposing a war like this after it has started isn't supporting the American troops, but hoping to be proven wrong. That, though, is the burden of pessimism on all subjects. As a skeptic, at the least, about Gulf War II, I do hope to be proven wrong. But it hasn't happened yet.

# BUSH'S WAR

Time, *April 21, 2003*

The "great man" theory of history has been out of fashion for decades. Historians trying to explain the course of human events point to geography or climate or technology. They explore the everyday life of ordinary people and the tides of change that sweep through whole populations. When they write about individual historical actors, the emphasis tends to be on psychology. Kings and Queens, Presidents and Prime Ministers may affect events at the margins, but the notion that history happens because someone decided it should happen is regarded as unenlightening if not simply wrong.

About Gulf War II and its consequences (whatever they may be), though, the "great man" theory is correct, and the great man is President George W. Bush. Great in this context does not necessarily mean good or wise. It does usually suggest a certain largeness of character or presence on the stage, which Bush does not possess. Whatever gods gave him this role were casting against type. But the role is his. This was George W. Bush's war. It was the result of one man's deliberate, sudden and unforced decision. Yes, Saddam Hussein deserves the ultimate moral blame, but Bush pushed the button.

Bush's decision to make war on Iraq may have been visionary and courageous or reckless and tragic or anything in between, but one thing it wasn't was urgently necessary. For Bush, this war was optional. Events did not impose it on him. Few public voices were egging him on. He hadn't made an issue of the need for "regime change" during the presidential campaign or made it a priority in the early months of his Administration. If he had completely ignored Iraq through the 2004 election, the price would have been a few disappointed Administration hawks and one or two grumpy op-eds. But something or someone put this bee in his bonnet, and from a standing start, history took off. Thousands died, millions were freed from tyranny (we hope), billions were spent, a region was shaken to its core, alliances ruptured, and the entire world watched it all on TV.

Compare America's other wars of the past sixty years. All of them had, if not inevitability, at least a bit of propulsion from forces larger than one man's desire. Gulf War I was provoked by an actual event: Iraq's occupation of Kuwait. George the Elder didn't have to make war, but he had to do something. Vietnam, famously, was never an explicit decision. Even the parody war in Grenada had a few captive American medical students to force its way onto the agenda. Some people believe that Franklin Roosevelt personally, deliberately and even dishonestly maneuvered a reluctant America into World War II. But World War II was history boiling over and impossible to avoid one way or another.

Why did Bush want this war? His ostensible reasons were unconvincing. Whatever we may find now in the rubble of Baghdad, he never offered any good evidence of a close link between Iraq and al-Qaeda or of weapons of mass destruction that could threaten the U.S. His desire to liberate a nation from tyranny undoubtedly was sincere, but there are other tyrants in the world. Why this one? On the other hand, the ulterior motives attributed to Bush by critics are even more implausible. He didn't start a war to serve his re-election campaign or avenge his father or enrich his oil buddies or help Israel. The mystery of Bush's true motives adds to the impression of a wizard arbitrarily waving his wand over history.

War on Iraq was optional for George W. Bush in another sense too. He could have easily chosen not to have it, in which case it wouldn't have happened, but when he decided to have it, that was it: we had it. The President's ability to decide when and where to use America's military power is now absolute. Congress cannot stop him. That's not what the Constitution says, and it's not what the War Powers Act says, but that's how it works in practice. The U.N. cannot stop him. That's not what the U.N. Charter says, but who cares? And who cares what America's allies think either?

Even more amazing than the President's pragmatic power over military resources is his apparent spiritual power over so many minds. Bush is not the only one who decided rather suddenly that disempowering Saddam had to be the world's top priority. When Bush decided this, so did almost every congressional Republican, conservative TV pundit and British Prime Minister. In polls, a large majority of Americans agreed with Bush that Saddam was a terrible threat and had to go, even though there had been no popular passion for this idea before Bush brought it up. You could call this many things, but one of them is leadership. If real leadership means leading people where they don't want to go, George W. Bush has shown himself to be a real leader. And he now owns a bit of history to prove it.

## Bill Bennett's Bad Bet

Slate, *May 4, 2003*

Sinners have long cherished the fantasy that William Bennett, the virtue magnate, might be among our number. The news over the weekend—that Bennett's fifty-thousand-dollar sermons and best-selling moral instruction manuals have financed a multimillion dol-lar gambling habit—has lit a lamp of happiness in even the darkest hearts. As the joyous word spread, crack flowed like water through inner-city streets, family court judges began handing out free divorces, children lit bonfires of *The Book of Virtues, More Virtuous Virtues, Who Cheesed My Virtue?, Moral Tails: Virtue for Dogs*, etc. And cynics everywhere thought, for just a moment: Maybe there is a God after all.

If there were a Pulitzer Prize for schadenfreude (joy in the suffering of others), *Newsweek*'s Jonathan Alter and Joshua Green of the *Washington Monthly* would surely deserve it for bringing us this story. They are shoo-ins for the public service category in any event. Schadenfreude is an unvirtuous emotion of which we should be ashamed. Bill Bennett himself was always full of sorrow when forced to point out the moral failings of other public figures. But the flaws of his critics don't absolve Bennett of his own.

Let's also be honest that gambling would not be our first-choice vice if we were designing this fantasy-come-true from scratch. But gambling will do. It will definitely do. Bill Bennett has been exposed as a humbug artist who ought to be pelted off the public stage if he lacks the decency to slink quietly away, as he is constantly calling on others to do. Although it may be impossible for anyone famous to become permanently discredited in American culture (a Bennett-like point I agree with), Bennett clearly deserves that distinction. There are those who will try to deny it to him. They will say:

1. He never specifically criticized gambling. This, if true, doesn't show that Bennett is not a hypocrite. It just shows that he's not a complete idiot. Working his way down the list of other people's pleasures, weaknesses, and uses of American freedom, he just happened to skip over his own. How convenient. Is there some reason why his general intolerance of the standard vices does not apply to this one? None that he's ever mentioned.

Open, say, Bennett's *The Broken Hearth: Reversing the Moral Collapse of the American Family*, and read about how Americans overvalue "unrestricted personal liberty." How we must relearn to "enter judgments on a whole range of behaviors and attitudes." About how "wealth and luxury . . . often make it harder to deny the quest for instant gratification" because "the more we attain, the more we want." How would you have guessed, last week, that Bennett would regard a man who routinely "cycle[s] several hundred thousand dollars in an evening" (his own description) sitting in an airless Las Vegas casino pumping coins into a slot machine or video game? Well, you would have guessed wrong! He thinks it's perfectly OK as long as you don't spend the family milk money.

2. His gambling never hurt anyone else. This is, of course, the classic libertarian standard of permissible behavior, and I think it's a good one. If a hypocrite is a person who says one thing and does another, the problem with Bennett is what he says—not (as far as we know) what he does. Bennett can't plead liberty now because opposing libertarianism is what his sundry crusades are all about. He wants to put marijuana smokers in jail. He wants to make it harder to get divorced. He wants more "moral criticism of homosexuality" and "declining to accept that what they do is right."

In all these cases, Bennett wants laws against or heightened social disapproval of activities that have no direct harmful effects on anyone except the participants. He argues that the activities in question are encouraging other, more harmful activities or are eroding general social norms in some vague way. Empower America, one of Bennett's several shirt-pocket mass movements, officially opposes the spread of legalized gambling, and the Index of Leading Cultural Indicators, one of Bennett's cleverer PR conceits, includes "problem" gambling as a negative indicator of cultural health. So, Bennett doesn't believe that gambling is harmless. He just believes that his own gambling is harmless. But by the standards he applies to everything else, it is not harmless.

Bennett has been especially critical of libertarian sentiments coming from intellectuals and the media elite. Smoking a bit of pot may not ruin their middle-class lives, but by smoking pot, they create an atmosphere of toleration that can be disastrous for others who are not so well-grounded. The Bill Bennett who can ooze disdain over this is the same Bill Bennett who apparently thinks he has no connection to all those "problem" gamblers because he makes millions preaching virtue and they don't.

3. HE'S DOING NO HARM TO HIMSELF. From the information in Alter's and Green's articles, Bennett seems to be in deep denial about this. If it's true that he's lost eight million dollars in gambling casinos over ten years, that surely is addictive or compulsive behavior no matter how good virtue has been to him financially. He claims to have won more than he has lost, which is virtually (that word again!) impossible playing the machines as Bennett apparently does. If he's not in denial, then he's simply lying, which is a definite non-virtue. And he's spraying smarm like the worst kind of cornered politician— telling the *Washington Post*, for example, that his gambling habit started with "church bingo."

Even as an innocent hobby, playing the slots is about as far as you can get from the image Bennett paints of his notion of the Good Life. Surely even a high-roller can't "cycle through" eight million dollars so quickly that family, church, and community don't suffer. There are preachers who can preach an ideal they don't themselves meet and even use their own weaknesses as part of the lesson. Bill Bennett has not been such a preacher. He is smug, disdainful, intolerant. He gambled on bluster, and lost.

## THE FABULIST

AN AMERICAN SUCCESS STORY.

Slate, *May 15, 2003*

President Bush, of course, is not a junior reporter for the *New York Times*. So maybe it doesn't matter if he makes up stories and puts them in the newspaper. After Ronald Reagan, it's almost a presidential tradition.

Bush was in New Mexico on Monday with a new answer to critics who complain that his tax cut proposal favors the rich. In two words: small business. "Most new jobs in America are created by small businesses." Therefore tax cuts "must focus on the entrepreneur." And thence to more familiar bromides: It's not "the government's money," it's "your money"; "our greatest strength" is "our individual citizens"; criticism is "just typical Washington, D.C., political rhetoric, is what it is."

The myth of small business is one of the more ridiculous bipartisan superstitions that influence government policy. Small businesses, by their nature, come and go. They create more jobs than big businesses and wipe out more jobs, too. Any small-business owner burdened by high taxes is, by definition, more affluent than the typical big-business owner, who is an ordinary working American with an interest in a retirement fund. Small businesses are swell. But special favors for small business make no sense in terms of either fairness or prosperity.

Bush gave his speech Monday at a company in Albuquerque called MCT Industries. "We're standing in the midst of what we call the American dream," he said. MCT is privately owned by the family of Ted Martinez, who founded it on a shoestring in 1973 and is now a wealthy VIP who hangs around with politicians. "The Martinez family is living that dream," Bush said.

Before we even get to the fantasy element, there is a logical problem here, isn't there? A successful "small" business makes an odd poster child for the proposition that the government is getting in the way of small business success. How did the Martinez family manage to achieve the American dream during a period when high taxes were supposedly thwarting that dream? If MCT Industries is so successful under current arrangements, why does it need a tax cut?

You don't need overdeveloped smell detectors to suspect that this story may be a bit more complicated. And the most casual stroll through the Internet and media databases enriches the narrative a lot. MCT Industries seems to be a weird collection of unrelated businesses whose only unifying theme is selling to government agencies or needing the approval of politicians. The Martinez family is wealthy because of tax revenues, not despite them.

No surprise, MCT is a member of the Rio Grande Minority Purchasing Council, a trade association for businesses looking to benefit from reverse discrimination. Racial favoritism for "disadvantaged" wealthy business owners is the most ridiculous and unjustifiable form of affirmative action and generally the only kind Republicans are enthusiastic about. Martinez is a GOP activist, but his company does not discriminate. At a 1997 conference of Hispanic CEOs, Clinton Energy Secretary Federico Pena boasted about how "MCT was able to secure a diesel-powered aircraft maintenance contract with the U.S. Air Force" thanks to the "assistance" of a federal agency.

Earlier this year, the Albuquerque City Council declined to authorize about $5 million of industrial revenue bonds for MCT. IRBs are a racket—legal, unfortunately—in which local governments use their right to issue federal-tax-exempt bonds in order to raise money for private companies. The company gets to borrow at a below-market interest rate, subsidized by the loss to the federal Treasury. In Albuquerque, the lucky companies get exempted from local property taxes and some state taxes to boot. MCT did not want the money for job-creating expansion but to refinance IRBs it already enjoys to get an even lower interest rate. Those IRBs helped to finance a factory to build maintenance equipment and do R & D, both for the Defense Department.

October 2002. MCT is one of the contributors to a PAC that paid for the mayor's family to visit China.

July 2002. The Bureau of Indian Affairs approves an MCT municipal garbage landfill on an Indian reservation. Also, the New Mexico Rural Development Response Council and several state agencies help MCT to acquire land for a factory to build platforms for aircraft repairs.

August 1999. *Waste News* reports that Albuquerque has a bizarre regulation requiring all city garbage trucks to be made out of a particular brand of steel. Only one company sells trucks made out of this material. Guess.

December 1998. The Energy Department (secretary: Bill Richardson, now governor of New Mexico) hires MCT to build magnets to be used in making tritium for nuclear warheads.

June 1997. MCT, as a local company, competes against a national waste-management firm for a local garbage-collection contract. It wins the contract and sells the business to the national firm the next day.

October 1996. Republican vice presidential candidate Jack Kemp holds a rally at MCT. Ted Martinez hands him a document asserting that almost a third of MCT's payroll goes to paying federal, state, and local taxes. In his speech, Kemp makes it "half."

October 1995. Giant defense contractor TRW announces that it has won a $185 million contract from the Air Force, which it will share with two "small disadvantaged businesses" including MCT.

December 1994. In congressional testimony about export assistance for small businesses, a Commerce Department official talks about how the federal government sponsored an exhibit by MCT at the Paris Air Show and subsequent Commerce Department shows in China and Dubai.

So you get rich with a dozen different types of tax-funded help, you become a Republican, and you live happily ever after complaining about how much you pay in taxes. Maybe President Bush was right after all, that is the American dream.

## SYMPATHY FOR THE *NEW YORK TIMES*

Slate, *May 21, 2003*

**A**lthough rarely reluctant to join in a schadenfreude festival, I nevertheless feel sorry for the *New York Times*. Duped by one of its own reporters, hemorrhaging rumors and leaks like the institutions it is used to covering, its extravagant public self-flagellation merely inviting flagellation by everyone else, the paper is at a low ebb. Much of the criticism and self-criticism is deserved. But after two weeks of *Times*-bashing, it's time for a bit of therapeutic outreach.

One reason the *Times* has my sympathy over being duped by a writer is that I've been there. And let me tell you: The clarity of hindsight is remarkable. A couple of years ago, *Slate* published a vivid, rollicking yarn about an alleged sport called "monkeyfishing." The author claimed to have used a rod and reel, with rotten fruit as bait, to catch monkeys living on an island in the Florida Keys.

As editor of *Slate* at the time, I read the piece before it was published and didn't like it—for a variety of wrong reasons. So I cannot even claim to have been blinded by enthusiasm. Others at *Slate* did like it and so we published it. When outsiders challenged it, I read it again.

It was like reading an entirely different article. Red flags waved from every line. At first the author stood by his story and we stood by him. But within days, poking around by ourselves and others made this position untenable, and so we both caved. The question remains, though, why my baloney-detectors didn't function beforehand, when they could have saved us considerable embarrassment. All I can say is: Congress is about to exempt dividends from the income tax—i.e., stranger things than monkeyfishing actually do happen.

Whatever the reason, reading an article with doubts raised is a different experience from reading it in its virginal pre-publication freshness. As *Slate*'s Jack Shafer has pointed out, most readers of Jayson Blair's *Times* articles did not spot the hints of fabrication or plagiarism either. This includes many of the critics who now say that the *Times* missed important clues because of institutional arrogance or political bias or an affirmative action mentality.

Of course readers are entitled to assume that published articles have been pre-skepticized. And Jayson Blair duped the *Times* again and again. But holding foresight to the standards of hindsight is a bit unfair.

My second reason for feeling sympathy for the *New York Times* is that it now wears the Scarlet P, for plagiarist, when in a way we are all plagiarizers of the *New York Times*. Plagiarism technically applies only to an article's words, not to the ideas and information contained in them. But the value of a newspaper article lies more in the ideas and information than in the precise words. And much or even most American news reporting and commentary on national issues derives—uncredited—from the *New York Times*.

Even if you don't read the *Times* yourself, you get your news from journalists at other media who do. The *Times* sets the news agenda that everyone else follows. The *Washington Post* and maybe one or two other papers also play this role, but even as a writer who appears in the *Washington Post*—a damned fine newspaper run by superb editors who are graced with every kind of brilliance, charm, and physical beauty—I would have to concede that the *Times* is more influential.

It's not just the agenda setting. Our basic awareness of what is going on in the world derives in large part from the *Times*. How do you even know that Baghdad exists? Have you been there? Touched it? How do I, sitting in Seattle, know the current status of the Bush administration's Mideast road map, about which I may choose to opine with seeming authority? Column-writing is an especially derivative form of journalism. But even the hardest of hard-news reporters starts with basic knowledge that probably comes more from the *Times* than her own two eyes.

It's true that the journalistic food chain runs both ways: Big media like the *Times* often pick up stories and information from smaller fish, often with insufficient credit or none at all. But it is the imprimatur of the *Times* or the *Post* that stamps the story as important before sending it back down to other papers—as well as up to the media gods of television.

This near-universal dependence on the *Times* helps to explain the schadenfreude (dependence causes resentment) as well as the more serious alarm about the *Times*' reliability. It also puts Jayson Blair's rip-offs of others, if not his fabrications, in perspective. No one gets ripped off more than the *New York Times*.

The social critic Dwight Macdonald, reminiscing about the left-wing *Partisan Review* crowd of the 1930s, wrote: "The N.Y. Times was to us what Aristotle was to the medieval scholastics—a revered authority, even though pagan, and a mine of useful information about the actual world." Today's equivalent of that sect-ridden, conspiracy-minded, alienation-proud political world is on the right. I was listening to a right-wing broadcast crank the other day as he carried on about how the *Times* can't be trusted about this and that. I don't know where he got his information, but I have a guess.

## SUPREME COURT FUDGE

Slate, *June 24, 2003*

Admission to a prestige institution like the University of Michigan or its law school is what computer types call a "binary" decision. It's yes or no. You're in, or you're out. There is no partial or halfway admission. The effect of any factor in that decision is also binary. It either changes the result or it doesn't. It makes all the difference, or it makes none at all. Those are the only possibilities.

For any individual, the process of turning factors into that yes-or-no decision doesn't matter. Any factor that changes the result has the same impact as if it were an absolute quota of one. It gets you in, or it keeps you out. And this is either right or it is wrong. The process of turning factors into a result doesn't matter here, either. In this sense, the moral question is binary, too.

For twenty-five years, since Justice Powell's opinion in the *Bakke* case, moderates on the Supreme Court and well-meaning people throughout the land have been pretending that it is possible to split a difference that cannot be split. This week's court ruling, in which Justice O'Connor contrasts the college and law-school admissions systems at Michigan and essentially reaffirms *Bakke*, shows how laughable that pretense has become.

Michigan's college admissions policy at the time this suit began was strictly numerical: You needed 100 points to get in, and you got 20 points for being an officially recognized minority. Flatly unconstitutional, the court declared. Michigan's law school, by contrast, "engages in a highly individualized, holistic review of each applicant's file." It "awards no mechanical, predetermined diversity 'bonuses' based on race or ethnicity." Instead, it makes "a flexible assessment of applicants' talents, experiences, and potential . . ." blah blah blah. This is how it should be done, the court said.

Yes, but does the law school give an advantage in admissions to blacks and other minorities? Well, says the court, quoting the law school's brief, it "aspires to 'achieve that diversity which has the potential to enrich everyone's education.'" The law school "does not restrict the types of diverse contributions eligible" for special treatment. In fact, it "recognizes 'many possible bases for diversity admissions.'"

Yes, yes, yes, but does the law-school admissions policy favor minorities? Well, since you insist, yes: "The policy does . . . reaffirm the Law School's longstanding commitment to 'one particular type of diversity,'" i.e., "racial and ethnic diversity." But O'Connor's opinion immediately sinks back into a vat of fudge, trying not to acknowledge that "racial and ethnic diversity" means that some people will be admitted because of their race and others will be rejected for the same reason—exactly as in the undergraduate admissions system the court finds unconstitutional. By ignoring the similarities, the court avoids having to explain coherently why it sees such profound differences.

The court actually seems to be in denial on this point. Although it forbids explicit racial quotas or mathematical formulas to achieve racial balance, it is happy enough to measure the success of its preferred fuzzier approaches in statistical terms. If a selection system is going to be judged by its success in approximating the results of a mathematical formula, how is it any different from using that formula explicitly? Elsewhere, arguing for the social value of affirmative action, O'Connor's opinion cites dramatic statistics about how few minority students there would be if it were ended. But don't those statistics imply that affirmative action is having an equal-and-opposite effect now? And isn't that good to exactly the extent that ending affirmative action would be bad? And if that extent can be measured and judged using statistics, why is it wrong to achieve the statistical goal through statistical means?

The majority opinion says that its preferred flexible-flier style of affirmative action does "not unduly harm members of any racial group." Well, this depends on what you mean by "unduly," doesn't it? As noted, we're dealing with an all-or-nothing-at-all decision here. Every time affirmative action changes the result, a minority beneficiary benefits by 100 percent and a white person is burdened 100 percent, in the only currency at issue, which is admission to the University of Michigan. This burden may be reasonable or unreasonable, but it is precisely the same size as the burden imposed by the mathematical-formula-style affirmative action that the court finds objectionable.

The Supreme Court took these Michigan cases to end a quarter century of uncertainty about affirmative action. What it has produced is utter logical confusion. The law-school dean testified that "the extent to which race is considered in admissions . . . varies from one applicant to another." It "may play no role" or it "may be a determinative factor." O'Connor cites this approvingly, but it is nonsense on several levels. First, "no role" and "determinative factor" are in fact the only possible options: There cannot be an infinite variety of effects on a yes-or-no question. Second, when race is determinative for one applicant, it is determinative for one other applicant, who may or may not be identifiable. Third, the same two possibilities—no factor and determinative factor—apply to any admissions system that takes race into account in any way, including by mathematical formula and even including an outright quota system. So, it says nothing special about the law school's admissions policy compared with any other.

Finally, the court is confused if it thinks that a subjective judgment full of unquantifiable factors is obviously fairer than a straightforward formula. But confusion seems to be a purposeful strategy. The court's message to universities and other selective, government-financed institutions is: We have fudged this dangerous issue. You should do the same.

## ABOLISH MARRIAGE

Slate, *July 2, 2003*

Critics and enthusiasts of *Lawrence v. Texas*, last week's Supreme Court decision invalidating state anti-sodomy laws, agree on one thing: The next argument is going to be about gay marriage. As Justice Scalia noted in his tart dissent, it follows from the logic of *Lawrence*. Mutually consenting sex with the person of your choice in the privacy of your own home is now a basic right of American citizenship under the Constitution. This does not mean that the government must supply it or guarantee it. But the government cannot forbid it, and the government also should not discriminate against you for choosing to exercise a basic right of citizenship. Offering an institution as important as marriage to male-female couples only is exactly this kind of discrimination. Or so the gay rights movement will now argue. Persuasively, I think.

Opponents of gay rights will resist mightily, although they have been in retreat for a couple of decades. General anti-gay sentiments are now considered a serious breach of civic etiquette, even in anti-gay circles. The current line of defense, which probably won't hold either, is between social toleration of homosexuals and social approval of homosexuality. Or between accepting the reality that people are gay, even accepting that gays are people, and endorsing something called "the gay agenda." Gay marriage, the opponents will argue, would cross this line. It would make homosexuality respectable and, worse, normal. Gays are welcome to exist all they want, and to do their inexplicable thing if they must, but they shouldn't expect a government stamp of approval.

It's going to get ugly. And then it's going to get boring. So, we have two options here. We can add gay marriage to the short list of controversies—abortion, affirmative action, the death penalty—that are so frozen and ritualistic that debates about them are more like Kabuki performances than intellectual exercises. Or we can think outside the box. There is a solution that ought to satisfy both camps and may not be a bad idea even apart from the gay-marriage controversy.

That solution is to end the institution of marriage. Or rather (he hastens to clarify, Dear) the solution is to end the institution of government-sanctioned marriage. Or, framed to appeal to conservatives: End the government monopoly on marriage. Wait, I've got it: Privatize marriage. These slogans all mean the same thing. Let churches and other religious institutions continue to offer marriage ceremonies. Let department stores and casinos get into the act if they want. Let each organization decide for itself what kinds of couples it wants to offer marriage to. Let couples celebrate their union in any way they choose and consider themselves married whenever they want. Let others be free to consider them not married, under rules these others may prefer. And, yes, if three people want to get married, or one person wants to marry herself, and someone else wants to conduct a ceremony and declare them married, let 'em. If you and your government aren't implicated, what do you care?

In fact, there is nothing to stop any of this from happening now.

And a lot of it does happen. But only certain marriages get certi-fied by the government. So, in the United States we are about to find ourselves in a strange situation where the principal demand of a liberation movement is to be included in the red tape of a gov-ernment bureaucracy. Having just gotten state governments out of their bedrooms, gays now want these governments back in. Mean-while, social-conservative anti-gays, many of them Southerners, are calling on the government in Washington to trample states' rights and nationalize the rules of marriage, if necessary, to prevent gays from getting what they want. The Senate Majority Leader, Bill Frist of Tennessee, responded to the Supreme Court's *Lawrence* deci-sion by endorsing a constitutional amendment, no less, against gay marriage.

If marriage were an entirely private affair, all the disputes over gay marriage would become irrelevant. Gay marriage would not have the official sanction of government, but neither would straight marriage. There would be official equality between the two, which is the essence of what gays want and are entitled to. And if the other side is sincere in saying that its concern is not what people do in pri-vate, but government endorsement of a gay "lifestyle" or "agenda," that problem goes away, too.

Yes, yes, marriage is about more than sleeping arrangements. There are children, there are finances, there are spousal job benefits like health insurance and pensions. In all these areas the law uses marriage as a substitute for other factors that are harder to measure, such as financial dependence or devotion to offspring. It would be possible to write rules that measure the real factors at stake and leave marriage out of the matter. Regarding children and finances, people can set their own rules, as many already do. None of this would be easy. Marriage functions as what lawyers call a "bright line," which saves the trouble of trying to measure a lot of amorphous factors. You're either married or you're not. Once marriage itself becomes amorphous, who-gets-the-kids and who-gets-health-care become trickier questions.

So, sure, there are some legitimate objections to the idea of priva-tizing marriage. But they don't add up to a fatal objection. Especially when you consider that the alternative is arguing about gay mar-riage until death do us part.

## WHO IS BURIED IN BUSH'S SPEECH?

Slate, *July 14, 2003*

Once again a mysterious criminal stalks the nation's capital. First there was the mystery sniper. Then there was the mystery arsonist. Now there is the mystery ventriloquist. The media are in a frenzy of speculation and leakage. Senators are calling for hearings. All of Washington demands an answer: Who was the arch-fiend who told a lie in President Bush's State of the Union speech? No investigation has plumbed such depths of the unknown since O.J. Simpson's hunt for the real killer of his ex-wife. (Whatever happened to that, by the way?)

Whodunit? Was it Col. Mustard in the kitchen with a candlestick? Condoleezza Rice in the Situation Room with a bottle of Wite-Out and a felt-tipped pen?

Linguists note that the question, "Who lied in George Bush's State of the Union speech?" bears a certain resemblance to the famous conundrum, "Who is buried in Grant's Tomb?" They speculate that the two questions may have parallel answers. But philosophers are still struggling to properly analyze the Grant's Tomb issue—let alone answer it. And experts say that even when this famous nineteenth-century presidential puzzle is solved, it could be many years before the findings can be applied with any confidence to presidents of more recent vintage.

Lacking a real-life analogy that sufficiently captures the complexity of the speech-gate puzzle and the challenge facing investigators dedicated to solving it, political scientists say the best comparison may be to the assassination of Maj. Strasser in the film *Casablanca*. If you recall, Humphrey Bogart is standing over the body, holding a smoking gun. Claude Rains says: "Maj. Strasser has been shot! Round up the usual suspects." And yet the mystery of who killed the major is never solved.

Ever since Watergate, a "smoking gun" has been the standard for judging any Washington scandal. Many a miscreant has escaped with his reputation undamaged—or even enhanced by the publicity and pseudovindication—because there was no "smoking gun" like the

Watergate tapes. But now it seems that the standard has been lifted. You would think that on the question of who told a lie in a speech, evidence seen on television by millions of people around the world might count for something. Apparently not. The Bush administration borrows from Chico Marx: "Who are you going to believe—us or your own two eyes?"

The case for the defense is a classic illustration of what lawyers call "arguing in the alternative." The Bushies say: a) It wasn't really a lie; b) someone else told the lie; and c) the lie doesn't matter. All these defenses are invalid.

1. Bushies fanned out to the weekend talk shows to note, as if with one voice, that what Bush said was technically accurate. But it was not accurate, even technically. The words in question were: "The British government has learned that Saddam Hussein recently sought significant quantities of uranium from Africa." Bush didn't say it was true, you see—he just said the Brits said it. This is a contemptible argument in any event. But to descend to the administration's level of nitpickery, the argument simply doesn't work. Bush didn't say that the Brits "said" this Africa business—he said they "learned" it. The difference between "said" and "learned" is that "learned" clearly means there is some pre-existing basis for believing whatever it is, apart from the fact that someone said it. Is it theoretically possible to "learn" something that is not true? I'm not sure (as Donald Rumsfeld would say). However, it certainly is not possible to say that someone has "learned" a piece of information without clearly intending to imply that you, the speaker, wish the listener to accept it as true. Bush expressed no skepticism or doubt, even though the Brits qualification was only added as protection because doubts had been expressed internally.

2. The Bush argument blaming the CIA for failing to remove this falsehood from the president's speech is based on the logic of "stop me before I lie again." Bush spoke the words, his staff wrote them, those involved carefully overlooked reasons for skepticism. It would have been nice if the CIA had caught this falsehood, but its failure to do so hardly exonerates others. Furthermore, the CIA is part of the executive branch, as is the White House staff. If the president—especially this president—can disown anything he says that he didn't

actually find out or think up and write down all by himself, he is more or less beyond criticism. Which seems to be the idea here.

The president says he has not lost his confidence in CIA Director George Tenet. How sweet. If someone backed me up in a lie and then took the fall for me when it was exposed, I'd have confidence in him too.

3. The final argument: It was only 16 words! What's the big deal? The bulk of the case for war remains intact. Logically, of course, this argument will work for any single thread of the pro-war argument. Perhaps the president will tell us which particular points among those he and his administration have made are the ones we are supposed to take seriously. Or how many gimmes he feels entitled to take in the course of this game. Is it a matter of word count? When he hits 100 words, say, are we entitled to assume that he cares whether the words are true?

## At Least Say You're Sorry

Slate, *Sept. 11, 2003*

President Bush will get his $87 billion for a year's worth of victory in Iraq and Afghanistan, but he will have to endure a lot of nyah-nyah-nyah and I-told-you-so along the way. He could have avoided all this irritation—and he is just the kind of man to find it incredibly irritating—with two little words in his TV address last Sunday evening: "I'm sorry." If he had acknowledged with a bit of grace what everyone assumes to be true—that the administration was blindsided by the postwar challenge in both these countries—this would have cut off a politically damaging debate that will now go on through the election campaign. And he would have won all sorts of brownie points for high-mindedness. Instead, he and his spokesfolk will be defending a fairly obvious untruth day after day through the election campaign.

Why do politicians so rarely apologize? Why in particular won't they admit to being surprised by some development? Lack of scruples can't explain it: Denying the obvious isn't even good unscrupulous politics. For that reason, it is beyond spin. If spinning involves an indifference to truth, what's going on here looks more like an actual preference for falsehood. The truth would be better politics, and the administration is spreading lies anyway.

This is not meant to be a partisan observation. Bush's predecessor was, if anything, a more flamboyant liar. What's going on here is something like lying-by-reflex. If the opposition accuses you of saying the world is round, you lunge for the microphone to declare your passionate belief that it is flat. Or maybe it has something to do with the bureaucracies that political campaigns have become. The truth, whatever its advantages, is messy and out-of-control. A lie can be designed by committee, vetted by consultants, tested with focus groups, shaped to perfection. Anyone can tell the truth. Crafting a good lie is a job for professionals.

This $87 billion request is a minefield of embarrassments, through which a simple "We got it wrong" would have been the safest route. After all, Bush either knew we'd be spending this kind of money for two or more years after declaring victory—and didn't tell us— or he didn't realize it himself. Those are the only two options. He deceived us, or he wasn't clairvoyant in the fog of war. Apparently, Bush would rather be thought omniscient than honest, which is a pity, since appearing honest is a more realistic ambition. Especially for him.

What's more, this would have been a truth without a tail. Telling one hard truth can lead you down, down, down into a vicious circle of more truth, revelation, embarrassment, and chagrin. That's one reason for the truth's dangerous reputation. But the Bush administration's failure to realize how much its postwar festivities would cost is a truth that doesn't lead anywhere in particular. Clearly knowing about the $87 billion bill for Year 2 would not have stopped Bush from conducting the war to begin with. Nor would this knowledge have stopped opponents from opposing it. Among supporters, there may be a few people who bought Bush's initial war-on-terrorism rationale, didn't mind the bait-and-switch to his revised freedom-and-democracy rationale, reveled in the military victory, and yet would have opposed it all if they'd known about the $87 billion. But it is an odd camel whose back is broken by this particular straw.

Bush needs some truth-telling points, because another aspect of this $87 billion request is driving him to dishonesty that he can't abandon so blithely. That issue is: If he gets the $87 billion, where will it have come from? Bush is sending Colin Powell around the world with a begging cup. But whatever can't be raised from foreigners apparently can be conjured out of thin air.

Raising taxes to pay the $87 billion would be a bad mistake, Bush says: Economic growth—fed by tax cuts—will cover the $87 billion and then some. But however miraculous Bush's tax cuts turn out to be, economic growth will not be $87 billion more miraculous just because that much more is suddenly needed in Iraq and Afghanistan. Nor does Bush plan, or even concede the necessity, to harvest this $87 billion at some point by raising taxes (or not cutting them) by that amount. And although he talks vaguely about spending restraint, he and the Congress controlled by his party have shown very little of it. He certainly has not pinpointed $87 billion in other spending that the new $87 billion can replace.

So, spending $87 billion costs nothing, apparently. This makes it even sillier to deny being blindsided. What difference does it make?

While apologizing to the citizenry, Bush could win even more brownie points, at almost no cost, by apologizing specifically to his predecessor. Bush ridiculed Bill Clinton's efforts to follow up military interventions with "nation-building." Believe it or not, this was a pejorative term, implying unrealistic ambitions. Now Bush talks about turning Iraq into a Jeffersonian democracy.

And if Bush wants credit for a Gold-Star Triple-Whammy Zirconium-Studded apology, he should apologize to his father, who stopped Gulf War I at the Iraqi border. Armchair Freudians believe that in going to Baghdad and toppling Saddam, George II was playing Oedipal tennis with George I. If so, junior has lost. The elder Bush's most notorious decision as president looks better every day. And not just because of the $87 billion.

## JUST SUPPOSIN'

IN DEFENSE OF HYPOTHETICAL QUESTIONS.

Slate, *Oct. 2, 2003*

One of the absurd conventions of American politics is the notion that there is something suspect or illegitimate about a hypothetical question. By labeling a question as "hypothetical," politicians and government officials feel they are entitled to duck it without looking like they have something to hide. They even seem to want credit for maintaining high standards by keeping this virus from corrupting the political discussion.

"If I've learned one thing in my nine days in politics, it's you better be careful with hypothetical questions," declared Gen. Wesley Clark in a recent Democratic presidential candidates' debate. He might have learned it on television, where "Never answer a hypothetical question" is one of the rules a real-life political strategist offered to real-life presidential candidate Howard Dean in HBO's fictional Washington drama *K Street*.

The question Clark was trying not to answer was "your vote, up or down, yes or no" on President Bush's request for $87 billion to finance the wars in Iraq and Afghanistan for another year. This question is only hypothetical in the sense that Clark doesn't literally get to vote on the matter. That kind of literalness could make almost any question hypothetical. The obvious purpose of the question was to elicit Clark's opinion on the $87 billion. And surely it is not unreasonable or "hypothetical" to expect candidates for president to express an opinion on whatever controversy surrounds the presidency at the moment.

Secretary of State Colin Powell was asked this week whether Americans would have supported the Iraq war if they'd known we weren't going to find those weapons of mass destruction the administration used to justify it. This really is a hypothetical question, as Powell labeled it in declining to answer, but it's a darned interesting one and one an honest leader in a democracy ought to be pondering about now, even if he doesn't care to share his thoughts.

Neither of these examples is the kind of hypothetical question that calls on the answerer to imagine a situation that is unlikely to occur, and one there would have been no good reason to think about. What if a man from Mars were running in the California recall election? What if President Bush were secretly writing a treatise on moral philosophy? And so on.

Avoiding questions (from reporters, from opponents, from citizens) is the basic activity of the American politician. Or rather, avoiding the supply of answers. Skill and ingenuity in question-avoidance techniques are a big factor in political success. Usually, avoiding the question involves pretending to answer it, or at least supplying some words to fill the dead space after the question has been asked. But if you can squeeze a question into one of a few choice categories, the unwritten rules allow the politician to not answer at all. There's national security. ("I'm sorry, but revealing the size of my gun collection might imperil our war on terrorism.") There's privacy. ("I must protect my family from the pain of learning about my other family.") There are legal proceedings. ("That arson allegation has been referred to the Justice Department, and I cannot comment further.") But only an allegedly hypothetical question may be dismissed because of its very nature, irrespective of subject matter.

This is silly. Hypothetical questions are at the heart of every election in a democracy. These are questions the voters must answer. Voters are expected to imagine each of the candidates holding the office he or she is seeking and to decide which one's performance would be most to their liking. Every promise made by a candidate imposes two hypothetical questions on the voter: If elected, will this person do as promised? And if this promise is kept, will I like the result? The voter cannot say, "I don't answer hypothetical questions." And voters cannot sensibly answer the hypothetical questions they've been assigned without learning the answers to some hypothetical questions from the candidates.

Hypothetical questions are essential to thinking through almost any social or political issue. In law school they're called "hypos," and the process is called "salami slicing." Imagine this situation, and tell me the result. Now change the situation slightly—does the result change? Now change it in a different way—same result, or different one? It's just like an eye exam, where you peer through a series of alternative lenses until you zero in on the correct prescription.

Yet even lawyers turn against the cherished hypo when nominated for prestigious judgeships. Then they say self-righteously that they cannot answer hypothetical questions about how they might rule. Once they are safely on the bench, of course, they issue public opinions every day that are, among other things, statements about how they analyze the issue at hand and strong indications, if not more, of how they will rule in the future.

A refusal or inability to answer hypothetical questions is nothing to be proud of. In fact, it ought to be a disqualification for public office. Anyone who doesn't ponder hypothetical questions all the time is unfit for the task of governing. In fact, it's hard to see how any halfway intelligent person can manage to avoid taking up hypothetical questions a dozen times a day.

But we can all name a few politicians we suspect are up to this challenge.

## FILTER TIPS

Slate, *Oct. 16, 2003*

To President Bush, the news is like a cigarette. You can get it filtered or unfiltered. And which way does he prefer it? Well, that depends on the circumstances. When he is trying to send a message to the public, Bush prefers to have it go out unfiltered. He feels, for example, that the "good news about Iraq" is getting filtered out by the national media. "Somehow you just got to go over the heads of the filter and speak directly to the American people," he said the other day. So, lately he has been talking to local and regional media, whom he trusts to filter less.

But when he is on the receiving end, Bush prefers his news heavily filtered. "I glance at the headlines, just to get kind of a flavor," he told Brit Hume of Fox News last month. But, "I rarely read the stories" because "a lot of times there's opinions mixed in with news." Instead, "I get briefed by [White House Chief of Staff] Andy Card and Condi [Rice, the national security adviser] in the morning."

The president concluded, "The best way to get the news is from objective sources. And the most objective sources I have are people on my staff who tell me what's happening in the world."

Bush's beef about news from Iraq is a variation on the famous complaint that the media never report about all the planes that land safely. And it's true: Many American soldiers have not been killed since the war officially ended. You rarely read stories about all the electricity that works, or the many Iraqis who aren't shouting anti-American slogans. For that matter, what about all the countries we haven't invaded and occupied in the past year? And what about the unreported fact that Saddam Hussein has been removed from power? Well, maybe that isn't actually unreported. But an unfilterish media would surely report it again and again in every story every day, in case people forgot.

Every president complains that the media are blocking his message, and the media complain that every administration wants to manage the news. It's not only presidents. Everyone who has something to say in our media-saturated culture (and who doesn't?) longs for ways to get that message out unmediated by someone else. In this media cacophony, the president probably has more ability to deliver his message without a filter than anyone else on earth. Anything the president says is automatically news. If he wants to commandeer all the TV networks for a speech in prime time, he can usually do it. The president can even hold a press conference, although this president rarely bothers.

Bush also will have a campaign war chest of $170 million that he can spend in the next year delivering any message he wants, completely unfiltered. Who can top that? Well, until recently there was Saddam Hussein. He could talk as long as he wanted and Iraqi television never cut away for a commercial, let alone bring on annoying pundits to pick and pick and pick. And the next day's Baghdad Gazette would publish every single word, also without any tedious analysis. A few others, such as Fidel Castro, still have this privilege. I was under the impression that George Bush found this distasteful—the sort of thing one might even tighten a boycott or start a war over.

George W. Bush doesn't really want people to get the news unfiltered. He wants people to get the news filtered by George W. Bush. Or rather, he wants everyone to get the news filtered by the same people who apparently filter it for him. It's an interesting epistemological question how our president knows what he thinks he knows and why he thinks it is less distorted than what the rest of us know or think we know. Every president lives in a cocoon of advisers who filter reality for him, but it's stunning that this president actually seems to prefer getting his take on reality that way.

Bush apparently thinks (if that is the word) that the publicly available media contaminate the news with opinion but Condi Rice and Andy Card are objective reporters. Anyone who has either been a boss or had a boss will find it easier, knowing that Bush believes this, to understand how he can also believe that things are going swimmingly in Iraq. And where does the Rice-Card News Service obtain its uncontaminated information? Bush conceded his shocking suspicion that Rice and Card "probably read the news themselves." They do? Whatever next? The president apparently is willing to tolerate the reading of newspapers by his staff members in the privacy of their own homes, as long as they don't flaunt this unseemly habit by bringing the wretched things into the White House or referring to them at staff meetings.

The president noted, though, that Rice and Card also get "news directly from participants on the world stage." ("Hi, Achmed—it's Condi. What's going on there in Baghdad? What's the weather like? And how's traffic? Thanks, I'll go tell the president and call you again in fifteen minutes.") The notion that these world-stagers are sources of objective opinion while newspaper reporters are burdened by insuppressible opinions and hidden agendas is another odd one.

When it comes to unfiltered news, the president says he can dish it out and actually brags that he can't take it. In fact, he can't do either one.


## TAKING BUSH PERSONALLY

Slate, *Oct. 23, 2003*

Conservatives wonder why so many liberals don't just disagree with President Bush's policies but seem to dislike him personally. The story of stem-cell research may help to explain. Two years ago, Bush announced an unexpectedly restrictive policy on the use of stem cells from human embryos in federally funded medical research. Because federal funding plays such a large role, the government more or less sets the rules for major medical research in this country.

Bush's policy was that research could continue on stem-cell "lines" that existed at the moment of his speech, in August 2001, but that otherwise, embryo research was banned. Even surplus embryos already in the freezer at fertility clinics—where embryos are routinely created and destroyed by the thousands every year—could not be used for medical research and would have to be thrown out instead.

Bush's professed moral concern was bolstered by two factual assumptions. One was that there were more than sixty stem-cell lines available for research. Stem cells are "wild card" cells. They multiply and evolve into cells for specific purposes in the human body. A "line" is the result of a particular cell that has been "tweaked" and is multiplying in the laboratory. The hope is to develop lines of cells that can be put back into human beings and be counted on to evolve into replacements for missing or defective parts. The likeliest example is dopamine-producing brain cells for people with Parkinson's disease. The dream is replacements for whole organs or even limbs. But each line is a crapshoot. So the more lines, the better. And it turns out that the number of useful lines is more like ten than sixty.

Bush also touted the possibility of harmlessly harvesting stem cells from adults. He said, "Therapies developed from adult stem cells are already helping suffering people." This apparently referred to decades-old techniques such as removing some of a leukemia patient's bone marrow and then reinjecting it after the patient has undergone radiation.

As for finding adult stem cells that could turn into unrelated body parts, that was just a dream two years ago, and now it is not even that. A new study, reported last week in *Nature*, concluded that when earlier studies thought they saw new specialized cells derived from adult stem cells, they were really seeing those adult cells bonding with pre-existing specialized cells. There's hope in this bonding process, too—but not the hope researchers had for adult stem cells, and nothing like the hope they still have for embryonic stem cells. Since Bush's speech, scientists have used embryonic stem cells to reverse the course of Parkinson's in rats.

Put it all together, and the stem cells that can squeeze through Bush's loopholes are far less promising than they seemed two years ago while the general promise of embryonic stem cells burns brighter than ever. If you claim to have made an anguished moral decision, and the factual basis for that decision turns out to be faulty, you ought to reconsider, or your claim to moral anguish looks phony. But Bush's moral anguish was suspect from the beginning because the policy it produced makes no sense.

The week-old embryos used for stem-cell research are microscopic clumps of cells, unthinking and unknowing, with fewer physical human qualities than a mosquito. Fetal-tissue research has used brain cells from aborted fetuses, but this is not that. Week-old, lab-created embryos have no brain cells.

Furthermore, not a single embryo dies because of stem-cell research, which simply uses a tiny fraction of the embryos that live and die as a routine part of procedures at fertility clinics. And actual stem-cell therapy for real patients, if it is allowed to develop, will not even need these surplus embryos. Once a usable line is developed from an embryo, the cells for treatment can be developed in a laboratory.

None of this matters if you believe that a microscopic embryo is a human being with the same human rights as you and me. George W. Bush claims to believe that, and you have to believe something like that to justify your opposition to stem-cell research. But Bush cannot possibly believe that embryos are full human beings, or he would surely oppose modern fertility procedures that create and destroy many embryos for each baby they bring into the world. Bush does not oppose modern fertility treatments. He even praised them in his anti-stem-cell speech.

It's not a complicated point. If stem-cell research is morally questionable, the procedures used in fertility clinics are worse. You cannot logically outlaw the one and praise the other. And surely logical coherence is a measure of moral sincerity.

If he's got both his facts and his logic wrong—and he has—Bush's alleged moral anguish on this subject is unimpressive. In fact, it is insulting to the people (including me) whose lives could be saved or redeemed by the medical breakthroughs Bush's stem-cell policy is preventing.

This is not a policy disagreement. Or rather, it is not only a policy disagreement. If the president is not a complete moron—and he probably is not—he is a hardened cynic, staging moral anguish he does not feel, pandering to people he cannot possibly agree with, and sacrificing the future of many American citizens for short-term political advantage.

Is that a good enough reason to dislike him personally?

## THE RELIGIOUS SUPERIORITY COMPLEX

Time, *Nov. 3, 2003*

"I knew that my god was bigger than his," said Lieut. General William Boykin, Deputy Under Secretary of Defense for Intelligence, referring to a Somali warlord he once crossed swords with. The echo of a famous dog-food commercial was unintentional, we must hope. Presumably, Boykin's God does not eat Ken-L Ration. But maybe Boykin does so himself, because he's a mighty frisky fella.

Boykin was caught on videotape speaking to church groups and saying things like, "The enemy is a guy called Satan." And, "They're after us because we're a Christian nation." Now—like so many Christian soldiers before him, sent to distant lands to bring the pagans around to our point of view—he's in hot water. Only this time it's the forces of Western civilization, not the natives, who want him for lunch.

Among other problems, Boykin's theo-babble muddies the waters of moral outrage over the latest rantings by the Prime Minister of Malaysia, Mahathir Mohamad, whose mouth is like a radio station where the anti-Semitic golden oldies never stop. Jews "rule the world by proxy." They "invented socialism, communism, human rights and democracy so that persecuting them would appear to be wrong." (Figure that one out!) The media don't report his criticism of Muslims, he explained, because Jews control the media. And so on. In fact, until the last outburst, Mahathir got great press as a supposedly moderate Muslim leader, although his views on Jews are not new. He was President Bush's poster boy for Muslim moderation.

Bush's moral outrage at both Mahathir and Boykin has been oddly muted. He claims to have told Mahathir that saying Jews succeed at the expense of Muslims is "wrong and divisive." Mahathir claims that Bush only apologized in private for having to criticize him in public, "unless my hearing is very bad." Which, he tartly added, it isn't. About Boykin, Bush said that the general's remarks "didn't reflect my opinion." The Pentagon has begun an official investigation into Boykin's remarks. What there is to investigate is a puzzle.

Everyone who gets caught in one of these ethno-controversies privately believes that he or she is being punished for having had the guts to tell a harsh truth. Any apology he or she coughs up, as Boykin did, only reinforces this feeling. No doubt even Mahathir has friends and sycophants who are telling him, "Mo, you're just a victim of political correctness. What is this world coming to when a simple Prime Minister can't say the Jews control everything without people making a ridiculous fuss?"

Bush ought to be furious at Boykin, because, until now, greater understanding and embrace of Islam have been real achievements of the Bush Administration. Even as America's victory in the Iraq war turns to ash, Bush can take pride that Americans have a greater appreciation that Muslims and their religion add to the richness of our great ethnic stew. And without Bush's special emphasis, the opposite might easily have happened.

At the same time, Bush has described the war on terror from the beginning in Manichaean terms not all that different from Boykin's. "Today, our nation saw evil," he said on Sept. 11, 2001. "Freedom and fear, justice and cruelty, have always been at war, and we know that God is not neutral between them," he told the nation nine days later. Boykin may be understandably perplexed about what line he crossed by referring to evil as "a guy called Satan."

As a devout believer, Boykin may also wonder why it is impermissible to say that the God you believe in is superior to the God you don't believe in. I wonder this same thing as a nonbeliever: Doesn't one religion's gospel logically preclude the others'? (Except, of course, where they overlap with universal precepts, such as not murdering people, that even we nonbelievers can wrap our heads around.) Although Boykin's version of Christianity seems less like monotheism than the star of a high school polytheism tournament, his basic point is that Christianity is right and Islam is wrong.

Doesn't the one imply the other? Pretending that my religion is no better than your religion may make for fewer religious wars, but it seems contrary to the very idea of religion. For this, you take a leap of faith?

Boykin's mistake was to put all these pieces together, implying that Islam itself is not merely mistaken but evil. Talking like this while in a U.S. military uniform was also pretty tactless. Mahathir's mistake, by contrast, was to open his trap at all.

## ATTACK GEOGRAPHY

### HEY, BUDDY, WHO DO YOU THINK YOU'RE CALLING "BUCOLIC"?

Slate, *Nov. 20, 2003*

Republicans have had a talent for geographical chauvinism since Nixon's southern strategy. Wherever a Democratic candidate happens to be from, that place turns out to be isolated and unrepresentative and not part of the real America. They are having a good time at the moment dissing Vermont, home of former Gov. Howard Dean. It's way up there in the Northeast somewhere. (Yeah, not too far south of the Bush family hangout in Maine.) It doesn't have any black people. Its best-known product is some hippie ice cream. Worst of all, it's (gasp!) "bucolic."

Odd, but I don't recall these points being made by any politician, Republican or Democrat, about New Hampshire, which is adjacent to Vermont. In the next few months, as always in election years, we will be hearing repeatedly about what a wonderful place New Hampshire is. Second only to Iowa. But, Vermont—now, that's a different story.

In 1988, Republicans painted Massachusetts as a foreign country and Democratic candidate Michael Dukakis as an elitist, compared with that po' boy from Texas, the elder George Bush. Massachusetts, to its credit, is a bit south of Vermont. On the other hand, it is full of universities. Need we say more?

When Bill Clinton emerged as Democratic front-runner in 1992, Republicans went to work denigrating Arkansas. "A failed governor of a small state," was the sound bite summary. "Failed" was disputable, and disputed. "Small" was beyond dispute. But so what? "Mine is bigger than yours" is the subtext of a lot that goes on in politics, but getting all puffed up about the size of your state seems especially ridiculous. Should mothers in small states go back to their children and say, "Sorry, I was wrong. You can't grow up to be president. Our state's too small"?

The semiserious notion here is that the governor of a small state hasn't done as much raw governing as the governor of a large state. If we're measuring governorship by the inch, though, we had better note that George W. Bush was governor for six years, whereas Dean was governor for eleven years—almost twice as long. So, measuring a governorship in population years, Bush of Texas (population at the last census: 20.85 million) scores 125 million, whereas Dean of Vermont (population: 609,000) scores, um, 6.7 million. Well, OK, but measuring in square-mile years of governorship, Bush of Texas (268,000 square miles) scores 1.6 million, whereas Dean of Vermont (9,600 square miles) scores . . . gosh, it really is a small state, isn't it?

Bush ought to sympathize with Dean a bit, though, because Dean is now getting the same grief that Bush got four years ago for the effrontery of being a governor at all. Governors have no foreign policy experience, it is said. How can they run for president when they've never been to Botswana? Senators, by contrast, know Washington. They know NATO. They may even know Botswana. But do they know how to run anything larger than their own offices? Even the state of Vermont is bigger than most congressional staffs, probably.

The experience of being president surely is more like the experience of running Vermont than it is like being, say, a member of the U.S. Senate. Senators, like journalists, enjoy jobs with a wonderful ratio of respectability to responsibility. There's a lot of the first, not much of the second. You can huff and puff all day, people are inclined to take you seriously, but if you're talking nonsense, no one gets hurt. Usually. A governor or a president, by contrast, makes decisions, and things tend to happen as a result. Usually. This can be disorienting and dangerous to a novice.

When they were going after Clinton, they portrayed Arkansas as the last place you would want your president from. Why? Well, it's in the South—out of the American mainstream. It's full of poor people. Everyone's married to his cousin. They eat horrible, fatty lower-class foods. My dear, it's Hicksville, plain and simple. Read your Faulkner—these people are sicko.

But now Vermont is in last place. Why? It's in New England—out of the American mainstream. There aren't enough poor people there. Everyone's married to her girlfriend—or will be soon. They eat horrible, fatty upper-class cheese. And, of course, that hoity-toity ice cream. Man, it's Snotsville. Read your Cheever or your John O'Hara—the guy really comes from Park Avenue after all. These people are wacko.

Dean does hail from New York City and state, which were still fairly large at the most recent census. But in the attack geography game, multiple locations are a subtractive process. Having experienced two places makes Dean doubly isolated from his country. The GOP will be making meat out of Dean's New York background, too. They will have a harder time of it since they have chosen to hold their convention in New York next summer. This was a cynical decision, intended to provide a backdrop for yet one more presidential victory lap in the war on terrorism. The cynicism may have been premature. But does anyone remember 1992? (Answer: No, of course not. I proceed anyway.) In that year there was a lot of Republican sneeriness over the Democrats' decision to hold their convention in New York. New York, it seemed, was not the real America. Urban. Ethnic. Noisy, crowded, dirty. The real America was . . . was . . . perhaps the word they were searching for back then was "bucolic." Like Vermont. The Republicans went to Houston that year. Now, I ask you.

The appropriate sentiment at this point is that we all live in the real America and share . . . something. What a generation of attack geography actually demonstrates is that none of us live in the real America. There is no part of the country that cannot be portrayed, with some accuracy, as a sealed society out of touch with the rest of the country. In fact, attack geography depends on this very ignorance and disdain wherever it decrees the Real America to be in this election cycle.

But whoever thought "bucolic" would be a fighting word?

## WHEN GOOD NEWS IS BAD NEWS

THE POLITICS OF MIXED EMOTIONS.

Slate, *Dec. 18, 2003*

It's a familiar human predicament. Dear old Aunt Maude—dear, rich old Aunt Maude—has staged a remarkable recovery. The doctors say she could live another thirty years. You are delighted, of course. And yet you can't help thinking about the money.

The Democratic presidential candidates woke up Sunday morning to learn that U.S. forces had captured Saddam Hussein. O joy! O joy! O ****! You cannot blame them for having mixed emotions. How long do you suppose each one spent relishing the good news for the world before dwelling on the bad news for their own political futures? And how long did President Bush spend savoring the boon for Iraqis before he started to savor the boon for his re-election campaign? It's obviously less of a challenge, though, to be and/or appear sincere when good news for the world is good news for you personally.

How to deal with mixed emotions is a bigger challenge to politicians than to the rest of us for a couple of reasons. One is that being and/or appearing concerned for the greater good is a basic qualification for their jobs. You cannot win an election if the voters suspect that you are wishing them ill, gleeful when bad things happen, and disappointed when things turn out well. Even admitting to mixed feelings—which are only human—would kill your ambitions. And yet almost any development in the news during an election campaign creates a similar dilemma for everyone except the incumbent.

It's the Law of Mixed Emotions: If you're the challenger, what's good for the voters is bad for you, and what's bad for the voters is good for you. When the stock market goes down, it buoys you up. When the market goes up, it brings you down. Or at least part of you must feel this way. There may be politicians so pure of heart that such cynical thoughts never cross their minds. But I certainly would not want anyone so wonderful representing me. Nor would I trust such an angel to protect my interests in this cold world.

So if you're a politician, how should you deal with good news that's bad news? Howard Dean's comments this week offer both a negative and a positive case study. He broke the most obvious rule: Pretend, at least, that you're enjoying the party. Don't stint or quibble. It may well be true, as Dean said, that capturing Saddam doesn't make America any safer than if he'd been left cowering in his spider hole for the next fifty years. The Bush administration certainly had given us the impression until this week that it believed the important thing was toppling him from power, not running him physically into the ground. But that's just cheap irony. Save it for the pundits. To be presidential, look gracious.

On the other hand, Dean won points in my book for another bit of straight talk. After calling Saddam's capture "a great day" for the military, for Iraqis, and for Americans generally, he added that it was "frankly, a great day for the administration." This is a rare example of a politician saying "frankly" and then saying something actually frank. It comes close to admitting the obvious: that this development helps Bush's chance of winning next year's election and therefore hurts Dean's.

It's a real mystery why politicians find it so hard to admit the obvious about the horse-race aspects of politics. No doubt it requires a dose of blind optimism to be a politician in the first place. Even Dennis Kucinich must think he has a 1-in-10,000 chance of becoming president, when his chance is actually much smaller. But there is also an annoying convention that you must pretend to a confidence you don't feel. Anyone who doesn't realize that this week's news has been a big boost for Bush's re-election is too stupid or blinded to be elected president. Yet the press will punish any candidate who says so, possibly because if the candidates take up stating the obvious, they're stealing our material. The pols need to be coy and evasive so that we can tell it to you straight.

Virtually every Democratic candidate, including Dean, followed another puzzling convention of American politics by saying that the capture of Saddam was a reason, or at least an occasion, to draw in other nations. Their most common complaint about the war has been that it isn't "multilateral." It's hard to see how this argument is affected one way or another by finding Saddam in a hole. (Well, this macho triumph by George W. seems to have cowed the Europeans and made them more cooperative—but that presumably was not the point his opponents were trying to make.)

Politicians reacting to a surprise in the news are always declaring that the unexpected development makes them believe even more deeply in the wisdom and urgency of whatever they have been saying all along. Bush inherited huge surpluses, and he called for a tax cut. Now there are huge deficits, and he calls for a tax cut.

Even when the cause-and-effect connection isn't totally implausible, a politician taking this line usually looks silly. If you had asked John Kerry a week ago whether it was even possible for him to feel more strongly than he already did about the need for a more "globalized" approach to the situation in Iraq, he probably would have said it isn't possible. He felt very, very, very strongly about it last week. Now we are supposed to believe that he feels very, very, very, very strongly. Is there any development that could make him feel only very, very strongly—or even make him change his mind?

# 2004

## Novak Agonistes

Slate, *Jan. 2, 2004*

Certain dramas are re-enacted again and again in Washington, like the Passion Play at Oberammergau. Or Groundhog Day. Or those huge Renaissance paintings on the walls of art museums. The Washington drama of the current moment involves two such familiar plot lines. Independently, they are the stuff of high seriousness. Together, they become farce.

So, imagine two giant canvases side by side. One is called "The Demand for a Special Prosecutor." It features a choir of angels in white robes. A light shining down from heaven reveals them to be editorial writers, the heads of non-profit good-government groups, and politicians of the opposition party. These angels all point an accusing finger at a figure cowering at the bottom right. This is the attorney general (generally portrayed as an animal, half-snake and half-jackass). In the background are mini-tableaux of various past scandals and present accusations.

The other canvas is called "The Reporter Protecting His Sources," and it shows columnist Robert Novak, dressed in a tunic, standing defiantly at the mouth of a cave. One hand thrusts forward in a gesture of "Halt!" The other hand squeezes his pursed lips. In the darkness behind him, we can just make out the presence of bodies—his sources—writhing in fear of exposure. In the foreground, helmeted and breast-plated soldiers prepare to cart him off to jail.

As you probably know, Novak wrote last July that "two senior administration officials" had told him that a woman named Valerie Plame was a CIA agent. The White House was furious at Plame's husband, former Ambassador Joseph Wilson, for publicly dissing President Bush's State of the Union assertion that Saddam Hussein was importing uranium from Africa. Wilson had led the investigation of the uranium question. The Bushies apparently thought it would be clever revenge to reveal that Plame had helped Wilson to get this assignment. (What kind of man lets his wife send him out for uranium?) Whoever talked to Novak either didn't consider or didn't care that revealing the name of a covert intelligence agent is against the law.

Democrats, of course, have been milking the issue. Novak, of course, says he will go to jail rather than reveal his sources. The Bush administration, of course, resisted calls for a special or independent prosecutor to investigate the leak and, of course, ultimately relented. On Tuesday, Attorney General John Ashcroft announced that he will recuse himself from the investigation. A semi-independent outside counsel will take over.

The Justice Department has already been beavering away for months on the Plame leak. There are four full-time prosecutors on the case. Their staffs have "sift[ed] through thousands of e-mails and documents." Dozens of White House officials have been interviewed. Now the independent counsel will start all over. This is costing millions of taxpayer dollars. All in pursuit of a question to which Bob Novak—a journalist whose vast output of writing and twenty-three-hours-a-day TV schedule ordinarily leave little opportunity for the unexpressed thought or unreported factoid—has the answer. Apparently so do several other Washington journalists who were similarly approached with the Plame story, according to the *Washington Post*.

The attitude of all right-thinking people about these developments is accurately reflected in the *New York Times* editorial page. The *Times* greeted Ashcroft's announcement with an editorial headlined, "The Right Thing, At Last." It complained of "an egregiously long delay" and worried that "we may never know what damage" these two months of inaction may have caused.

The *Times* is also an ardent defender of special legal protections for journalists. (Its name is on the seminal Supreme Court ruling in this area, 1964's *New York Times v. Sullivan*, which gave reporters limited immunity from libel laws.) *Times* editorials have celebrated the expansion of these protections and deplored attempts to scale them back. A very distinguished *New York Times* writer once told me that if the *Times* ballet critic, heading home after assessing the day's offerings of pliés and glissades, happens to witness a murder on her way to the Times Square subway, she has a First Amendment right and obligation to refuse to testify about what she saw.

So, put it all together and you get: 1) the anonymity of Novak's sources must be protected at all costs for the sake of the First Amendment; and 2) the White House leakers must be exposed and punished at all costs for the sake of national security. Unfortunately for the striking of heroic postures, these two groups are the same people. Either we think they should be named, or we think they should not be named. Which is it?

It is no solution to say, as some do, that it is journalist's job to protect the identity of his or her sources and it is the government's job to expose them. This isn't a game. There is no invisible hand to guarantee that the struggle of competing forces will achieve the correct balance. Journalists ought to be concerned about national security, and government officials ought to be concerned about the First Amendment. When these interests conflict, those involved ought to have an obligation to strike the balance for themselves.

The purpose of protecting the identity of leakers is to encourage future leaks. Leaks to journalists, and the fear of leaks, can be an important restraint on misbehavior by powerful institutions and people. This serves the public interest. But there is no public interest in leaks that harm national security, or leaks that violate the law, or leaks intended to harm blameless individuals. There is no reason to want more of these kinds of leaks. So, there is no reason to protect the identity of such bad-faith leakers.

From a distance, it smells as if the national security hoop-de-do about the Valerie Plame leak is exaggerated. On the other hand, the personal malevolence and Borgia-like scheming behind the leak is impressive. I'm not sure where I would come out on protecting the source of this leak. But it doesn't matter where I would come out because I don't know who the leakers were. Novak and others do know. They should either tell us who or tell us why not.

## BLIND, DEAF, AND LAME

NO ONE LISTENED TO PAUL O'NEILL. HERE'S WHY.

Slate, *Jan. 15, 2004*

"Paul, I'll be blunt," said Alan Greenspan to Paul O'Neill in January 2001, according to Paul O'Neill. "Your zipper's undone, and you have something hanging from your nose." No, actually, says O'Neill, the Fed chairman told him, "Paul, I'll be blunt. We really need you down here."

That's blunt? Yes, because O'Neill, you see, did not want to be secretary of the treasury. According to *The Price of Loyalty* (written by journalist Ron Suskind, but entirely from O'Neill's point of view), he preferred life at his "tasteful, sprawling colonial" in Pittsburgh, and he felt that Washington had become infested with politics and corruption since he first worked there in the prelapsarian innocence of the Nixon administration. "As one of the country's most Washington-savvy CEO's he was bored by the process of influence-peddling that keeps the lights on in this town." That's why he needed to be romanced. "Paul," Greenspan pressed on—batting his eyelashes seductively (or so one imagines the scene) and perhaps bringing out his saxophone for a few bars of "Stardust"—"Paul, your presence will be an enormous asset in the creation of sensible policy."

O'Neill, according to O'Neill, is a man on whom praise and compliments fall thick as a winter snowstorm. "Paul, you have the balls of a daylight burglar," he quotes a subordinate as telling him years ago. He also quotes himself telling the story to another subordinate. Elsewhere he recounts, with prim disapproval, watching George W. Bush call on White House Chief of Staff Andy Card to rustle up some cheeseburgers. O'Neill believes, he says, that a CEO should be judged by how he treats "whoever is at the very bottom," a remark Card may find somewhat more insulting than the cheeseburgers that inspired it. Later, with characteristic subtlety, O'Neill quotes himself offering to get his secretary a cup of coffee. Very nice. But she might be thinking that getting her own coffee—or even getting his—would be a small price to pay if it meant not having to hear and praise the boss' self-congratulatory anecdotes again and again.

Asked to be treasury secretary, O'Neill is filled with foreboding. He alerts the president-elect about his legendary reputation for straight talk. "In 1986, I gave a speech that was reported in the *Atlanta Journal-Constitution*. . . ." he begins. Thus forewarned, in more ways than one, Bush offers him the job anyway, and O'Neill decides his country needs him. "I think I'm going to have to do this," he tells his wife. Among other reasons, O'Neill feels called upon to play ambassador between the new president and his father, the former president. "He was uniquely qualified to finesse this delicate and defining relationship." His unique qualifications included having never even met George W. except for once, briefly, at President Clinton's education summit in 1996.

Describing his time as treasury secretary, O'Neill sounds, of course, like Capt. Renault. But the character in *Casablanca* was a cynic who knew perfectly well that there was gambling going on in Rick's cafe. O'Neill seems genuinely surprised to discover that Bush actually does intend to cut taxes (as he promised repeatedly in his campaign); that the administration wants "regime change" in Iraq (as did the previous administration and almost everyone else in the world—the question was what to do about it); that the president would, on balance, prefer to be re-elected; and so on. Not a single weapon of mass destruction was wheeled into his office during his entire two-year tenure.

It's true that George W. Bush has turned out to be a more radical president than everyone predicted. But O'Neill has no insights about why it turned out this way or why we should have seen it coming. His theme, in fact, is that he was blindsided more than anyone. O'Neill deserves the credit for the Bush presidency's most pleasant surprise—serious financial and diplomatic engagement in the battle against AIDS in Africa—and he takes it. No doubt O'Neill would be responsible for Bush's new initiative to promote marriage on Mars, or whatever, if he were still there (in the administration, not on Mars).

Speaking of blindsided, howzabout that killer quote describing Bush in Cabinet meetings as being "like a blind man in a roomful of deaf people"? O'Neill says this is "the only way I can describe it," and I fear that may be the case. It's vivid, and it certainly sounds insulting enough. But what on Earth does it mean? According to the *New York Times* and the *Los Angeles Times*, it means Bush is "disengaged." The *Washington Post* story began, "President Bush showed little interest in policy discussions in his first two years in the White House, leading Cabinet meetings 'like a blind man in a roomful of deaf people.' . . ."

I'm sorry, but how is being uninterested in policy like being a blind man in a roomful of deaf people? Are blind people uninterested in policy? Or, more accurately, do blind people become less interested in policy when they find themselves in a room with deaf people? Does a blind man surrounded by deaf people talking policy issues think: "Oh, hell. These folks are going to go on and on and on about the problems of deaf people. Who needs that? I've got problems of my own." Is that O'Neill's point? And even if there is something about a room full of deaf people that makes a blind man disengage from policy issues, what does this have to do with President Bush and his Cabinet?

As described by Paul O'Neill, life inside the Bush administration is like life itself (according to Macbeth): "a tale told by an idiot, full of sound and fury, signifying nothing." The only solid punch he lands on President Bush is unintentional: What kind of idiot would hire this idiot as secretary of the treasury?

## "I'M NOT A QUITTER!"

CANDIDATES WHO CAN'T TAKE A HINT.

Slate, *Jan. 29, 2004*

NOTE: *On CNN the night of the New Hampshire primary, a spokeswoman for Joe Lieberman said with a straight face that the candidate was encouraged by his third-place showing in Greater Manchester.*

Q: Governor, in light of your seventh-place showing in five successive primaries, some people are saying it's time for you to withdraw from the race. What is your reaction to that?

A: Larry, the American people have spoken, and I have heard them loud and clear. They want change, they want leadership, and they demand accountability from all of us who have the privilege of asking for their votes for the highest office in this great country. To withdraw now, simply because the going is tough, would betray everything I stand for. I cannot let down my supporters in that way and still call myself "that krazy kick-ass comeback kid."

Q: Many people have been hoping you would stop calling yourself that anyway.

A: Well, they hope in vain. I am that krazy kick-ass comeback kid. I always have been and always will be. You have to be true to yourself, Larry, to who you really are. Because the American people can spot a faker. You know, Larry, unlike some of my rivals who went to fancy prep schools, my family didn't have a lot when I was growing up . . .

Q: Yes, we know, we know.

A: . . . we didn't have a lot of money for things like tracking polls and negative advertising. But my poppa used to say, "We don't need focus groups to tell us what's right." My parents raised me not to give up. I'm a fighter. And I'll keep on fighting for my message of hope and for the American people.

Q: But nobody's voting for you, Governor. At what point do you say, "They've heard my message and they just don't like it"?

A: How can they not like it? I mean, let's get real here. It's a message of hope and a message of change. It's a message with every cliché that's worked for every winning candidate of both parties. How can it not be working for me? I mean, let me ask you that. Why isn't it working? Why, why?

Q: You tell me, Governor. Why isn't it working?

A: Who says it's not working? It is working. It's working all over this country. It's working hard, just like the American people. And working people are responding to a message that works as hard as they do.

Q: They are? What's your evidence for that?

A: Larry, in the Nebraska primary, I came in third among Hispanic homeowners living in metropolitan Lincoln. That's an amazing showing for a white guy like me who rents a studio apartment.

Q: Your wife got the house, I believe.

A: That's right, Larry. Thanks for reminding me. But as I was saying, only a month ago I was coming in fourth among Hispanic homeowners in Lincoln, Neb. Yet I ended up a strong third in that crucial demographic. This says to me, "Kid, you've got the momentum.

Don't give up now!" Not that Hispanics or any other Americans can be reduced to the status of a demographic. They are people—never forget that. And people are what this election is all about, no matter what my opponents may say.

Q: How many Hispanic homeowners from Lincoln voted in the Nebraska Democratic primary?

A: Seven, although we're still waiting for Mrs. Menendez's absentee ballot.

Q: And weren't there only two other candidates on the ballot in Nebraska?

A: Yes, and they own two homes each, because they're rich. What's your point?

Q: Well, leaving Hispanic homeowners aside, how did you manage to finish fifth among three candidates?

A: There's a strong write-in tradition in Nebraska. In fact, we felt we were putting ourselves at a disadvantage by registering to appear on the ballot. But we did it because it was the right thing to do. Can we move on now?

Q: Don't you have to actually win some primary somewhere if you're going to claim your party's nomination?

A: I agree with you, that's the conventional wisdom. But we couldn't afford a lot of conventional wisdom when I was growing up. My mama used to say, "We don't need conventional wisdom. Homespun bromides will do just fine." And that's why I believe it's not over 'til it's over. Would it be better to win a primary than to lose all of them? Would it be better to come in second or third than fourth or fifth? And Larry, I truly believe we will come in a solid fourth in at least one of the fourteen primaries happening tomorrow.

Sure, a lower number like one or two is better than a higher number like four or five under the cockamamie and corrupt electoral system we operate under. That's one of the things that has to change in this country, if we're going to move into the twenty-first century. We face competition from other nations with much more sophisticated approaches to elections, such as not having them at all. In 2000, our own country tried the experiment of holding an election and ignoring the result. Many Democrats found that solution unsatisfactory. We must do better. For ourselves, for the world, and most importantly for our children.

When I am president, I will appoint a high-level commission to meet in secret and refuse subpoenas for documents. It will address this issue, along with all other issues that might arise during my presidency, so that I can concentrate on continuing to tell the American people how wonderful they are. Which they are, by the way. Some of my opponents in this primary season—and everyone in the other party—appear to believe that the American people are only wonderful during election years. When I am president, the American people will be wonderful all the time.

Q: Thank you, Governor. And America Votes 2004 continues. Coming up next: Our distinguished panel of journalists will discuss, Is there any way to stop this thing from becoming a foregone conclusion and giving us nothing to write about between now and the conventions? Don't go away. Please, please, don't go away. Wait! Come back. Come back . . .

## Take This Column, Please

Time, *April 4, 2004*

As the scythe of scandal continues to cut off the careers and other vital parts of reporters and editors at the nation's major newspapers, those of us who peddle opinions for a living rather than facts are starting to get nervous. When will the spotlight turn on us? Every time another malefactor is exposed, we feel a chill and think we hear the tumbrels roll. We know in our hearts that we are uniquely vulnerable.

We opinionistas are a diverse bunch: newspaper editorial writers draped in cardigan sweaters and clutching pipes, columnists dictating a few trenchant paragraphs on cell phones while striding self-importantly through Reagan National Airport, troll-like TV commentators with ill-fitting teeth, fat and angry radio talk-show hosts . . . We all agree on very little. But we share a common bewilderment about the venom attached to these recent accusations of plagiarism and fabrication.

What we don't get is this: If you're not supposed to take it from someone else and you're not supposed to make it up yourself, where are you supposed to get it? From this perspective, reporters have it easy. There is always something new to report. Life itself supplies a regular stream of events—roughly 3.2 billion an hour, according to scientists. With the advent of computers, it has become a simple matter to rank all events in order of their suitability as news, using the famous Gannett scale, developed by the well-known newspaper chain and involving such factors as the impact of an event on other events, the number of proper names that are difficult to spell (a negative factor), and the involvement of people from diverse backgrounds (a plus, obviously).

But pity the opinionmeister! Opinions don't flare and quickly die like fireworks. Opinions come and stay, leaving little room for new ones. There are only five opinions you can have about abortion, according to a report prepared for the Opinion League of America. There are only two possible opinions (sometimes characterized as yes and no) on capital punishment, just one on matters implicating the American flag. Under these circumstances, it would be annoying to be told that it is unacceptable for an opinion to be used more than once. Worse than annoying, it would be wasteful. Call it plagiarism if you like; we prefer to think of it as recycling. Facts are like air: they can be polluted, but there is no danger that we will actually run out of the stuff. Opinions, by contrast, are like water or oil: the danger of running out is real.

A confession: I have often lifted opinions from others, even from other members of the Opinion League itself. On the other hand, I have also invented opinions out of whole cloth. Before the ethics cops come to arrest me, let me point out one of the wonderful things about opinions: people who produce them like to have them stolen! Facts are very different in this regard. Let's say I find out and report that Attorney General John Ashcroft was on the golf course on 9/11 and finished the last three holes before helicoptering back to his office to start reading the Constitution, looking for loopholes. And suppose you publish a news story containing the same information, without crediting me. I would feel violated and accuse you of plagiarism. But suppose I express the opinion that Ashcroft is the finest Attorney General since John Mitchell. This certainly would be an original viewpoint. And suppose you echo it, even without credit. That is not plagiarism, that is influence! And I am not insulted, I am flattered. Furthermore, suppose I make up that story about the Attorney General, as indeed I did. A total fabrication, just like the alleged Gannett scale. I would be in trouble if I actually presented it as fact. On the other hand, if I dream up an equally far-fetched opinion about Ashcroft, people are likely to declare that they will defend to the death my right to possess it.

At a time when the U.S. faces an imminent flood of cheap foreign opinion from places like China (whose reasoning tends to break down at the first turn in the argument), it is vital for this country to protect opinion journalism from the jihad sweeping through the newsroom full of factniks down the hall. For this reason, the Opinion League of America has voted to merge with our traditional rivals, the International Brotherhood of Blowhards and Allied Trades. With some opinion production being outsourced to places like Bangladesh, where children as young as six or seven spend fifty or more hours a week expressing views on everything from international finance to local school-board elections, we need the Blowhards, and they need us. Together we will fight to protect the sacred right of opinion professionals to make up their opinions, steal them from others and do whatever else may be necessary to guarantee that Americans will continue to enjoy the finest opinions in the world.

## PARADISE LOST

New York Times Book Review, *May 23, 2004*

NOTE: *This is a review of* On Paradise Drive *by David Brooks. I regarded it as mixed at worst. Brooks regarded it as hostile. My wife agreed with Brooks. You be the judge.*

For several years, in the world of political journalism, David Brooks has been every liberal's favorite conservative. This is not just because he throws us a bone of agreement every now and then. Even the most poisonous propagandist (i.e., Bill O'Reilly) knows that trick. Brooks goes farther. In his writing and on television, he actually seems reasonable. More than that, he seems cuddly. He gives the impression of being open to persuasion. Like the elderly Jewish lady who thinks someone must be Jewish because "he's so nice," liberals suspect that a writer as amiable as Brooks must be a liberal at heart. Some conservatives think so too.

There is a prize for being the liberals' favorite conservative, and Brooks has claimed it: a column in the *New York Times*. With Brooks, the *Times* continues its probably unintentional experiment in reinventing the political column. First came Frank Rich, who added culture, high and low, to the traditional tired stew of Washington concerns. Maureen Dowd added psychiatry—trying to understand politicians as real people, usually not to their advantage. Thomas Friedman added parables, circling the globe in search of small but sturdy anecdotes to support huge structures of metaphor.

Brooks adds social anthropology. His distinctive combination of wisdom and wisecracks, now available to readers of this newspaper, was perfected in his previous book, Bobos in *Paradise*, a funny examination of the 1960's generation as it negotiates the twin perils of aging and prosperity. His new book, *On Paradise Drive: How We Live Now (and Always Have) in the Future Tense*, applies the Brooks technique to the whole darn country. He starts by slicing and dicing the American population into categories and subcategories, each with its own values and habits and sartorial preferences. Then he turns around and puts us all back together again, reinterpreting his previous examples of our differences as evidence of our essential similarity. It's a bravura performance and always entertaining, if not always convincing.

The Brooks sociological method has four components: fearless generalizing, clever coinage, jokes and shopping lists. In the April issue of *Philadelphia Magazine*, the journalist Sasha Issenberg nailed Brooks, a local boy, pretty hard on some of his generalizations. Checking out the assertions in a couple of magazine articles that were partly incorporated into this book, Issenberg reported that, contrary to Brooks, people in blue states (those that went Democratic in 2000) don't read more books than people in red (Republican) states. Nor do reds buy more items on QVC. "When it comes to yardwork," Brooks had written, "they have rider mowers; we have illegal aliens." Part of Brooks's charm is that he often includes himself (disingenuously, but that makes the gesture even grander) in groups he is mocking. But Issenberg reports that red states tend to have more illegal aliens than blue ones.

Brooks defends his generalizations as poetic hyperbole and got disappointingly pompous with Issenberg when confronted with their inaccuracy. But this won't do. When he says that a store in a suburban mall is "barely visible because of the curvature of the earth," that is poetic hyperbole. When he claims that it is impossible to spend more than $20 for dinner in a Red Lobster, that is just wrong, and mystifyingly so. As Issenberg points out, these little factoids are credibility crutches. They are the difference between sociology and shtick. America's cities needn't actually be full of "African bistros where El Salvadoran servers wearing Palestinian kaffiyehs serve Virginia Woolf wannabes Slovakian beer" in order to justify this typical Brooks formulation. But there ought to be one Salvadoran server somewhere who routinely wears a kaffiyeh—and I wonder if there is one.

At the very least, Brooks does not let the sociology get in the way of the shtick, and he wields a mean shoehorn when he needs the theory to fit the joke. Among some of the formerly young, "the energy that once went into sex and raving now goes into salads." O.K., that's funny. So is essentially the same joke a few pages later, when Brooks writes that "bathroom tile is their cocaine." Except that now he's referring to a different one of his demographic slices, which undermines the claim to sociology. And when another joke surfaces three times, it undermines the shtick as well. The "16-foot refrigerators with the through-the-door goat cheese and guacamole delivery systems"? Ha ha. A large Home Depot salesman "looking like an S.U.V. in human form"? Ha ha ha. S.U.V.'s "so big they look like the Louisiana Superdome on wheels"? Enough already.

"In America, it is acceptable to cut off any driver in a vehicle that costs a third more than yours. That's called democracy." True? Funny? Wouldn't the joke work just as well the other way? ". . . a third less than yours. That's called capitalism." And if it works both ways as a joke, it must not work at all as a sociological insight.

In his fondness for coining phrases and his show-off use of commercial brand names as shorthand for demographic nuances, Brooks clearly takes after the country's greatest living conservative social observer, Tom Wolfe. Like the factoid bubbles so skillfully burst in

*Philadelphia Magazine*, the brand names are there as evidence that you're not talking through your hat. So the nuances had better be right. As far as I know, most of Brooks's are. As far as I know is not very far in some shopping areas. I must take his word about Corian countertops. But in the case of Trader Joe's, to which Brooks devotes a multipage riff, I feel more at home. And Brooks has failed to solve the mystery of this appealing but hard-to-define California-based food chain.

The term "Bobos" (short for "bourgeois bohemians") almost joined Tom Wolfe classics like "the right stuff" and "radical chic" in the Coinage Hall of Fame. The test of a successful coinage (I state with Brooksian bluff-authority) is whether many people use the term without knowing where it came from. If "Bobos" ultimately fell short, keep in mind that the challenge was daunting. It would have had to displace a beloved and long-established incumbent— "yuppies"—describing roughly the same phenomenon. The near miss must have hurt. In his new book, Brooks flings coinage after coinage up against the zeitgeist, hoping that one will stick. Among the more promising contenders are the "crunchy zone" (one of his suburban slices), the "meatloaf line" (between distant suburbs, where they allegedly don't eat meatloaf, and real rural America, where they do), "Patio Man" (from an already famous Brooksian epic about purchasing a barbecue at Home Depot) and "conquest shopping" (from the same saga).

When he turns from the task of subdividing Americans to the task of stitching us back together, Brooks becomes as incomprehensible as the subtitle of this book. (What does it mean to "live in the future tense"?) Near as I can tell, Brooks's argument is a variation on the famous Turner thesis. The historian Frederick Jackson Turner wrote in 1893, just as America's western expansion was more or less complete, that the empty West had served as the country's defining fact and safety valve. The ever-present possibility of picking up and moving west had made Americans free and equal, and had spared us the conflicts of class and nation that infected the Old World of Europe.

Brooks's thesis—to give it more clarity than he does, at the risk of getting it wrong—seems to be that the suburbs and exurbs play a similar role in twenty-first-century America. Although sometimes he seems to be saying that the "move on" energy of Americans comes from technology like the Internet, or is more spiritual than geographical or material anyway. In any event, our defining—and uniting—characteristics as Americans, according to Brooks, are that we'd rather leave than fight, and we're always thinking about the future instead of dwelling on the past. That means the enormous gulfs in values, aspirations, understanding of the world and food preferences he outlines so wittily in the first part of *On Paradise Drive* don't turn Americans against one another (as they would the folks of some clotted and backward Old World nation). We all prosper in our various cultural cul-de-sacs (or as Brooks puts it, much better: "Everybody can be an aristocrat within his own Olympus"), and we don't trouble ourselves about what the folks in the next cul-de-sac might be up to. No skin off our backs.

The Brooks thesis, if I've got it right, is a lovely, sweet thesis, as genial as the author himself. But a better answer to the question of why, if Americans are so diverse, we get along so much better than those foreigners, might be, "What in the world are you talking about?" It certainly is not obvious that the spirit of live-and-let-live is stronger in America than elsewhere. The citizens of other countries at our economic level, like those in the old nations of Europe, seem generally better than we are, not worse, at not rubbing one another raw. Maybe that is because they know they will be rubbing up against one another in any case.

Brooks almost makes this point himself a while later: "America is not only the nation where you can get a supersize tub of French fries to go with our 32-ounce double cheeseburger, it is also just about the only nation where people blow up abortion clinics." But this comes while he is riffing about Americans' inclination toward excess, rather than our mystical ability to get along. So that's different.

Brooks has a wise and funny few pages turning the familiar golf concept of "par" into a universal suburban state of grace:

> Your DVD collection is organized, and so is your walk-in closet. Your car is clean and vacuumed, your frequently dialed numbers are programmed into your cordless phone, your telephone plan is suited to your needs, and your various gizmos interact without conflict. Your spouse is athletic, your kids are bright, your job is rewarding, your promotions are inevitable, everywhere you need to be comes with its own accessible parking. You look great in casual slacks.

Unfortunately, he couldn't resist doing practically the same clever thing with a remark from the autobiography of Ray Kroc, the founder of McDonald's, about the importance of French fries. Brooks conjures up a mystical concept called "Fry!," defined roughly as monomania about some business goal, preferably one that seems shallow or pointless in the larger scheme of things. This he also presents as a spiritual state of grace, and he credits the business executives who religiously "Follow Your Fry!" with America's economic success.

These riffs will not win prizes for internal consistency. In the Fry! discussion, there are detours into the culture of frequent flier points and the obsession with upgrades, among other topics. These are hilarious, but Brooks seems to forget his premise that Fry! is about monomania. That hardly matters if he's not trying to be serious. But he is trying to be serious, at least sometimes. He says he wants to rescue American civilization from the charge that it is shallow, and his main argument against that charge is that seemingly shallow behavior like shopping for the perfect barbecue or marketing the perfect French fry is actually a deeply spiritual quest, on a continuum with those of the Pilgrims arriving from the east and the pioneers heading west. We're certainly not going to buy that notion if the author himself can be distracted from it whenever the possibility of a good joke floats by.

"Is he serious?" is an interesting question about David Brooks. But a more important question, for Brooks himself and for all of humanity (now that he is a *Times* columnist), is "Is he conservative?" Although Brooks's mockery is genial rather than sneery and distancing like Tom Wolfe's, there is no doubt that if a professed liberal *New York Times* columnist, say Paul Krugman, were to describe the products and culture of capitalism the way Brooks does, his lines would be cited and denounced on every right-wing radio talk show.

When he ridicules consumer appetites, Brooks is safely within the permissible, rueful conservative critique of capitalism's "contradictions." When he writes of the "tediousness of pod after pod of the highway-side office parks" and the "sheer existential nothingness of an office-park lobby," he sounds quaintly like the cultural critics of American capitalism in the 1950's and 60's. But when he declares that hard-working business executives are living their "whole lives" in a furrow—"in that furrow, your personality becomes a mere selling device. Friendships become contacts. The urge to improve deteriorates to mere acquisitiveness. Money becomes the measure of accomplishment"—well, frankly, that sounds more than a bit like Karl Marx, doesn't it?

And it gets even worse. In an uncharacteristically heavy-handed passage, Brooks imagines an effete French intellectual confronting a straightforward, honest, rough-hewn Nevada trucker. Boy, does that Frog learn a thing or two. Brooks's complaint is not that the French hate Americans, but that they love us for the wrong reasons:

> Our eager openness to everything, our capacity for mindless fun. . . . The convertible nation, ripping off our tube tops, yipping like banshees as we cruise down the freeway from cineplex to surf shop. How charming! How wild! How seductive the Americans are, with all their careless money and ingenuous vitality!

Brooks calls this a "pro-American insult," but it is alarmingly close to his own pro-American critique. And when he goes on to imagine his French intellectual "posing like a great Gallic hunter" next to a "bon mot he has bagged on the American desert," the appalling truth becomes unavoidable.

David Brooks is not merely a liberal. He's French.

J'accuse.


## THE TROUBLE WITH OPTIMISM

Washington Post, *June 22, 2004*

Everyone agreed during the recent Reaganalia that one of Ronald Reagan's best qualities was optimism. For Reagan's longtime supporters, optimism is a key element in the official hagiography. He lifted the atmosphere of doom and "malaise" perpetrated by his predecessor, Jimmy Carter. For those who did not especially admire the late president when he was alive, this was something nice they could say in all sincerity, instead of or as an introduction to what they really thought of him.

Reagan's death took what was already a festival of optimism in American politics and turned it into an orgy. Optimism has long been on every short list of "quintessentially American" qualities. After Reagan's two sweeping victories, it became a great cliche of political analysis as well: The more optimistic candidate almost always wins. This insight is like those studies showing that the taller presidential candidate almost always wins (the 2004 election will be an interesting test of that one), with the crucial difference that you can't do much about your height. By contrast you can ladle on the optimism all you want. Thanks to Reagan, optimism is considered an essential ingredient of any presidential candidate's public self-presentation. They all say they have it; their opponents accuse them of lacking it. A typical American politician would sooner admit to being a bigamist than a pessimist.

The climactic TV commercial in President Bush's spring saturation bombing campaign against Sen. John Kerry is titled "Pessimism" and begins with Bush declaring, "I'm optimistic about America because I believe in the people of America"—a sentiment that would work just about as well the other way ("I believe in the people of America because I'm optimistic about America"). The ad then attempts to out Kerry as a pessimist, based on the evidence that he talks about the Great Depression. "One thing's sure," Bush's ad notes. "Pessimism never created a job." Meanwhile, Kerry is running an ad titled "Optimists," asserting that he is as optimistic as the next guy.

Could there be an emptier claim made on behalf of someone hoping to lead the United States of America than to say that he is "optimistic"?

Optimism may well be part of the American character, but it is pretty insufficient as either a campaign promise or a governing principle. If the objective situation calls for optimism, being optimistic isn't much of a trick or a distinction. If the objective situation calls for something closer to pessimism, the last thing we want is some Micawber whistling past the Treasury Department.

It's a bit of a cheat for the incumbent to accuse his opponent of pessimism. By the very nature of elections, the side in power is going to argue that things are going well, and the side in opposition is going to argue that things are going badly. It is awfully convenient for the side in power if the canons of optimism forbid any assertion that things are going badly—even if they are. That, of course, is the whole idea of Bush's optimism offensive. Kerry has brought up the Great Depression to point out that Bush, as of now, is the first president since then to suffer a net loss of jobs. Bush says the important issue here isn't the loss of jobs, or even the truth of Kerry's statement (which he doesn't challenge), but the very reference itself.

No one starts out as an incumbent. In 1980 even Ronald Reagan saw bleakness and defeat everywhere. The greatest alleged success of Reagan's presidency—victory in the Cold War—is widely misrepresented as a triumph of optimism. Even if you credit Reagan for that victory (which I don't), the rhetorical theme of his military buildup was pessimism, not optimism. It wasn't that communism just needed one last push, it was that communism was triumphing throughout the world. Democracy was in peril. The Soviets were on the verge of nuclear superiority. Complacency—misplaced optimism—is what the Reaganites accused their critics of.

As recently as the 2000 election, today's President Georgie Sunshine was eager to spread pessimism and gloom. And apparently he remained optimism-deficient until recently. What else can explain the job losses of his first three years as president?

We don't want a president who sees the silver lining in every cloud. We want a president who sees the cloud and dispels it. We want someone who will make the objective situation justify optimism, not someone who is optimistic in any objective situation. If optimism is hard-wired into the American character, it should be especially important to have someone sober at the wheel of the car. Of course, such clear-headedness is a hopeless ideal. But it is odd that politicians of every stripe now promise that their vision will be clouded.

And if forced to choose between a leader whose vision is clouded by optimism and one whose vision is clouded by pessimism, there is a good case that pessimism is the more prudent choice. Another name for pessimism is a tragic sensibility. It is a vivid awareness that things can go wrong, and often have. An optimist thinks he can pop over to Iraq, knock Saddam Hussein off his perch, establish democracy throughout the Middle East, and be home in time for dinner. A pessimist knows better.

## A GOOD EDITORIAL

*Unpublished, June 23, 2004*

NOTE: *This was a memo to the editorial writers of the* Los Angeles Times, *written when I started my job there as editorial and opinion editor. It got a very chilly reception.*

These are some thoughts about what makes a good editorial. They are supposed to be the start of a discussion, which I hope we will continue via email. I also hope to start a similar discussion about the op-ed page and the Sunday section. Most of this is nothing new, and none of it is meant as criticism of the page now. And none of it is a hard-and-fast rule. No doubt many brilliant editorials violate all of these guidelines except the big one I start with.

The essential quality of any piece of opinion journalism is intellectual honesty. Intellectual honesty is to an editorial or op-ed what factual accuracy is to a news story: the gold standard. Obviously editorials should be accurate, and news stories should be honest. But a dishonest argument rots an opinion piece even more than a factual error does. Intellectual honesty includes things like:

- Sincerity (do you truly believe what you're writing?)
- Coherence (have you thought hard and thought it through?)
- Consistency, or Sauce for the Goose (does this opinion fit with your opinions on other matters? are you prepared to apply the same logic in circumstances where it leads to a less agreeable conclusion?)
- Skepticism (have you considered the counterarguments?)

An unsigned editorial is a particular type of opinion piece. What is the point of this somewhat odd genre? To express the view of the newspaper, obviously. Except that the newspaper, in all its other pages, prides itself on having no view. So in a way, it makes even less sense for a newspaper to produce an official or semi-official opinion on the issues of the day than for, say, an auto company or a restaurant chain to do so. These businesses at least have no business interest in being thought unopinionated.

And why should anyone care about an opinion expressed in an unsigned editorial? Many people don't care. The editorial page is often one of the least read parts of a newspaper. It is published to some degree as an indulgence of tradition. Our goal should be to make editorials more valuable to the reader and therefore to the company. A signed opinion piece can draw readers with its style or with its author's reputation. It may be possible for an unsigned editorial to have similar appeal, but it certainly is harder. A better approach (or so it seems to me) is for editorials to offer something clearly different from signed opinion pieces. Something readers also cannot get from news stories and analysis.

What is that something? Call it maybe "order in the universe." The editorial page should be a place readers want to come to for a sense (inevitably false, but genuinely attempted) that someone has it all figured out. That despite the chaos of the news and the cacophony of the op-ed page, a general understanding of the way the world is and a coherent opinion of how it ought to be are both possible. Editorials have unsung advantages over news stories, and even so-called news "analysis": they are allowed to state facts as a given, without the citations and quotations and counter-quotes required by the conventions of news writing. And, of course, they are not required to come to a screeching halt before tumbling into a conclusion. Even their brevity can be an advantage, if it forces concision.

In short, a good editorial is one that explains and clarifies an issue in the news. It can—in fact it should—have an opinion. But ideally it also should give readers the understanding they need to disagree intelligently. Here are some of the specific elements of a good editorial:

1. A framework of analysis. You can't always cover the big picture when you're reacting to some specific controversy or event, but you can try to hint at it. And you should have it in mind whether you are able to discuss it or not. Over time, the editorial page should have a coherent worldview in which, e.g., our view on driver's licenses for illegal immigrants fits in with our position on immigration policy in general, which in turn fits with our views on trade, on the minimum wage, and so on. This is a matter of intellectual honesty and disci-

pline, but it also is a marketing tool. The world is a puzzle, and we'll show you how all the pieces fit together.

2. An intellectual problem. ("Intellectual" just means a problem that needs to be solved by reasoning. It needn't be hoity-toity.)
- The problem should arise from the news, or from some larger public concern. No doubt there are brilliant editorials awakening readers to issues that have been wrongly ignored. But the usual effect of trying to make the readers care about an issue in order to tell them what to think about it is the opposite of awakening.
- Disagreement. If no one or almost no one disagrees, it also is probably not a good subject for an editorial. Of course events sometimes require commemoration but defy argument—tragic natural disasters, for instance. But even when unavoidable, such editorials are likely to be boring.

3. An analysis and argument.
- The argument should be intellectually honest, as per above.
- It should be consistent with what we have said before on this issue and others. If it departs from previous editorials, this should be acknowledged and explained. There are only two possible explanations: circumstances have changed, or we have decided that we were wrong. If it is the second, the editorial should say so and say why.
- The argument should address the core of the problem, not some side issue—even if in practice the side issue could be determinative. In an editorial, there is no point in winning the argument on a technicality. The point is to help people understand. Editorials about small aspects of a larger problem should illuminate the larger problem.
- "Polls show that people overwhelmingly support our position" is not an argument. The goal of an editorial is to affect public opinion, not to reflect it. In fact, if people overwhelmingly support the position we think is correct, there may be no need for an editorial. The work has been done. On the other hand, we will often want to take positions that are not supported by public opinion, and we don't concede that this makes our argument invalid.
- "Experts support our position" is also not an argument. Ditto

organizations of almost any sort. If someone or some group has a persuasive point, or useful information, there is nothing wrong with borrowing these and citing the source. But the unadorned fact that someone shares your conclusion rarely belongs in an editorial. Making a decision based on endorsements is a (sometimes necessary) substitute for thinking it through yourself. An editorial should think it through.

4. A conclusion. The problem should be solved, at least to our satisfaction.
- There should be a "should" or a call to action.
- The call to action does not have to be directed necessarily to a person who actually reads the *Los Angeles Times*. But it should be aimed at someone within our general sphere of influence who might plausibly take the action being recommended. (The *Economist* is always calling on the Taliban to adopt capitalist democracy, and so on. Avoid that.)
- The following, or variants, do not count as conclusions:
  - "There are no easy answers" or "only time will tell" or the right answer "remains to be seen." Any question with more than one easy answer probably shouldn't be the subject of an editorial in the first place.
  - Delay, further study, or anything involving a panel of experts.
  - The parties involved should lay aside their differences, or negotiate in good faith.
  - "Fundamental reform is needed" may sometimes be the correct conclusion, but should be used sparingly, because it's anticlimactic. Think about changing topics.

5. Clarity over cleverness! Editorials are the voice of the group, or even the institution. And their goal is understanding and persuasion on difficult issues. So the structure should be straightforward, and the voice should be fairly consistent across different authors. Don't deny yourself a really good joke or pleasing turn of phrase. But show restraint.
Some specific small tips:
- It isn't essential that every editorial be structured as problem/argument/conclusion, but that's not a bad general model.
- Avoid backing in to the subject with a discursive lead about the

weather or the last time this regulatory body was enmeshed in controversy.

- Avoid making your real message the "but" of a sentence that starts out saying the opposite. (Two bullets up, see an example of what not to do.)
- Don't assume that the readers are familiar with the topic, but don't assume either that they need to be made familiar with it in all its glorious detail.

6. Concision.

- Try to avoid a lot of who-struck-John about how the committee voted and who might be replaced and how it used to work before the notorious 1954 reforms. Write about the substantive issue, not about the process.
- Avoid color and human interest. You need every line you've got to explain why drug-testing regulations are excessive, or inadequate. You do not have space for Mary Doe, forty-seven, of San Luis Obispo, who took a pill and almost died, or was cured, or whatever.
- Use the editorial writer's privilege: you don't need to buttress every assertion with a quote from someone else. The premise of an editorial is that you, the writer, are the voice of authority. If the reader doesn't trust your judgment more than that of Helene Knightly, chairwoman of Citizens for Cleaner Mailboxes, or Professor Roger Jordan of the University of Manitoba Pocket Nuclear Bomb Lab, there's no point.

7. Topics. We publish three (or so) editorials every day. Ask yourself, is this one of the three most important things a responsible citizen needs to be thinking about tomorrow? Or if not, is it one of the three most interesting things an active mind wants to be thinking about? If neither, why are we writing about it?

- Unless it is something like the 9/11 Commission, the fact that a group has issued a report is rarely a good topic. Especially if all we have to say is that the report is interesting and/or we agree with it.
- Ditto the meeting of some group, or the publication of an article in a trade journal.
- Ditto legislation introduced that has no chance of passage.

- Ditto the intermediate stages in some endless bureaucratic saga.
- National and local: try to have your cake and eat it too. Look for California topics with national implications, and national topics with a specific or disparate impact on California.

8. Counterarguments. Give the case for the other side, as objectively as possible, and explain why it's wrong. This is not, or not just, a matter of fairness. It is to make your own case stronger. A piece that makes it seem as if no reasonable person could possibly disagree is unconvincing when the reader knows that there actually are reasonable people who do disagree.

Or do you disagree?

## THE CASE AGAINST GEORGE W. BUSH

Time, *Sept. 5, 2004*

NOTE: *This was for a "Bush pro and con" during the 2004 election in* Time. *Charles Krauthammer wrote the "pro."*

What do we know about George W. Bush that we didn't know four years ago, when most of us voted for someone else? We ought to know a lot more. Never has anyone become President of the United States less pretested by life. And never has any President been tested so dramatically so soon after taking office.

He was born at the intersection of two elites—the Eastern Wasp establishment and the Texas oiligarchy. He gimme'd his way through America's top educational institutions. In his forties, he was still a kid, hanging around his father's White House with not much to do. A decade later, without actually winning the most votes, he was President himself. The average gas-station attendant struggled harder to get where he or she is than did George W. Bush. Then came Sept. 11.

The heroic saga writes itself, with help from Shakespeare's Henry V and the life story of Harry Truman. This small man, this wastrel youth, finds himself leading his nation as it faces one of its greatest challenges. And in the fire of great events, he finds the fire of greatness within himself. Take it away, Peggy Noonan.

It's a swell story line, but it won't wash. Against a backdrop of great events, even a mediocrity can seem great for a while. After Sept. 11, there was certainly a great flurry of activity. War on terrorism was declared. An actual war was started in Iraq and still goes on. A Department of Homeland Security was founded. Various American freedoms have been suspended. More than $100 billion has been spent. At the rate things are going, the toll of American lives lost responding to 9/11 may exceed the toll of 9/11 itself. The toll of innocent foreigners is higher already.

But what has it all amounted to? As the most powerful nation in the world, we have managed to track down and kill a few members of al-Qaida. No more airliners have been flown into skyscrapers in the three years since 9/11, but then that was true in the three years before 9/11 as well. Are we safer from terrorism than we were before? The only honest answer is, Who knows?

You may approve or disapprove of the invasion and occupation of Iraq, but it is clear beyond dispute that Iraq had nothing to do with 9/11. By turning the world in general and the young people of the Muslim world in particular against us, the decision to respond to al-Qaida by toppling Saddam Hussein could have made future terrorism more likely, not less.

Subtract the war on terror, including Iraq, and the Bush presidency looks small indeed. Buying short-term prosperity by goosing the economy with heavy borrowing is no trick at all, yet it's not clear that Bush has pulled off even this (except the borrowing). His party has controlled Congress for most of his term. Aside from the traditional Republican wealth-friendly tax cut, can you name a single major successful legislative initiative? O.K., prescription drugs for seniors. Starting in 2006. If it works, which many experts doubt.

And what have these four years taught us about Bush as a person? Some fortunate folks whose lives do not require struggle have used the gift of ease to become better people: wiser than if they had had bills and laundry cluttering their minds, kinder and gentler—in the famous formulation of George Bush the Elder—than if they had needed sharp elbows to get somewhere. Bush the Younger never seemed noble in this way. But as we got to know him in 2000, the ease of his life had seemed to make him affable, undogmatic and pleasantly underinvested in anything as vulgar as an agenda. And then there was all that amiable chatter about "compassionate conservatism." The forecast was for a laconic, moderate presidency.

How wrong this was. Bush's obvious lack of interest in policy issues makes him more dogmatic, not less so. Intellectual laziness stiffens the backbone as much as ideological fervor does. Hand him his position on an issue, and he can cross it off his list. Bush's intellectual defenders compare him to Ronald Reagan, who was simpleminded (they say) in the best sense. Reagan whittled down the world's complexities into a few simple truths. But Reagan pondered those complexities on his way to simplicity. He stopped thinking only after a fair amount of thought. Bush's advisers deliver ideas to him like a pizza. His stove has never been lit. And four years have not illuminated the meaning of compassionate conservatism. It remains an insult to conservatives and a mystery to everybody else. On every big social issue that has arisen during his term (gay marriage, for example, and stem-cell research), Bush has been steadfast in taking the hard-conservative line.

The Wasp graciousness, the good-ole-boy affability, even the obviously sincere religious conviction run about a quarter-inch deep. In four years, this small man had two historic opportunities to reach for greatness, to lead this country to a new and better place, and he passed up both. The first was when the Democrats patriotically bowed to a Supreme Court decision they believed to be wrong, if not corrupt, so that the U.S. could avoid a further constitutional crisis. What a moment for bipartisanship! Maybe put more than a token Democrat in the Cabinet? Not a chance.

George W. Bush's second opportunity came on Sept. 11, 2001. Past grievances suddenly seemed petty, current disagreements seemed irrelevant, and, even among Bush's opponents, desperate hope replaced sullen doubts that our nation's leader would be up to the task. Bush got this gift from the opposition—the suspension of dislike and disbelief—without doing anything to deserve it. He could have asked for and got anything he wanted in the weeks and months after 9/11. And he decided to invade Iraq.

For once, George W. Bush was tested. And he flunked.

## SOCIAL SECURITY PRIVATIZATION WON'T WORK

THAT'S NOT AN OPINION—IT'S A MATHEMATICAL CERTAINTY.

Los Angeles Times, *Dec. 19, 2004*

NOTE: *As an experiment, when President Bush proposed privatizing part of Social Security, I sent this memo out to several leading political blogs, asking them to publish it and inviting their readers to prove me wrong if they could. Several tried, but none did (in my opinion).*

MY CONTENTION: Social Security privatization is not just unlikely to succeed, for various reasons that are subject to discussion. It is mathematically certain to fail. Discussion is pointless.

The usual case against privatization is that 1) millions of inexperienced investors may end up worse off, and 2) stocks don't necessarily do better than bonds over the long run, as proponents assume. But privatization won't work for a better reason: It can't possibly work, even in theory.

The logic is not very complicated:

1. To "work," privatization must generate more money for retirees than current arrangements. This bonus is supposed to be extra money in retirees' pockets and/or it is supposed to make up for a reduction in promised benefits, thus helping to close the looming revenue gap.

2. Where does this bonus come from? There are only two possibilities—from greater economic growth or from other people.

3. Greater economic growth requires either more capital to invest or smarter investment of the same amount of capital. Privatization will not lead to either of these.
   a. If nothing else in the federal budget changes, every dollar deflected from the federal treasury into private Social Security accounts must be replaced by a dollar that the government

raises in private markets. So the total pool of capital available for private investment remains the same.

b. The only change in decision-making about capital investment is that the decisions about some fraction of the capital stock will be made by people with little or no financial experience. Maybe this will not be the disaster that some critics predict, but there is no reason to think that it will actually increase the overall return on capital.

4. If the economy doesn't produce more than it otherwise would, the Social Security privatization bonus must come from other investors, in the form of a lower return.

a. This is in fact the implicit assumption behind the notion of putting Social Security money into stocks, instead of government bonds, because stocks have a better long-term return. The bonus will come from those saps who sell the stocks and buy the bonds.

b. Why would anyone sell their stocks and buy government bonds when the government itself is out there saying that stocks will earn a better return? In other words, privatization means betting the nation's most important social program on a theory that cannot be true unless many people are convinced that it's false.

c. Even if the theory were true, initially, privatization would make it false. The money newly available for private investment would bid up the price of (and thus lower the return on) stocks, while the government would need to raise the interest on its bonds in order to attract replacement money.

# 2005

## The Century's Greatest Love Story

Washington Post, *April 10, 2005*

Grace Kelly and Prince Rainier of Monaco (who died last week) were your textbook royal marriage. But for a royal romance that reaches depths of profound emotion that seem almost human, give me Charles and Camilla any day.

Could it all be a brilliant PR stratagem? Years of tawdry royal shenanigans have drastically reduced the British people's interest in being patronized by the royal family. But maybe some royal functionary (Keeper of the Queen's Spin?) had the brilliant insight that patronizing this collection of odd ducks and losers can be just as effective a bond as being patronized by them. What an adorable pair of doofuses!

Under the British system of government, the royal family is supposed to keep the nation supplied with gossip on the one hand and serve as a positive moral example on the other. This is a tough combo.

Here in the United States, by contrast, we believe in checks and balances. So we split these responsibilities. We have Hollywood celebrities to supply the fodder for gossip, and politicians to supply the positive moral. . . . Well, we have politicians to supply the gossip, and business leaders to supply the positive. . . . Okay, we have business leaders to supply the gossip and clergymen to supply. . . . Oh heck, I guess it's up to journalists to supply the positive moral example.

Here in the United States we don't split the role of head of government from the role of head of state. In Britain they do. And this is the best defense of the monarchy: People can express their love of country by adoring the queen, without implying any view either way about the prime minister. This is pleasant for the queen. And it's healthy for the prime minister. Keeps him humble. Or at least humbler.

By contrast, the U.S. presidency is an ego-inflating machine. The president moves in a vast imperial cocoon, unsurpassed in grandeur since the pharaohs. It would take a level of humility incompatible with running for public office in the first place for a president not to think, "Hey, I'm a pretty cool guy." Every time George W. Bush hears "Hail to the Chief," the odds go up that some unsuspecting country is going to find itself getting violently democratized.

By making itself a laughingstock, the British royal family has adapted to the needs of the current moment. We don't worry too much these days about the problem of politicians being held in excessively high regard. Thanks to modern political science, we enjoy politicians who dangerously overvalue themselves and a citizenry that dangerously undervalues them at the same time.

Once again, the royal family is there to help. Instead of an outlet for surplus admiration, the family turned itself into an outlet for excessive mockery and contempt. This allows the politicians to retain a minimum of dignity and respect as they go about the people's business.

British journos are doing their best, mocking Camilla Parker Bowles's dowdiness, Prince Charles's eccentricity, the bumbled details of the wedding. But they can't destroy the romance of a love story that exposes Charles and Diana, and King Edward VIII and Wallis Simpson as the cold, calculated contrivances they were.

There's no special magic about a prince approaching middle age who marries a young society beauty. The more we learn about Princess Diana, the less magical that story seems. And the abdication tale remains far from inspiring.

Now, what about a prince who marries a young beauty out of his sense of duty, who waits for decades until a car crash frees him and then marries the woman he really loves—a woman who almost everyone else in the world finds remarkably unattractive; a woman he didn't need to marry in order to enjoy her companionship as he had for decades; a woman his family and the world didn't want him to marry. And what about a woman who watched her longtime lover marry a much younger beauty; who married someone else herself out of some kind of bitter realism; who fell in love with a young future king but is marrying an old weirdo who very likely won't ever occupy the throne; a woman who is inviting a lifetime of public mockery for every aspect of her public appearance. . . . Now that is a love story.

And an instructive one. It teaches us about the virtue of patience, about the shallowness of physical appearance, about the courage to resist fashion. Camilla's values aren't original—they're the values of the British upper class, and they're not as innocent as they seem. The shabby clothing and the perennial bad hair day are not the ingenuous result of indifference to fashion; they are a calculated statement of superiority to fashion.

But this isn't 1805. The global forces of fashion and celebrity are way more powerful these days than the once-triumphant British upper class. What once might have been seen as insufferable snobbery (and what may even now be intended as snobbery, which is endearingly hopeless right there) seems charming and touching.

So I'm going out on a limb here and declaring Camilla and Charles the greatest love story of the twenty-first century, so far. And they had better live happily ever after.


## NO SMOKING GUN

THE DOWNING STREET MEMO.

Washington Post, *June 12, 2005*

NOTE: *Nothing else I have written has ever received as hostile a response as this piece. The hostility was from the Left, where the Downing Street Memo seems to play the same role as the New Testament in some fundamentalist Christian sects: It must be accepted as the literal truth, or you're going to hell. I found this annoying for a couple of reasons. First, whether the Iraq war is a bad idea and whether the DSM is important proof of Bush's warlike intentions are two separate questions, with little overlap in the evidence. It is more than possible to decide "yes" to the first and "no" to the sec-*

*ond. The fact that almost no one does suggests either that people on both sides of the Iraq debate aren't really opening their minds to the evidence anymore, or a spectacular breakdown in the law of averages. Second, as this book demonstrates (and many columns on this theme were left out to avoid repetition), I have been writing against the Iraq war consistently since the beginning. That this one column should put me beyond the pale demonstrates once again the maxim that the Left looks for heretics while the Right looks for converts.*

*In an exchange with Mark Danner in the* New York Review of Books *(August 11, 2005), I said I appreciated the frustration of DSM enthusiasts. They say they have proof that Bush was planning to go to war in the summer of 2002, and some critics dismiss this as untrue while others dismiss it as obviously true. Just to be clear, I am in the second camp.*

After about the two hundredth e-mail from a stranger demanding that I cease my personal coverup of something called the Downing Street Memo, I decided to read it. It's all over the blogosphere and Air America, the left-wing talk radio network: This is the smoking gun of the Iraq war. It is proof positive that President Bush was determined to invade Iraq the year before he did so. The whole "weapons of mass destruction" concern was phony from the start, and the drama about inspections was just kabuki: going through the motions.

Although it is flattering to be thought personally responsible for allowing a proven war criminal to remain in office, in the end I don't buy the fuss. Nevertheless, I am enjoying it, as an encouraging sign of the revival of the left. Developing a paranoid theory and promoting it to the very edge of national respectability takes a certain amount of ideological self-confidence. It takes a critical mass of citizens with extreme views and the time and energy to obsess about them. It takes a promotional infrastructure and the widely shared self-discipline to settle on a story line, disseminate it and stick to it.

It takes, in short, what Hillary Clinton once called a vast conspiracy. The right has enjoyed one for years. Even moderate and reasonable right-wingers have enjoyed the presence of a mass of angry people even further right. This overhang of extremists makes the moderates appear more reasonable. It pulls the center of politics, where the media try to be and where compromises on particular issues end up, in a rightward direction. Listening to extreme views on your own side is soothing even if you would never express them and may not even believe them yourself.

So, cheers for the Downing Street Memo. But what does it say? It's a report on a meeting of British Prime Minister Tony Blair and some aides on July 23, 2002. The key passage summarizes "recent talks in Washington" by the head of British foreign intelligence (identified, John Le Carré–style, simply as "C"). C reported that "military action was now seen as inevitable. Bush wanted to remove Saddam, through military action, justified by the conjunction of terrorism and WMD. But intelligence and facts were being fixed around the policy. . . . There was little discussion in Washington of the aftermath after military action."

C's focus on the dog that didn't bark—the lack of discussion about the aftermath of war—was smart and prescient. But even on its face, the memo is not proof that Bush had decided on war. It says that war is "now seen as inevitable" by "Washington." That is, people other than Bush had concluded, based on observation, that he was determined to go to war. There is no claim of even fourth-hand knowledge that he had actually declared this intention. Even if "Washington" meant actual administration decision makers, rather than the usual freelance chatterboxes, C is saying only that these people believe that war is how events will play out.

Of course, if "intelligence and facts were being fixed around the policy," rather than vice versa, that is pretty good evidence of Bush's intentions, as well as a scandal in its own right. And we know now that this was true and a half. Fixing intelligence and facts to fit a desired policy is the Bush II governing style, especially concerning the war in Iraq. But C offered no specifics, or none that made it into the memo. Nor does the memo assert that actual decision makers had told him they were fixing the facts. Although the prose is not exactly crystalline, it seems to be saying only that "Washington" had reached that conclusion.

And of course Washington had done so. You don't need a secret memo to know this. Just look at what was in the newspapers on July 23, 2002, and the day before. Left-wing *Los Angeles Times* columnist Robert Scheer casually referred to the coming war against Iraq as "much-planned-for." The *New York Times* reported Defense Secretary Donald Rumsfeld's response to an earlier story "which reported preliminary planning on ways the United States might attack Iraq to topple President Saddam Hussein." Rumsfeld effectively confirmed the report by announcing an investigation of the leak.

A *Wall Street Journal* op-ed piece declared that "the drums of war beat louder." A dispatch from Turkey in the *New York Times* even used the same word "inevitable" to describe the thinking in Ankara about the thinking in Washington about the decision "to topple President Saddam Hussein of Iraq by force."

Poor *Time* magazine, with a cover date of July 22 but actually published a week earlier, had the whole story. "Sometime last spring the President ordered the Pentagon and the CIA to come up with a new plan to invade Iraq and topple its leader." Originally planned for the fall, the war was put off until "at least early next year" (which is when, in fact, it happened). Unfortunately, *Time* went on to speculate that because of a weak economy, the war "may have to wait—some think forever," and concluded that "Washington is engaged more in psy-war than in war itself."

Some people you have to hit over the head. Hey, you folks at *Time*, why are you ignoring the Downing Street Memo?

## NIGER-SCOOTER-PLAME-GATE

Slate, *Oct. 28, 2005*

NOTE: *Judy Miller testified that she could not read her notes.*

**C**onfused? Sure. Who isn't? One entertaining aspect of the story that reaches some sort of climax today is the struggle of the media to summarize or label it (hence, "the story that reaches some sort of climax today"). Once upon a time, someone went to Niger, which is not Nigeria, and off we go in time and space. Even Fox News has been driven to compound sentences.

All the glam elements are there: a secret agent, international intrigue, sex (if you know where to look), blogs, moral dilemmas, movie-of-the-week dialogue at the White House. (Aide: "Mr. President, somebody has inserted a lie into your State of the Union address!" The President: "This is clearly the work of al-Qaida. We must invade Iraq immediately. Or is it Iran?") But somehow all these elements don't cohere. Alfred Hitchcock coined the term "McGuffin" to describe the gimmick that keeps the plot moving. He said you need one. The trouble here is not the lack of a McGuffin but too many.

You can't knock the names, though. Above all, there is the wonderfully Pynchonesque Valerie Plame. Plame: headline writers and copy editors seeking a short label for this saga were drawn like moths to this mysterious beauty, a one-syllable word of only five letters. And yet the eponymous heroine of the Plame Affair or Plame Controversy has actually been off-stage the entire time. Except for a brief appearance in *Vanity Fair*, posed rakishly with her husband in a sports car, it's been *Hamlet* without the Prince of Denmark.

The husband's name is forgettably bland. Joe Wilson? John Roberts? Something like that. Then there is the aide to the vice president who answers to the call of "Snooker." Or is it Smoky? Or maybe Sunshine? In the typical movie about Washington, a character labeled as an aide to the vice president might just as well carry a sign saying, "I get killed off in the first five minutes." And yet Snotty, or Skipper, or Snappy starts out as an obscure minor character and floats up steadily to the point where he is the central figure of the entire drama.

Anyway, let's recap. Two and a half years ago, Robert Novak published the name of an undercover CIA agent in his column. He then joined Plame off-stage, where he has mysteriously remained ever since. Since he has known the answer all along, he may have been murdered to assure his silence. Although there is no evidence for this, it makes as much sense as any other explanation for his disappearance from the story line.

Enter the liberal media establishment, led by the *New York Times*. First seen charging up a hill, demanding the appointment of a special prosecutor to get to the bottom of this outrage, it soon was charging back down the hill, complaining that the special prosecutor was asking journalists to finger the leaker. Who else would you ask?

Judith Miller of the *Times* was the only reporter who declined any deal, at least at first, and went to jail rather than testify. An expert on germ warfare (the subject of her most recent book), she said that revealing her source would inevitably lead to a pandemic that would wipe out all of humankind. Or something like that. My notes are a bit hard to interpret.

Everyone assumed that Miller's source was Snapper. Him and/or Karl Rove (another great name, especially for the official bad guy: a double rifle shot with the "K" in Karl lending a Teutonic flourish). He said he didn't mind if she testified. She apparently didn't hear this, so a couple months later he said it louder and she said OK. Then she testified that she couldn't remember who told her that Valerie Plame was an undercover CIA agent, but it wasn't Skippy. And she conceded that much of what she reported in the run-up to the Iraq war, relying on administration leaks, was wrong. So, she went to jail to protect a "source" who didn't give her the crucial fact at issue for a story she didn't write, but did give her inaccurate information for other stories. Huh?

The *New York Times* has started quietly, nervously backing away from Miller, like hikers trying to escape a rattlesnake. The rest of the media are fleeing without restraint. She's not a good poster child for the cause. But the cause itself remains somewhat bewildering. Why should you go to jail to protect the identity of a source who has used anonymity systematically and successfully to deceive you and your readers? Why should Scooter Libby go to jail—involuntarily—for having a conversation with you that you think the Constitution should protect and even encourage? Either this whole prosecution is nuts, or the mainstream media's view of reporters' rights is nuts. Which is it?

The Republicans have their own plotline they'd like to impose on this confusing blur of events. It's actually a dusted-off plotline from the Reagan Iran-Contra scandal of the 1980s: all about an "overzealous prosecutor" and "bitter partisans" on the other side who want to "politicize policy differences." But two intervening developments have overroasted these chestnuts: Bill Clinton and Yahoo! When Sen. Kay Bailey Hutchison pre-emptively mocked perjury as what prosecutors charge you with if they can't find a real crime, it was the work of minutes for bloggers to find and post her comments from the Clinton impeachment about the transcendent seriousness of a perjury rap.

But despair not. Many of these contradictions and ambiguities will surely be resolved in Act 2. Please take your seats. The performance is about to begin.

# HOW CONSERVATIVE IS "TOO CONSERVATIVE"?

Slate, *Nov. 4, 2005*

The Democrats have declared war on President Bush's latest Supreme Court candidate, Samuel Alito, without much in the way of weapons. Only two, really: the filibuster and the power of persuasion. And the filibuster—because it seems (and is) unfair and anti-democratic—will backfire unless people are persuaded that it is saving them from something really bad.

And to make the challenge even more daunting, most of the usual tools of persuasion aren't available this time. Alito seems like a fine fellow, personally. His credentials and qualifications are beyond dispute. Unlike Robert Bork, he is not scary-looking. And another Anita Hill is too much to hope for. Those are the cheap shortcuts. All that's left is a serious argument: Alito is simply too conservative.

The Republican counterargument will be fourfold: a) He is not very conservative; b) no one knows how conservative he is, and no one is going to find out, because discussing his views in any detail would involve "prejudging" future issues before the court; c) it doesn't matter whether he is conservative—even raising the question "politicizes" what ought to be a nonpartisan search for judicial excellence; and d) sure he's conservative. Very conservative. Who won the election?

Actually d), the most valid argument, is one you will never hear, although the Harriet Miers detour showed what happens if Republican activists suspect that a nominee really might not be onboard the ideological train.

The other Republican arguments are laughable. Of course Alito is very conservative. That's why he got nominated. The process of choosing justices is no more political in the Senate than it is in the White House. Alito has been a judge for fifteen years and has written opinions on hundreds of subjects. If that is not "prejudging," answering questions at a confirmation hearing certainly is not.

So, how conservative is "too conservative"? Democrats like the phrase "outside the mainstream." They also like to emphasize that the next justice will be replacing Sandra Day O'Connor, an icon of swing-vote moderation. The notion is that presidents of all stripes are under some kind of vague, floating obligation to keep the court in ideological balance. This, unfortunately, is a party-out-of-power fantasy. There is no requirement of moderation in the abstract. President Bush needn't nominate a compromise candidate just to show he's a good sport.

"Too conservative" may just mean anti-abortion. Maybe this is all about *Roe v. Wade* and nothing more. But if you're really looking for a standard to judge whether someone is too conservative to sit on the Supreme Court, you need to distinguish between three different kinds of judicial conservatism.

First, conservatism can mean a deep respect for precedent and a reluctance to reverse established doctrines. All judges are supposed to be bound by precedent, and it's a bit of a mystery when and why they feel empowered to change course. But this meaning of conservatism is mainly advanced by liberals, who like the idea that conservatism itself will stay the hand of conservative judges in reversing great liberal precedents.

Of course each of these liberal precedents—school desegregation, Miranda warnings, abortion choice, and so on—was a precedent-buster in its day, making the argument a bit hypocritical. But recent Supreme Court nominees have found that asserting a deep respect for precedent is a great way to reassure senators that they won't overturn *Roe*, whatever they might think of it on the merits, and whatever they actually intend.

Second, a conservative can mean someone who reads the Constitution narrowly and is reluctant to overrule the elected branches of government. Republicans have been waving this flag for decades, reverencing "strict constructionism" and the framers' "original intent" while condemning "activist" judges who are "legislating from the bench." The belief is not just that the conservative theory of constitutional interpretation is better than the liberal theory. It's that conservative judges have a theory, while liberal judges are just on an unprincipled power grab. This conceit is what allows President Bush to insist that he does not impose any ideological litmus test on judges, as long as they agree with him.

The truth is that Republicans do not have a simple machine that turns the framers' words into instructions for judges, and Democrats are not entirely bereft of judicial philosophy. It is probably true that if you rated all constitutional rulings on a scale of literal-minded-ness, it would show that, on average, Democratic appointees are more inclined than Republican appointees to take metaphorical leaps from the framers' exact words. It may even be true that judges picked by Republicans are on average less likely to tell the elected branches what they may and may not do.

But only on average. On some hot issues—such as affirmative action, or property rights, or gun control—it is Republicans calling for judges to interfere and Democrats who want them to keep their hands off.

The third meaning of conservative as applied to judges is a conser-vative judicial activist: someone who uses the power of the courts to impose conservative policies, with or without the benefit of a guiding philosophy. A judge who preaches judicial restraint but practices activ-ism would be a good example of how to be "too conservative." But so is a judge whose philosophy of restraint leaves injustices unrectified. Restraint isn't always good, and activism isn't always bad.

Judicial power is like government spending: People hate it in the abstract but love it in the particular. That makes an honest debate hard to have, and harder to win. Nevertheless, it would be nice to have one.

### GUESS WHO'S NOT COMING TO DINNER?

Guardian, *Nov. 15, 2005*

NOTE: *Jonathan Powell was an aide to Prime Minister Tony Blair. His brother, Charles Powell, served similarly for Margaret Thatcher.*

Can the Special Relationship survive the revelation that three years ago Britain's Ambassador to the United States was reduced to vulgar obscenity in order to claim his rightful place at a dinner party? The words are chiseled on our hearts like the lapidary phrases inscribed in stone all over town. Told by the prime minister's chief of staff,

Jonathan Powell, that the chair he had been planning to occupy at a dinner that night with President Bush at the White House was being redeployed, Sir Christopher Meyer said: "If this happens, you will fucking cut me off at the fucking knees."

Wow. It's not your classic British understatement, is it? Nor is it the usual diplomatic newspeak. It's Yes Minister Meets the Sopranos. It's Anthony Trollope in cowboy boots. It's West Wing a la West End. And no reporter had to go to jail to protect the source of this anecdote. The source is Sir Christopher himself, in last week's *Guardian* excerpts from his forthcoming memoirs. And he does not seek anonymity. Quite the opposite. He must think he sounds pretty cool, pretty tough, pretty American, almost black, issuing unveiled threats of violence with a chorus of copulation in the background.

All fucking aside, though, Sir Christopher bungles the job. A proper threat is: get me into this dinner, or I will cut you off at the knees. Sir Christopher's version is: get me into this dinner party or *you* will cut *me* off at the knees. The best that can be said is that this has a sweet English futility about it. As a threat, it is unimpressive, and possibly even counterproductive.

The tragedy, of course, is that it was all so unnecessary. Sir Christopher could have made his essential point—which was, "Oh, puleeze let me come to that dinner. Oh, please, please, pretty please"—in truly British ways, without resorting to potty mouth. For example, Sir Christopher might have tried upper-class verbal shambling: "You know, Jonathan, old sock, I wouldn't half-mind going to that White House dinner tonight, funnily enough. I don't suppose that anybody will be there. It's just that . . . oh well never mind. Only a thought. Terrible idea, actually. No, you go. Have a wonderful time."

Or he could have gone for a bit of retired-colonel-style bluster. "Now see here, my good man. Do you know who I am? Fetch me an invitation pronto or—mark my words—the prime minister will hear about it. And I warn you, she is a close personal friend of mine. And what do you mean, sir, parading around here pretending to be Sir Charles Powell? Now there is a fine fellow. He knows who to invite to a dinner party."

If he was feeling creative, Sir Christopher might have attempted a Wildean approach. "Not to be invited to a dinner party is one thing. To be invited then disinvited is quite another. The one is merely insulting while the other is . . . is . . . Well, it's just so fucking rude, isn't it? Look, I don't have time for this Oscar Wilde shit. Just get me a fucking seat at the fucking table—all right, matey?"

Or he even could have retreated into globalony, the dialect of English used by diplomats and bureaucrats. "I regret to inform you, Jonathan, that sub-paragraph 4, clause 8, of the Special Addendum to the United Nations Charter relating to the Care and Feeding of Ambassadors specifically provides that, you know, to get a fellow's hopes up and all, and then to crush them like a . . . , well, it's torture, Jonathan. Yes it is, yes it is. It's torture, nothing more and nothing less. And I don't care whether the UN Charter really says anything about it or not. Are you writing this down? Say, be a good fellow and make that 'the fucking UN Charter.' Thanks awfully."

Even when he is doing a bad Clint Eastwood imitation, though, "Sir Christopher Meyer" is a great comic character in the British tradition that ranges from Shakespeare's Malvolio to Ricky Gervais's David Brent in *The Office*. All these characters suffer from self-importance without self-awareness. Sir Christopher's conviction that Britain's entire future depends on his attendance at a dinner party to which he hasn't been invited is a comic premise worthy of Peter Sellers as Inspector Clouseau. His eye-rolling disdain for the "pygmies" fate has forced him to work with is an almost direct rip-off of Rowan Atkinson's *BlackAdder*. His exasperated disquisition about why it's perfectly acceptable to send four people to fill three places at a White House dinner—which he delivers to the reader and then quotes himself delivering again to the prime minister—is Basil Fawlty to a T.

And when Tony Blair finally says he really doesn't care who comes to this dinner, Sir Christopher loftily labels this sensible response as "unhelpful," and you can almost hear John Cleese declaring sarcastically, "Oh, well that's very helpful. Thank you so very much indeed," and under his breath, mumbling, "Git." Or maybe "Fucking git."

## CHENEY WEIGHS IN

Slate, *Nov. 26, 2005*

"**O**ne might also argue," said Vice President Cheney in a speech on Tuesday, "that untruthful charges against the Commander-in-chief have an insidious effect on the war effort." That would certainly be an ugly and demagogic argument, were one to make it. After all, if untruthful charges against the president hurt the war effort (by undermining public support and soldiers' morale), then those charges will hurt the war effort even more if they happen to be true. So, one would be saying, in effect, that any criticism of the president is, essentially, treason.

Lest one fear that he might be saying that, Cheney immediately added, "I am unwilling to say that"—"that" being what he had just said. He generously granted critics the right to criticize (as did the president this week). Then he resumed hurling adjectives like an ape hurling coconuts at unwanted visitors. "Dishonest." "Reprehensible." "Corrupt."

"Shameless." President Bush and others joined in, all morally outraged that anyone would accuse the administration of misleading us into war by faking a belief that Saddam Hussein possessed nuclear and/or chemical and biological weapons.

Interestingly, the administration no longer claims that Saddam actually had such weapons at the time Bush led the country into war in order to eliminate them. "The flaws in intelligence are plain enough in hindsight," Cheney said on Tuesday. So-called WMDs (weapons of mass destruction) were not the only argument for the war, but the administration thought they were a crucial argument at the time. So, the administration now concedes that the country went into war on a false premise. Doesn't that mean that the war was a mistake no matter where the false premise came from?

Cheney and others insist that Bush couldn't possibly have misled anyone about WMDs since everybody had assumed for years, back into the Clinton administration, that there were WMDs in Iraq. That's why any criticism of Bush on this point is corrupt, reprehensible, distasteful, odiferous, infectious, and so on. But this indignation is belied by Cheney's own remarks in the 2000 election. In the vice presidential debate, for example, Cheney was happy to agree with Bush that Saddam's possession of WMDs would be a good enough reason to "take him out." But he did not assume that Saddam already had such weapons. And he certainly did not assume that this view was the general consensus. "We'll have to see if that happens," he said. "It's unfortunate we find ourselves in a position where we don't know for sure what might be transpiring inside Iraq. I certainly hope he's not regenerating that kind of capability."

If you're looking for changed stories, don't waste your time on the war's critics. Look up Cheney's bitter critique of President Clinton's military initiatives in the 2000 campaign, and specifically the need for more burden-sharing by allies and a sharply defined "exit strategy." At the time, about eleven thousand American troops were in Bosnia and Kosovo working alongside about fifty-five thousand soldiers from allied countries. If only!

Until last week, the anti-war position in the debate over Iraq closely resembled the pro-war position in the ancient debate over Vietnam. That is: It was a mistake to get in, but now that we're in, we can't just cut and run. That was the logic on which Richard Nixon and Henry Kissinger took over the Vietnam War four years after major American involvement began and kept it going for another five. American "credibility" depended on our keeping our word, however foolish that word might have been. In the end, all the United States wanted was a "decent interval" between our departure and the North Vietnamese triumph—and we didn't even get that. Thousands of Americans died in Vietnam after America's citizens and government were in general agreement that the war was a mistake.

We are now very close to that point of general agreement in the Iraq war. Do you believe that if Bush, Cheney, and company could turn back the clock, they would do this again? And now, thanks to Rep. John Murtha, it is permissible to say, or at least to ask, "Why not just get out now? Or at least soon, on a fixed schedule?" There are arguments against this—some good, some bad—but the worst is the one delivered by Cheney and others with their most withering scorn. It is the argument that it is wrong to tell American soldiers risking their lives in a foreign desert that they are fighting for a mistake.

One strength of this argument is that it doesn't require defending the war itself. The logic applies equally whether the war is justified or not. Another strength is that the argument is true, in a way: It is a terrible thing to tell someone he or she is risking death in a mistaken cause. But it is more terrible actually to die in that mistaken cause.

The longer the war goes on, the more Americans and "allies" and Iraqis will die. That is not a slam-dunk argument for ending this foreign entanglement. But it is worth keeping in mind while you try to decide whether American credibility or Iraqi prosperity or Middle East stability can justify the cost in blood and treasure. And don't forget to factor in the likelihood that the war will actually produce these fine things.

The last man or woman to die in any war will almost surely die in vain: The outcome has been determined, if not certified. And he or she might die happier thinking that death came in a noble cause that will not be abandoned. But if it is not a noble cause, he or she might prefer not to die at all. Stifling criticism that might shorten the war is no favor to American soldiers. They can live without that kind of "respect."

## THE NEW CORRUPTION

Slate, *Dec. 2, 2005*

It used to be said that the moral arc of a Washington career could be divided into four parts: idealism, pragmatism, ambition, and corruption. You arrive with a passion for a cause, determined to challenge the system. Then you learn to work for your cause within the system. Then rising in the system becomes your cause. Then finally you exploit the system—your connections in it, and your understanding of it—for personal profit.

And it remains true, sort of, but faster. Even the appalling Jack Abramoff had ideals at one point. But he took a shortcut straight to corruption. On the other hand, you can now trace the traditional moral arc in the life of conservative-dominated Washington itself, which began with Ronald Reagan's inauguration and marks its twenty-fifth anniversary in January. Reagan and company arrived to tear down the government and make Washington irrelevant. Now the airport and a giant warehouse of bureaucrats are named after him.

By the twentieth anniversary of their arrival, when an intellectually corrupt Supreme Court ruling gave them complete control of the government at last, the conservatives had lost any stomach for tearing down the government. George W. Bush's "compassionate conservatism" was more like an apology than an ideology. Meanwhile Tom DeLay—the real boss in Congress—openly warned K Street that unless all the choice lobbying jobs went to Republicans, lobbyists could not expect to have any influence with the Republican Congress. This warning would be meaningless, of course, unless the opposite was also true: If you hire Republican lobbyists, you and they will have influence over Congress. And darned if DeLay didn't turn out to be exactly right about this!

No prominent Republican upbraided DeLay for his open invitation to bribery. And bribery is what it is: not just campaign contributions, but the promise of personal enrichment for politicians and political aides who play ball for a few years before cashing in.

When Rep. Randy "Duke" Cunningham pleaded guilty this week to accepting a comic cornucopia of baubles, plus some cash, from defense contractors, the vast right-wing conspiracy acted with impressive speed and forcefulness to expel one of its most doggedly loyal loudmouths and pack him off to a long jail term. Even President Bush, who possesses the admirable quality of an affable capacity for understanding and forgiveness on the personal level, seized an unnecessary opportunity to wish the blackguard ill. There was no talk of "sadness"—the usual formula for expressing sympathy without excusing guilt.

This astringent response would be more impressive if the basic facts about Cunningham's corruption hadn't been widely known for months. The *San Diego Union-Tribune* reported last June that a company seeking business from the Pentagon had bought Cunningham's southern California house from him, held it unoccupied briefly, and sold it—in the hottest real estate market in human history—for a $700,000 loss. You didn't need to know that Duke's haul included two antique commodes to smell the stench. Yet all the Republican voices now saying that Cunningham deserves his punishment were silent until he clearly and unavoidably was going to get it.

Like medieval scholastics counting the angels on the head of a pin, Justice Department lawyers are struggling with the question of when favors to and from a member of Congress or a congressional aide take on the metaphysical quality of a corrupt bribe. The brazenness of the DeLay-Abramoff circle has caused prosecutors to look past traditional distinctions, such as that between campaign contributions and cash or other favors to a politician personally. Or the distinction between doing what a lobbyist wants after he has taken you to Scotland to play golf, and promising to do what he wants before he takes you to Scotland to play golf.

These distinctions don't really touch on what's corrupt here, which is simply the ability of money to give some people more influence than others over the course of a democracy where, civically if not economically, we are all supposed to be equal. So, where do you draw the line between harmless favors and corrupt bribery?

It's not an easy question, if you're talking about sending people to prison. But it's a very easy question if you're just talking: The answer is that it's all corrupt bribery. People and companies hire lobbyists because it works. Lobbyists get the big bucks because their efforts earn or save clients even bigger bucks in their dealings with the government. Members of Congress are among the world's greatest bargains: What are a couple of commodes compared with $163 million of Pentagon contracts?

Perhaps conceding more than he intended, former Democratic Sen. John Breaux, now on K Street, told the *New York Times* that a member of Congress will be swayed more by two thousand letters from constituents on some issue than by anything a lobbyist can offer. I guess if it's a lobbyist versus nineteen hundred constituents, it's too bad for the constituents. That seems fair.

# 2006

## Wendy

*Unpublished. Jan. 2006*

Surely other visitors to Wendy Wasserstein's hospital room in recent weeks had the same reaction I did, that it was like wandering into one of her plays.

*A sunny, flower-filled room on the top floor of the Memorial Sloan-Kettering Cancer Center on the Upper East Side. This is like the concierge level of a hotel—everything is just a bit nicer—except that most of the customers are dying. WENDY lies peacefully in bed, tucked in up to her neck, breathing softly, apparently asleep. She has been like this for weeks. Nevertheless, she looks good: thin. The only other person in the room is CHARLIE, a private nurse.*

MIKE enters, carrying a sad, small bouquet. He sees the lavish flower displays and quickly stuffs his own offering into a wastebasket. He spots Charlie.

MIKE: So is this 9-G, Wendy Wasserstein's room? I just walked into the room next door, accidentally, and a man I've never seen before told me that I must be his wife's second cousin from Rhode Island. His wife is dying, and relatives he doesn't even know are showing up. He says they just want to see what it's like to die on the top floor of Sloan-Kettering. They were married for forty-two years and he never met her cousins in Rhode Island . . . [spotting Wendy] oh! [A pause.] Can she hear us?

CHARLIE (slowly, trying to guess what answer Mike wants to hear): Yes? Perhaps? Well, actually we don't know. But [he brightens, nurse-like] anything's possible. Most of her visitors want to talk to her, and we tell them it can't do any harm.

MIKE (who has been staring): She looks as if she is going to just wake up and start talking any second.

CHARLIE (bored—he hears this all day—but kindly): As I told you, anything is possible.

MIKE: In your experience, has that ever happened in a case like this? Do people ever just wake up and resume their lives?

CHARLIE: Well, no . . . but [looking at the bright side again] I'm a bit new to cancer. I mostly worked with terminal AIDS patients until those cases dried up. But I'll leave you two alone.

CHARLIE exits. MIKE pulls a chair up to WENDY's bed, sits, and speaks.

MIKE: Wendy . . .

I won't try to compete any further with the leading playwright—the Neil Simon and the Arthur Miller—of our generation, who died Monday of lymphoma at the inadequate age of fifty-five. But I think Wendy would have loved the situation for its innate mixture of tragedy and comedy, or for its dramatic possibilities (the Mike character might make humiliating confessions; the Wendy character's mother might emerge from behind an arras). She also might relish a clever technical solution to the problem of the soliloquy: how to let your characters speak their inner thoughts aloud without seeming stagy and ridiculous.

Wendy was a craftswoman. If you knew her and her family, you could see how she turned life into art—not through anything like crude transcription, but by creating an alternate universe that drew from ours and reflected a wise light back on it. When she started work on her play about Washington, *An American Daughter*, she asked me to round up some local types for her inspection. So I had a party that was actually an audition—not to play a character but to be a character. And several Washington characters are easily identifiable in the play that emerged. But all are transformed, complex, poignant, with, if anything, more human dimensions than their real-life models.

Wendy took no shortcuts to epiphany. In her plays, angels do not pop down from the scaffolding. Especially in later works like *The Sisters Rosensweig*, Wendy offered audiences something that fashion and economics have almost wiped out: what one of her older characters might call a "real evening in the theater." That means more than one or two realistic characters, performing on a realistic set, wearing realistic costumes, and following realistic conventions. Time moves forward, just as in real life. Characters are introduced and tested, problems arise and are resolved. A happy ending is not out of the question.

Wendy's plays fit into another neglected genre as well. Although they seem intensely personal, they are what the British call "State of the Nation" plays: they use plot and character to assess some aspect of the national condition. Wendy did this most overtly in *An American Daughter*, derived from the experience of Zoe Baird, who lost a chance to be President Clinton's attorney general because she hadn't paid the Social Security tax for her babysitter.

A couple of months ago, I set up a Google news alert set for "Wendy Wasserstein." A grim technological death watch. But it turned out to be a life watch as well. Every day brought e-mails with news clips announcing a college production of *The Heidi Chronicles* in New Zealand or a Wasserstein season at the repertory company in some American city far from Broadway. The products of Wendy's imagination will be alive and strutting the world's stages for a long time—maybe forever. By contrast, who even remembers what this column was about two weeks ago? Not me.

Let's be honest: Wendy's characters do not span much of the human condition. Even her one major black character (the heroine's best friend in *An American Daughter*) is Jewish—and a doctor, no less. But her audiences always felt that she was telling, play-by-play, the story of their lives. Our lives. And now we'll never know how it comes out.

## THE FUTURE OF NEWSPAPERS

Slate, *Jan. 7, 2006*

**S**omewhere in the forest, a tree is cut down. It is loaded onto a giant truck and hauled a vast distance to a factory, where the trees are turned into huge rolls of paper. These rolls are loaded onto another truck and hauled another vast distance to another factory, where the rolls of paper are covered in ink, chopped up, folded, stacked, tied, and loaded onto a third set of trucks, which fan out across cities and regions dropping bundles here and there.

Printing plants no longer have the clickety-clack of linotype machines and bubbling vats of molten lead. The letterpress machines that stamped the ink on the paper have been supplanted by offset presses that transfer it gently. There is computer-controlled this and that. Nevertheless, the process remains highly physical, mechanical, complicated, and noisy. As we live through the second industrial revolution, your daily newspaper remains a tribute to the wonders of the first one.

Meanwhile, back to those bundles. Some of them are opened and the newspapers are put, one-by-one, into plastic bags. Bagged or unbagged, they are loaded onto a fourth set of vehicles—bicycles by legend, usually these days a car or small truck—and flung individually into your bushes or at your cat. Other bundles go to retail establishments. Still other newspapers are locked into attractive metal boxes bolted into the sidewalk. Anyone who is feeling lucky and happens to possess the exact change has a decent shot at obtaining a paper or, for the same price, carting away a dozen.

What happens next is aided by a flat surface, especially on a Sunday near Christmas. The proud owner of up to four or five pounds of paper and ink begins searching for the parts he or she wants. The paper has multiple sections, each of which is either folded into others or wrapped around others according to an ancient formula known only to newspaper publishers and designed to guarantee that no one section can either be found on the first go-through or removed without putting half a dozen other sections into play. Newspaper-industry regulations do not require any particular labeling system for sections, but they do require that if letters are used, the sections cannot be in alphabetical order.

And so, at last, there are two piles of paper: a short one of stuff to read, and a tall one of stuff to throw away. Unfortunately, many people are taking the logic of this process one step further. Instead of buying a paper in order to throw most of it away, they are not buying it in the first place.

Bill Gates says that in technology things that are supposed to happen in less than five years usually take longer than expected, while things that are supposed to happen in more than ten years usually come sooner than expected. Ten years ago, when I went to work for Microsoft, the newspaper industry was in a panic over something called Sidewalk—a now-forgotten Microsoft project to create Web site entertainment guides for a couple dozen big cities. Newspapers were convinced that Microsoft could and would put them out of business by stealing their ad base. It didn't happen. The collapse of the Internet bubble did happen. And, until very recently, the newspapers got complacent. Some developed good Web sites, some didn't, but most stopped thinking of the Web as an imminent danger.

Ten years later, newspapers are starting to panic again. But merely slobbering after bloggers may not be enough. In 1996, the oldest Americans who grew up with computers and don't even understand my tiresome anecdotes about how people used to resist them ("What's a typewriter, Mike?") were just entering adulthood. Now they are most of the working population, or close to it.

The trouble even an established customer will take to obtain a newspaper continues to shrink, as well. Once, I would drive across town if necessary. Today, I open the front door and if the paper isn't within about ten feet I retreat to my computer and read it online. Only six months ago, that figure was twenty feet. Extrapolating, they will have to bring it to me in bed by the end of the year and read it to me out loud by the second quarter of 2007.

No one knows how all this will play out. Newspapers have got the content. The first time I heard myself called a "content provider," I felt like a guy who'd been hired by the company that makes Tupperware to make sure there was plenty of Jell-O salad in the world. As a rule, anyone who uses the term "content provider" without a smirk needs to consider getting content from someone else.

But it is hard to believe that there will be room in the economy for delivering news by the Rube Goldberg process described above. That doesn't mean newspapers are toast. After all, they've got the brand names. You gotta trust something called the "Post-Intelligencer" more than something called "Yahoo!" or "Google," don't you? No, seriously, don't you? OK, how old did you say you are?

## GIVE ME LIBERTY OR LET ME THINK ABOUT IT

Washington Post, *Jan. 13, 2006*

Most of us are not Patrick Henry and would be willing to lose a great deal of freedom to save our lives. It's not even necessarily deplorable. Giving up a certain amount of freedom in exchange for the safety and comfort of civilized society is what government is all about, according to guys like Hobbes and Locke, who influenced the Founding Fathers. And that's good government. Many people live under bad governments that take away more freedom than necessary, and these people choose not to become heroes. That is not a contemptible choice, especially if we're talking France or maybe even China, and not Stalin's Russia or Hitler's Germany. The notion that freedom is indivisible—if you lose a little you have lost it all; if one person is deprived of liberty then we all are—is sweet, and useful for indoctrinating children. But it just isn't true.

The current debate about government wiretapping of U.S. citizens inside the United States as part of the war on terrorism—like the debate before it about the torture of terror suspects, and the debate about U.S. prisons in foreign countries—is all about the divisibility of freedom. The arguments all seem to pit hard practicality on one side against sentiment, if not empty sentimentality, on the other. There are the folks who are fighting a war to protect us from a terrible enemy and there are the folks getting in their way with a lot of fruity abstractions. You can note all you want the irony of the government's trampling American values in the name of protecting them. But that irony can be turned on its head. If the cost of losing the war and the cost of winning it are measured in the same currency—American values, especially freedom—then giving up some freedom to avoid losing all of it is obviously the right thing to do.

Arguing for abstractions while the other side argues for practicality is, to some extent, just a burden that civil libertarians—or even liberals in general—will always have to bear. In the old days, liberals at least had the luxury of the easy, tempting argument in the economic sphere—"here is some money from the government"—while conservatives were stuck with long-term abstractions such as fiscal responsibility. Now conservatives promise tax cuts starting yesterday and liberals are left defending big government and fiscal responsibility as well.

The good guys need to frame their argument in ways that don't require people to be heroes—to give up something practical and immediate, such as safety from terrorism, in exchange for an abstraction, such as liberty, especially the liberty of someone else (like a young Arab swept off the streets of Baghdad and locked up in a secret prison).

The argument starts with the traditional, and still powerful, slippery slope: Today it's him, tomorrow it's you; or, today it's your international phone conversations, tomorrow it's your desk drawers. The Bush administration is helping to prevent slippery-slope arguments from seeming paranoid by slipping and sliding before our very eyes. We gave it the thuggishly titled Patriot Act and now it claims constitutional authority to ignore the act's safeguards.

And the slippery slope extends beyond civil liberties, which not everyone fetishizes, to the rule of law generally, which is more popular. That Congressional Research Service report last week is a meticulous and deadpan analysis of the administration's express and implied reasoning in claiming a right to wiretap conversations at will. No legal restriction on presidential power of any sort could survive the administration's logic, which skips with ease over statutes and the Constitution itself.

The Fourth Amendment is typical of laws protecting civil liberties in that it doesn't forbid the government to invade people's privacy, or lock them up or take their property. Rather, it requires the government to be "reasonable" and to explain its reasons to someone else.

In short, it requires a reality test. It recognizes that even freedom exists in a world of trade-offs. But it does not necessarily trust the government in power to make those trade-offs correctly.

This is the second answer of the soft-hearts to the hard-heads: We're not as otherworldly as you think. We do recognize that there is a trade-off between the values we celebrate and the practical demands of protecting those values. We just need a reality test. Is the enemy in the war on terrorism really worse, justifying greater violations of civil liberties and human rights, than the enemy in World War II was?

Here, once again, the Bush administration helps to make the softies' case. It could have jumped through the required hoops and been wiretapping away about five minutes later. Or if the administration didn't like the way some court was interpreting the law, it could have gotten a law tailor-made from Congress just the way it liked. ("I'll take it medium rare, with cuffs but no pleats, and hold the right to a jury trial.") But that was too much trouble.

## WHY LAWYERS ARE LIARS

THEY DON'T WANT TO: IT'S THEIR ETHICAL OBLIGATION!

Slate, *Jan. 20, 2006*

As a loyal member—well, as a member—of the District of Columbia Bar for more than a quarter of a century, I was aware of the tension between advocacy and honesty. But until the recent controversies over Supreme Court nominees, I was unaware of the scope and depth of my professional obligation to avoid telling the truth. Sometimes this merely means evasion, but often it encourages or even requires outright lying. In other lines of work—journalism, for example—the truth is a standard that is not always met. But for lawyers, judging from the arguments made successfully for John Roberts and Samuel Alito, and unsuccessfully for Harriet Miers, the truth is something you must constantly struggle to overcome.

Suppose you are a star at law school and start your career as a Supreme Court law clerk. Roberts clerked for his predecessor, William Rehnquist, who had clerked for Justice Robert Jackson. That was in 1954, the year of *Brown v. Board of Education*. Rehnquist wrote Jackson a memo saying, "I realize that this is an unpopular and unhumanitarian position . . . but I think *Plessy v. Ferguson* [the precedent upholding racial segregation] was right and should be re-affirmed." Asked about this at his own confirmation hearings, Rehnquist said he was just writing what Jackson might say if Jackson favored upholding racial segregation, which Jackson did not and neither did Rehnquist, according to Rehnquist. This established the principle that you don't need to really believe anything you write as a Supreme Court clerk. (The only alternative explanation would be that Rehnquist was against *Brown* and a liar to boot.) At Roberts' hearings last year, his role as a Supreme Court clerk barely came up. What would be the point?

So life goes on and now you're a young lawyer applying for a job. Let's say you're in the Justice Department, and you want a promotion to deputy assistant attorney general. It's 1985, you're Sam Alito, and Reagan is president. You write that "the Constitution does not protect a right to an abortion," and you tout your past efforts to overturn *Roe v. Wade.* You say this is work "in which I personally believe very strongly." A non-lawyer might leap from this to the conclusion that in 1985, at least, Alito opposed abortion and wanted to overturn *Roe.* But that is not the case at all. He told skeptical Democrats twenty years later that he was just "seeking a job." The scope of this "seeking a job" exception to the general obligation to tell the truth is not clear. Does it, for example, cover a nominee "seeking a job" as a Supreme Court justice?

Even when not seeking a job, it appears that Justice Department lawyers have responsibilities far weightier than telling the truth. Roberts also served in the Reagan Justice Department and wrote briefs taking the conservative side on a variety of hot issues such as abortion. He signed a brief declaring that *Roe v. Wade* was "wrongly decided and should be overruled." But, as the conservative Committee for Justice reassured liberals during Roberts' confirmation, "Roberts, as one of several attorneys on the brief for the government, was simply arguing the position of the United States, his client." Alito, in a similar job, described himself as a "line attorney," invoking an image of lawyers along a conveyor belt, tightening an argument here and adding a precedent there to whatever legal and moral claptrap came along.

Legal briefs filed for a client are one thing, but internal memos to a client are another. Or so you might think. But I'm afraid not. Roberts' defenders—his defenders—insisted during his confirmation that memos he wrote to his boss when he worked in the White House itself should not be taken seriously as a reflection of his true beliefs. The memos gave the appearance of urging the Reagan administration to take a more conservative line on issues such as school prayer and employment discrimination. But White House Press Secretary Scott McClellan revealed that these were actually Reagan's views already: "I think what those files show is a young White House staffer helping to provide legal analysis in support of the President's agenda, President Reagan's agenda." In other words, Roberts supplied reasons for Reagan to believe what he believed anyway, but kept his more nuanced views for himself.

When, in the course of a long, varied, and successful career do lawyers become free to have their own agendas and say what they really think? Not when they leave the government and enter private practice. Roberts told the Senate Judiciary Committee that "the positions a lawyer presents on behalf of a client should not be ascribed to that lawyer." He also noted that he had once helped some welfare recipients to get their benefits restored. Presumably that was to make clear that he does not necessarily support welfare benefits.

What if that practicing lawyer should be appointed as a judge? Alito warned senators not to assume that the decisions of a lower federal court reflect a judge's true beliefs, because lesser judges are bound by rulings of the Supreme Court. And if that lower court judge is nominated to join the Supremes? We all know that in the confirmation process, etiquette, if not ethics, requires evasion, if not outright lying, because to reveal any actual legal view would amount to "prejudging" possible future cases.

And finally, even Supreme Court justices are bound, to some extent, by the doctrine of stare decisis, which is the judicial equivalent of papal infallibility. Rulings lose the mystical authority they depend on when people start to get the idea they can be reversed at will. The actual power of stare decisis in restraining Supreme Court justices from saying and doing what they believe is unclear. The capstone untruth of a successful legal career is promising, under stare decisis, to suppress your true beliefs more than you really will.

How did we get to this situation where the princes of the law claim a lifetime of insincerity while their enemies accuse them of having told the truth all along? It's partly the result of various confusions and evasions now baked into the confirmation process. Not expressing a view does not equal not having one. For a Supreme Court nominee to have thought about legal issues and reached some provisional conclusion is not a scandal. It is admirable and probably inevitable. For senators to learn these views and exercise "advice and consent" on that basis is not a scandal either. That's how it is supposed to work.

There is a difference between a general political philosophy and a judicial philosophy—a view about the role of judges. Neither is a bad thing for judges to have. Neither amounts to "prejudging." In fact, a judicial philosophy is essential. Judges should rule based on their judicial philosophy, not their political ideology. For that reason, trying to determine a judge's judicial philosophy is a perfectly legitimate part of the Senate confirmation process. And that includes following that philosophy to specific conclusions on specific issues. You want judges to be open-minded, not empty-headed.

For a lawyer to advocate the client's views, rather than his or her own, is also how it is supposed to work. And the obvious corollary is that lawyers often don't believe what they say. But, as a member of the Bar, I wish Supreme Court nominees would stop pointing that out. It could wreck the whole system.

## THE AYATOLLAH JOKE BOOK

SO, THE PROPHET MOHAMMED WALKS INTO A BAR . . .

Slate, *Feb. 10, 2006*

**A**yatollah Ali Khamenei, the noted wit, expert on freedom, and unelected religious leader—the leader who counts—of Iran, observed the other day that in the West, "casting doubt or negating the genocide of the Jews is banned but insulting the beliefs of 1.5 billion Muslims is allowed." He apparently thought this was a devastating point. Touché, Ayatollah Khamenei.

The worldwide fuss over twelve cartoon images of the Prophet Mohammed (some mocking, some benign) that ran in a Danish newspaper has already killed at least ten people. Many self-styled voices of Islam have made the bizarre comparison between showing pictures of the Prophet Mohammed and expressing doubt about the Holocaust. A government-controlled Tehran newspaper announced a contest for cartoons about the Holocaust, asking "whether freedom of expression" applies to "the crimes committed by the United States and Israel." In a spirit of "see how you like it," a European Muslim group posted on the Web a cartoon of Anne Frank in bed with Hitler.

Muslim complaints about a Western double standard would be more telling if the factual premise was accurate. But it is not. In fact, it is nearly the opposite of the truth. Nothing is easier and more common in the West, including the United States, than criticizing the United States—except for criticizing Israel. A few Western countries have stupid laws, erratically enforced, against denying the Holocaust, but that hasn't stopped Holocaust denial from becoming a literary industry and cultural phenomenon. This is distressing to many Jews and others because making sure that the world remembers the Holocaust has become the main strategy for trying to prevent another one. The willingness of so many people to disbelieve the reality of a historical event as relatively recent and well-documented as the Holocaust leads you to despair of the human capacity for reason, along with more or less every advance in human affairs since the Dark Ages. Nevertheless, there has been no rioting about the historical reality of the Holocaust. No one has died over it.

Meanwhile, whatever point these European Muslims were making with their cartoon of Hitler and Anne Frank is more or less disproved by their very exercise. No one tried to stop them from putting the cartoon on the Web. The notion that jokes about Anne Frank are beyond the pale is provably false. There's a play running in New York right now called *25 Questions for a Jewish Mother*. It's a monologue written and acted by stand-up comic Judy Gold, who says on stage every night that her mother used to read to her from a pop-up version of Anne Frank's diary and would say, "Pull the tab, Judith. Alive. Pull it again. Dead." Maybe you had to be there. But the *New York Times* reviewer called the play "fiercely funny, honest and moving" and did not demand that the author be executed, or even admonished.

By contrast, in a spectacular exercise of self-censorship, almost every major newspaper in this country is refraining from publishing the controversial Danish cartoons, even though they are at the center of a major news story that these papers cover at length every day. The Danish paper that originally published the twelve cartoons has apologized and editors in France and Jordan who published some of them have been fired. In tomorrow's paper, you're more likely to see a picture of Anne Frank or Hitler or both in bed with Eleanor Roosevelt, all three of them naked and performing unconventional sex acts, than you are to see a perfectly respectful picture of the Prophet

Mohammed. An editorial in the *Times* on Wednesday said that not publishing the cartoons was "a reasonable choice" since they would offend many people and "are so easy to describe in words." I am looking at a front page photo in today's *Times* (as I write on Thursday) of Mariah Carey singing into a microphone. Words do it justice, I think, but they ran the picture anyway.

Of course it is not Western values that are trampling freedom of expression: It is the ayatollah's own values, combined with the threat of violence. The other problem with his little joke about double standards, and with the whole supposedly mordant comparison between denying the Holocaust and portraying the prophet, is that the offended Muslims do not want a world where people are free to do both. They don't even want a world where people are not free to do either, which would at least be consistent. They want a world where you may not portray the Prophet Mohammed (even flatteringly, slaying infidels or whatnot) but you may deny the Holocaust all day long.

The bewildered prime minister of Denmark, trying to calm the whirlwind that has descended on his innocent, unsuspecting country, gets it spectacularly wrong when he reassures disgruntled Muslims that Denmark supports "freedom of religion" and is "one of the world's most tolerant and open societies." Tolerance, openness, and freedom of religion are not what they have in mind.

A lively debate is going on about whether Islam really does forbid any portrayal of the prophet, however benign, or whether that is a recent innovation of some subset of the faithful with possible ulterior motives. This debate misses the point. Some Christians believe they are required to wear particular sorts of clothing. Some Jews and Muslims don't eat pork. They don't claim that their religion requires other people to wear special clothing or avoid eating pork. Tolerance and ecumenism can only do so much. They have nothing to offer a Muslim in Afghanistan who is personally insulted and enraged about an image that appears in a newspaper in Denmark.

The shameful American position on all this is boilerplate endorsement of free expression combined with denunciation of the cartoons as an "unacceptable" insult. When three protesters died this week in a confrontation at a U.S. military base in Afghanistan, an American spokesman there said that Afghans "should judge us on what we're doing here, not on what some cartoonist is doing somewhere else."

But the limits of free expression cannot be set by the sensitivities of people who don't believe in it. How can President Bush continue to ask young Americans to sacrifice their lives for freedom in the Muslim world, if he won't even defend freedom verbally when forces from that world are suppressing it in our own?

## WHAT'S YOUR THEORY?

Slate, *Feb. 24, 2006*

The hideous complexity of President Bush's prescription-drug program has reduced elderly Americans—and their children—to tears of bewildered frustration. The multiple options when you sign up, each with its own multiple ceilings and co-payments; the second round of red tape when you actually want to acquire some pills; the ludicrously complex and arbitrary standards of eligibility, which play a cruel and pointless game of hide-and-seek as they lurch up and down the graph paper like drunks: Suddenly a mystery is solved—so, this must be what he means by "compassionate conservatism."

Thus Bush's only major domestic accomplishment in six years as president has not achieved its intended purpose of cementing the affection of senior citizens for the Republican Party. Many Republicans are sobbing with frustration, too. It is one thing to put aside your principles and spend hundreds of billions of taxpayer dollars on the largest expansion of the welfare state since the Great Society if it is going to help you to win elections (so you can pursue your dream of smaller government). It is another to sell your soul and not get anything for it. No one looks more foolish than a failed cynic.

But, look on the bright side, say the Bushies. The wretched thing does seem to be restraining drug prices and costing the government less than it was supposed to. The current cost estimate is only $678 billion over ten years. That's down 8 percent from the previous estimate of $737 billion. Cool. But when the prescription-drug benefit was enacted in 2003, it was supposed to cost $400 billion over ten years. As disenchanted conservative Bruce Bartlett retails in his new book about the Bush presidency, delicately entitled *Impostor*, there was a mini-scandal and an official investigation when it came out that the administration was hiding its own estimate of $534 billion. When the dust settled, that figure had become $557.7 billion.

Who believes any of these numbers? Do you? I will bet anyone a month's supply of Lipitor, collectible in 2016, that the ten-year bill will be more than $678 billion. Any takers?

What's shocking about this, more than the numbers (hundreds of billions of dollars are hard to fathom), is that Bush's drug benefit comes without even a theory about how it will be paid for. Even after nearly three decades of Republican abracadabranomics, this may be a first. A transparently phony theory at least pays tribute to the hypothesis that money doesn't grow on trees. Not even to bother coming up with a phony theory is an arrogant insult to democracy. It raises "because I said so" to a governing philosophy.

The classic Republican phony theory is, of course, supply-side economics. Every proposed tax cut from before Reagan until Bush's own has been defended on the grounds that it will pay for itself by stimulating new economic activity. This is a theory based more on faith than on evidence, but at least it's a theory.

Bush's other big attempt at a domestic initiative—Social Security privatization—came with a theory: Investing in stocks pays better than government bonds. So, you can close the looming gap between Social Security revenues and benefits—and even give the oldsters a bit extra—by letting folks invest for themselves at least part of what the government is now investing for them in those dismal bonds. The theory had a comically obvious flaw: How can society as a whole divert money from government bonds to private stocks as long as the government is still spending and borrowing as much as ever? But, at least, as I say, it was a theory. At least it paid us the compliment of obfuscation. Better to be duped than ignored. Bush's proposed Health Savings Accounts—as a way to cover the uninsured and restrain the rise in health costs—come with a theory that may even have some merit.

But the drug program has no theory. It addresses none of the conundrums of the pharmaceutical age. Pills are increasingly central to medical care, and many more miracles await. But pills are also a characteristic postindustrial product, like software or movies: They can cost billions to develop but can be mass distributed for practically nothing. Conventional supply-and-demand economics offers a compelling explanation of how an "invisible hand" sets the price and distribution of brooms or spaghetti sauce so that the benefit to society and individuals is maximized. But it has almost nothing to say about Fosamax or Windows or *Brokeback Mountain*. Conventional compassion, however sincere, is little guide to what you do about a lifesaving drug that costs $100,000 a year. And spraying government subsidies on the insurance industry and other big companies does not equal using the power of the free market to solve these problems.

Without a theory, the prescription-drug benefit is—like most government now—a straightforward matter of writing checks. Nothing wrong with that, in my book. But even if this subsidy to senior citizens survives its rocky premiere, it is doomed. Simple transfers of money cannot keep up with the rising cost—and rising benefit—of pharmaceutical drugs.

Long ago, in 1988, a Republican president and Congress enacted a bill to address the other missing piece in Medicare: insurance against the cost of long-term or catastrophic illness. But seniors, initially delighted, recoiled in horror when they discovered that they were actually expected to pay premiums to cover the cost of this insurance. The benefit program was repealed the next year, amid much embarrassment. It didn't occur to them back then to pass the benefit and ignore the cost. That's progress.

## M1 AND ME

AN EXCLUSIVE EXCERPT FROM ALAN GREENSPAN'S $8.5 MILLION MEMOIR.

Slate, *March 10, 2006*

NOTE: *Penguin Press is reportedly paying $8.5 million for the memoirs of former Federal Reserve Board Chairman Alan Greenspan. During eighteen years at the Fed, until his retirement in January, Greenspan captivated Washington and the world with his pronouncements about the economy, delivered in a style that came to be known as "oracular obscurity." According to the Yale literary critic*

*Harold Bloom—no mean practitioner himself, according to some observers—"Oracular obscurity combines the spoken traditions of Homer and Shakespeare with the writing style of postwar French pomposité grandiloquente and just a dash of Latin American magic realism to produce an entirely new phenomenon that has reinvented congressional testimony as a literary genre." But experts say it is not clear how well the oracular-obscurist style will adapt itself to the genre of autobiography. The book is due to be published in September of next year. According to publishing industry sources, Greenspan's working title is* Considerations. *The publisher's working title is* Is Your Money Supply Expanding, or Are You Just Glad to See Me? *This column has obtained an early sample of the contents.*

CHAPTER 1: THE BEGINNING

Although developments in human biology are always—and, in the view of many experts, perhaps not un-including myself, quite properly—subject to a variety of interpretations, the evidence does tend to suggest, with only a limited amount of ambiguity, that I was born.

About the year in which this happenstance may or may not have occurred, we must be prepared to accept a somewhat larger margin of error. It is possible to extrapolate backwards from my current age of eighty-one and reach a tentative conclusion based on the primitive but widely accepted methodology sometimes referred to as subtraction. Such a calculation, allowing for a reasonable margin of error, would, in layman's terms, start with the year of publication, alleged to be approximately 2007, and remove years sufficient to allow for my being eighty-one. Is that clear? No? Good. If I may continue, such a calculation would place my birth somewhere perhaps midpoint in the range of 1921 to 1931, although we have the testimony of many who have played tennis with me that I couldn't possibly be as old as that. Such anecdotal data is usually of limited value and must be regarded with extreme skepticism. However, in this case we should, I think, be prepared to give limited but not unlimited credence to the possibility that I am somewhat younger than simple subtraction might suggest.

At any rate, let me be clear about one thing. Or maybe not. Never mind. Where was I?

Considerations of birth lead inexorably to the difficult issue of parentage. Recent research has cast considerable doubt on the popular folklore that one is necessarily the child of those who one has been led to consider as one's parents. Prudence therefore dictates that we give only moderate credence to my memories of growing up in a Jewish family in New York. Although I was present throughout my childhood, until the age of four I lacked the necessary grounding in statistics and advanced calculus that might allow me to identify my parentage with sufficient certainty to justify inclusion of such a hypothesis in a book such as this one. However, given the relatively (in fact, completely) total lack of evidence to support any other hypothesis, we must, in my opinion, err on the side of prudence and accept the conventional view of my upbringing.

Many Americans have asked me over the years: "Who is this Prudence you seem to be so enamored of?" Concern has been expressed that, with her apparent fondness for dictation, she might have had an inappropriate and, through myself, disproportionate influence over our nation's financial affairs. I can only say, Senator—I mean, Dear Reader—that in this as in all other circumstances, I have chosen my words with great care. When, as on many occasions, I have had the honor of hectoring distinguished senators and members of Congress to "err on the side of prudence," that was exactly what I meant. I did not mean to be urging public officials to "err at the side of Prudence." Such an interpretation is both unwise as economic policy and unfair to a lovely woman who was, as she once put it, when I knew her many decades ago, "a sucker for a saxophone player." Some people find it hard to believe that Alan Greenspan used to be a professional jazz saxophonist. Where do they think I learned how to riff?

And if Penguin Press thinks that they're going to get any more from me about that relationship for their $8.5 million, they can think again. There is too much that I am eager to say about the relationship between M1, housing starts, and Chinese exports in the third quarter of last year. Let us therefore return to the nettlesome question of my birth, and agree if we can that—as a first approximation—I was born in New York in 1926. In Chapter 2 we will consider what is known, or at least known to be knowable, about my first 10 minutes of life . . .

## THE TWILIGHT OF OBJECTIVITY

Slate, *March 31, 2006*

CNN says it is just thrilled by the transformation of Lou Dobbs—formerly a mild-mannered news anchor noted for his palsy-walsy interviews with corporate CEOs—into a raving populist xenophobe. Ratings are up. It's like watching one of those "makeover" shows that turn nerds into fops or bathrooms into ballrooms. According to the *New York Times*, this demonstrates "that what works in cable television news is not an objective analysis of the day's events," but "a specific point of view on a sizzling-hot topic." Nicholas Lemann, dean of Columbia Journalism School, made the same point in a recent *New Yorker* profile of Fox News' Bill O'Reilly. Cable, Lemann wrote, "is increasingly a medium of outsize, super-opinionated franchise personalities."

The head of CNN/US, Jonathan Klein, told the *Times* that Lou Dobbs' license to emote is "sui generis" among CNN anchors, but that is obviously not true. Consider Anderson Cooper, CNN's rising star. His career was made when he exploded in self-righteous anger while interviewing Louisiana Sen. Mary Landrieu after Hurricane Katrina and gave her an emotional tongue-lashing over the inadequacy of the relief effort. Klein said Cooper has "that magical something . . . a refreshing way of being the anti-anchor . . . getting involved the way you might." In short, he's acting like a human being, albeit a somewhat overwrought one. And now on CNN and elsewhere you can see other anchors struggling to act like human beings, with varying degrees of success.

Klein is a man who goes with the flow. Only five months before anointing Cooper CNN's new messiah (nothing human is alien to Anderson Cooper; nothing alien is human to Lou Dobbs), he killed CNN's long-running debate show *Crossfire*, on the grounds that viewers wanted information and not opinions. He said he agreed "wholeheartedly" with Jon Stewart's widely discussed and uncharacteristically stuffy remark that *Crossfire* and similar shows were "hurting America" with their occasionally raucous displays of emotional commitment to a political point of view.

But that's just a personal gripe (I worked at *Crossfire* for six years), easily resolved by a slavish apology. More important is that Klein is right in sensing, on second thought, that objectivity is not a horse to bet the network on. Or the newspaper, either. The newspaper industry is in the midst of a psychic meltdown over the threat posed by the Internet. Internet panic is a rolling contagion among the established media. It started with newspapers, now it's spreading to magazines, and within a year book publishers will be in one of their recurring solipsistic frenzies.

No one seriously doubts anymore that the Internet will fundamentally change the news business. The uncertainty is whether it will only change the method of delivering the product, or whether it will change the nature of the product as well. Will people want, in any form—and will they pay for—a collection of articles, written by professional journalists from a detached and purportedly objective point of view? The television industry is panicky as well. Will anyone sit through a half-hour newscast invented back when everyone had to watch the same thing at the same time? Or are blogs and podcasts the cutting edge of a new model for both print and video—more personalized, more interactive, more opinionated, more communal, less objective?

Objectivity—the faith professed by American journalism and by its critics—is less an ideal than a conceit. It's not that all journalists are secretly biased, or even that perfect objectivity is an admirable but unachievable goal. In fact, most reporters work hard to be objective and the best come very close. The trouble is that objectivity is a muddled concept. Many of the world's most highly opinionated people believe with a passion that it is wrong for reporters to have any opinions at all about what they cover. These critics are people who could shed their own skins more easily than they could shed their opinions. But they expect it of journalists. It can't be done. Journalists who claim to have developed no opinions about what they cover are either lying or deeply incurious and unreflective about the world around them. In either case, they might be happier in another line of work.

Or perhaps objectivity is supposed to be a shimmering, unreachable destination, but the journey itself is purifying, as you mentally pick up your biases and put them aside, one-by-one. Is that the idea? It has a pleasing, Buddhist flavor. But that's no substitute for sense.

Nobody believes in objectivity, if that means neutrality on any question about which two people somewhere on the planet might disagree. May a reporter take as a given that two plus two is four? Should a newspaper strive to be open-minded about Osama Bin Laden? To reveal—to have!—no preference between the United States and Iran? Is it permissible for a news story to take as a given that the Holocaust not only happened, but was a bad thing—or is that an expression of opinion that belongs on the op-ed page? Even those who think objectivity can be turned on and off like a light switch don't want it switched on all the time. But short of that, there is no objective answer to when the switch needs to be on and when it can safely be turned off.

Would it be the end of the world if American newspapers abandoned the cult of objectivity? In intellectual fields other than journalism, the notion of an objective reality that words are capable of describing has been going ever more deeply out of fashion for decades. Maybe it doesn't matter what linguists think. But even within journalism, there are reassuring models of what a post-objective press might look like.

Most of the world's newspapers, in fact, already make no pretense of anything close to objectivity in the American sense. But readers of the good ones (such as the *Guardian* or *Financial Times* of London, to name the most obvious English-language examples) come away as well-informed as the readers of any "objective" American newspaper. Another model, right here in America, is the newsmagazine. *Time* long ago abandoned the extreme partisanship and arch style of its founder, Henry Luce, but all the newsmags produce outstanding journalism with little pretense to objectivity.

Opinion journalism can be more honest than objective-style journalism because it doesn't have to hide its point of view. It doesn't have to follow a trail of evidence or line of reasoning until one step before the conclusion and then slam on the brakes for fear of falling into the gulch of subjectivity. All observations are subjective. Writers freed of artificial objectivity can try to determine the whole truth about their subject and then tell it whole to the world. Their "objective" counterparts have to sort their subjective observations into two arbitrary piles: truths that are objective as well, and truths that are just an opinion. That second pile of truths then gets tossed out, or perhaps put in quotes and attributed to someone else. That is a common trick used by objective-style journalists in order to tell their readers what they believe to be true without inciting the wrath of the Objectivity cops.

Abandoning the pretense of objectivity does not mean abandoning the journalist's most important obligation, which is factual accuracy. In fact, the practice of opinion journalism brings additional ethical obligations. These can be summarized in two words: intellectual honesty. Are you writing or saying what you really think? Have you tested it against the available counterarguments? Will you stand by an expressed principle in different situations, when it leads to an unpleasing conclusion? Are you open to new evidence or argument that might change your mind? Do you retain at least a tiny, healthy sliver of a doubt about the argument you choose to make?

Much of today's opinion journalism, especially on TV, is not a great advertisement for the notion that American journalism could be improved by more opinion and less effort at objectivity. But that's because the conditions under which much opinion journalism is practiced today make honesty harder and doubt practically impossible. Like the mopey vicar in Evelyn Waugh's novel *Decline and Fall*, who loses a cushy parish when struck by a case of "doubts," TV pundits need to radiate certainty for the sake of their careers. As Lou Dobbs has demonstrated, this doesn't mean you can't change your mind, as long as you are as certain in your opinion today as you were of the opposite opinion a couple of days ago.

## WIN A DATE WITH E. J. DIONNE

Slate, *April 21, 2006*

**N**icholas Kristof writes a man's column. As he describes his life twice a week in the *New York Times*, Kristof (who just won this year's Pulitzer Prize for commentary) actually lives the fantasy that seduced us all into the column racket in the first place. Partying all night while accepting large bribes from businessmen who don't want to be mentioned in print and movie stars who do? No, no. That fantasy comes later. I mean: stripping down to your loincloth and swinging through the trees to some distant place of misery that those other lazy bastards are too fat and old and weak to get to, and rescuing victims of oppression with your superpower of worldwide publicity. No joke, he does good. But also: cool!

Not that Kristof ignores women's issues, either. He opposes rape, for example. Chicks love that.

So naturally I was intrigued by a promotion the *Times* has been running: "Win a Trip with Nick Kristof." Gosh. Me? On a trip with Nick Kristof?? Wowie. Nick himself writes: "I'm looking for a masochist. If your dream trip doesn't involve a five-star hotel in Rome or Bora-Bora, but a bedbug-infested mattress in a malarial jungle as hungry jackals yelp outside—then read on." He adds, "Don't expect comfort so much as diarrhea." How on earth did Kristof know about my bedbugs-and-jackals-and-diarrhea fantasy? Bob Woodward promised me he wouldn't tell anyone else.

The rules say you have to be over eighteen and a college or graduate student, but I can fake both of those. And Nick reassures us that those "boring" lawyers have "nixed" some of his usual favorite activities, such as "hiking through Afghan minefields, riding a camel through Darfur, or sneaking illegally into Zimbabwe." And all it takes is "a seven-hundred-word essay on why you're the perfect traveling companion for Nick Kristof." Very tempting. I wouldn't have to tell them that I snore. And I could use a few tips on how to win a Pulitzer Prize.

Then I try to picture the scene. It's the middle of the night. We're in a small tent pitched on the rocky slope of a mountain trail: me, Nick, our trusty guide, three prostitutes we've rescued from a life of sex slavery, and four local businessmen unjustly accused of insider trading on the village's primitive, hand-pumped stock exchange. Outside, the jackals are yelping. Inside, nature is calling. Urgently. Am I man enough to face the jackals, or masochist enough to wait until morning? Answer: Whatever. I'm tough. I can handle either of these. But ultimately, the jackals are less terrifying than the thought of one more minute listening to Nick's tales of all the real adventures he's been on that make this one seem like a game of paddycakes. I flee the tent, am devoured by the jackals, and Kristof gets a column out of it.

No, in the end, I have to be honest with myself. These days, my dream doesn't involve bedbugs and jackals, but a five-star hotel in

Rome. That's why I have decided instead to enter the *Times'* next contest: "Win a Trip with Tom Friedman."

Tom writes: "The world, as you know, is flat. If you're not afraid to fall off the edge, if you dream of running up travel expenses that would finance Hannibal's army, if you fantasize about meeting presidents and prime ministers and reminding them that the world is flat, if you can go to Davos and Aspen and Bilderberg and still get it up for the Bohemian Grove, then you may be the right person to accompany me on a unique 'World Is Flat World Tour.' We will be staying in the best hotels and interviewing world leaders day and night. You may find yourself discoursing in Arabic about the flatness of the world with a group of Saudi princes, or even asking the Pope himself, 'Do you agree with Tom Friedman that the world is flat?' All it takes to apply is a seven-hundred-word essay on 'Why the World is Flat.'" Tom himself will choose the winner, and they'll immediately be off to St. Petersburg, where you will get to operate the PowerPoint for Tom's presentation titled: "Flatter Will Get You Nowhere: The Limits of World Flatness."

Or maybe I should wait and Win a Trip with Maureen Dowd. Maureen writes: "Are you girl enough to come shopping with me and my best friend, Jill? Can you dis the defense department and find the shoe department at the same time?"

The *Washington Post* has chosen, so far, not to subject its columnists to this kind of embarrassment. But how long can it hold out? I'm psyched for "Win a Trip with George Will." Finally admitting his uncanny resemblance to Mr. Peabody, the scholarly time-traveling dog on the *Rocky and Bullwinkle* cartoon show, George takes a lucky companion back to the eighteenth century, where they will explain the original meaning of the Declaration of Independence to its signers.

Join David Broder in a tour of Midwestern capitals. You'll interview more lieutenant governors than there are stars on the flag. Or take seething lessons from Charles Krauthammer. Or write an essay on, "Why I have no interest in a trip with Robert Novak." Novak writes: "I'm looking for people who want to travel with me as little as I want to travel with them." The lucky winner won't have to.

## ABOVE THE LAW

THE PRESIDENT ISN'T, BUT JOURNALISTS ARE?

Slate, *May 5, 2006*

NOTE: *The* Globe *article discussed in this piece won its author, Charlie Savage, a Pulitzer Prize.*

If there is anything scarier than a president who thinks he is above the law, it is a president who thinks that journalists aren't. That is the combined message from two major newspapers this week.

Last Sunday's *Boston Globe* carried an alarming 4,500-word front-page article about President Bush and the Constitution. It seems that Bush has asserted the right to ignore "vast swaths of laws," simply because he thinks that these laws are unconstitutional. Through the veil of objectivity, it is hard not to detect a note of disapproval here. Four times the article says that Bush has asserted this right "quietly," a word often used in news stories to imply menace. Quoted against Bush are people such as "legal scholars" and "many legal scholars," including "a professor who has studied the executive power claims Bush made during his first term," a "professor who studies executive power," and a "professor who specializes in executive-power issues." Quoted in his defense are "former administration officials" and "[s]ome administration defenders," as well as others who have served in or support the Bush administration.

The article is specifically about "signing statements," in which the president offers his interpretation of an act of Congress as he signs it into law. This was an innovation of the Reagan administration, intended to give courts something other than a law's legislative history—that is, Congress' side of the story—in any future dispute over its meaning. Bush often signs a law and says that parts of it are unconstitutional at the same time. Sneaky!

To put pursuers off the scent, the *Globe* reports, Bush often obeys and enforces the very laws he says are unconstitutional. Even the fact that Bush has never vetoed a single act of Congress is part of his quiet executive power grab, because it denies Congress the "chance to override his judgments."

The *Globe* does not report what its cadre of professors of executive power think that a president should do when called upon to enforce or obey a law he or she believes to be unconstitutional. It's not an easy question. Some connoisseurs of "quiet" constitutional power grabs point to *Marbury v. Madison*, the 1803 case in which the Supreme Court established its power to have the last word in constitutional interpretation, as the beginning of a power grab by the judicial branch. That judicial power is not in the Constitution in so many words. The logic of *Marbury* was that every officer of the government has an obligation to follow the Constitution, and courts get the last word in any dispute over its meaning simply because their opportunity to express a view comes last procedurally. The Constitution is like a hot potato, and the judges are holding it when the music stops.

The tradition of judicial review is almost universally accepted, and it has served this country very, very well. What was dangerous about the Reagan administration's signing-statements initiative was the claim that a president is entitled to govern according to his or her own interpretation of the Constitution even after the courts have ruled. This is a recipe for near-dictatorial executive power, not to mention governmental chaos, in which no fundamental issue can ever be resolved. But the *Globe* does not even suggest that Bush is claiming the right to thumb his nose at the courts in this way.

The complications come when the courts haven't, or haven't yet, ruled on the subject at hand. In that situation, shouldn't the president—who swears to "preserve, protect, and defend" the Constitution—follow his own sincere beliefs about what the Constitution requires? Well, yes and no. It depends on how unclear the issue really is and how plausible the president's interpretation. A president shouldn't force the courts to rule again and again on some issue because the specific facts of each case are slightly different. More than that: After 220 years of constitutional interpretation, the doctrines are pretty thick on the ground. As a general rule, even on some novel issue, the president ought to follow the Constitution as he sincerely imagines that the courts will see it, rather than as he wishes they would see it. On the other hand, even the Supreme Court does change its mind occasionally. And the president, like anyone else, has the right to present a test case. But this is a right best used sparingly.

Bottom line: It is not necessarily an outrage for the president to run the government according to his own interpretation of the Constitution. And it is certainly not an outrage for the president to simply state his view and then do nothing about it. Legitimate outrage comes when the president acts in flagrant violation of the Constitution, defending his actions unconvincingly, disingenuously, or not at all. And Bush has offered plenty of grist for this mill in his assertion of the right to kidnap people off the streets, keep them locked up for years without a trial or even a public acknowledgment of their existence, to torture them, and so on. But nailing him simply for stating his views on a constitutional issue, without even asking whether those views are right or wrong, is wrong.

It's wrong especially when contrasted with another current fever running through the nation's editorial pages: the ongoing issue of leaks and anonymous sources. Many in the media believe that the Constitution contains a "reporter's privilege" to protect the identity of sources in circumstances, like a criminal trial, in which citizens ordinarily can be compelled to produce information or go to jail. The Supreme Court and lower courts have ruled and ruled again that there is no such privilege. And it certainly is not obvious that the First Amendment, which seems to be about the right to speak, actually protects a right not to speak. Yet many in the media not only believe that it does. They believe passionately that it is not merely OK but profoundly noble to follow their own interpretation and ignore the Supreme Court's.

Why must the president obey constitutional interpretations he disagrees with if journalists don't have to? Upholding the Constitution is actually part of his job description. It is not part of theirs.

Last Sunday, the same day as the *Globe* piece, the *New York Times* had a front-page article about the other shoe waiting to drop in these leak cases. The Bush administration might go beyond forcing journalists to testify about the sources of leaks. It might start to prosecute journalists themselves as recipients of illegal leaks. As with the *Globe* story, this turns out to be a matter of pugnacious noises by the Bush administration. Actual prosecutions of journalists for receiving or publishing leaks are "unknown," the *Times* article concedes. But this could change at any moment.

Well, maybe. It would be odd for the Bush administration to take up this particular cause at this particular moment, since the fellow most eager for evidence from journalists is the special prosecutor investigating the Bush administration. But it wouldn't be constitutionally crazy. Maybe you can find an implied journalist's privilege in the First Amendment's guarantee of a free press, but you've got to look pretty hard. Why should the Constitution allow the government to prosecute the provider of stolen government information but not the knowing recipient or to prosecute all other recipients of such information (like two lobbyists currently under investigation) but not journalists?

Maybe journalists sincerely believe they are entitled to such constitutional special treatment. Maybe they are even right about this, and the courts are wrong. But who wants to live in a society where every citizen and government official feels free to act according to his or her own personal interpretation of the Constitution, even after the Supreme Court has specifically said that this interpretation is wrong? President Bush would top my list of people I don't want wandering through the text and getting fancy ideas. But why should he stay out of the "I say what's constitutional around here" game if his tormentors in the press are playing it?

## PLEASE DON'T REMAIN CALM

IN A CRISIS, SHOULD YOU BE A HERO? OR OBEY THE RULES?

Slate, *May 12, 2006*

The story of United Flight 93, more than any other tale—true or fable—of our lifetime, makes you wonder about yourself. These were not young soldiers in battle. This was not the culmination of some long crisis with time to ruminate and firm up your resolve. These were ordinary, middle-class, and (mostly) middle-aged Americans going about their everyday lives, when—bang!—they faced the ultimate test. And passed. "Once to every man and nation comes the moment to decide," goes the old hymn. But usually it's not literally just a moment. These people were not just courageous. They were instinctually courageous.

I think I'd flunk. Oh, perhaps optimistically, I give myself a 50–50 chance of having the courage to rise from my seat and join a charge toward the cockpit (once I'd concluded I was almost certainly going to die anyway). What I find harder to imagine is disobeying the instructions from authority figures—flight attendants, anonymous voices over the public-address system, telling me to stay seated and remain calm.

In retrospect, this was bad advice. Similar instructions were even worse advice at the World Trade Center, where people who called 911 were told to remain at their desks. Many ignored or didn't wait for this advice, fled anyway, made it partway down the emergency stairs, and then were told to go back to their desks, or to wait at assembly points in the doomed buildings. Hundreds did as they were told and died as a result. Other hundreds defied authority, proceeded out of the buildings, and went about the rest of their lives.

So, what's the lesson? Is it to defy authority and follow your own instincts in an emergency? If so, we haven't learned it. For a while after 9/11 there was talk of changing the official policy regarding hijackings and to start encouraging the passengers to whack the hijackers with their pillows, and so on. An urban myth sprouted about an airplane captain who gave the passengers detailed instructions in guerilla warfare at thirty thousand feet. But today, airline passengers are still told at the start of every flight that in an emergency they should remain calm and follow instructions from anyone in a uniform or—in the case of United—even inanimate objects ("lighted signs and placards").

Poking around the Web, I stumbled across the official "Hijacking Survival Guidelines" for employees of the U.S. Department of Agriculture. They say, "Stay calm and encourage others around you to do the same. Do not challenge the hijackers physically or verbally. Comply with their instructions. Do not struggle. . . . Blend in with the other airline passengers." (There's no telling, I suppose, how an emotionally volatile hijacker might react to the discovery that there is an Agriculture Department employee on board.)

So the U.S. government is kicking in millions of dollars for a memorial to the heroes of United 93. But meanwhile it is officially encouraging people not to do what these heroes did, should the occasion arise. "Don't try this at home" might be a sensible policy if the United 93 passengers had been specially selected or trained. But they were an utterly random collection of Americans, just like you or me or the employees of the Ag Department. If they are heroes, why are we being told not to do what they did?

It is the nature of authorities to assert authority, and it's hard to imagine officials of anything urging people to pay no attention to official instructions. But there is also some logic here. The policies followed by police and fire officials at the World Trade Center (at the cost of their own lives as well as others') seem very wrong in hindsight. But these rules themselves were the product of hindsight. During the first World Trade Center bombing, back in 1993, rescue attempts and fire control were frustrated by the anarchy of thousands fleeing unnecessarily down narrow emergency stairs. Emergency planners are like generals—always fighting the last war. But what other choice do they have? Let he who anticipated that the next four hijacked planes would be pointed at major office buildings cast the first stone.

With convenient symmetry, it also seems to be the nature of most people, most of the time, to obey authority. The famous Stanley Milgram experiments at Yale in 1961 demonstrated that it is frighteningly easy to induce ordinary people—good people—to inflict pain on others, when ordered to do so by some authority figure. Sept. 11 demonstrated that most people will sit tight and obey orders even unto their own deaths. The defiance of authority is a big reason the United 93 story is so thrilling. This was heroism, American-style. Dissing the Man on your way out the door. These folks were cowboys. John Wayne and Clint Eastwood don't have time for the rules, and neither did they.

But instinct aside, people who choose to obey authority in crises may do so because of a conscious and rational decision that it is the right thing to do. If, in an airplane emergency, the flight attendant told me to remain in my seat with my seat belt buckled high across my waist and my seat back and tray table in the full upright and locked position, I would be strongly inclined to assume that a trained flight attendant knew more about what was going on, and the best way of dealing with it, than I did. She, far better than I, could assess the ever-present danger of items shifting in the overhead bins. The incantatory power of these familiar phrases no doubt enhances their persuasiveness. As a fairly enthusiastic fan of the rule of law generally—in a democratic society, that is—I would probably regard being caught in the middle of a crisis like 9/11 as a test of my principles in extremis. And I would be inclined, even for high-minded reasons, to do as told.

And sometimes obeying authority is the counsel of courage while defying it is the counsel of cowardice. It probably took more courage to climb back up to your office in the World Trade Center than it did to proceed down and out of the building. Foolish courage, as it turns out, but you never know. I suspect that many emergencies are what game theorists call a "prisoner's dilemma" situation, where everybody is best off if most people obey the rules, but the few that disobey are even better off—as long as they're only a few. In a situation like the World Trade Center, for example, the most lives might be saved by an orderly evacuation, but your best shot at saving your own life is to escape before order collapses because everyone else is doing what you do.

Courage and cowardice, obeying instructions and defying them, are all unreliable guides in an unimaginable crisis like 9/11. In a way, that's comforting. You can't really get it wrong. You're in the hands of fate (or faith, if you've got it). We celebrate the passengers who rebelled on United 93 for their choice, but we surely don't, or shouldn't, blame any of the folks on any of those planes for arriving at a different decision, or none at all.

The closest I've come to such a crisis was a big earthquake in Seattle a few years ago. I was at a meeting in a ground-floor conference room at Microsoft when the tremors started. People shouted, "Don't run outside, don't run outside"—that being the one piece of official advice everybody remembers. Then, after a very long two or three seconds, everybody ran outside. Including me. That's not courage, and it may not be wisdom. But it's instinct and it's irresistible. I'd do it again, whatever they may say.

## How I Spent My Summer Vacation

Time, *July 16, 2006*

Like NASA before the first moon landing, I have been soliciting advice about what to say when I wake up from brain surgery. That's right, brain surgery—it's a real conversation stopper, isn't it? There aren't many things you can say these days that retain their shock value, but that is one of them. "So, Mike—got any summer plans?" "Why, yes, next Tuesday I'm having brain surgery. How about you?" In the age of angioplasty and Lipitor, even the heart has lost much of its metaphorical power, at least in the medical context. People are willing to accept it as a collection of muscles and blood vessels rather than—or at least in addition to—the seat of various emotions. But the brain remains the seat of the self itself in physical reality as well as in metaphor. And the brain as metaphor looms so large that there isn't much room left for the simultaneous physical reality that the brain is material, performs mechanical functions, can break down and sometimes can be repaired.

So brain surgery remains shocking and mystical. People don't expect to run into someone who's having brain surgery next week squeezing the melons at Whole Foods. (Unless, of course, he's squeezing them and shrieking, "Why don't you answer? Hello? Hello?") Self-indulgently, I've been dropping the conversational bomb of brain surgery more often than absolutely necessary just to enjoy the reaction. And why not? I deserve that treat. After all, I'm going to be having brain surgery.

Brain surgery is a license for self-indulgence. Cancel that dentist's appointment; you've suffered enough. (Though technically, before you go under, you haven't actually suffered at all.) Take out the trash? "C'mon, honey, I've got BRAIN SURGERY next week." Writers devote a lot of creative energy to dreaming up reasons not to write. One of the all-time best came recently from *Washington Post* columnist Anne Applebaum, who told her readers that she was going to stop writing the column for a while because her husband had become Defense Minister of Poland, and she was moving to Warsaw. Sure, Anne, and I'm taking the summer off because I'm having brain surgery. In Cleveland.

But it's true. The operation is called deep-brain stimulation (DBS). They stick a couple of wires into your head, run them around your ears and into batteries that are implanted in your chest. Then current from the batteries zaps some bad signals in your brain so that good signals can be heard by the rest of your body. When it works, as it generally does, it greatly reduces the symptoms of Parkinson's disease. I wrote in *Time* four and a half years ago about having PD and adopting a strategy of denial: pretending to myself and others that I didn't have it. By now my symptoms are past the point where dishonesty and self-deception are a useful approach. But maybe this operation will get me back there.

As I write, surgery is a few days off. But you can assume, if you are reading this, that it went well. And thank you for your concern. Now, where was I? Oh, yes, brain surgery. Thinking I would give self-deception one more shot, I tried to convince myself that DBS isn't really brain surgery. They don't crack open your skull; they just drill a couple of small holes to put the wires through. Tiny holes. Itsy-bitsy holes. Teensy-weensy little holes. The propaganda they give you when you sign up for the operation describes the holes as "dime-sized." That took me aback. The dime, there's no denying, is a seriously undersized coin. But frankly, I wasn't thinking coins at all. I was thinking grains of sand. A dime is huge! The hospital printout of all the things you can't do afterward describes it as "major brain surgery." Is there minor brain surgery?

To an American middle-class professional of the twenty-first century, what is scariest about brain surgery isn't the ever present risk of disaster or even the chance of unexpected side effects. It's the danger that people will look at you differently. We are all brain snobs, and we are all—those of us over twenty or so—losing brain cells. But if you're walking around with wires in your head and batteries flanking your chest, every senior moment when you can't remember the term for, you know, when they drill holes in your skull—right, brain surgery—is . . . is . . . is . . . well, it's going to seem significant to others and to you.

That's why my first words coming out of surgery are so important. They have got to tell the world—and convince myself—that I am all there. Of course, there are the obvious jokes about brain surgery ("Well, it wasn't exactly rocket science") and about those wires in my head ("Can you hear me now?"). There is Dada ("I am the Defense Minister of Poland. Who the hell are you?"). And slapstick ("I feel as if I've lost ten pounds . . . uh oh"). I'm still working on it.

Editor's note: Kinsley's surgery took place on July 12 and went fine. His first words were, "Well, of course, when you cut taxes, government revenues go up. Why couldn't I see that before?"

## YROTCIV IN IRAQ

Slate, *Sept. 22, 2006*

Harold Pinter wrote a play a while back called *Betrayal*. (Rent the movie: It's terrific.) The plot was a fairly mundane story about an adulterous affair among affluent London literati. What gives the tale its haunting magic is that Pinter tells it in reverse: starting with the couple breaking up and ending with that first, ambiguous flirtation.

Others have tried this device. Martin Amis used it in a novel called *Time's Arrow* to make some point or other about the dangers of nuclear war. There is a Stephen Sondheim musical called *Merrily We Roll Along*, which starts with the hero as an unattractive middle-aged Hollywood power player and ends with him as an idealistic youth gazing toward "the hills of tomorrow." A clever movie several years ago called *Memento* used the time-backward trick as a way to imitate for the audience the effect of amnesia.

So, it's been used by some of the masters. And it's a good trick: disorienting, as modern art is supposed to be, and with built-in poignance. But that doesn't mean that anyone can pull it off. Frankly, I would have pegged George W. Bush—whose awareness of his own weaknesses is one of his more attractive traits—as just about the last person in the world who would try this literary jujitsu. But in his own narrative of his own war (the one in Iraq), he has done it. If you trace the concept of "victory" in his remarks on Iraq, and those of subordinates, you discover a war that was won three and a half years ago, and today has barely started.

Return with me, if you will, to May 1, 2003. That was the day Bush landed on the aircraft carrier *Abraham Lincoln*, and—under a banner declaring "Mission Accomplished"—declared that "major combat operations in Iraq have ended" and "the United States and our allies have prevailed. (Applause.)" (This is from the official White House transcript.) The White House claimed that the banner was somebody else's idea and that Bush didn't declare victory in so many words. But Bush did use the word "victory," saying that Iraq was "one victory in a war on terror . . ." And as I recall, the occasion was pretty triumphal. Perhaps you remember differently. And in his radio address two days later, Bush used the term "victory" unabashedly.

Soon, however, the concept of "victory" became more fluid. There is not just one victory, but many. Or, as then–press secretary Scott McClellan put it in August 2004, "Every progress made in Iraq since the collapse of Saddam's regime is a victory against the terrorists and enemies of Iraq." And there was a subtle shift from declaring how wonderful victory was to emphasizing how wonderful it will be. "The rise of democracy in Iraq will be an essential victory in the war on terror," the vice president said in April 2004.

During his 2004 presidential campaign, Bush said repeatedly that one reason to vote for him over Sen. John Kerry was that he, Bush, had "a strategy that will lead to victory. And that strategy has four commitments." By October 2005, these four "commitments" had been honed down to three "prongs." Then they metastasized into four "categories for victory. And they're clear, and our command structure and our diplomats in Iraq understand the definition of victory." It's nice that someone does.

It was during the 2004 campaign that Bush offered his most imaginative explanation for why victory in Iraq looked so much like failure. "Because we achieved such a rapid victory"—note that it is once more, briefly, a victory—"more of the Saddam loyalists were [still] around."

On May 1, 2006, the third anniversary of "mission accomplished," White House press secretary Scott McClellan was asked whether "victory" had been achieved in Iraq. He said, "We're making real progress on our plan for victory. . . . We are on the path to victory. We are winning in Iraq. But there is more work to do." Democrats should shut up because their criticism of the president "does nothing to help advance our goal of achieving victory in Iraq." (Once victory is achieved, presumably, it will be OK for Democrats to criticize.) And make no mistake: "[W]hen the job in Iraq is done, it will be a major victory."

On Aug. 28, criticizing "self-defeating pessimism," Vice President Cheney said there are "only two options in Iraq—victory or defeat." On Aug. 31, Bush said that "victory in Iraq will be difficult and it will require more sacrifice." He predicted that "victory in Iraq will be a crushing defeat for our enemies"—which, as a tautology, is a safe bet.

Which brings us to last week, and Bush's television speech on the fifth anniversary of Sept. 11, 2001. "Bush Says Iraq Victory Is

Vital" was the *Washington Post*'s accurate headline. And Bush was eloquent. "Once more into the breach, dear friends, once more . . ." Well, maybe not that eloquent. But his point was the same as Henry V's: Don't give up now! "Mistakes have been made in Iraq," he conceded. He even conceded that "Saddam Hussein was not responsible for the 9/11 attacks." But let us not, for mercy's sake, learn anything from five years of experience. Instead, let's just pretend it all never happened. After all, we won this war back in 2003.

## War and Embryos

Slate, *Sept. 29, 2006*

It was, I believe, Rep. Barney Frank, Democrat of Massachusetts, who first made the excellent, bitter, and terribly unfair joke about Ronald Reagan: that he believed in a right to life that begins at conception and ends at birth. This joke has been adapted for use against various Republican politicians ever since. In the case of President George W. Bush, though, it appears to be literally true.

Bush, as we know, believes deeply and earnestly that human life begins at conception. Even tiny embryos composed of half a dozen microscopic cells, he thinks, have the same right to life as you and me. That is why he cannot bring himself to allow federal funding for stem-cell research, or even for other projects in labs where stem-cell research is going on. Even though these embryos are obtained from fertility clinics where they would otherwise be destroyed anyway, and even though he appears to have no objection to the fertility clinics themselves, where these same embryos are manufactured and destroyed by the thousands, the much smaller number of embryos needed and destroyed in the process of developing cures for diseases like Parkinson's are, in effect, tiny little children whose use in this way constitutes killing a human being and therefore is intolerable.

But President Bush does not believe that the deaths of all little children as a result of U.S. policy are, in effect, murder. He thinks that some are, while very unfortunate, also inevitable and essential.

You know who I mean. Close to fifty thousand Iraqi civilians have died so far as a direct result of our invasion and occupation of their country, in order to liberate them. The numbers are actually increasing as the country slides into chaos: more than sixty-five hundred in July and August alone. These numbers are from reliable sources and are not seriously contested. They include many who were tortured and then killed, along with others blown up less personally by car bombs and suicide bombers. The number does not include the hundreds of thousands who have died prematurely as a result of a decade and a half of war and embargos imposed on the Iraqi economy. Nor does it include soldiers on both sides, most of whom are innocent, too. Last week the number of American soldiers killed in Iraq and Afghanistan surpassed the number of people who died in the terrorist attacks of Sept. 11, 2001.

Bush is right, of course, that the inevitable loss of innocent life in wartime cannot be a reason not to go to war, or a reason not to fight that war in a way intended to win. Eggs, omelettes, and all that. "Collateral damage" should be a consideration weighed in the balance, of course. But there is no formula to determine when you have the balance right. It does seem to me that both of our wars in Iraq were started and conducted with insufficient consideration for the cost in innocent blood. Callousness, naiveté, isolation of the decision makers from democratic accountability, and isolation of the citizenry from the consequences, or even the awareness, of what is being done in their name—all have played a role. I don't see anything coming out of this war that is worth fifty thousand innocent lives, although a case can be made, I guess.

But it is hard—I would say it is impossible—to reconcile Bush's absolutism over alleged human life when it is a clump of unknowing, unfeeling cells with his sophisticated, if not cavalier, attitude toward the loss of innocent human life when it is children and adults in Iraq.

In all discussions weighing the cost of something-or-other in terms of human life, a philosopher pops up at this point and says that the crucial difference is a matter of intentions. Terrorists purposely target innocent civilians. We try hard not to kill innocent civilians, even if we know it can't be avoided. They're worse, even if our score is sadly higher.

But are stem cells any different? Stem-cell researchers don't want to kill embryos. They know that the deaths of embryos are a consequence of what they do, and they think that curing terrible diseases is worth it—just as President Bush thinks that bringing democracy to Iraq is worth it. In the case of stem cells, there is the added element that the embryos in question will be killed (or pointlessly frozen indefinitely) anyway if they are not used for research. And—oh, yes—there is still the question of whether a clump of a half-dozen cells you can't see without a microscope is actually a human being in the same sense as a six-year-old girl blown up as she skips off to kindergarten in Baghdad.

A commander in chief who must face life-or-death questions like these deserves a bit of sympathy. I would sympathize a bit more with President Bush if his answers weren't so preening and struggle-free. It is very wonderful to be so morally pure that you won't allow a single embryo to be destroyed in the quest for medical cures that could save lives by the thousands. You are way beyond Gandhi, sweeping the path ahead to avoid stepping on an insect: Insects have more human characteristics than a six-cell embryo.

And regarding Iraq, you are quite the man—aren't you?—"making the tough decisions." A regular Harry Truman, consigning thousands to death in order to bring democracy and freedom and peace to millions. But Truman actually produced democracy and freedom and peace, whereas you want credit for your hopes. That's not how it works. If you want to be the hard-ass, you get judged by results. And you can't be Gandhi and Truman at the same time.

# 2007

## IN GOD, DISTRUST

New York Times Book Review, *May 13, 2007*

Observers of the Christopher Hitchens phenomenon have been expecting a book about religion from him around now. But this impressive and enjoyable attack on everything so many people hold dear is not the book we were expecting.

First in London thirty or more years ago, then in New York and for the last couple of decades in Washington, Hitchens has established himself as a character. This character draws on such familiar sources as the novels of P. G. Wodehouse, Evelyn Waugh and Graham Greene; the leftist politics of the 1960s (British variant); and—of course—the person of George Orwell. (Others might throw in the flower-clutching Bunthorne from Gilbert and Sullivan's *Patience*, but that is probably not an intentional influence.) Hitchens is the bohemian and the swell, the dashing foreign correspondent, the painstaking literary critic and the intellectual engagé. He charms Washington hostesses but will set off a stink bomb in the salon if the opportunity arises.

His conversation sparkles, not quite effortlessly, and if he is a bit too quick to resort to French in search of le mot juste, his jewels of erudition, though flashy, are real. Or at least they fool me. Hitchens was right to choose Washington over New York and London.

His enemies would like to believe he is a fraud. But he isn't, as the very existence of his many enemies tends to prove. He is self-styled, to be sure, but no more so than many others in Washington—or even in New York or London—who are not nearly as good at it. He is a principled dissolute, with the courage of his dissolution: he enjoys smoking and drinking, and not just the reputation for smoking and drinking—although he enjoys that too. And through it all he is productive to an extent that seems like cheating: twenty-three books, pamphlets, collections and collaborations so far; a long and often heavily researched column every month in *Vanity Fair*; frequent fusillades in *Slate* and elsewhere; and speeches, debates and other public spectacles whenever offered.

The big strategic challenge for a career like this is to remain interesting, and the easiest tactic for doing that is surprise. If they expect you to say X, you say minus X.

Consistency is foolish, as the man said. (Didn't he?) Under the unwritten and somewhat eccentric rules of American public discourse, a statement that contradicts everything you have ever said before is considered for that reason to be especially sincere, courageous and dependable. At the *New Republic* in the 1980s, when I was the editor, we used to joke about changing our name to "Even the Liberal New Republic," because that was how we were referred to whenever we took a conservative position on something, which was often. Then came the day when we took a liberal position on something and we were referred to as "Even the Conservative New Republic."

As this example illustrates, among writers about politics, the surprise technique usually means starting left and turning right. Trouble is, you do this once and what's your next party trick?

Christopher Hitchens had seemed to be solving this problem by turning his conversion into an ideological "Dance of the Seven Veils." Long ago he came out against abortion. Interesting! Then he discovered and made quite a kosher meal of the fact that his mother, deceased, was Jewish, which under Jewish law meant he himself was Jewish. Interesting!! (He was notorious at the time for his anti-Zionist sympathies.) In the 1990s, Hitchens was virulently, and somewhat inexplicably, hostile to President Bill Clinton. Interesting!!! You would have thought that Clinton's decadence—the thing that bothered other liberals and leftists the most—would have positively appealed to Hitchens. Finally and recently, he became the most (possibly the only) intellectually serious non-neocon supporter of George W. Bush's Iraq war. Interesting!!!!

Where was this train heading? Possibly toward an open conversion to mainline conservatism and quick descent into cliché and demagoguery (the path chosen by Paul Johnson, a somewhat similar British character of the previous generation). But surely there was time for a few more intellectual adventures before retiring to an office at the Hoover Institution or some other nursing home of the mind. One obvious possibility stood out: Hitchens, known to be a fervid atheist, would find God and take up religion. The only question was which flavor he would choose. Embrace Islam? Too cute. Complete the half-finished Jewish script? Become a Catholic, following the path well trodden by such British writers as Waugh and Greene? Or—most daring and original—would he embrace the old Church of England (Episcopalianism in America) and spend his declining years writing about the beauty of the hymns, the essential Britishness of village churchyards, the importance of protecting religion from the dangers of excessive faith, and so on?

Well, ladies and gentlemen, Hitchens is either playing the contrarian at a very high level or possibly he is even sincere. But just as he had us expecting minus X, he confounds us by reverting to X. He has written, with tremendous brio and great wit, but also with an underlying genuine anger, an all-out attack on all aspects of religion. Sometimes, instead of the word "religion," he refers to it as "god-worship," which, although virtually a tautology (isn't "object of worship" almost a definition of a god?), makes the practice sound sinister and strange.

Hitchens is an old-fashioned village atheist, standing in the square trying to pick arguments with the good citizens on their way to church. The book is full of logical flourishes and conundrums, many of them entertaining to the nonbeliever. How could Christ have died for our sins, when supposedly he also did not die at all? Did the Jews not know that murder and adultery were wrong before they received the Ten Commandments, and if they did know, why was this such a wonderful gift? On a more somber note, how can the "argument from design" (that only some kind of "intelligence" could have designed anything as perfect as a human being) be reconciled with the religious practice of female genital mutilation, which posits that women, at least, as nature creates them, are not so perfect after all? Whether sallies like these give pause to the believer is a question I can't answer.

And all the logical sallies don't exactly add up to a sustained argument, because Hitchens thinks a sustained argument shouldn't even be necessary and yet wouldn't be sufficient. To him, it's blindingly obvious: the great religions all began at a time when we knew a tiny fraction of what we know today about the origins of Earth and human life. It's understandable that early humans would develop stories about gods or God to salve their ignorance. But people today have no such excuse. If they continue to believe in the unbelievable, or say they do, they are morons or lunatics or liars. "The human wish to credit good things as miraculous and to charge bad things to another account is apparently universal," he remarks, unsympathetically.

Although Hitchens's title refers to God, his real energy is in the subtitle: "religion poisons everything." Disproving the existence of God (at least to his own satisfaction and, frankly, to mine) is just the beginning for Hitchens. In fact, it sometimes seems as if existence is just one of the bones Hitchens wants to pick with God—and not even the most important. If God would just leave the world alone, Hitchens would be glad to let him exist, quietly, in retirement somewhere. Possibly the Hoover Institution.

Hitchens is attracted repeatedly to the principle of Occam's razor: that simple explanations are more likely to be correct than complicated ones. (E.g., Earth makes a circle around the Sun; the Sun doesn't do a complex roller coaster ride around Earth.) You might think that Occam's razor would favor religion; the biblical creation story certainly seems simpler than evolution. But Hitchens argues effectively again and again that attaching the religious myth to what we know from science to be true adds nothing but needless complication.

For Hitchens, it's personal. He is a great friend of Salman Rushdie, and he reminds us that it wasn't just some crazed fringe Muslim who threatened Rushdie's life, killed several others and made him a virtual prisoner for the crime of writing a novel. Religious leaders from all the major faiths, who disagree on some of the most fundamental questions, managed to put aside their differences to agree that Rushdie had it coming. (Elsewhere, Hitchens notes tartly that if any one of the major faiths is true, then the others must be false in important respects—an obvious point often forgotten in the warm haze of ecumenism.)

Hitchens's erudition is on display—impressively so, and perhaps sometimes pretentiously so. In one paragraph, he brings in Stephen Jay Gould, chaos theory and Saul Bellow; pronounces the movie *It's a Wonderful Life* "engaging but abysmal" (a typical Hitchens aside: cleverly paradoxical? witlessly oxymoronic? take your pick) in the way it explains to a "middlebrow audience" Heisenberg's uncertainty principle; and winds down through a discussion of the potential of stem cells. Nevertheless, and in spite of all temptations, he has written an entire book without a single reference to Sir Isaiah Berlin, the fox or the hedgehog.

But speaking of foxes, Hitchens has outfoxed the Hitchens watchers by writing a serious and deeply felt book, totally consistent with his beliefs of a lifetime. And God should be flattered: unlike most of those clamoring for his attention, Hitchens treats him like an adult.


## WE TRY HARDER (BUT WHAT'S THE POINT?)

New York Times, *May 16, 2007*

NOTE: *The history of Avis has been an obsession of mine. I don't know why. An article in my previous collection,* Big Babies, *told the Avis story as far as it had gotten by then.*

In 1946, Warren E. Avis (who died last month at the age of ninety-two) had an idea: rental cars should be available at airports. So he founded Avis Airlines Rent-a-Car. In 1954, he sold the company to another businessman, Richard Robie. Two years later, in 1956, Robie sold Avis to an investment group led by a company called Amoskeag. In 1962, the investment banking firm Lazard Frères bought Avis. In 1965, Lazard sold Avis to the giant conglomerate ITT Corporation.

Since 1946, Avis has been sold or reorganized seventeen or eighteen times, depending on how you count. Each time Avis changed hands or structure, there have been fees for bankers and fees for lawyers, bonuses for the top executives and theories about why this was exactly what the company needed.

In 1972, ITT spun off Avis as a publicly traded company. Then, in 1977, the company was bought by another giant conglomerate, Norton Simon. In 1983, a company called Esmark (formerly Swift & Co.) bought Norton Simon. In 1984, Esmark was bought by Beatrice

Foods, and in 1986, Beatrice was bought by the leveraged buyout firm Kohlberg Kravis Roberts & Company.

Kohlberg Kravis Roberts immediately sold Avis to an investment group called Wesray. Wesray sold Avis's fleet leasing business to a company called PHH Group. Then it spun off Avis's foreign operations and took them public as a company called Avis Europe P.L.C. And then, in 1987, Wesray sold Avis to its employees under an employee stock ownership program. Wesray more than tripled its money in fourteen months.

Two years after the stock ownership deal, the company sold General Motors a complicated security that effectively gave it a 26 percent stake in Avis. Apart from that, Avis's employee ownership experiment lasted nine years, until 1996, when Avis sold itself to a company called HFS. Employees got an average of $26,000 each. Eighty or ninety current and former Avis executives got an average of $1.75 million each.

A year later, in 1997, HFS took Avis public. (The initial public offering raised just over $330 million. The banker Bear Stearns charged $15 million for its services.) In 1999, Avis bought PHH. Remember PHH? That was the company Avis sold its fleet leasing operation to in 1987. PHH was owned by Cendant, a company that had been formed in 1997 by the merger of HFS—right, the company that had spun off Avis in 1997—and another company called CUC. HFS had retained 19 percent of the company's stock when it took Avis public. With the stock portion of Avis's purchase price for PHH, Cendant now owned 34 percent of Avis.

A couple of years later, Cendant bought the roughly two-thirds of Avis that it didn't already own and made Avis a wholly owned subsidiary.

In 2006, Cendant split itself into four independent companies, one of which was the Avis Budget Group. (Somewhere along the line, Cendant had also acquired Budget Rent a Car.) The Avis Budget Group became the parent company of Avis Budget Car Rental.

Modern capitalism has two parts: there's business, and there's finance. Business is renting you a car at the airport. Finance is something else. More and more of the news labeled "business" these days is actually about finance, and much of it is mystifying. Even if you can understand—just barely—how it works, you still wonder what the point is and why people who do it need to get paid so much. And you strongly suspect that the swirl of financial activity around Avis for the past six decades has had little or nothing to do with the business of renting cars.

Last September, a week after the Avis Budget Group began trading on the New York Stock Exchange, the *Wall Street Journal* reported that the new company was "ripe for the picking." Carl Icahn, another wily financier from the 1980s, had acquired a $100 million stake in the company and would not comment about his intentions.

The *Journal* warned, "If a buyout or acquisition deal doesn't materialize for Avis, stock and bond investors will have to focus on the fundamentals of its car-rental business." Goodness! Anything but that!

## How Many Divisions Has the Congress?

Washington Post, *June 2, 2007*

**W**hat are you supposed to do, according to supporters of the Iraq war, if you think that war is a dreadful mistake? Suppose you are an actual member of Congress, elected by constituents who also, like most Americans according to opinion polls, oppose the war. Is there any legitimate action you can take? Or must you simply allow the war to go on and let young Americans continue dying in what you regard as a bad cause? What are your options?

The Constitution says that "the Congress shall have the Power . . . to declare War." That power does not mean much unless it includes the power *not* to declare war as well. But presidents of both parties have pretty much stolen Congress's war power, with the ordinarily "strict constructionist" Republicans taking the lead. Congress has stood by and not done much—but what could it do? As Stalin supposedly said about military advice from the Vatican, "How many divisions has the Pope?"

Last week President Bush condescended to sign a bill authorizing $100 billion for his war, but only after any serious timetables or criteria or deadlines for withdrawal were stripped from the legislation. There was a time, circa 1999, when Republicans considered it the height of naivete, irresponsibility, and indifference to the fate of American soldiers to commit any troops to action in a foreign country without what used to be called an "exit strategy." That was when the president was a Democrat. Now, it is considered the height of naivete, irresponsibility, and indifference to the fate of American soldiers to suggest the possibility of any exit strategy short of triumph. If you do, you are betraying the troops. In our current war, no one sees actual triumph in the cards, so there is no exit strategy.

Woe betide any politician who suggests that waiting for complete triumph might not be the only alternative—just in case democracy, prosperity, peace, and brotherhood don't flower in Iraq next week. Senators Hillary Clinton and Barack Obama opposed the war funding bill because it lacked even the mealymouthed timetables in an earlier version that Bush vetoed. For this they got crocodile tears from Senator John McCain. Squandering a bit more of his war-hero capital, McCain came close to accusing the two leading Democratic presidential candidates of treason: "I was very disappointed to see Senator Obama and Senator Clinton embrace the policy of surrender. . . ." Former Governor Mitt Romney, with no known foreign policy expertise or even interest (unless you count his "mission" to France after college, trying to convert the French to Mormonism), attributed Clinton's and Obama's votes to "an inexperienced worldview on national security."

A confused *Wall Street Journal* editorial on Saturday seemed to be addressing this question of how an elected representative might legitimately oppose a war in our democracy. It began by accusing House Speaker Nancy Pelosi and Senate Majority Leader Harry Reid of cowardice. They "claim to oppose the war and want it to end, yet they refuse to use their power of the purse to end it." So there is a "power of the purse," you see. Congress can cut off funds for a war people don't like. In this connection, older readers might recall the Iran-Contra affair, in which sources of money were found to keep the Contra war going in Nicaragua without Congress even knowing about it. This met with the enthusiastic approval of the *Wall Street Journal*, even though funds you do not know about are hard to cut off. But what happens if you, as a member of Congress, do attempt to use the power of the purse? Senators Clinton, Obama, and Chris Dodd (also running for president) voted against the final

Iraq funding bill because all meaningful deadlines and timetables had been stripped out so that President Bush would agree to sign it. Last Saturday's editorial accuses these three Democratic Senators of "vot[ing] to undermine US troops in the middle of a difficult mission." If this is true of last week's vote, it will always be true of any attempt to cut off a war by cutting off funds. Unless the *Journal* is in favor of "undermining US troops," this makes the alleged "power of the purse" unusable.

Advocates of the current war who enjoy the spectacle of war opponents caught in this trap of laws and logic had better hope that every military action a president chooses to engage in from here on out is as wonderful to them as the current war in Iraq. Because there is nothing war-specific about this line of argument. It would work just as well on an invasion of Canada or an aerial bombardment of Portugal. The president can do it if he wants, and no one can legitimately stop him.

Of course the president is elected, and in that sense he is acting as proxy for the citizens when he decides to take our country into a war. Right? Well, not quite. Let's leave aside the special voting anomalies of the 2000 election. When this president first ran for national office, he campaigned on a platform of criticizing his predecessor for engaging in military action (in Kosovo and Somalia) without an exit strategy. He mocked the notion of trying to establish democracy in distant lands. He denounced the use of American soldiers for "nation building." In 2000, if you were looking for a way to express your disapproval of the policies and prejudices that subsequently got us into Iraq, your obvious answer would have been to vote for George W. Bush.

Check and mate.

# INDEX

Avis Airlines Rent-A-Car, 332
Avis Budget Car Rental, 333
Avis Budget Group, 333–34
Avis Europe P.L.C, 333
Axelrod, Robert, 108–9

Baden-Powell, Robert, 151
Baird, Zoe, 292
Baker, James, 65, 67, 73
Bakke case, 218
Bandar, Prince, 154
Barnes, Fred, 33, 35
Barr, Bob, 76
Bartlett, Bruce, 303–4
Bartley, Robert, 128
Baucus, Max, 26
Bauer, Gary, 129
Bear Stearns, 333
Beatrice Foods, 332–33
Bellow, Saul, 331
Bennett, William, 73–74
    gambling habit of, 210–12
Berlin, Irving, 77
Berlin, Isaiah, 332
Betrayal (Pinter), 323
Bias: A CBS Insider Exposes How the
    Media Distort the News (Gold-
    berg), 127–28, 132
Big Test, The (Lemann), 101
Bill and Melinda Gates Foundation,
    xiii
Bin Laden, Osama, 104–5, 108, 109, 110,
    114, 115, 119, 137, 156–57, 310
Black Adder (television series), 284
Blair, Jayson, 216–17
Blair, Tony, 92, 174–75, 276, 282, 284
Blix, Hans, 196
Bloom, Harold, 305–6
Bob Jones University, 192
"Bobos," as term, 256
Bogart, Humphrey, 223
Book of Virtues, The (Bennett), 210
Bork, Robert, 73, 280
Bosnia, 24, 286
Boston Globe, 314–16
Botswana, 238
Boxer, Barbara, 52
Boykin, William, 235–37
Boy Scouts, 151

Bradley, Bill, 79
Branch Davidians, 13
Brandeis, Louis, 21
Breaux, John, 289
Brent, David, 284
Brinkley, David, 161
Broder, David, 313
Brokaw, Tom, 141, 161
Broken Hearth, The: Reversing the
    Moral Collapse of the American
    Family (Bennett), 211
Brooks, David, 253–59
Brown v. Board of Education, 297–98
Buchanan, Pat, 133
buckraking, 6–10
Budget Rent a Car, 333
Bureau of Indian Affairs, 214
Bush, George H. W., 33, 40, 41, 164,
    168, 177, 188, 209, 227, 237, 268
    lying of, 149–50
    standards for impeachment of, 17,
        18–19
Bush, George W., xiv, 17, 43, 45, 47, 51,
    53, 76, 77, 92, 104, 109, 111, 117,
    118, 122, 124, 126, 139, 180, 188,
    190, 191, 192, 206, 213, 215, 238,
    240, 242, 246, 283, 303, 325
    as above the law, 314–17
    Alito nominated by, 280–81
    anti-Semitism charge against, 32–33
    axis of evil, coinage of, 196
    born again faith of, 33–35
    Boykin religious controversy and,
        235–36
    case against, 267–69
    compassionate conservatism of, 197,
        268–69, 288, 303
    and decision for war, 203–5, 208–9
    Downing Street Memo and, 274, 276
    election results controversy and,
        61–71
    Iraq War debate and, 170–71, 174–75,
        177–78
    leadership of, 209–10
    liberals' personal dislike of, 232–35
    lying style of, 149–51
    media criticized by, 230–32
    mission accomplished declaration of,
        323–24

MICHAEL KINSLEY is a columnist for *Time* magazine, where he has been an essayist since 1986. He spent the better part of two decades (1976–1995) at the *New Republic,* including two stints as editor. During that time he left the *New Republic* twice, to be editor of *Harper's* and American editor of the *Economist.* For many years he wrote a weekly column that appeared in the *New Republic, Washington Post,* and other newspapers. He also has written regular columns for the *Wall Street Journal* and the *Times* of London. From 1989 through 1995 he was the liberal host on the CNN program *Crossfire.* He also was for many years an interlocutor on William Buckley's *Firing Line* and the moderator of the *Firing Line* debates on PBS. In 1995, he went to work for Microsoft to start what became *Slate,* now owned by the Washington Post Company. In 2004–2005 he was editorial and opinion editor of the *Los Angeles Times.* His writing has appeared in all of these publications as well as the *New Yorker, Reader's Digest, Condé Nast Traveler,* and other publications. He is a member of the Screen Actors Guild and the District of Columbia Bar. He lives in Seattle and Washington, D.C., with his wife, Patty Stonesifer, who is CEO of the Bill and Melinda Gates Foundation.